A STUDENT'S GUIDE TO ACCOUNTING FOR LAWYERS

THIRD EDITION

(or, "Numbers frighten me. Just give me the bottom line.")

Daniel Lipsky, CPA
Professor Emeritus
The City University of New York

David A. Lipton
Professor of Law
The Catholic University of America

STUDENT GUIDE SERIES

1998

MATTHEW◆BENDER

Library of Congress Cataloging-in-Publication Data

Lipsky, Daniel
  A student's guide to accounting for lawyers / Daniel Lipsky, David A. Lipton. — 3rd ed.
    p.   cm. (Student guide series)
  Includes index.
  ISBN 0-8205-3054-9
  1. Accounting.   I. Lipton, David A., 1945– .   II. Title.   III. Series.
HF5635.L726 1997
657'08 .024'334—dc21   97–43524
                                                                    CIP

MATTHEW◆BENDER

MATTHEW BENDER & CO., INC.
EDITORIAL OFFICES
2 PARK AVENUE, NEW YORK, NY 10016-5675 (212) 448-2000
201 MISSION ST., SAN FRANCISCO, CA 94105-1831 (415) 908-3200

LEGAL EDUCATION PUBLICATIONS

ADVISORY BOARD

Dedicated

to BADS

AUTHOR'S PREFACE
(with apologies to Robert Frost)

Something there is about a law student that just doesn't love accounting. Maybe it's the numbers. Perhaps law students don't feel comfortable with the mathematics, albeit limited, upon which accounting relies. After all there is a basic equation and some addition and subtraction. Discomfort with numbers should not be unexpected since law students have chosen a profession which thrives on the malleability of language, whereas, in mathematics, there is usually but one correct answer.

Then again, maybe this notorious lack of fondness grows out of the language accountants employ. What a lawyer calls "earned surplus," an accountant today refers to as "retained earnings." What is "profit" to an attorney constitutes "net income" to the accountant. How can attorneys be expected to respond favorably to a field whose practitioners arbitrarily seem to revise nomenclature with which the lawyer is otherwise familiar?

Perhaps law students dislike accounting because they don't like the clothes that they imagine accountants wear . . . too much polyester and too many green visors. Even lawyers are not immune from the tendency to stereotype.

For whatever reason, or reasons, the reality is that many law students and young lawyers suffer a certain amount of "accounting-phobia." They do not enjoy the subject. They disparage the study of accounting. And, most troubling, they avoid learning the basics of accounting.

This aversion to accounting is unfortunate. We say this not because we believe that accounting is imbued with inherent magical qualities that make it universally enjoyable to those who engage in its study. Rather, we believe that the law student's accounting phobia is unfortunate because accounting plays such a pivotal role in the lawyer's work and the law student's studies.

In broad terms, accounting is critical to the lawyer because it provides the lawyer with the tools necessary to evaluate the financial condition of businesses, whether for profit or not-for-profit, whether publicly or privately owned, whether large or small. More specifically, the accounting process provides the attorney with the data necessary to permit advice to be given upon legal questions in a far-ranging variety of contexts. The corporate lawyer who represents the large corporation wishing to sell securities to the public must be in a position to interpret and evaluate the financial statements upon which the public will rely in purchasing those securities. The labor lawyer, bargaining for employees, must be able to analyze the earnings record of the employer's business in order to effectively negotiate a salary increase. The estate lawyer who probates a decedent's will has to be able to compute the net worth of the decedent's estate. The social activist lawyer who represents a non-profit community development organization seeking a government grant must be able to demonstrate financial need in terms of anticipated expenditures and revenues. The generalist who has been asked by the joint owners of a small manufacturing corporation to determine if they can issue themselves dividends must be able to evaluate the solvency of the business or perhaps measure the amount of earnings retained by that business.

Appreciating both the importance of accounting to the lawyer as well as the lawyer's aversion to the subject, we decided to design a manual that would invite the law student and the beginning attorney to gain a familiarity with the subject without provoking any of the tell-tale side effects of "accounting intimidation" and "ennui." We chose not to overwhelm the reader with many of the technical aspects of record keeping and preparation of financial statements, activities in which lawyers would typically not engage. (The accountant half of us thought that it might be wise to include the specifics of double-entry record keeping in an Appendix for those readers who seek to understand more fully the accounting recording process. The lawyer half agreed that it made sense but thought he caught a shadow of a green visor over his co-author's forehead).

We also determined that, as frequently as it is possible, we will discuss the issue at hand in language and concepts that lawyers and law students will understand. The accounting problem under inspection will generally be examined through discussions and questions that are part of an approach with which law students will be familiar. This book is not designed to prepare the reader to talk and think like an accountant, but rather to allow the reader to understand about what the accountant is talking and thinking.

Finally, we generally try to show why a particular accounting idea or technique is important to the lawyer. We want the reader to understand what the accountant is doing. But, perhaps more importantly, we want the reader to appreciate how the accountant's work impacts on the lawyer's work.

If the reader's appetite is whetted by this manual, he certainly could go deeper into the study of accounting. However, if the reader's interest is in understanding enough accounting to enable him or her to respond to the financial issues with which he or she will be confronted as a law student and a beginning attorney, this manual will supply most of the essentials.

Daniel Lipsky
David A. Lipton

INTRODUCTION

Those readers who have examined the preceding Authors' Preface should have an understanding of the purpose of this Guide and the approach to accounting followed herein. Essentially, the authors have committed themselves to a de-mystification of the accounting process. What is not immediately apparent from the Preface, and what the authors would like to address within this Introduction, is when and how this Guide should be used.

This Guide has been written to be read and utilized by three distinct audiences. First, the Guide will provide a valuable tool for students and lawyers who want to engage in a general initial study of or refamiliarization with accounting on their own in order to acquire the basic knowledge necessary to pursue other legal studies and to practice law. For those students who seek a general knowledge of basic accounting, this Guide is best read in the order in which it is written. Chapter I introduces the reader to the basic accounting equation and explains how this equation is central to the preparation of the financial statements upon which the lawyer relies. In Chapters II and III, the reader is guided through a more detailed discussion of the elements of the basic equation — assets, liabilities and equities. As an important aside, Chapter IV explains the concept of generally accepted accounting principles, which concept plays a frequent role in the exposition of basic accounting practices.

Having an understanding of basic terms, the reader can then progress to an analysis of three of the financial statements — the balance sheet (Chapter V), the income statement (Chapter VI), and the increasingly important statement of cash flows (Chapter VII). During the discussion of the income statement, the concepts of expenses and revenues as well as accruals and deferrals are developed.

At this juncture, the reader is instructed in how to apply the accounting knowledge so far gained to specific needs and problems confronting attorneys. Thus, in Chapter VIII, the reader is introduced to financial and ratio analysis in order to develop an ability to evaluate the financial condition of a business enterprise. In Chapters IX and X, the Guide explores state-imposed restrictions on distributions and share issuances — two concerns of the corporate attorney which require an understanding of some basic accounting principles. These restrictions are examined in jurisdictions which rely upon concepts of par as well as those jurisdictions which have eliminated the concept of par from their corporate statutes.

This third edition of the Student's Guide includes a chapter on accounting for partnerships, Chapter XI, and a chapter on accounting for not-for-profit corporations, Chapter XII. While many accounting principles are applicable to a broad variety of business forms, previous chapters in this Guide have primarily focused upon accounting as applied to for-profit corporations. Attorneys, however, frequently have to be familiar with the financial operations of other business forms. The chapters on partnerships and the not-for-profit corporations provide the basic information necessary to interpret the financial statements of these business entities.

A second use of the Guide is as a supplement for students who are taking either Business Associations, Corporations, Securities, Partnership, Taxation, Corporate Finance, Not-for-Profit Corporations or other business-related courses and who have had no previous accounting. It will provide these students with the preparation necessary to deal with questions regarding basic corporate financial statements, corporate distributions, share issuance, asset valuation, balance sheet interpretation, financial analysis, and assist their understanding of financial statements of partnerships and not-for-profit corporations. If the Guide is used on a supplemental basis for a particular course, the readings might be assigned selectively, depending upon which substantive areas the course was designed to emphasize. For example, Chapters II and III, which cover the basics of accounting, Chapter VIII which discusses ratio analysis, and Chapters IX and X dealing with state corporate statutes might be particularly relevant for a course on Corporations. An instructor who sought to provide greater depth in accounting might consider including Chapter VII on the statement of cash flows and Chapter XI on accounting for partnerships.

Finally, the Guide may be used as a primary text for the growing number of law schools that are offering accounting "mini-courses" to introduce students to the basics of accounting. Such abbreviated courses typically run between seven and fourteen hours and are usually offered during the law students' third term. They are designed to provide law students with the basics of accounting so that they may successfully complete the business-related courses taught at law school. For such courses, the materials in this Guide may be used selectively or in their entirety. Some instructors of these abbreviated courses might prefer to emphasize the first two chapters dealing with the basic equation and asset valuation. Other instructors might seek to include as well the chapters on financial statements and financial analysis.

For all of these audiences, the problems and solutions accompanying the Guide should prove to be of significant assistance as a learning device. Working through the problems provides the reader with a needed opportunity to apply the principles and procedures introduced in the body of the Guide to specific fact patterns. In addition, the problems, together with the solutions, frequently expand upon ideas presented in the Guide and advance these ideas one step further. Finally, through the problems and the accompanying solutions, the reader can evaluate her or his comprehension of the subject matter presented in the Guide.

The various readers of this Guide should keep in mind the existence and utility of the two matters covered in the Appendices. Appendix A provides an introduction to the mechanics of accounting — debits and credits, ledgers and journals, and double entry bookkeeping. Although the authors believe that an understanding of the mechanics of accounting is not critical for an understanding of the accounting process itself, there will be some readers who will undoubtedly benefit from pursuing a study of the technical aspects of recording financial data. Those readers intent upon learning the mechanical aspects of accounting might even choose to read Appendix A before reading the body of the Guide, since learning the methods for recording financial data can assist in learning about the accounting process which relies upon this recorded data.

Appendix B is a reprint of the financial statements found in a recent annual report of a major manufacturing firm. In the text, when discussing financial statements, or the recording of assets and liabilities, or the auditor's report, frequent reference will be made to Appendix B. Flipping back through the book to this Appendix will then allow the reader to examine a practical application of a specific substantive discussion about accounting practices.

Appendices C and D are reprints of the financial statements of a typical not for profit corporation after and before significant changes were made in the guidelines for the preparation of such statements.

Throughout this Guide, footnote citations will be found to the official pronouncements of various bodies which set accounting standards. These pronouncements are part of the common law of accounting and are referred to collectively as "generally accepted accounting principles." Their development and importance are described more fully in Chapter IV. Also, in Chapters IX and X, dealing with corporate distributions and share issuances, reference will frequently be made to popular state laws pertinent to these subjects, as well as to the Model Business Corporation Act.

Accounting does not have to be "fun" for the law student. However, it is a critical subject matter for the law school curriculum. This Guide is designed to provide a palatable, if not at times enjoyable, vehicle by which a broad range of students can learn this vital subject.

(Matthew Bender & Co., Inc.)

TABLE OF CONTENTS

CHAPTER I — THE ACCOUNTING PROCESS

CHAPTER II — AN AMPLIFICATION OF ASSETS AND LIABILITIES

CHAPTER III — A FURTHER EXAMINATION OF CORPORATE EQUITY

CHAPTER IV — GENERALLY ACCEPTED ACCOUNTING PRINCIPLES

CHAPTER V — A FURTHER EXAMINATION OF THE BALANCE SHEET

CHAPTER VI — A FURTHER EXAMINATION OF THE INCOME STATEMENT

CHAPTER VII — THE STATEMENT OF CASH FLOWS

CHAPTER VIII — FINANCIAL ANALYSIS

CHAPTER IX — PUTTING THE ACCOUNTING PROCESS TO WORK TO ASSIST IN MAKING LEGAL DECISIONS ABOUT DISTRIBUTIONS

CHAPTER X — SHARE ISSUANCE AND CAPITAL CONTRIBUTION REQUIREMENTS

CHAPTER XI — ACCOUNTING FOR SOLE PROPRIETORSHIPS AND PARTNERSHIPS

 (Pub.642)

CHAPTER XII — ACCOUNTING FOR NON-PROFIT ORGANIZATIONS

APPENDIX   A — THE MECHANICS OF ACCOUNTING

CHAPTER I

THE ACCOUNTING PROCESS

A. INTRODUCTION: ACCOUNTING AND THE ATTORNEY

Reliance upon the Financial Statements

Accounting is carried out for all types of entities — not only for profit-seeking business enterprises, but also for governmental units, not-for-profit organizations, individuals, and private households. This manual, however, is primarily concerned with accounting done for business enterprises.

Specifically, this book will focus upon those functions of accounting that are essential to the legal decisions that attorneys make based upon the financial condition of a business enterprise. Even more narrowly, this manual will emphasize the general accounting concepts underlying a specific business enterprise — the corporation (though Chapter XI specifically deals with accounting for partnerships and Chapter XII specifically deals with accounting for not-for-profit corporations). Most of the accounting functions that are relevant to the corporation are generic in nature and will have an application to all business enterprises. Their specific application to corporations, as well as the broader nature of these functions will be discussed and developed.

The accountant's evaluation of the financial condition of any business enterprise is essential to the attorney's work. The attorney's interaction with the accounting process, however, is generally limited to the financial statements which constitute the end product of the accounting process. The basic statements typically include a balance sheet, an income statement, perhaps a statement of retained earnings, and, in many situations, a statement of cash flows. These statements may be supplemented with various supporting schedules or analyses.

B. THE INTERPLAY BETWEEN THE ACCOUNTING PROCESS AND FINANCIAL STATEMENTS

Why the Financial Statements are Significant

The financial statements are useful for the attorney in evaluating the condition of a business entity because they summarize the numerous financial events that occur in the life of the entity. Thus, by studying the financial statements, the attorney is able to evaluate the aggregate impact on a business enterprise of its financial activities over a period of time. Collectively, the financial statements can be used by an attorney to determine the condition of a business at a specific point in time, to evaluate the performance of a business over a set period of time and, when two or more financial statements from different time periods are compared, to gauge the changes in performance from one time interval to another or the changes in condition from one point of time to another.

The financial events that are summarized in the financial statements are initially recorded pursuant to a method which is referred to as the "accounting process."[1] The accounting process is a system that has been developed to accumulate and classify the financial data for a given business entity. The data are obtained from a variety of financial transactions such as purchases or sales of goods and services, acquisitions

---

[1] In this Guide, a distinction will be made between the "process" by which financial data is recorded and summarized and the "mechanics" underlying this process. This Guide focuses on explaining the process. Understanding the mechanics is not critical to an understanding of the process. The mechanics of accounting are explained in Appendix A.

or dispositions of securities, land, buildings or equipment, distributions of dividends, and borrowings or repayments of cash.

Before we seek to understand the financial statements, we must examine the accounting process upon which the financial statements are based.

C. AN ASIDE ON TERMINOLOGY

Their Language, Our Language

The terms employed in accounting are taken, to a considerable extent, from ordinary everyday language. When used, however, in a technical sense, within the accounting framework, these terms may acquire a more limited or precise meaning than they have in general usage. As a precaution against misunderstanding, these ordinary terms will be briefly explained or defined, where appropriate, in the course of this text.

As a further precaution, the reader is warned that accounting terminology has been subject to review and modification over the years with the aim of improving clarity. Consequently, older judicial cases and statutes often employ terminology no longer favored in current accounting practice. For this reason, both earlier and current terminology will be indicated when relevant.[2]

D. THE ACCOUNTING PROCESS AND THE FUNDAMENTAL ACCOUNTING EQUATION

In the Beginning, there was a Basic Equation

The entire accounting process rests on the simple concept that the sum of equities is always equal to the sum of the assets.

Assets are the economic resources owned by the enterprise, such as cash on hand or in the bank, accounts receivable, merchandise inventory, land, building and equipment. Equities are claims made against the assets. Equities include (1) the amounts owed by the enterprise to the creditors and (2) the interest of the owners in the enterprise (the claims of the owners on the enterprise). The amounts owed to the creditors are customarily termed "liabilities" and include such items as accounts payable, unpaid taxes, and amounts owed on a mortgage. The interest of the owners in an enterprise is referred to as the ownership equity or net worth. In the corporation, the owners are the shareholders and so the ownership equity is designated "shareholders' equity."

The fundamental equation can be expressed as follows:

Assets = Equities.

Equities are divisible, as already indicated, into equities of creditors and ownership equity, so that the equation can be expressed as:

Assets = Equities of creditors + Ownership equity.

If the commonly used alternative terminology is employed, the equation may be expressed as:

Assets = Liabilities + Net Worth.

If we are referring to a corporation, we would say:

Assets = Liabilities + Shareholders' Equity.

The fundamental equation can also be stated in a form which gives greater definition to net worth or ownership equity by subtracting liabilities from assets. Thus:

Assets − Liabilities = Net Worth.

It is in this last form, that the basic, self-evident nature of the fundamental equation is best seen. For in this last formulation, we are essentially saying that if you add up all the resources owned by an enterprise

---

[2] The American Institute of Certified Public Accountants conducts an annual survey of the financial statements of 600 industrial and merchandising corporations to observe trends in the usage of terminology and format in these statements. The results are published in an annual publication called "Accounting Trends and Techniques." Reference will be made to the 1996 edition of this survey edited by G. L. Yarnall and R. Rikert.

and then subtract from that sum everything the enterprise owes to its creditors, the remainder represents the ownership interest in the enterprise. The truth of the equation becomes apparent.

Assets less liabilities are also frequently referred to as "net assets." ("Net" means the remainder that results after relevant deductions are made.) By simple substitution: Net Assets = Net Worth (or Ownership Equity or Shareholders' Equity).

[Note: It should be understood that there are instances where the liabilities of an enterprise exceed the assets. In these circumstances, the net worth is to be viewed as a deficiency or a negative quantity.]

In the accounting process, this fundamental equation essentially becomes the vehicle by which all financial events are recorded. Whatever the financial activities in which a business enterprise engages — buying goods, selling goods, issuing stock, paying debts or whatever — there is an impact on the business' assets, liabilities, or net worth, or any combination of the three.

Each financial event is recorded in terms of its effect on these three elements of the basic equation. But since these three elements are interrelated, what affects one affects the others. As we will see, an increase or decrease in one element, must be offset by a countervailing addition or subtraction in another element of the equation that maintains the overall equality of the equation.

E. ILLUSTRATIVE TRANSACTIONS

How Daily Transactions are Integrated into the Accounting Equation

To illustrate how the accounting process is used to accumulate and categorize financial data, let us consider a series of transactions which might have taken place in a merchandising corporation during the three months ended August 31, —. We will analyze and explain each transaction in terms of its effect on the basic accounting equation.

The transactions are entered and summarized below in Exhibit 1.1, Summary of the Effects of Transactions on the Accounting Equation. The reader should refer to this Exhibit with each transaction, to observe the effect of each transaction on the accounting equation. Later, we will examine how the basic financial statements build upon these numerous transactions by summarizing them and presenting their cumulative effect.

It is important to observe that the fundamental accounting equation remains in balance after each and every transaction.

Transaction group 1

Davidson and Earling agreed to join in a merchandising business. Upon the advice of their attorney, the business was incorporated as the Best Selling Corporation. Davidson and Earling each invested $12,500 and each received 1250 shares of common stock. After these transactions, the accounting equation shows cash of $25,000, an asset, balanced by the shareholders' equity in this asset. The equity is represented solely by the shareholders' equity or net worth, designated as Paid-in Capital of $25,000. In this transaction, the asset side of the equation increased by $25,000 and the equity increased by the same amount. Thus, the basic equation maintained its balance.

Transaction group 2

Merchandise was purchased from various vendors at intervals during the course of the three-month period under consideration. Some of the vendors insisted on immediate payment. These cash purchases are summarized in transaction group 2 for a total of $10,000. The effect on the equation was to decrease the asset cash by $10,000 and to increase the asset merchandise by the same amount. In essence, one type of asset was exchanged for another; the total amount of assets, however, remained constant. There was no change in equities. The equation now shows two types of assets — cash of $15,000 and merchandise of $10,000 — balanced by the equity, capital stock, of $25,000.

EXHIBIT 1.1 BEST SELLING CORPORATION
Summary of the Effects of Transactions on the Accounting Equation
For the three months ended August 31, 19____

	ASSETS				Liabilities		Shareholders' Equity	
	Cash +	Accounts + Receivable	Merchandise	=	Accounts Payable	+	Paid in + Capital	Retained Earnings (Earned Surplus)
1 Investment	+ 25,000						+25,000	
2 Merchandise purchased for cash	− 10,000		+ 10,000					
Balances	15,000		10,000	= 25,000			25,000	
3 Merchandise purchased on credit			+ 100,000		+100,000			
Balances	15,000		110,000	= 125,000	100,000		25,000	
4 Sales on credit		+ 125,000	− 75,000					+50,000
Balances	15,000	125,000	35,000	= 175,000	100,000		25,000	50,000
5 Collections of accounts receivable	+ 102,000	− 102,000						
Balances	117,000	23,000	35,000	= 175,000	100,000		25,000	50,000
6 Payments of accounts payable	− 80,000				− 80,000			
Balances	37,000	23,000	35,000	= 95,00	20,000		25,000	50,000
7 Payment for rent, salaries and other expenses	− 34,600							− 34,600
Balances	2,400	23,000	35,000	= 60,400	20,000		25,000	15,400
8 Declaration and Payment of a dividend	− 800							− 800
Final Balances	**1,600**	**23,000**	**35,000**	**= 59,600**	**20,000**		**25,000**	**14,600**

(Matthew Bender & Co., Inc.)

Transaction group 3

Additional merchandise purchases were made during the period, but these were made on credit. These transactions are summarized in Exhibit 1.1 as credit purchases of $100,000. As for the equation, assets were increased by $100,000 of merchandise and there was an equal increase in equities, represented by the liability to vendors, of $100,000. Liabilities to vendors are generally termed "accounts payable."

Transaction group 4

In the course of the three months ended August 31, 19 —, there were a large number of sales of merchandise. All of the sales were on credit and totaled $125,000; the cost of the merchandise sold was $75,000. The amounts receivable from customers are generally termed "accounts receivable." In this set of transactions, the asset of accounts receivable increased by $125,000, while the asset merchandise decreased by $75,000. As we see, assets did not remain constant. A profit was made on the sale of merchandise and this increased the total sum of assets. Essentially then, the ownership interest in the corporation was increased by this increment in assets. Merchandise costing $75,000 was sold at $125,000 for a profit of $50,000. This profit increased the ownership equity by $50,000. In the case of a corporation, as contrasted with a sole proprietorship or partnership, changes in ownership equity arising from revenues and expired costs are not reflected in capital stock but are accumulated in Retained Earnings or, as the attorney would phrase it, "Earned Surplus."[3] Thus, the ownership equity of the Best Selling Corporation includes two elements — the original capital contribution and the net earnings from operations or profits.

After the entry is made on Exhibit 1.1 for this group of transactions, the accounting equation shows assets — cash, accounts receivable and merchandise — totalling $175,000 balanced by equities — accounts payable, capital stock, and retained earnings — also totalling $175,000.

Transaction group 5

Of the $125,000 accounts receivable, $102,000 was paid, leaving an accounts receivable balance of $23,000. Although the accounts receivable asset decreased, the asset — cash — increased by the same amount. The cash balance increased to $117,000. There was no net change in assets and thus no countervailing changes in either liabilities or shareholders' equity.

Transaction group 6

The payments to creditors of $80,000 made during the period reduced the liability — accounts payable — and reduced the asset — cash — by the same amount. The equation now shows assets and equities each totalling $95,000.

Transaction group 7

Expenses during the period for rent, salaries and various other items, totalled $34,600 and were paid in cash. All expenses were paid as they arose. Thus, there was no increase or decrease in liabilities. The effect of these transactions, then, was to reduce cash and to reduce the ownership equity, or retained earnings, by the same amount — $34,600.

Transaction group 8

Dividends totaling $800 ($.32 per share for 2500 shares) were declared by the Board of Directors and were paid, reducing cash by $800 and reducing earned surplus or retained earnings by the same amount. After this entry, as after each of the prior entries, the equation remains in balance. As demonstrated in

---

[3] In 1953, the American Institute of Certified Public Accountants recommended the term "earned surplus" be replaced in financial reports by either the term "retained earnings" or a similar term. American Institute of Certified Public Accountants, Accounting Terminology Bulletin No.1, par. 69 (1953). By 1995 only one of the 600 firms surveyed by the AICPA still used the term "earned surplus" in their balance sheet captions. Accounting Trends and Techniques, *supra*, note 1, at 262.

Various accounting bodies have promulgated accounting standards of one sort or another like those found in the Accounting Terminology Bulletin. These promulgations are a part of generally accepted accounting principles and are occasionally cited as footnotes to this Guide. These principles, their promulgation, and their significance are discussed *infra* in Chapter IV.

Exhibit 1.1, assets total $59,600. These are balanced by accounts payable of $20,000, capital stock of $25,000 and retained earnings (earned surplus) of $14,600, also totalling $59,600.

F. PERIODIC FINANCIAL STATEMENTS

How The Daily Transactions Are Summarized In the Financial Statements

As stated earlier, financial statements summarize the events which have been recorded in accordance with the accounting process. Financial statements, as a rule, are prepared at the end of each fiscal year. Interim statements are often prepared quarterly and, for management purposes, may also be prepared on a monthly basis. The balance sheet, the income statement, the statement of retained earnings and the statement of cash flows are discussed below. An illustrative balance sheet, income statement, and statement of retained earnings all for the Best Selling Corporation have been prepared. Inasmuch as only a few simple transactions were included in the preceding section to illustrate the functioning of the fundamental equation, the resulting financial statements are not as involved as those generally encountered in published corporate reports.

1.   **The Balance Sheet.** A balance sheet, as its name suggests, essentially presents a compilation of the balances appearing in the fundamental equation. It thus groups all assets of an enterprise in one location and all the claims against the assets (liabilities and owners' equity) in another. As with the fundamental equation, the two groups must logically always be in equality. The figures are typically arranged in one of two conventional formats — the "account form" and the "report form." In the more common account form, a "T" pattern is employed in which, below the title heading, the assets of the enterprise are listed on the left side of the balance sheet and all the claims against the assets (liabilities and owners' equity) are located on the right. The total assets always equal the total liabilities plus owners' equity.

The report form is an alternative presentation utilizing a vertical arrangement in which assets are listed first, followed by liabilities and then by ownership equity. A balance sheet, particularly one in the report form, may also be referred to as a Statement of Financial Position.[4]

Note that the balances apply to a given moment in time. A balance sheet is customarily dated as of the last day of a fiscal period and the balance is understood to be as of the close of business on the date indicated in the heading of the balance sheet. (Occasionally, in special circumstances, one encounters a balance sheet dated as of the beginning of a fiscal period. In such cases, the balance moment would be before the business day commenced.)

The balance sheet shown in Exhibit 1.2 is in the account form. It includes the assets and equities of the Best Selling Corporation at the close of business on August 31, —. Thus, the Exhibit 1.2 balance sheet summarizes the impact on the Best Selling Corporation of the various transactions discussed in the prior section and presents a picture of the financial position of the Best Selling Corporation after the completion of those transactions. Assets are listed in order of their ease of convertibility into cash in the normal course of business operations (liquidity), with the most liquid assets being listed first. Liabilities are listed in general order of their due dates, with the earliest maturities listed first.

---

[4] Of the 600 companies surveyed in 1995 by the American Institute of Certified Public Accountants, 162 used the Account Form balance sheet, 436 used the Report Form, and none used the Financial Position Form. Accounting Trends and Techniques, *supra* note 1, at 141.

EXHIBIT 1.2

BEST SELLING CORPORATION

Balance Sheet
August 31, 19____

ASSETS		LIABILITIES AND SHAREHOLDERS' EQUITY		
Cash	$ 1,600	Accounts payable		$20,000
Accounts receivable	23,000			
Merchandise inventory	35,000	Paid-in capital	$25,000	
		Retained earnings	14,600	
		Total shareholders' equity		39,600
		Total liabilities and shareholders' equity		
Total assets	$59,600			$59,600

It is important not to be confused about the entries on the right hand side of the balance sheet. An entry of $14,600 in Retained Earnings does not mean that there is a pool of cash on the asset side equal to that amount. Similarly, the $20,000 Accounts Payable is not represented by an asset entry of that amount. Recall that the $20,000 is the remainder of a $100,000 obligation which was incurred to buy $100,000 worth of merchandise. Much of that merchandise was sold on credit and the corporation's accounts receivable increased. Some of the merchandise remains. Of the accounts receivable created by the sales, some were paid and some of the cash receipts were used to pay off a portion of the accounts payable. Some of the cash receipts were applied to other expenses and to dividends. All that the right hand entries provide is a means for recording the sources of the collective assets on the left hand side. We will discuss this relationship further when we explore the equity entries.[5]

2. The Income Statement. An income statement summarizes the revenues and expenses of an enterprise for a fiscal period. Essentially, "revenues" are the increases in net assets (which, you recall, are equal to ownership equity) resulting from the profit-seeking operations of a business. More explicitly, revenues arise from the sale of goods and services in the regular course of business and "gains" from transactions which are peripheral to ordinary business transactions, such as dispositions of assets other than products, which could include sale of plant assets (land, buildings and equipment) or investments. "Expenses," in contrast, are decreases in net assets (or ownership equity) relating to the sales of goods or services in the regular course of business, such as the cost of goods sold, the costs of selling and administration, and "losses" from transactions which are peripheral to ordinary business operations, such as the sale of major assets or investments at a loss. Expenses arise out of activities designed to create revenues. (The definition of revenues and expenses will be expanded upon in Chapter VI; and revenues and expenses will be distinguished from gains and losses.)

Total revenues less total expenses equals net income or profit. This net income increases ownership equity (or shareholders' equity). The revenues of the Best Selling Corporation for the three months ended August 31, 19—, and the related expenses are sorted out and listed in Exhibit 1.3. (Needless to say, if expenses exceeded revenues, the Corporation would suffer a loss and ownership equity would be decreased.)

It should be noted that, although the capital contribution of the stockholders increased shareholders' equity, this increase does not constitute revenue (since it did not arise from sales of goods and services or gains on disposition of assets) and therefore is not reflected in the income statement. Similarly, although the declaration of a dividend decreased shareholders' equity, this particular decrease does not represent an

---

[5] See Chapter III, *infra*.

expense (since it does not arise from ordinary revenue-producing operations) and is not reflected in the income statement. Dividends are returns on the owner's capital.

It warrants emphasis that an income statement applies to a *period of time* as contrasted with a balance sheet which applies to a *moment* in time.

EXHIBIT 1.3

BEST SELLING CORPORATION

Income Statement
Three months ended August 31, 19_____

Sales	$125,000
Deduct: Cost of sales	75,000
Gross Margin	50,000
Deduct: Rent, salaries and other expenses	34,600
Net Income	$ 15,400
Earnings Per Share of Common Stock (2500 Outstanding)	$ 6.16

[Note 1: The term "gross margin" is used today in place of the term "gross profit." Both terms mean the same thing. They stand for an intermediate profit figure that is derived by subtracting the cost of products sold from the revenues received from the sales. The gross margin is the profit that arises from sales before the indirect expenses of selling, such as rent and salaries, are deducted from the sale revenues.]

[Note 2: For purposes of simplification, the effect of income taxes on the profits of the Best Selling Corporation are not shown in this Income Statement. However, since a corporation is taxed as a separate legal entity, an actual corporate income statement would show "Net Income" both before and after taxes.]

3. **The Statement of Retained Earnings.** A statement of retained earnings or earned surplus reconciles balances of retained earnings at the beginning and the end of a fiscal period. The retained earnings statement essentially reports the increase or decrease in retained earnings (earned surplus) that the corporation experiences during a given period of time. A Statement of Retained Earnings for the Best Selling Corporation, covering the three months ended August 31, 19—, appears as Exhibit 1.4.

EXHIBIT 1.4

BEST SELLING CORPORATION

Statement of Retained Earnings (Earned Surplus)
Three months ended August 31, 19_____

Retained earnings, June 1, 19_____ (Earned surplus)		-0-
Net income for the period	$15,400	
Less dividends declared	800	
Increase in retained earnings (Earned surplus)		$14,600
Retained earnings, August 31, 19_____ (Earned surplus)		$14,600

[Note: Since this period constituted the first three months of operation, the retained earnings at the beginning of the period were zero. The statement of retained earnings for the next three-month period would start with a beginning retained earnings of $14,600. To this amount would be added the net income of the next period reduced by the dividends declared in that period.]

[Where there have been changes in paid-in capital during the period, there may also be a statement explaining such changes. Such changes in paid-in capital would occur were there additional shares sold by the corporation during the period. The statement explaining the changes might be combined with the Statement of Retained Earnings under a title such as Statement of Changes in Shareholders' Equity.]

4. The Statement of Cash Flows. Within the past several decades, a fourth type of financial statement — a Statement of Cash Flows — has begun to be included as a basic statement in annual financial reports.[6] This fourth type of statement presents a summary of the source and use of all funds by a corporation during a specified period. This statement is derived from the income statement, the beginning and ending balance sheets, and other financial records and presents a different type of information than appears in either the income statement or the balance sheet. For a further discussion of the statement of cash flows, see Chapter VII, *infra*.

---

[6] In 1971, the Accounting Principles Board directed that the Statement of Changes in Financial Positions be considered a basic financial statement. American Institute of Certified Public Accountants, Opinions of the Accounting Principles Boar, No. 19 (Mar. 1971). In November 1987, the Financial Accounting Standards Board adopted the Statement of Cash Flows, replacing the Statement of Changes in Financial Positions effective for fiscal years ending after July 15, 1988. Statement of Financial Accounting Standards No. 95, "Statement of Cash Flows" (Financial Accounting Standards Boards, 1987). The Statement of Cash Flows is required every time a company prepares an income statement.

CHAPTER II

AN AMPLIFICATION OF ASSETS AND LIABILITIES

A. INTRODUCTION: WHY WE NEED TO KNOW MORE ABOUT ASSETS AND LIABILITIES

Or, Just When You Thought It Was Safe to Go Back Into the Water

In the first Chapter, when we discussed assets and liabilities in the context of the basic equation, our explanation of these fundamental terms was uncomplicated and brief. Later in that chapter, when we initially explored the nature of a balance sheet, the assets and liabilities which we carried on our illustrative balance sheet were limited in variety, thus making our balance sheet simple in nature. As we will see in a moment, however, the practical reality is that the balance sheet of a typical business entity, while not devastatingly complex, is rarely so uncomplicated. We need a further amplification of the varieties and classifications of assets and liabilities that we may find on a balance sheet. We also need an explanation of the valuation process used to determine the dollar value of the corporation's assets and liabilities.

We require these further explanations for several reasons. In part, we have to understand the additional varieties and classifications of assets and liabilities that exist in order to be able to comprehend a typical balance sheet. Furthermore, a full understanding of the classification of "current" and "noncurrent" assets and liabilities (only hinted at in Chapter I) is critical to developing techniques for analyzing and evaluating the financial condition of a corporation (such as a corporation's ability to pay its short term debts as they become due).[1]

In addition, in understanding how assets and liabilities are valued, we gain further insight into the nature of the restrictions that exist upon the distributions that a corporation can make. Such restrictions are delineated, in part, by the amount of assets, relative to liabilities, of a corporation. In understanding how a determination is made regarding the book value of assets or liabilities, we gain a greater understanding of what these restrictions are indeed regulating. Such distribution restrictions are also often dependent upon the earnings history of the corporation, which history in turn is also affected by asset and liability valuation.[2] Such restrictions also respond, in part, to a corporation's being able to pay its obligations as they become due.[3] And again, a determination of a corporation's ability to pay its obligations as they become due can only be made after current assets are distinguished from noncurrent assets. The valuation process is also essential in determining whether the total assets of a corporation exceed its total liabilities[4] and this determination is also frequently essential to computing distribution restrictions.

Finally, in recognizing the alternative methods by which some assets are valued, we will be able to understand how the valuation of assets can impact upon a business's income. This impact upon income, in turn, will be seen as affecting the taxes that a business must pay.

---

[1] See, for example, Section E of this chapter, *infra*, on working capital. Also, for a discussion on evaluating the financial health of a corporation, see Chapter VIII, *infra*, on financial analysis.

[2] For a discussion of restrictions on distributions, see Chapter IX, *infra*, on corporate distribution.

[3] For a discussion of distribution restriction provisions based upon equity insolvency tests, see Chapter IX, Section C, par. 4, *infra*.

[4] For a discussion of distribution restrictions based upon bankruptcy insolvency tests, see Chapter IX, Section C, par. 4, *infra*.

B. CURRENT ASSETS

A Classification Based Upon Convertibility Into Cash

A distinction is frequently made on the balance sheet between "current" assets and other than current assets. Current assets can be understood as those assets which are either already in the form of cash or which can be readily converted into cash in the normal course of business operations. The normal course of business operations contemplates the regular, continuing operations of a going concern. Thus, current assets would not include equipment that a business had used in a now discontinued operation even though the business plans to sell this equipment for cash within the near future.

A current asset might be converted into cash in a number of instances, such as when a current asset (say, inventory) is consumed in the manufacture of a product which in turn is sold for cash (or on credit giving rise to an account receivable); or when a current asset (such as a marketable security) is sold for cash; or when an account receivable is collected by the business entity.

In short, current assets are those assets that a business entity has available in the normal course of business to pay off short term obligations as they become due. Segregating assets into current assets and noncurrent assets allows the reader of a balance sheet to determine the amount of assets a corporation has available for current operations. It informs a reader, such as a creditor or supplier, of the ability of a business to pay its bills and loans as they become due.

The accountant defines current assets in terms of the "operating cycle" of a business. The operating cycle of a business is the average period of time in which a business entity produces and sells its product, measured from the time of acquisition of materials and services to the realization of cash from accounts receivable.[5] Those assets which are either converted into cash, sold or consumed within an operating cycle are current assets. A typical operating cycle would involve the expenditure of cash by a business entity to purchase materials, supplies, and labor in order to produce commodities or services, the sale of which would give rise to accounts receivable from which cash would ultimately be collected.

Current assets,[6] then, include cash available for current operations; marketable securities representing short-term investment of cash available; trade notes and accounts receivable; inventories of finished goods; goods in process; raw materials and operating and maintenance supplies; and prepaid expenses, such as insurance, interest, rents, and general supplies.[7] The listing on a balance sheet would generally be in order of the ease by which such assets can be converted into cash in the normal course of business operations. Cash, which requires no conversion, is listed first on the balance sheet. It might be useful at this point to examine the balance sheet of the H.J. Heinz Company reproduced in Appendix B to see how current assets are carried on a typical balance sheet.

---

[5] Where there are several operating cycles within one year, a one-year cycle is used for distinguishing current assets from other than current assets. Where a business has an operating cycle that is longer than one year, such as the lumber business or shipbuilding, the longer period is used. Where a business has no clearly defined operating cycle, a one-year cycle is presumed. American Institute of Certified Public Accountants, Accounting Research Bulletin No. 43, Ch. 3 (June 1953).

[6] The American Institute of Certified Public Accountants provides the following definition of current assets: "[C]ash and other assets or resources commonly identified as those which are reasonably expected to be realized in cash or sold or consumed during the normal operating cycle of the business." American Institute of Certified Public Accountants, Research Bulletin No. 43, Ch. 3 (June 1953).

[7] Prepaid expenses include supplies that a business has on hand which are not yet being utilized and advance payment for services. If a business pays for its lease rental six months in advance, the prepaid rent is an asset. Cash will not have to be expended during that period to cover the rental costs of that period. The American Institute of Certified Public Accountants has explained that "[p]repaid expenses are not current assets in the sense that they will be converted into cash but in the sense that, if not paid in advance, they would require the use of current assets during the operating cycle." American Institute of Certified Public Accountants, Accounting Research Bulletin No. 43, Ch. 3 (June 1953).

C. NONCURRENT ASSETS

Those That are Not Current

"Noncurrent assets" include those assets that are either consumed or used in the operations of an entity over a period of time lasting longer than an operating cycle. A typical manufacturing firm might own land, buildings, machinery and vehicles, all of which would be used over and over again in its operations.[8]

While the term "current assets" will almost always appear on a balance sheet, the term "noncurrent assets" will not frequently be used. Instead of the term "noncurrent assets," an entity might list the various types of assets owned by the entity that are other than current assets. Thus, a typical balance sheet might first list current assets and then list various other assets each of which might be considered noncurrent assets. Examples of assets which are other than current include:

1. Land, Buildings and Equipment. These assets are sometimes referred to as "plant assets" or "fixed assets." These assets are all used by the entity for the production of goods and services. With the exception of land, these fixed assets wear out over time or eventually lose their usefulness. Fixed assets include real property, buildings, furniture, fixtures, machinery, equipment, and vehicles, but do not include land, buildings, or equipment held for investment or disposal.

2. Intangible Fixed Assets. These assets are usually carried on a balance sheet separately from the tangible fixed assets. They are assets used in the operations of a business (as opposed to being held for investment or sale), which have no physical qualities. They include intangibles with fixed lives, such as patents, copyrights and franchises, as well as intangibles with indefinite usefulness, such as goodwill.

3. Deferred Charges. These assets are long-term prepaid expenses. As discussed above, prepaid expenses which are expected to benefit the business entity only for a short period of time are carried as current assets. When prepayment is made on a future expense for a time period that exceeds the entity's operating cycle, the benefit that the entity will receive beyond the operating cycle is carried on the balance sheet, among other than current assets, as a deferred charge. For example, assume a corporation with a one-year operating cycle prepays its annual rent of $1,000 for a manufacturing building for three years. The prepayment of the $1,000 for the first year is a prepaid expense to be included among current assets. The $2,000 prepayment for the following two years is a deferred charge to be included among noncurrent assets. At times, the division of prepaid expenses between current and noncurrent assets is not so simple. For example, prior to 1974, research efforts, the results of which would benefit the entity for several years, could be carried in part as current assets and in part as noncurrent assets. Judgment was required to determine how the allocation should be made.[9]

4. Investments and Funds. These are investments which are not of a short-term nature and for which there is no expectation that they will be converted into cash. These assets are not always integrally utilized in the business operations of an entity. Included in this category would be long-term investments in real property or other tangible assets not used in current operations; stocks and bonds held for long-term purposes, including stocks and bonds of subsidiaries and of companies in which management decides to maintain a voting interest; and cash and securities set aside in funds for bond retirement, pensions and other special

---

[8] The term "noncurrent assets" includes more than merely those assets which have an extended use in operation. For example, an unused building which an entity owns but which is no longer being utilized in production and perhaps is being held for sale, would not be treated as a current asset. This building will not provide extended use in operation. It is still owned by the entity, however, and it still has value and it is therefore a resource of the entity. We would include this unused building in our category of noncurrent assets. Thus, the term "noncurrent assets" is really a catchall phrase which essentially means, as its name indicates, all assets which are other than current assets.

[9] Since 1974, generally accepted accounting principles dictate that research and development costs are not to be treated as assets. After that time, research and development costs are to be treated as expenses, incurred during the period of time in which such research is conducted and serving to reduce net income for that period. Financial Accounting Standard Board, Statements of Financial Accounting Standards No. 2 (Oct. 1974).

purposes. This category, sometimes simply referred to as "investments," commonly is listed first among the noncurrent assets. If securities are purchased by an entity merely as a temporary means of investing excess cash, these securities would not be carried as the noncurrent asset "investment," but rather as the current asset "marketable securities" which was mentioned above in our discussion of current assets.

Note: Although, generally, manufacturing, merchandising and service organizations will classify the assets on their balance sheets into current assets and categories other than current, this classification is not necessarily employed by other businesses. For example, financial institutions such as banks, brokerage firms, and insurance companies typically will not utilize this classification. In a sense, almost all of the assets of a financial institution, including its long-term investments, are part of its business operations and hence are current assets.]

Also, merchandising, manufacturing and most service enterprises tend to arrange their balance sheets by placing current assets before other than current assets. However, public utilities emphasize plant investment and, consequently, many list this category first on the balance sheet.

D. LIABILITIES

A Mirror Image

Parallelling the classification of assets, liabilities are also grouped into "current" or "short-term" liabilities and "noncurrent" or "long-term" liabilities.

1. Current Liabilities. The definition of "current liabilities" is dependent upon the term "current assets": Liabilities which are expected to be satisfied by the application of current assets are called "current liabilities." In other words, current liabilities generally are obligations which fall due or "mature" within a year or within the length of an operating cycle, if longer. Current liabilities include loans or bond or note installment payments maturing within a year; accounts payable which arise from the purchase of goods and services in the ordinary course of business; and rent and taxes due as of the date of the balance sheet. Current liabilities are usually presented in the same order as the examples just described.

2. Noncurrent Liabilities. "Noncurrent" or "other" liabilities include all liabilities not classified as current. Most commonly, there are "long-term debts," that is debts which have a maturity date beyond the current operating cycle or beyond one year. Noncurrent or other liabilities, however, might also include pension obligations, deferred income taxes, and contingent liabilities (which frequently appear only in the notes). The term "noncurrent liabilities" will often not appear on a balance sheet. Instead, the various types of noncurrent liabilities will be listed.

The most common long-term debts are bonds or long-term notes. If repayment of the principal of a long-term debt is to be made over a period of years, only that portion of the debt that matures beyond the current operating cycle is classified as a long-term debt. The portion maturing sooner is a current liability. Even if a debt will mature before the expiration of the current operating cycle, however, if it is to be re-funded (*i.e.*, if a new debt will be incurred in order to pay off the old debt) rather than paid off, it will be considered a long-term debt, since cash will not be diverted within the current operating cycle.

Deferred income tax liabilities are also primarily noncurrent liabilities. These liabilities result from legitimate differences between treatment of expenses for financial reporting purposes and treatment of these same expenses for tax purposes.[10] These differences can give rise to diminished taxes in a current accounting period, which would be offset by somewhat augmented taxes in a later period. The future additional taxes must be carried as a liability on the balance sheet as of the end of the current accounting period.

Contingent liabilities are liabilities as to which there is uncertainty whether they will actually arise and they generally are noncurrent. Such contingencies can include potential direct liabilities such as those that

---

[10] For example, for tax purposes, a firm might use an accelerated depreciation method (see Section G, *infra*), thus reducing current taxable earnings. For financial reporting purposes, the same firm might employ a straight line depreciation method which would reduce current taxable earnings by a lesser amount.

might arise from an unsuccessfully defended lawsuit or a government action for violations of regulations, or claims arising from a warranty.[11] Contingencies might also include secondary liabilities, such as those that might arise from a guaranty contract for which the primary obligor has failed to make payment. Contingencies must be reflected on a financial statement when (i) it is probable that the loss will occur and when (ii) the amount of loss can reasonably be estimated. If both the requirements for reflecting the contingency are not met, but the contingency is still reasonably possible, then a disclosure must be made in the notes to the financial statement.[12]

Note: Just as financial institutions do not classify their assets into current and noncurrent, they do not typically classify their liabilities into current and noncurrent.

Also, noncurrent liabilities are usually shown on the balance sheet after current liabilities. Just as public utilities reverse this practice for their assets, however, they also, on the equities side of the balance sheet, present shareholders' equity and long-term liabilities first, followed by current liabilities.

E. WORKING CAPITAL

A Definition Derived from our Classifications of Assets and Liabilities

One of the advantages of having identified current assets and current liabilities is that we can now define "working capital." Very simply, working capital or "net working capital" allows a reader of a balance sheet to appreciate what portion of the liquid assets of a business will constitute a margin of safety beyond what is necessary for meeting obligations as they become due within the current operating cycle. Working capital is the amount of liquid capital a business has with which to survive bad times, respond to unexpected problems, or take advantage of unexpected opportunities. A determination of working capital can readily be made once current assets and current liabilities have been compiled.

For example, let us assume that a particular business's current assets total $2,500 and its current liabilities total $1,100. We would know that the business had working capital of $1,400. In other words, this business would have $1,400 available in current assets beyond what will be necessary to meet the $1,100 of obligations that will mature before the end of the current operating cycle.

The concept of working capital is important in analyzing the financial health of an entity.[13]

F. VALUATION OF ASSETS AND LIABILITIES ON THE BALANCE SHEET

Now That We Know What the Terms Mean We Still Have to Plug in the Numbers

Identifying assets or liabilities and placing them in their respective categories is an essential step in setting up a balance sheet. Before specific assets or liabilities can be recorded on a balance sheet, however, an amount must be assigned to the particular item. The amount at which an asset appears on a balance sheet is referred to as "book value" or "carrying value."

One could devise a number of logical methods for assigning a book value to items on a balance sheet. For example, assets could be valued in terms of what it would cost to replace them, or at what they would be sold for in the ordinary course of business, or maybe for what they would be sold in a forced sale (*i.e.*, liquidation).

Each of these valuation techniques would involve a considerable degree of estimation. Different individuals with the same basic data might arrive at a different book value for the same items, thus creating financial reports lacking in uniformity. Financial reports which lack uniformity would possess significantly reduced utility for creditors or investors seeking to evaluate the condition of a business entity.

---

[11] Warranty claims that are regularly recurring would most likely be treated as current liabilities.

[12] Financial Accounting Standards Board, Statements of Financial Accounting Standards No. 5 (March 1975).

[13] For a further discussion of how working capital is employed to analyze the health of a business, see Chapter VIII below, on ratio analysis.

(Matthew Bender & Co., Inc.)

The above valuation techniques would also require the presentation of vast amounts of data in order to explain the assumptions upon which the estimations would depend. This data would be too detailed for a convenient display on a balance sheet. Accountants, over the years, have developed a widely accepted framework for assigning a book value to assets and liabilities. The method, although somewhat arbitrary, provides relatively objective and consistent results. The practice employed by accountants is to account for assets and liabilities on the basis of "actual" cost or "historical cost."

Historical cost is the amount paid by an enterprise for an asset. It is the acquisition price of an asset. If an asset is acquired other than by a cash purchase, the historical cost is determined by the fair market value at the date of acquisition of the assets given in exchange.

To illustrate, when a parcel of land is acquired by an entity, (i) it may be bought by payment of $100,000 cash; (ii) it may be bought at an agreed price of $100,000 with part of the purchase price being in the form of interest-bearing notes at the market interest rate at the time of purchase; or (iii) it may instead be acquired by issuance of corporate shares with a total market price of $100,000. In each case, the land will be carried in subsequent balance sheets at its acquisition price or historical cost of $100,000. The acquisition price is determined, in the first instance, by the cash that was exchanged for the land and in the second and third instances by the fair market value of the notes or the shares exchanged for the land.

Notice that in all three instances, the focus of the inquiry for determining historical cost is on the value of the consideration exchanged for the land. Even if the land were bought at either a bargain price or an excessive price, the historical cost would be determined by the value of the consideration given in exchange rather than by some presumed fair value of the land.

The concept of historical cost applies also to liabilities in the sense that the liability is recorded in an amount equal to the cost to the enterprise of the assets or services received in exchange when the liability was created. With liabilities, as with assets, there are alternative valuation methods that might have been chosen to record liabilities but were not chosen because of the lack of uniform results they would provide or because of the voluminous data upon which these valuation methods would rely.

To say that all assets and liabilities are recorded at actual or historical cost is too simplistic and perhaps somewhat misleading. Although original recordings are made at historical cost, there are generally accepted modifications which are made to these original recordings. Such modifications arise from adjustments to historical costs to reflect changes that occur in the value of certain assets carried on the balance sheet. Other modifications might merely reflect the fact that for some assets there is more than one method for assigning value, and in different circumstances, different methods are employed. The impact of these modifications is apparent either in the balance sheet itself or in the notes explaining the financial statements. The book value of assets is determined by starting with the original historical cost and applying to that original cost the appropriate modification.

In the next several sections, there will be a discussion of these modifications as they apply to plant assets, inventories, accounts receivable, marketable securities and the intangible asset goodwill.

G. MODIFICATIONS OF HISTORICAL COSTS — PLANT ASSETS

Depreciation

1. What is This Thing Called "Depreciation"? Plant assets (*e.g.*, land, buildings, equipment, furniture and fixtures) are initially recorded on the balance sheet at cost. Cost includes not only the price paid for an item, such as machinery, but also installation costs necessary to make that machinery operational.

All plant assets, with the exception of land, ultimately lose their utility. Plant assets lose their usefulness over time either as a result of physical factors (wear and tear of operation or deterioration over time) or of functional factors (obsolescence or inadequacy because of change in operations). In effect, they are consumed in operations.

As when other assets are consumed in operations (*e.g.*, when raw materials are utilized in production), the partial consumption of plant assets over time is an expense which is incurred by a business entity and which needs to be periodically recognized by the business entity over the useful life of the assets. This expense is called "depreciation expense," and it appears upon the income statement of the business.

In addition to providing information as to the costs allocated to operations during a specific time period, the depreciation expense amount serves a second purpose. It offers an arbitrary measurement of the decline in the service potential of the asset. Thus, the sum of the periodic allocations for depreciation, "accumulated depreciation," is shown on the balance sheet as a deduction from the original cost of the particular asset. Accumulated depreciation, or "Allowance for Depreciation," is referred to as a "contra account" because it is offset against the "Plant Asset" account. On a typical balance sheet, the plant asset "Equipment" with its corresponding contra account for Accumulated Depreciation might appear as follows:

Equipment	$10,000
Less: Accumulated depreciation	2,000
	$8,000

Thus plant assets are carried at historical cost less accumulated depreciation.

Although the historical cost of an asset less its accumulated depreciation might, in some instances, provide an approximation of the fair market value of the asset, that is not the purpose of depreciating assets. Rather, depreciation is essentially a method for allocating the historical cost of an asset to expenses over the anticipated useful life of the asset. As additional depreciation expenses are "charged" against revenue, the accumulated depreciation account (which is deducted from the asset's historical cost) is augmented and the value of the asset on the balance sheet is diminished. The $8,000 at which the equipment in the above example is carried on the balance sheet might equal market value of the equipment, but that would be largely coincidental. This is because that $8,000 figure is derived not by investigating the remaining value of the equipment, but merely by subtracting from its acquisition costs the periodic expenses allocated to its use.

It is important to bear in mind that the depreciation expense is incurred without any cash flowing out of the business entity. Rather, the depreciation expense is merely the allocation over time of the cost of an asset, which has already been acquired. Because of this, the net income (which is derived in part by subtracting this arbitrary depreciation expense) of a business may be less than the actual funds available to it. As an example, suppose a business consists entirely of the operations of a single trailer truck used for hauling. It receives $40,000 in revenues in the course of a year. It has $14,000 of expenses during the year, but this includes $4,000 of depreciation for the year. The business will have a net income of only $26,000 for the year. But it will have available funds amounting to $30,000. The depreciation expenses reduce income, but they do not require a present outlay of cash.

2. How to Determine the Amount of Depreciation. Once the acquisition cost of an asset is known, to determine the depreciation charge for that asset to be allocated in each period, it is necessary to know the estimated value of the asset at the end of its useful life or its "salvage value," the estimated useful life of the asset,[14] and the method of depreciation that will be employed.

One of the most common methods in financial reports for allocating depreciation expenses is the "straight line" method. This approach spreads the depreciation expenses equally over the estimated life of an asset. Under the straight line method, the yearly depreciation charge is computed by subtracting the estimated

---

[14] It is important to emphasize that, prospectively, both salvage value and useful life of an asset are only estimates. These estimates have at times proved to be wrong. In the early 1970's, computers owned by some computer leasing companies were found to have a far shorter useful life than what was predicted, because they had become obsolete in the face of unanticipated technological advancements in the industry. Contrariwise, in the 1960's, the estimated useful lives of the jet planes owned by some commercial airlines were found to be too short. The airline industry was discovering that some of the early passenger jet airplanes were lasting longer than anticipated.

Generally accepted accounting principles direct that changes in estimates of useful life or in salvage value be treated only prospectively in financial statements. American Institute of Certified Public Accountants, Accounting Principle Board Opinion No. 20, par. 31 (July 1971). Thus, if the annual depreciation charge for an asset had been too small because the estimate of the useful life was too long, instead of correcting past charges, the amount of depreciation for the remaining period of useful life should be proportionately increased.

salvage value from the actual cost and dividing the remainder by the estimated number of years of use. The formula to determine depreciation would be:

$$\text{Yearly Depreciation Charge} = \frac{\text{(Cost) less (Salvage Value)}}{\text{Years of Useful Life}}$$

To see how this formula would work, consider a firm which uses small trucks in its operations, each truck costing $11,000. The firm will maintain and repair these trucks for a period of ten years, after which time the firm has determined that it makes sense to buy new trucks and sell the old ones. The firm estimates that, after ten years, the resale, scrap or salvage value of the trucks will be $1,000 each. Under the straight line method of depreciation, this firm's depreciation charge would be $1,000.

$$\text{Yearly Depreciation Charge} = \frac{\$11,000 - \$1,000}{10} = \$1,000 \text{ per year}$$

At the end of ten years, the cost of each truck, less its salvage value, will have been allocated to expense.[15]

An alternative approach to depreciation is to use an "accelerated" approach. Accelerated methods allocate more cost to the earlier years of service and less to the later years. There are a number of justifications for this approach. The primary explanation regards assets as being most efficient when new and hence depreciation as greatest during this time. In addition, since repair costs generally increase as an asset ages, decreasing depreciation costs with age results in a more constant total operational cost of an asset.

3. The Impact of and Calculation of Accelerated Depreciation. For business managers, an accelerated depreciation method might be attractive, since it results in a greater expense during the early years of ownership of a plant asset and hence lower taxable earnings (without any less available funds than under the straight line method) and consequently lower income taxes. Admittedly, the reduced taxes might well be offset by higher taxes in the later years of ownership of the asset, but in the interim, the firm using the accelerated method will have the use of a greater sum of money than it would have with the straight line depreciation method.[16]

As an illustration, we can apply an accelerated depreciation method to the same firm discussed above which purchases small trucks for $11,000 and depreciates them over a ten-year life. One of the two commonly employed accelerated methods is the "sum of the years' digits method." Under this method, the amount of depreciation charged each year as an expense is a decreasing fraction of the actual cost of the asset less salvage value.[17] In the first year of depreciation under this method, $1,818 would be charged

---

[15] Under the straight line depreciation method, the annual depreciation and book value of the above-discussed truck would appear as follows:

Year	Annual Depreciation	Remaining Cost (Book Value)
1	$ 1,000	$10,000
2	1,000	9,000
3	1,000	8,000
4	1,000	7,000
5	1,000	6,000
6	1,000	5,000
7	1,000	4,000
8	1,000	3,000
9	1,000	2,000
10	1,000	1,000 (estimated salvage value)
Total	$10,000	

[16] Similar tax savings can be effected by using a shorter rather than longer estimated useful life for a depreciable asset. The shorter the life employed, the greater the depreciation expense each year and the less taxable income. The Internal Revenue Service is, of course, concerned about the degree of acceleration that is employed in a depreciation method, as well as the length of the estimated life that is employed. It has established guidelines for both of these variables.

[17] The denominator of this fraction equals the sum of all the digits from one to that number which equals the estimated life of the asset. The numerator decreases each year and equals the number of years remaining in the life of the asset as measured

as a depreciation expense. This would represent a considerably greater expense than the $1,000 which would be charged under the above-described straight line method. In the tenth year of depreciation, however, the accelerated method would permit a depreciation expense of only $182. Under the straight line method, the depreciation expense remains constant at $1,000.

The book value of an asset under the accelerated technique obviously declines faster than under the straight line method. The increased depreciation expense in the early years of depreciation under an accelerated method results in a greater amount of accumulated depreciation which is deducted from the original cost of an asset. The accelerated technique, accordingly, initially creates a lower book value than what would be created under a straight line depreciation approach. Thus, at the end of five years, the above-discussed truck would be carried at $3,727 under the sum-of-the-years' digit method and at $6,000 under a straight line method.

It is apparent that the choice of a depreciation method has a significant impact upon both the earnings and the net assets of a business at certain points in time. Were the same firm to carry the same truck as discussed above under the sum-of-the-years' digit method as opposed to a straight line method, it would have $2,273 less net assets and also $2,273 less retained earnings after the first five-year period. (At the end of the useful life of the truck, however, under both methods, the net assets of the firm as well as its retained earnings would be identical.)

To carry our understanding of the impact of various depreciation methods one step further, we can see that the choice of depreciation method could impact upon a corporation's ability to make distributions.[18] Both retained earnings and net assets are measurements of the financial condition of a corporation, which measurements are employed in determining if distributions can be made. The use of an accelerated depreciation method might give a diminished picture of the retained earnings and net assets of a corporation during the early years of the depreciable life of a particular major asset. Thus, during the early years of

---

by the year which has just passed. So for the truck in the above example, the denominator would equal the sum of the digits of its useful life which would be 1+2+3+4+5+6+7+8+9+10, or 55. The numerator in the first year would be 10 and in the last year would be 1. So, in the first year, $^{10}/_{55}$ of the actual cost of the truck less salvage value would be charged as a depreciated expense. In the last year, $^{1}/_{55}$ of the actual cost less salvage value would be charged as a depreciated expense, In total, 100% of the cost less salvage value would be allocated to depreciation.

Under the sum-of-the-years' digit depreciation method, the annual depreciation and book value of the above-discussed truck would appear as follows:

Year	Annual Depreciation	Remaining Cost (Book Value)	
1	$ 1,818	$ 9,182	
2	1,636	7,456	
3	1,455	6,091	
4	1,273	4,818	
5	1,091	3,727	
6	909	2,818	
7	727	2,091	
8	545	1,546	
9	364	1,182	
10	182	1,000	(estimated salvage value)
Total	$10,000		

Another frequently utilized accelerated depreciation method is the declining balance method. Here a depreciation rate is employed that is some multiple of the straight line rate. As an example, the double rate for an asset with a 10-year life would be 20% (double the straight line rate of $^1/_{10}$ or 10%). This rate is applied against the book value of the asset at the beginning of each period. Since the book value decreases each year, there is a lower depreciation charge each year. This depreciation process goes on until the book value is reduced to the approximate salvage value.

[18] For a discussion of restrictions on a corporation's ability to make distributions, see Chapter IX, infra.

the depreciation of this asset, the corporation might be more restricted in its ability to make distributions than if it used a straight line method of depreciation.[19]

Businesses are permitted to use an accelerated depreciation method for tax purposes while employing a straight line method for preparation of financial reports. Thus, the use of an accelerated method of depreciation for tax purposes might have no impact at all on a corporation's ability to make distributions.

4.   Some Remaining Concerns About What is Depreciable. It is clear that when a plant asset is acquired by a firm, the cost of that asset is allocated over time by a depreciation method. It is not always clear, however, how costs of repairs for fixed assets should be allocated. Should the addition of a new roof to a factory be treated as a repair, the entire cost of which would be charged against revenues during the period in which the repair is made? Perhaps the new roof should be considered a replacement of a portion of a fixed asset, the cost of which will be allocated over time through depreciation. Hinging on the outcome of the accounting treatment of the cost of the new roof is the size of the net income of the firm during the period in which the roof is improved and during the time for which the cost might be depreciated. If the entire cost of a roof is charged against revenues during a single fiscal period, net income will be more greatly reduced for that fiscal period than if the cost of the roof were added to the asset value of the factory and then allocated as an expense over time.

The primary factor that is considered in determining whether to "capitalize" (*i.e.*, add the cost of the total value of the roof and depreciate it) or "expense" (*i.e.*, charge the cost of the roof as an expense for that year) a repair, is whether the repair will benefit the firm for more than one operating cycle. Another consideration, in some situations, might be whether the cost seems to restore an asset to its original performance capabilities or whether it creates a new asset with better performance potential (*e.g.*, was the replacement of old, flammable, heat-absorbing shingle with modern, fireproof and non-heat-absorbing shingle?). One might also examine whether the cost is recurring (*e.g.*, is the repair a new coat of tar that is applied each year?). Relatively small expenditures are more likely to be expensed than capitalized inasmuch as they are not material in amount.

5.   Cost Allocation Concepts for Other than Plant Assets. Similar to the depreciation of plant assets, costs of assets represented by natural resources, such as petroleum, mineral deposits and timber (which assets are exhausted as they are used) are allocated to expenses as the resources are consumed (*i.e.*, mined or cut down). This allocation is termed "depletion." Costs of intangibles, such as patents or copyrights, are also allocated over time. This allocation is termed "amortization."[20]

H.   MODIFICATIONS OF HISTORICAL COSTS — INVENTORY

Methods of Valuing Inventory

Inventory is another asset the historical cost of which will typically be modified when recorded on a balance sheet. As with the impact that alternative methods of depreciation can have upon plant assets, the method employed for calculating inventory can have a significant impact upon the financial positions of a firm as reflected on the balance sheet as well as the income statement.

1.   What is Inventory and Why is the Determination of Historical Cost Not a Simple Matter? Inventory of a merchandising firm includes all of those goods which the firm holds for sale in the ordinary course of business. In the instance of a manufacturing firm, besides goods held for sale, inventory also includes goods which are in the process of production, as well as raw materials and supplies that will be

---

[19] Under some statutes, assets may be valued for purposes of determining whether distributions can be made both by the method employed in preparation of the corporation's financial statements, as well as by other fair valuation methods. See, for example, the Revised Model Business Corporation Act, § 6.40, Official Comment, § 6. Thus, under such statutes, even if an accelerated depreciation method is used to value assets for the financial statement, a fair market value can arguably be employed for a distribution test.

[20] For a discussion of the amortization of the intangible asset, goodwill, see Section K of this Chapter, *infra*.

consumed in the production of goods for sale. For example, the inventory of a firm that manufactures toy blocks for children might include the new supplies of wood that will be used to make the blocks, the blocks in process that have been cut and not yet painted and packaged, as well as the packages of completed blocks that are ready for distribution.

The cost of inventory for a merchandising firm is comprised of the purchase price of the inventory plus all additional costs (*e.g.*, transportation and transit insurance) incurred in acquiring the merchandise. For a manufacturing firm, the cost of inventory includes the cost of raw materials plus the cost of labor that has been applied to the raw materials plus an aliquot share of overhead costs. For convenience of discussion, we will focus upon the inventory of merchandising firms.

2.   Methods for Determining the Quantity of Inventory. Since the amount and value of the firm's inventory is critical for determining profits and the cost of its assets, firms maintain records as to the amount of inventory that is held by the business. There are two basic means of keeping track of the physical quantity of inventory. In some businesses, the nature of the inventory is such that the firm is able to maintain a record as to the acquisition and sale of each item of inventory it holds as such acquisition and sale occur. An example of a business that would be able to maintain such current records would be an automobile dealership. This method of keeping track of inventory is referred to as "the perpetual inventory method" because it can provide a running total of the amount of inventory on hand, as well as its dollar value.

More frequently, inventory is so numerous that it is inconvenient to keep a running record of the disposition of every item of inventory. Instead, a physical count of inventory is periodically taken. This method of keeping track of inventory is referred to as the "periodic inventory method."[21]

3.   How Inventory Impacts upon Assets and Profits. Businesses keep track of the quantity of inventory in order to know the amount to record on the balance sheet, as well as to determine gross (margin) profits for the period. When the cost of inventory at the end of a period is subtracted from the cost of starting inventory plus purchases made during that period, a determination can be made of the cost of goods sold during the period. When the cost of goods sold during a period is subtracted from the total sales for that period, a business can determine gross profits for that period. As an example, assume that a building supply company that sells bricks begins a year with an inventory of bricks that cost the company $10,000. Also assume that, during the year, the company makes several purchases of bricks for its inventory, totalling $25,000. If the company finishes the year with an inventory that cost $8,000, one can readily determine that the cost of the bricks sold during the year was $27,000.

Beginning inventory	$10,000
Purchases	25,000
Bricks available for sale	35,000
Less: Ending inventory	8,000
Cost of bricks sold	$27,000

If the company received $41,000 during the year from its sale of bricks, then gross profits on the bricks sold can be readily determined.

Sales	$41,000
Less: Cost of bricks sold	27,000
Gross (margin) profit on sales	$14,000

Thus, we see that ending inventory can assist in determining the amount of assets on a balance sheet as well as in calculating gross profits for the income statement.

---

[21] With modern computerized accounting systems, it is easier to keep a continuous record of physical units which should be on hand, and even the cost of these units. Periodic physical counts are necessary, however, from time to time to determine the accuracy of the book balance of the perpetual inventory record.

(Matthew Bender & Co., Inc.)

4. Methods for Determining the Cost of Inventory. Although it was not mentioned above, as a practical matter, the cost of inventory remaining with a firm at the end of a business period is not necessarily a simple matter to compute. Merely possessing quantity and cost of inventory at the beginning of a period, quantity and cost of purchases made during the period, and quantity of inventory remaining at the end of a period does not, without further analysis, automatically provide a monetary figure representing the cost of the ending inventory. Costs of units of inventory vary over time. During the course of a year, the per unit cost of bricks that our building supply firm bought in the above example might be different from the per unit cost of the bricks in the firm's beginning inventory. Unless expensive and inconvenient detailed records are kept, a firm will not know the order in which its bricks were sold. When the firm sold its bricks during the year as described above, it might have been selling bricks which it had in its inventory at the beginning of the year. It might also have been selling bricks it purchased in the course of the year. Consequently, it would be impossible for the firm to know the actual cost of either the bricks that were sold during the year or the cost of the bricks that remained at the end of the period. To compensate for these uncertainties, accountants have developed valuation methods for inventory which are based upon arbitrary assumptions as to the order in which inventory is utilized by a business.

5. Methods for Determining the Costs of Inventory Sold or Consumed. There are four generally accepted methods for assigning a cost to inventory utilized by a business. The withdrawal from stock can be treated under the first-in, first-out rule (FIFO), the last-in, first-out rule (LIFO), on an average basis, or on a specific cost basis.

Under FIFO, the cost arbitrarily assigned to the unit being withdrawn is the acquisition cost of that unit remaining in inventory which has been held the longest. As a consequence, the residual units remaining in inventory carry the cost of the most recently purchased units.

Conversely, under LIFO, the cost assigned to the item being withdrawn is the cost of the most recently acquired unit in stock. And it follows that the units remaining in inventory will carry acquisition costs applicable to units acquired at the earliest time, sometimes several years prior to the current balance sheet date.

Under an average cost technique, the cost assigned to inventory withdrawn is the weighted average of the costs of units purchased during the period and the units in inventory at the beginning of that period.

The specific cost method for valuing inventory withdrawn requires that each unit of inventory be specifically marked with its acquisition price. Under this method, the cost assigned to each item withdrawn from inventory is identical to the specific cost of the item withdrawn.

To be able to determine the impact of these various methods we can examine the purchases and sales of a hypothetical dealer in bushels of wheat during a period of time in which prices were rising for the wheat inventories purchased. We will compute the cost of goods sold and the cost of remaining inventories under the two most frequently employed accounting methods, FIFO and LIFO.

Purchase Date	Bushels Bought	Price per Bushel	Cost
January 10	500	$ 1.00	$ 500.00
March 3	400	1.20	480.00
June 15	500	1.30	650.00
August 30	600	1.40	840.00
November 18	300	1.60	480.00
	2300		$2950.00

Assume that, during the same period, the wheat dealer sold 1600 bushels of wheat, leaving 700 bushels in its inventory (the price at which the wheat is sold is irrelevant). The cost of the wheat sold under the FIFO method would be calculated by adding up the cost of the earliest purchases until 1600 bushels is reached.

500 bushels	January 10	@ $1.00	$ 500.00
400 bushels	March 3	@ $1.20	480.00

500 bushels	June 15	@ $1.30	650.00
200 bushels	August 30	@ $1.40	280.00
1600 bushels			$1910.00

The cost of the wheat remaining in inventory could be determined by adding up the cost of the most recent purchases until 700 bushels is reached (or, more simply, by subtracting the cost of the wheat sold from the total cost of the wheat purchased).

300 bushels	November 18	@ $1.60	$ 480.00
400 bushels	August 30	@ $1.40	560.00
700 bushels			$1040.00

The cost of the remaining wheat would be carried on the balance sheet as the cost of the wheat inventory of the business at the close of the period.

Under the LIFO method, the process would be reversed and the cost of the 1600 bushels sold would be determined from the cost of the most recent purchases.

300 bushels	November 18	@ $1.60	$ 480.00
600 bushels	August 30	@ $1.40	840.00
500 bushels	June 15	@ $1.30	650.00
200 bushels	March 3	@ $1.20	240.00
1600 bushels			$2210.00

And the cost of the 700 bushels remaining would be determined from the cost of the earliest purchases (or, again, by subtracting the cost of the wheat sold from the total cost of the wheat purchased).

500 bushels	January 10	@ $1.00	$ 500.00
200 bushels	March 3	@ $1.20	240.00
700 bushels			$ 740.00

6. The Significance of the Different Inventory Valuation Methods. One can see that the particular accounting method employed gives markedly different results as to the cost of the inventory sold and, necessarily, the cost of inventory remaining. Some of the differences in results can be summarized as follows:

(a) In the rising market described above, the LIFO method produced a cost of inventory sold that was $300 more than that derived under the FIFO method. Cost of goods, when subtracted from sales, equals gross (margin) profit. All else being equal, gross (margin) profit under the LIFO method would have to be $300 less than under the FIFO method. (Thus, the use of LIFO rather than FIFO in a market of rising costs would result in decreased profits.) Reduced gross profit would result in lower taxable income. Thus, in a rising market, the LIFO method will result in less tax than the FIFO method.

The significance of these various methods of calculating the cost of inventory is fully appreciated by business. In the early 1970's, when the nation's economy began to experience considerable inflation, many firms switched over to the LIFO accounting method because of the tax savings involved.

(b) Under LIFO, the oldest inventory costs remain on the balance sheet. Under FIFO, the most recent inventory costs remain on the balance sheet. Thus, in a rising market, LIFO produces a lower figure for the value of inventory than would be produced under the FIFO method. Obviously, these statements about the impact of the various accounting methods on the income statement and the balance sheet would be reversed in a market in which the unit price of inventory was falling.

(c) Under a LIFO method of inventory accounting, the cost of goods sold reflects recent price changes. Under the FIFO system, one has to wait a longer time to reflect price changes since the cost of goods sold reflects the price of the earliest remaining inventory. One could conclude that the LIFO method provides a more realistic idea of what it currently costs to sell or consume specific inventory, but a less realistic idea of the current cost of remaining inventory.

Generally accepted accounting principles[22] permit changes in the method of inventory accounting. The nature of the change, however, must be disclosed in the financial statements and the justification for the change must be discussed.[23]

As opposed to the flexibility that the Internal Revenue Service affords businesses that chose to employ different depreciation methods, the Service required that if the LIFO accounting method is employed for income tax purposes, it must also be utilized in the income statement of the business that is transmitted to its shareholders.[24]

I. MODIFICATION OF HISTORICAL COSTS — ACCOUNTS RECEIVABLE

Providing for Bad Debts

Most businesses of any size which sell goods or services make a portion of these sales to its customers on credit. The businesses will exchange for the asset, inventory, an asset in the form of a promise to pay or an account receivable. Initially, these accounts will be carried on the balance sheet at the amount billed to the customers. Even if care is taken to screen out poor credit risks, however, inevitably, a portion of these accounts receivable will not be paid. The Accounts Receivable account on the balance sheet needs to be adjusted in order to allow for the uncollectible receivables. The Accounts Receivable account which at first equals the amount billed to the customers is later reduced by an Allowance for Uncollectible Accounts or an Allowance for Bad Debts. This Allowance for Uncollectible Accounts is carried on the balance sheet as a negative asset account or a "contra" account. Thus, a business which has $5,000 worth of receivables, of which $400 are estimated to be uncollectible, would have an entry on its balance sheet that appeared as follows:

Accounts receivable	$5000.00
Less: Allowance for uncollectible accounts	400.00
Net accounts receivable	$4600.00

There are two basic methods for accounting for bad debts. Under the direct write-off method (primarily used by firms doing a limited credit business) an allowance is not made for the potential bad debt. Rather, the account receivable is written off when it is determined to be uncollectible. Thus, the provision for the bad debt might not be entered for a considerable period of time after the actual sale has been made and the credit extended.

For firms doing a greater amount of credit business, an estimate can be taken, based upon past experience, of what portion of accounts receivable (or perhaps, what portion of all sales) will prove to be uncollectible. This percentage is then carried as the Allowance for Uncollectible Accounts. In using this estimation method, higher percentages are likely to be employed the older an account receivable becomes. This is because a long outstanding account is less likely to be paid than an account outstanding for a shorter time. Under the estimation method, the provision for uncollectibles may be recorded during the same period in which the sales giving rise to the accounts receivable are recorded.

Regardless of which method is employed for bad debts, either at the time that the account receivable is reduced under the direct write-off method or at the time the allowance for bad debts is established under the estimation method, an expense is recorded for the business. In other words, the loss suffered or anticipated from the uncollectible receivables is considered to be a cost of extending credit. Again, we see that an adjustment to the assets also impacts upon the firm's income.

---

[22] For a discussion of generally accepted accounting principles, see Chapter IV, *infra*.

[23] American Institute of Certified Public Accountants, Accounting Principles Board Opinion No. 20 (July 1971).

[24] Internal Revenue Code § 472 (1992).

J. MODIFICATION OF HISTORICAL COSTS — MARKETABLE EQUITY SECURITIES

Different Methods of Valuation Depending Upon Classification

Businesses that have cash on hand beyond immediate needs might invest that cash for a temporary period of time in marketable securities such as government securities, commercial paper, or relatively liquid equity securities (*i.e.*, equity securities for which there are ready buyers and sellers). As we discussed above in this chapter, these securities are carried as current assets and management might sell them as the need for cash arises.

There is concern with how to carry the equity securities on a balance sheet since the market price of these securities tends to fluctuate. This concern with market fluctuation compels a business to at times carry marketable equity securities at an amount other than cost.

Until 1994, marketable securiries were carried in the balance sheet at the lower of cost or market. In 1993, however, the Financial Accounting Standards Board issued Statement No. 115, Accounting for Certain Investments in Debt and Equity Securities.[25] Under the rules expressed in Statement No. 115, all investments in debt securities and investments in equity securities having readily determinable fair values[26] are to be classified as follows:

Held-to-maturity,

Trading securities, or

Available-for-sale.

Held-to-maturity includes debt securities with the intent and ability to be held to maturity. Such securities are to be carried in the balance sheet at amortized cost.

Trading securities comprise debt and equity securities bought and held primarily for a sale in the near term. These securities are to be carried at fair (market) value. The carrying values are to be adjusted periodically with unrealized gains or losses included in earnings.

The available-for-sale category includes debt and equity securities not classified as held-to-maturity or trading securities. Available-for-sale securities are to be carried at fair value, but the unrealized gains or losses are not to be included in earnings but are to be reported as a separate component of shareholders' equity.

Investments in subsidiaries or affiliates are generally not marketable in the ordinary course of business and are not to be included in the forgoing categories. As discussed in section D of chapter V, Consolidated Financial Statements, investments exceeding 50% are eliminated in the process of consolidation.

Investments of less than 50% in the voting stock of another corporation (the "investee" corporation) might be intended for other than short-term means of utilizing excess cash. At times, these investments are intended for the purpose of gaining voting influence in the investee corporation. As discussed earlier in this chapter, such investments are carried as long-term assets. This significant economic relationship between the investing business and the investee corporation is recognized by carrying the securities of the investee corporation by the "equity method" on the books of the investing corporation.

Under the equity method, the investment is originally carried at cost. This account is then increased by the investor's proportionate share of earnings of the investee and decreased by the investor's proportionate share of losses of the investee and payment of dividends by the investee.[27] The equity method of accounting

---

[25] Financial Accounting Standards Board, Statement of Financial Accounting No. 115 (May, 1993).

[26] Generally, sales prices or bid-and-asked quotations on a recognized securities exchange.

[27] For example, assume Corporation B has 500,000 shares of stock outstanding. At the beginning of 20____, Firm A acquires 200,000 of these shares (40% of the amount outstanding) for $600,000. If, in that year, B earns $800,000 and pays dividends of $1 a share, the investment would be carried on A's balance sheet as of December 31, 20____ at $720,000. The original cost of $600,00 was increased by $320,000 or 40% of the total earnings of B and reduced by $200,000 of dividends received by A on the stock of B.

is most appropriate when the investor's investment enables the investor to influence the operations or financial decisions of the investee corporation. An investment of greater than 20% is required to trigger the presumption that the investor has a sufficient position to influence the investee.[28] At that point, the investor is considered to have that degree of responsibility for the return of its investment as to allow the investor to include in the results of its operations its share of earnings or losses of the investee.

K.　MODIFICATION OF HISTORICAL COSTS — THE INTANGIBLE ASSET CALLED GOODWILL

How to Carry a Reputation on Your Balance Sheet

Goodwill is one of many intangible assets which might be carried as an asset on the balance sheet of a business. Other intangible assets include patents, copyrights, licenses, trademarks and franchises. Intangible assets, in an accounting sense, are not easy to define. For certain, they have no physical presence. But assets other than intangible assets, such as accounts receivable and long-term investments, also have no physical presence. Some accountants further define intangible assets by the high degree of uncertainty as to the future benefits that a business can derive from such assets.

Goodwill is that particular intangible asset reflected in certain advantages a business might possess arising from such factors as location, reputation, good labor relations, or superior management, among others. Goodwill exists when a business, because of an intangible factor, is able to earn a greater rate of return on its assets than comparable businesses lacking the factor would be able to earn.

Intangible assets in general may be purchased, or they may be developed within a business. In either instance, as with other assets, they are recorded initially at cost. Thus, the cost of a patent on a balance sheet is carried at the price paid for the patent. If a patent is developed internally, it is carried at the cost of the legal fees that arise from registering the patent.[29]

Accountants, however, treat goodwill more conservatively than other intangible assets. Goodwill cannot really be identified as an asset that is severable from the total business. Unlike a specifically identifiable asset such as a copyright, goodwill cannot be sold without selling the entire business. Furthermore, attempting to associate specific costs with the development of goodwill is a very uncertain endeavor. In some instances, goodwill may exist even in the absence of development costs. Consequently, goodwill is only recorded when it is purchased in conjunction with the acquisition of a business. It is only at this point that we have an objective measurement of the cost of goodwill. We identify the cost of goodwill as the excess of the purchase price over the fair value of the identifiable net assets acquired.

In some instances, the effects of this practice of only reflecting goodwill on the balance sheet when a business is purchased, could be that two very identical businesses with very identical reputations might have significantly dissimilar balance sheets. A restaurant business that developed its reputation itself over time could not carry goodwill as an asset on its balance sheet. An identical restaurant business, however, if purchased at a price exceeding the market value of its identifiable assets less liabilities, could present a balance sheet which carried the asset goodwill in addition to the previously carried assets. The balance sheet of the predecessor restaurant business prior to sale might appear as follows:

Balance Sheet Just Prior to Sale:

Assets		Liabilities and Owners' Equity	
Equipment	400,000	Debts	200,000
Other Assets	100,000	Equity	300,000

[28] American Institute of Certified Public Accountants, Accounting Principles Board Opinion No. 18 (March 1971).

[29] Since it is difficult to identify the specific research costs associated with the internal development of a patent, generally accepted accounting principles dictate that such costs be charged to income ("expensed") when they occur and not carried as part of the cost of the patent ("capitalized"). Financial Accounting Standards Board, Statement of Financial Accounting Standards No. 2 (Oct. 1974).

Assume the restaurant business is then sold for $350,000. The purchase price is $50,000 greater than the net asset value of the firm and it is understood that this additional amount is to pay for the reputation of the business. The balance sheet of the successor business just after the sale would appear as follows:

Balance Sheet Just After the Sale:

Assets		Liabilities and Owners' Equity	
Equipment	400,000	Debts	200,000
Other Assets	100,000	Equity	350,000
Goodwill	50,000		

The accountant's unwillingness to record on the balance sheet of a business goodwill that the business has self-generated is reflective of the generally conservative nature of accounting principles.[30] If accounting principles permitted the recording of goodwill in the absence of a purchase of a business, there could be great uncertainty in demonstrating both the existence and amount of goodwill. An uncertain amount of self-developed goodwill permitted to appear on a business's balance sheet could mislead investors and creditors as to the financial condition of the business.[31] In addition, if the business were a corporation, the recorded self-developed goodwill could provide a portion of the legal justification for the corporation's making a distribution to its shareholders,[32] even though the true worth of the goodwill might be extremely speculative.

To even permit a business to record goodwill as an asset when the business is acquired is not entirely logical. The value of goodwill is dependent upon the business remaining a "going concern" and were the various assets of the business sold individually at a liquidation sale, there would be no goodwill upon which purchasers could bid. Goodwill is frequently dependent upon temporary factors, such as the style of a particular management or a fleeting public fad. The logic of allowing goodwill to be recorded if a business is acquired, however, is that at least at the moment of purchase, the buyers were willing to pay a premium which can be roughly computed and which would be reflective of the objective value of goodwill to that particular purchaser.

Intangible assets, like other assets, are amortized over a period of time. Thus, the cost of acquiring or developing intangible assets is charged to expenses in a systematic manner over time as the intangible asset is utilized. It is relatively easy to determine the useful life of some intangibles for amortization purposes. A patent would be amortized over its legal life of 17 years unless its useful life were somehow less than its legal life (e.g., were the patent to become obsolete).

It is somewhat more difficult to determine the useful life of goodwill. If the goodwill were dependent upon the personalities of certain managers, the goodwill would last for as long as those managers were associated with the business. If the goodwill were dependent upon a public fascination with the product or services sold by a business, the goodwill would last as long as the public fascination lasted. In some instances, where it arises from location and an efficiently run business, goodwill can last for a significant period of time. Accountants agree, however, that the value of goodwill should eventually be removed from the balance sheet.[33]

To determine the useful life of goodwill or any other intangible asset, generally accepted accounting principles direct that a reasonable estimate be made of the asset's useful life. The period of amortization, however, should in no instance exceed 40 years.[34] Thus, as the useful life of goodwill passes, the recorded

---

[30] See Chapter IV, Section B, infra.

[31] Arguably, financially sophisticated investors and creditors would know to discount the value of the assets to the extent of goodwill.

[32] For a discussion of how the amount of assets impacts on a corporation's ability to make distributions, see Chapter IX, Section C, infra.

[33] Actually, if the goodwill was acquired prior to October 31, 1970, it need not be amortized and can thus be carried indefinitely on the balance sheet. American Institute of Certified Public Accountants, Accounting Principles Board Opinion No. 17 (Aug. 1970).

[34] Id.

value of the asset will decrease each year by a fraction equal to the number one over the estimated number of years of useful life. If we assume that the goodwill (of $50,000) associated with the above-described restaurant that was purchased has a useful life of 40 years, then goodwill would be reduced each year on the balance sheet by $50,000 over 40 or $1,250. The decrease in goodwill would be charged as an expense against income.[35]

L. HISTORICAL COST AND ITS DEFICIENCIES

Can't Accountants Invent a Better Mousetrap?

Although the method of recording assets at historical cost with various modifications has the virtue of being relatively objective and simple, it has its drawbacks.

Historical cost of plant assets, as adjusted by depreciation, does not take into consideration the impact that inflation might have on the value of certain assets.[36] The historical method of allocating cost might thus mislead creditors and investors as to the true value of the assets of a business. The book value of major assets of businesses frequently is carried at significantly less than their market value or the cost of replacing them.

The failure of historical cost accounting to reflect inflation can also result in misleading financial information regarding net income. If the cost of an asset under historical accounting does not reflect inflation, the periodic depreciation expense, charged against income, also will not reflect inflation. Depreciation expense, you recall, is determined by dividing the acquisition cost of an asset, less its salvage value, over the years of useful life of the equipment. Were the acquisition cost to reflect the current price of an asset, rather than its historical cost, the periodic depreciation charge would be increased.

Consider equipment bought in 1990 for $100,000 with a useful life of 10 years and no salvage value. If that equipment is depreciated on a straight line basis, the annual charge to income for depreciation would be $1/10$ of $100,000 or $10,000. Assume that in 1995, because of inflation, equipment purchased in 1990 for $100,000 can now only be purchased at $130,000. Were the balance sheet adjusted to reflect the present day value of this equipment, the annual depreciation charge would be $1/10$ of $130,000 or $13,000 instead of $10,000. If net earnings exclusive of depreciation had remained constant during this period, the real net earnings of the business (after the effect of the adjusted depreciation) would show a decline of $3,000. Since historical costs do not reflect current prices, depreciation charges based on historical costs do not reflect current costs to a business utilizing certain assets and, consequently, net earnings do not reflect current costs.

To accommodate this concern with inflation, generally accepted accounting principles were changed in 1986 to encourage but not require companies to disclose supplementary information on the effects of changing prices.[37] Prior to that time, there were a brief number of years during which large public companies were required to supplement their financial statements with additional information which would restate financial data so as to take into consideration the effects of inflation.[38] Today, if inflation is discussed, it typically appears in Management's Discussion and Analysis in the report to the shareholders.[39]

Just as the market value of a particular asset might be greater than the book value due to inflation, market value may also be less than book value. Market value is driven by supply and demand. The market value price of an asset need not have a great deal of correlation with book value, which is dictated by historical

---

[35] Although the annual amortization costs of intangibles may, for tax purposes, be charged against income, this is not true of the amortization costs of goodwill. Internal Revenue Code 167 (1992) does not permit deductions for goodwill amortization expenses. Thus, recording and amortizing goodwill does not result in tax benefits.

[36] For a discussion of the limited situations in which a revaluation of capital is permitted, see Chapter IX, Section C, par. 8, *infra*, on distributions.

[37] Financial Accounting Standards Board, Statement of Financial Accounting Standards No. 89 (Dec. 1986).

[38] Financial Accounting Standards Board, Statement of Financial Accounting Standards No. 33 (Sept. 1979).

[39] Accounting Trends and Techniques reports that "many" of the companies surveyed include their discussion of inflation in the Management's Discussion and Analysis section of the annual report. Accounting Trends and Techniques 139 (AICPA 1996).

cost less depreciation. Oversupplies within the market for specific equipment or declines in purchaser interest in such equipment can drive down the market price of such assets. Sellers of a company's assets can not always wait to obtain the best price for the assets, particularly when the business is in a liquidation mode. Accordingly, the book value of an asset can be viewed as relatively arbitrary and not necessarily a good prediction of market price.

CHAPTER **III**

A FURTHER EXAMINATION OF CORPORATE EQUITY

A. SUB-CATEGORIES OF SHAREHOLDERS' EQUITY

Divisions Based upon Source of Equity

To complete our understanding of the elements of the balance sheet of the corporation, we need to further explore the various categories of corporate equity. In the first chapter, when we developed the concept of the accounting equation and later the balance sheet, we referred to the ownership interest in the corporation as "shareholders' equity." We further sub-categorized equity into paid-in capital (*see* Chapter I, Section E, Transaction Group 1) and "earned surplus" or "retained earnings" (*see* Chapter I, Section E, Transaction Group 4).

In dividing equity into these various categories (and others, as we shall see), the accountant is maintaining a record of the sources of shareholders' equity. Thus, the accounting system is able to distinguish between (i) that portion of shareholders' equity that is contributed to the corporation when the corporation raises funds through the sale of its shares (paid-in capital) and (ii) that portion of shareholders' equity that arises from the corporation's earnings (earned surplus or retained earnings). In categorizing equity by source, the accounting process is able to provide more specific ownership interest information to management, shareholders, prospective investors and creditors. At the same time, this categorization enables corporations to comply with various state statutory restrictions governing corporate distributions which often require the examination of one or more of a corporation's equity categories (or "equity accounts") before determining whether there is compliance with the statute. Let us examine these categories of equity more closely.

1. Paid-in Capital. The source of that portion of equity referred to as "paid-in capital" can be the contribution of assets of any kind. These contributed assets are most commonly in the form of cash, but they can also be in the form of merchandise, land, buildings or equipment, patents, copyrights, secret processes, trademarks, goodwill, shares of other corporations, as well as other items. The impact of such contributions on the accounting equation is to increase one or more categories of assets (or "asset accounts") and to increase shareholder equity by the same amount.

These "contributions" are typically purchases made by investors who, in consideration for their contributions, receive ownership interests in (or shares of) a corporation,[1] thus becoming shareholders. These shareholders can be the original investors in a corporation who purchase shares when the corporation is being created, or they can be investors who subsequently purchase shares from the same corporation when it issues additional stock.

Note: It is important to recognize that the corporation receives the contribution paid by an investor for shares in that corporation only when it is the corporation itself that has sold the shares to the investor. Investors do not buy shares solely from the corporation. Shares once issued by the corporation can be resold

---

[1] Less commonly, contributions to capital are donated to the corporation as gifts without any consideration. Such a contribution might come from a large shareholder who is seeking to assist a corporation in financial difficulty. The individual shareholder, in order to retain the value in the investment he has already made, might contribute cash or other assets to bolster the corporation's financial position. Such capital might be distinguished from paid-in capital by referring to it as "donated capital," although the distinction is not of great relevance for our purposes.

over and over again by shareholders. Only those purchases which are made directly from the corporation result in an increase in corporate assets. Subsequent resales by shareholders do not impact upon the corporation's balance sheet, but rather, result in funds being transferred from new investors to prior investors.

2. Earned Surplus (Retained Earnings). The source of that portion of equity that is referred to as "earned surplus" or "retained earnings," as the names imply, are the earnings of the corporation. The term "earnings," however, is used broadly. It includes not only earnings or profits from regular operations, but also gains from extraordinary transactions, such as the sale of an asset like a parcel of land or a building. Essentially then, earned surplus or retained earnings represent the ownership interest that arises from the profits and gains of a corporation or the undistributed return on the shareholders' investment. Of course, a corporation can also experience negative earnings, or losses. An accumulation of losses, a significant single-year loss, or an initial loss in the first year of operation can result in an overall corporate deficit in retained earnings. This deficit would be presented on the balance sheet as an item under shareholders' equity. To determine shareholders' equity, one would subtract the deficit from paid-in capital.

B. FURTHER DIVISIONS OF EQUITY

Sub-Categorizations of Paid-In Capital Based upon Par Value

1. When Par is Stated. Not only is shareholders' equity divided into "paid-in capital" and "retained earnings," but paid-in capital itself is further divided into various sub-categories. These sub-categories refer to an arbitrary and somewhat anachronistic monetary figure called "par value." Par value, in jurisdictions that continue to use this term, represents the minimum amount that must be received by the corporation for each share of stock upon original issuance of the stock for the shares to be considered fully paid. This fixed amount is identified in the Certificate of Incorporation. State statutes which utilize par typically prohibit the issuance of stock at less than par. It should be noted, however, that such legal restrictions apply only to the original issuance of shares by a corporation. Subsequent resale by the shareholder may be at any price, whether below or above par.

The use of par value is anachronistic because although originally designed to protect shareholders[2] and later to protect creditors,[3] as we shall see,[4] it really does neither. Par value is an arbitrary figure, since most jurisdictions, which make reference to par, grant corporations a broad degree of flexibility in the amount per share that can be set as par for any specific issuance of securities.

While par represents the minimum amount that must be contributed for a single share, there are no legal limits on the maximum amount at which a share may be issued or sold by a corporation. Corporations may, and frequently do, issue par value stock at an amount in excess of par or at a "premium."

The par value of stock multiplied by the number of shares issued is referred to as "stated capital," "legal capital," or, sometimes, just "capital."[5] The amount of capital contributed that exceeds stated capital is referred to as "capital surplus"[6] or "additional paid-in capital" or "capital in excess of par" or "paid-in surplus." These sub-categories of paid-in capital have relevance, as we shall see, in determining when distributions can be made by a corporation. *See* Chapter IX, Section C, *infra*.

---

[2] The concept of par value was developed in the late nineteenth century as a means of protecting shareholders by insuring that all shareholders pay in a specific amount of capital per share before having the right to enjoy the benefits of owning such shares. See B. Manning and J. Hanks, Legal Capital 23 (3d ed. 1990).

[3] Par was thought to protect creditors to the extent that most state laws (i) require that, at a minimum, funds equal to par times the number of shares outstanding must have been contributed to the corporation and (ii) prohibit distributions that might be made from these funds.

[4] Chapter IX, Section C, par. 8, *infra*.

[5] One will not usually find an item entitled "stated capital" or "legal capital" on most balance sheets. Rather, the term "capital stock" will frequently be used. As an example, see the balance sheet of the H.J. Heinz Company in Appendix B. There, stated capital is equal to the total amount of capital stock.

[6] Capital surplus may also be created when contributions are made to the corporation without consideration. See Section A of this Chapter, *supra*. Such capital surplus may be referred to as "Donated Surplus."

To confuse matters somewhat, terminology in this critical categorization process is not consistent. For example, the term "capital" is not used merely as a synonym for stated capital. It also is often employed in the place of the term "paid-in capital." In addition, "capital" is sometimes used to refer to the combination of paid-in capital and earned surplus. In other words, in different contexts, "capital" might mean "legal capital," "paid-in capital," or "shareholders' equity." Similarly, the term "surplus" might refer to earned surplus or to both earned surplus and capital surplus.

Numerous other inconsistent uses are made of the various terms for the different categories of equity. At times, intricate problem-solving must be employed merely to determine the intended meaning of the terms employed. For purposes of this manual, let us use the terms "paid-in capital," "stated capital," "capital surplus," and "earned surplus" or "retained earnings" as they have been described above.

2. When Par is Not Stated. Most jurisdictions, which make reference to par, still permit stock to be authorized without a par value. Such "no-par" stock can usually be issued and sold without any restrictions as to price. Statutes generally require directors to assign to such no-par stock a "stated value." The stated value of the no-par shares multiplied by the total number of shares equals stated capital. Statutes also indicate that the amount of consideration paid in for such no-par shares in excess of the assigned stated value shall become "capital surplus" or "excess above stated value."

If an assignment of stated value is not made by the directors for an issuance of no-par stock, then the entire consideration paid in constitutes stated capital.

Caveat: Listing of the terms "stated capital," "capital surplus," and "earned surplus" as specific categories of equity on the right-hand side of the balance sheet does not mean that there exist equivalent specific funds within the assets listed on the left-hand side of the balance sheet. The equity accounts do not provide information regarding the specific composition of the assets on the balance sheet. What they do is furnish a means of measuring ownership interest in the totality of assets minus liabilities.

For example, when one first studies financial statements, there is a tendency to believe that a corporation with an earned surplus of $10,000 from past earnings, necessarily has on the asset side of the balance sheet an account of "liquid" assets, such as cash or short term investments, that is also $10,000 in amount. In fact, the $10,000 of earnings which were retained in the corporation might have long ago been used to finance a new piece of equipment for the corporation, purchase additional inventory, or, perhaps, reduce outstanding debt liability. The categories of equity serve only as a means of (i) keeping track of the source of the assets giving rise to the equity of a corporation and (ii) allocating paid-in capital between that amount necessary to satisfy the par value requirements and that amount contributed in excess of the par requirements. Of course, while the amount in any category of equity does not imply the existence of any specific type of asset, there is always a representation that total shareholders' equity equals total assets less liabilities.

C. BALANCE SHEET REPRESENTATION OF SHAREHOLDERS' EQUITY

How Do I Know One If I See One

It might be helpful to examine how the various categories of shareholders' equity are presented on the balance sheet. When we discussed the balance sheet in Chapter I, in a simplified manner, we listed under Shareholders' Equity only Paid-in Capital and Retained Earnings. A more involved balance sheet might well include several of the items discussed above in Section B.

The first item to appear in the shareholders' equity section of a balance sheet is a listing of the capital stock of the corporation. Within this entry (or perhaps within supporting notes) should be found: (i) the number of shares authorized;[7] (ii) the number of shares issued;[8] (iii) whether the stock carries a par value and, if so, the amount of par; (iv) if the stock is no-par, whether there is a stated value and, if so, the

---

[7] Shares are "authorized" if the certificate of incorporation provides the board of directors with authority to issue such shares.

[8] When the board of directors exercises its authority and actually sells or otherwise distributes the shares to shareholders, the shares are considered "issued."

amount of such value. When a corporation has more than one class of stock, each class generally will be separately stated. Notice, in Appendix B, that the H.J. Heinz Company lists one class of preferred stock as well as its common stock in its balance sheet under "capital stock." The total amount(s) presented for capital stock is equal to the stated capital of the corporation.

After the capital stock should be listed "capital surplus," which might also be referred to as "additional paid-in capital" or "capital in excess of par or stated value," or perhaps "paid-in surplus." The term used on the balance sheet in Appendix B is "Additional Capital." In other instances, other terms are also used, all seeking to identify that contributed capital which is in excess of the stated capital — *i.e.*, the par or the stated value of the securities issued. The stated capital and the capital surplus together comprise paid-in capital and collectively they are, at times, so identified.[9]

The last item listed under shareholders' equity which we need to mention at this point is "retained earnings" or "earned surplus." As indicated above, accountants rarely use the term "earned surplus" anymore, preferring "retained earnings," "reinvested earnings," "accumulated earnings" or similar titles. Attorneys, however, steadfastly adhere to their old ways. As a consequence, in this manual, we will use the terms interchangeably (and, at times, together) depending upon the context.

Portions of retained earnings may be "reserved" or "restricted." This means that a limitation has been placed on that portion of retained earnings and that the total amount of retained earnings is no longer available for distribution. The amount that is so limited is essentially segregated from the rest of the retained earnings and cannot be distributed until the limitation is removed. Limitations can be placed on retained earnings for a number of different reasons:

1.   Legal Restrictions. Many jurisdictions require that retained earnings be restricted in an amount equal to the cost to a corporation of reacquiring its own shares. The repurchase is viewed as a distribution of retained earnings and the restriction limits the corporation's ability to distribute the same retained earnings twice. For a fuller discussion of restrictions resulting from the purchase by a corporation of its own shares, see paragraph 5 on stock repurchases in Chapter IX, Section C.

2.   Contractual Restrictions. Certain debt instruments might require that a specified amount of retained earnings be reserved each year in anticipation of eventual repayment of the debt obligation.

3.   Financial Planning. As a discretionary matter, the board of directors might choose to place a limitation on distribution of retained earnings in order to preserve retained earnings, perhaps for future expansion or perhaps to maintain a strong financial position for current operations.

4.   Protection in Event of Losses. The board of directors may also, as a discretionary matter, choose to limit retained earnings in anticipation of possible losses due to declines in business, lawsuits, or other contingencies.

The accountant may reflect any of the above limitations either in a note to the balance sheet or as a formal "appropriation" of retained earnings. This formal appropriation may be referred to on the balance sheet as an "appropriation," a "restriction," or a "reserve." The terminology will not necessarily be consistent from one corporation's balance sheet to another.

As an example of how all of the above information might be presented on a balance sheet, let's examine, in Exhibit 3.1 below, the shareholders' equity section of the Hypothetical Corporation. The Hypothetical Corporation has the following characteristics: (i) Preferred Stock, with a $5.00 par, for which 20,000 shares are authorized and 10,000 issued, the corporation having sold the shares for $10.00 per share; (ii) Common Stock, with no par and a stated value of $3.00, for which 20,000 shares are authorized and 1,000 shares are issued, the corporation having sold the shares for $3.00 per share; and (iii) an earned surplus of $25,000,

_____

[9] Donated capital, if any, might appear separately under Shareholders' Equity after capital surplus and be identified as "donated capital" or "donated surplus."

of which $5,000 has been reserved to finance the corporation's repayment of long-term debt instruments when they become due.[10]

EXHIBIT 3.1

Hypothetical Corporation

Shareholders' Equity Section of the Balance Sheet

Shareholders' Equity:
  Paid-in capital:

Preferred stock ($5 par value; 20,000 shares authorized: 10,000 shares issued)	$50,000	
Common stock (no-par, stated value $3.00, 20,000 shares authorized, 1,000 shares issued)	3,000	
Capital in excess of par or stated value Premium on preferred stock	50,000	
Total paid-in capital		$103,000

Retained earnings:
  Appropriated:

For bond redemption fund	$ 5,000	
Unappropriated:	20,000	
Total retained earnings		25,000
Total shareholders' equity		$128,000

---

[10] Today, as a practical matter, it is more typical for appropriations, restrictions, and reserves of retained earnings to be disclosed in notes to the financial statements, rather than as separate items on the face of the balance sheet.

CHAPTER IV

GENERALLY ACCEPTED ACCOUNTING PRINCIPLES

A. THE RULES BY WHICH ACCOUNTANTS OPERATE

The Accountants' "Common Law"

This chapter will constitute a slight deviation from the flow of this Guide. Some readers might choose to merely skim the material herein. Other readers however, might have been asking questions regarding what dictates certain accounting practices. The answer can frequently be found in a framework of conventions, rules, and procedures which are commonly referred to as "generally accepted accounting principles." These principles are the subject of this chapter.

These principles help determine how accounting information is to be presented on financial statements. The existence of these principles gives consistency to the financial statement of different companies, thus providing some comparability in their financial statements. Accounting principles are not immutable. Rather, they have evolved and continue to evolve "in response to changes in economic and social conditions."[1]

There are various elements that make up accounting principles. There are broad assumptions or conventions which affect all financial statements. There are some principles and procedures which have only a limited application. The accounting community uses different terms to describe the various elements that make up accepted principles. The elements are referred to, in different contexts, as conventions, assumptions, principles, axioms, standards, rules, practices and other terms as well. Different meanings are frequently ascribed to the several terms. The distinctions that are made between the terms, however, are not always clearly delineated, and the various terms are often used interchangeably. For our purposes, we can refer to the pervasive principles as *conventions* or *assumptions* and the more narrowly applied standards as *rules* or *principles*. Most of the rules and some of the conventions have in effect been codified in the statements promulgated by the various standard-setting bodies for the accounting profession.

In this chapter, we will briefly explore some basic conventions and rules which are relevant to the accounting practices we analyzed in earlier chapters. We will also identify the various accounting bodies which have codified many accounting conventions and rules. These codified conventions and rules are frequently cited in the footnotes to this Guide. Both the codified and uncodified conventions and rules are collectively referred to as "generally accepted accounting principles." When auditors examine the financial statements of an accounting entity, and render an unqualified opinion, they confirm that the statements have been prepared in conformity with generally accepted accounting principles. (For a discussion of auditors' opinions, see Chapter V, Section C, par. 4, *infra*).

B. ACCOUNTING CONVENTIONS

Principles that Underlie Most Accounting Practices

Many of the basic conventions that underlie accounting practices are so obvious that we tend to take them for granted. They blend so into our understanding of accounting that we neglect to recognize them as defined standards. After completing this Guide, many readers will find it instructive to reflect upon discussions regarding asset valuation, income determination, and the preparation of financial statements to see how the conventions which we are about to examine influence specific accounting practices. Some of the more essential conventions or assumptions are the following:

---

[1] American Institute of Certified Public Accountants, Accounting Principles Board Statement No. 4, par. 32 (Oct. 1970).

1. Separate Entity. The accounting process always relates to a specific accounting entity. Thus, in a sole proprietorship, the assets and liabilities appearing on a balance sheet will be only those of the business enterprise conducted by the owner, and not the personal assets and liabilities of the owner. For example, the assets of a sole proprietorship will include the building and equipment used in the business, but not the home in which the owner resides. Likewise, the income and expense items in the income statement should be only those of the specific business entity. These distinctions hold true for partnerships and corporations as well. The separation of identity between the owners of a corporation and the corporation itself is a recognized legal principle, as well as an accounting rule.

There are instances in which several accounting entities may be combined for financial reporting purposes into a single entity. The several subsidiaries of a large manufacturing corporation may each, by themselves, constitute separate legal and accounting entities. For certain financial reporting purposes, however, the financial statements of the parent corporation and its subsidiaries may be consolidated.[2] For accounting purposes, an entity can be composed of a business which is not a separate legal entity (*e.g.*, a sole proprietorship), one which is a separate legal entity (*e.g.*, a corporation), or several separate legal entities consolidated for financial reporting purposes (*e.g.*, a parent corporation and its subsidiaries).

2. Going Concern (or Continuity). Many of the valuations and allocations of expenses and revenues made by accountants are premised on the assumption that the particular accounting entity is not expected to be liquidated in the foreseeable future. The accountant does not base this assumption upon a premise that the business will last indefinitely, but rather, that it will last long enough to fulfill its current objectives and commitments. This convention provides the basis for the accountant's valuation of assets. When we examine historical cost accounting and see that the accountant values plant assets of a business on the basis of their cost less an arbitrary allowance for depreciation which is allocated over successive time periods, we will understand that the accountant is assuming the continued operation of the entity.[3] Were the business going to be liquidated in the near future, it would be wiser to value the assets at their current sale price less the cost of disposal.

3. Periodic Reporting. In most cases, a business enterprise has an indefinite life span extending over many years. Ultimate profitability cannot really be determined until a business ceases to exist and all of its assets are consumed or liquidated and all of its liabilities are paid or settled. One cannot defer financial reporting until final business liquidation, however. Business managers, owners and creditors, government taxing agencies, economists, analysts and society in general, all need more frequent and regular reporting. As a consequence, the accountant provides periodic reports.

The revolution of the earth about the sun and the seasonal cycles of nature provide us with a natural period for reports — *i.e.*, the year. Accordingly, financial statements are conventionally prepared for business enterprises on an annual basis. Most enterprises, however, also arrange for interim statements. Such interim statements are commonly prepared for stockholders of publicly held corporations on a quarterly basis and at even shorter intervals for management purposes.

The division of the business life span into time segments obliges the accountant to divide financial activities into arbitrary time periods. Consequently, it is necessary to defer and accrue income and expenses, since various income and expense items will not necessarily be received or incurred during the same time period in which they should be recognized.[4] Similarly, the convention of periodic reporting requires the accountant to make estimates of the useful life and salvage value of certain assets, the depreciation costs of which will then be allocated over various time periods. Usually, the longer the time span involved in any reporting period, the greater the reliability of the income statement.

---

[2] For a further discussion of consolidation of financial statements, see Chapter V, Section D, *infra*.

[3] Historical cost accounting and depreciation are discussed in Chapter II, *supra*.

[4] For a discussion of accrual accounting, see Chapter VI, Section F, *infra*.

4. Unit of Measurement. Accounting is based on the assumption that money provides an appropriate basis for measuring and analyzing economic activity. This conventional practice of equating various assets, liabilities and ownership elements into the common monetary denominator is all pervading in our economic environment. In this respect, the accounting process merely conforms to general practice in modern society.

Accountants take society's practice of measuring assets and equities in money terms one step further by adopting the convention that the unit of measure, the dollar, is relatively stable. Thus, dollars earned currently are treated as having the same value as dollars earned ten years previously. When the accountant totals the worth of a business, assets bought ten years previously, with an historical cost of $100 dollars, are viewed as having the same value as assets bought only a year earlier with an historical cost of $100. This practice continues even though, due to inflation, $100 could buy more ten years ago than it could one year ago. In the light of high levels of inflation some years ago, accounting practices were developed to disclose the affects of inflation and changes in prices upon certain of business operations.[5] On an experimental basis beginning in 1979, some large corporations were required to report in supplementary disclosures on the impact of inflation upon certain of their operations. After review in 1986, FASB concluded that such supplementary disclosures "should be encouraged, but not required."[6]

5. Consistency. Accounting principles require that financial statements be prepared from one period to another on a consistent basis. If the LIFO method of inventory accounting is employed in one period, it would be consistent to employ the same method in consecutive periods. If statements are prepared on a consistent basis, then the information retrievable from these statements will be comparable and the reader of these statements will be able to evaluate various trends and other relationships (*e.g.*, growth or decline in income, working capital, and price-to-earnings ratios).

Changes in accounting procedures are typically explained in the notes to the financial statements so that the reader will understand in what regard the statements are not consistent. As we will see in our discussion of the auditor's report,[7] the accountant must opine whether the accounting entity's financial statements are in conformance with generally accepted accounting principles applied on a consistent basis. If the auditor finds that accounting principles are not consistently applied, he is required to qualify his opinion.

6. Conservatism. Frequently, in accounting practice, choices must be made as to which acceptable alternatives should be employed for recognizing assets and liabilities or for recording expenses and revenues. Investors and creditors have, historically, preferred that accounting lean in the direction of understating rather than overstating net income and net assets. This pessimism or "conservatism" continues today as accounting attempts to prudently insure that uncertainties in business situations are resolved in the least optimistic manner. Thus, generally accepted accounting principles direct that when two estimates regarding a financial evaluation are equally likely, the less optimistic estimate should be employed.[8] This principle of conservatism does not require deliberate understating of results but, rather, selection of the more pessimistic result among equally valid alternatives.

7. Matching. To develop the most accurate assessment of the income of an accounting entity, accountants attempt, as closely as possible, to allocate expenses against appropriate revenues. In other words, accounting seeks to match expenses incurred within a fiscal period with the revenues actually earned during that period.

Sometimes this task is relatively easy, as when we match the expired portion of prepaid insurance expense with the revenues generated from the goods and services sold during the period covered by that portion. At other times the matching procedure is more complicated. To illustrate, in the manufacturing process,

---

[5] Financial Accounting Standards Board Statement of Financial Accounting Standards No. 33 (Sept. 1979).

[6] Financial Accounting Standards Board, Statement of Financial Accounting Standards No. 89 (Dec. 1986).

[7] For a discussion of the auditor's report, see Chapter V, Section C, par. 4, *infra*.

[8] Financial Accounting Standards Board, Concept No. 2, par. 95 (May 1980).

it is generally necessary to allocate labor costs between finished goods and goods in process. Finished goods can be sold and their sales will generate revenues. Against these revenues, the accountant wants to charge only those labor costs which went into the goods sold. He does not want to include the cost of labor that went into goods in process, which goods will not generate revenues until completed and sold. The accountant also does not want to include the cost of labor that went into finished goods which have not yet been sold and have thus not yet generated revenues.

If expenses are mismatched with revenues, expenses for that period can be inflated or deflated. Similarly, judgmental errors in allocating expenses over a period of time can distort income for that time period.

C. PROFESSIONAL PRONOUNCEMENTS OF ACCOUNTING CONVENTIONS AND RULES

A "Codification" of Generally Accepted Accounting Principles

For over a half century, various committees and boards established by the accounting profession in an effort to standardize existing practices and to advance new accounting principles have attempted to systematically codify accounting, practices. The efforts of these accounting bodies have been supplemented by releases promulgated by the Securities and Exchange Commission. Although the products of these various standard-setting entities typically deal with specific rules, part of the codification effort has also sought to restate the broad accounting conventions and assumptions.

The products of these accounting bodies serve as a kind of "Restatement" of accounting. The subject matter of these works is a part of generally accepted accounting principles. The focus of these principles runs the entire range of accounting practices. Throughout this Guide, we make frequent reference, primarily in the footnotes, to these generally accepted accounting principles. We can see that matters dealt with by these principles cover a variety of subjects ranging from accounting for inflation, to alternate acceptable depreciation methods, to terminology for accounting principles.

The American Institute of Certified Public Accountants (AICPA), the national professional organization for certified public accountants, has created several boards for establishing standards. From 1938 until the late 1950's, the AICPA's Committee on Accounting Procedures and its Committee on Accounting Terminology issued a total of 51 Accounting Research Bulletins (ARB's) and four Accounting Terminology Bulletins on a wide range of accounting topics. Many of these bulletins are still relevant today.

In 1959, rather than continue with an approach that addressed a series of unrelated problems, the AICPA established the Accounting Principles Board (APB) to formulate a set of overall accounting principles. Unlike the ARB's, the Opinions and Statements of the APB were based upon research and represented more than merely the consensus of the Board members. By 1973, the APB had issued a total of 31 Opinions and 4 Statements. The APB required that material deviations from APB Opinions be disclosed in notes to financial statements.

Concerned with the lack of independence of the APB from the business community which the accounting firms represented and the lack of full-time members on the APB, a private independent board — The Financial Accounting Standards Board (FASB) — was created in 1973. The members of the FASB are appointed by an independent charitable foundation called the Financial Accounting Foundation. The members cannot maintain any employment ties outside of the FASB. Standards issued by the FASB are considered generally accepted accounting principles. Opinions, statements, and bulletins of the Accounting Principles Board, as well as those of the Committees on Accounting Procedures and Accounting Terminology, remain in effect to the extent that they have not been amended or superseded by pronouncements of later bodies.

Although the Securities and Exchange Commission has the authority under Section 19(a) of the Securities Act of 1933 to create principles of accounting reporting, it has chosen to rely primarily on the profession to develop these principles. SEC Regulation S-X prescribes specific disclosure methods for reports under the 1933 Securities Act and 1934 Securities Exchange Act. The Commission also publishes accounting opinions in its Financial Reporting Releases. These opinions generally deal with accounting issues not covered by the pronouncements of the boards created by the profession.

Generally accepted accounting principles have been in a state of flux as they have been examined and reevaluated by the above-described bodies. The principles remain a fluid body of rules and, as the profession continues to study its rules, further changes can be anticipated.

CHAPTER V

A FURTHER EXAMINATION OF THE BALANCE SHEET

A. STRUCTURE AND USE OF THE BALANCE SHEET

Building upon What We Have Learned about Assets and Liabilities

As a practical matter, the second Chapter, which provided a discussion of the varieties of assets and liabilities and an explanation of their valuation, also expanded our understanding of the balance sheet. The same could be said regarding the third Chapter which explored the various categories of equity. Assets, liabilities and equities are elements of the balance sheet and an analysis of the elements of a balance sheet also serves to analyze the balance sheet itself. What we want to additionally explore, however, in this Chapter is how the balance sheet is structured and utilized and the nature of the information that supplements the balance sheet.

The balance sheet provides a picture of the financial position of a business at a specific point in time. It identifies, as of a designated date, the nature and size of the business' resources, the obligation of the business to its creditors, and the claims of the owners of the business.

The information presented in the balance sheet is vital for creditors and investors. From the balance sheet, lenders or potential lenders can assess the nature, amount and liquidity of the business's assets and determine the amount, immediacy and relative priority of the business's obligations. Taken together, these various assessments permit present and potential creditors to determine the degree of risk to which they presently are exposing, or to which they would expose, monies loaned to the business.

For the investor or potential investor, the balance sheet provides information about the availability of an enterprise's resources to pay dividends or expand operations. Investors analyze the balance sheet together with the income statement to determine what return on their investment the business provides. Investors also examine the balance sheet and the other financial statements to help determine the degree of risk to which their investment is exposed.[1]

The existence of the balance sheet with all of the information it provides encourages both credit extension and capital investment. Without the knowledge available from the balance sheet, creditors and investors would be more uncertain about, and consequently more reluctant to extend credit to and make investments in, a business.

B. WHAT IS INCLUDED ON THE BALANCE SHEET

Everything Is Included Except What Is Not

An overly facile description of a balance sheet is that it lists the assets and liabilities of an enterprise with their respective values at a specific point in time. Based upon what we have already discussed about assets and liabilities, we recognize the limitations of this description. For example, because accountants use an historical basis for valuing assets, most assets are listed not at current market value but at original

---

[1] See Chapter VIII, *infra*, for a more complete analysis of how investors and creditors employ certain ratios, derived from the balance sheet, to evaluate the advisability of making loans to and investments in various businesses.

cost less depreciation or other valuation adjustments.[2] Furthermore, the impact of inflation is not reflected, except in limited instances and then only in supplementary reports.[3]

In addition, as we have seen, the cost valuation that appears on a balance sheet is often highly subjective in nature. Estimates must be made of the useful life of plant assets which are often a large proportion of total assets.[4] Judgments must be made about the percentage of accounts receivable for which payment will be collected.[5] Choices are required regarding alternative methods for valuing inventory.[6] Each of these estimates and choices will have an impact upon the cost at which an asset is carried on the balance sheet. Thus, the valuation of assets is more subjective than might be implied by the brief description of the balance sheet above.

Some assets are not even recorded on the balance sheet. Intangible assets can be of significant value to an enterprise but are never recorded because their value is difficult or impossible to quantify. Included in such unrecorded assets would be the experience of personnel, marketing or manufacturing "now how," and working relations among personnel. Other unrecorded intangibles would include company reputation and goodwill.[7] The expenditures which helped create these unrecorded assets went for employee salaries, training programs and advertising, and were treated as expenses and not capitalized (*i.e.*, accounted for as an asset and depreciated over time). Thus, despite their value to the business, there is no recording of these intangible assets.

One might anticipate that the generally accepted accounting principle of conservatism[8] would not sanction any omission of actual or potential liabilities. As we saw in our discussion of contingent liabilities,[9] however, if a liability is either uncertain to occur or its amount cannot be reasonably estimated, the contingency need not be reflected on the balance sheet. A disclosure must be made, however, in the notes to the financial statement.[10] To obtain a complete picture of the potential claims against the assets of a business, the reader of financial statements should examine the notes for contingent liabilities.

Another instance in which liabilities have not always appeared on the balance sheet involves employer obligations to pay certain, non-pension, post-retirement benefits. Prior to 1990, under then-existing generally accepted accounting principles, there was no requirement that the balance sheet reflect liabilities arising from obligations of employers to pay future benefits of this type. Some accountants believed that this procedure made sense, since the determination of future obligations is very subjective. Other accountants believed that non-reporting of such liabilities distorted the balance sheet of some businesses, since it did not provide full disclosure of all liabilities. In 1990, the Financial Accounting Standards Board promulgated a standard which provided mandatory alternatives for reporting on the balance sheet these certain post-retirement benefits.[11]

---

[2] For a discussion of historical cost accounting, see Chapter II, Section F, *supra*.

[3] For a discussion of the consideration given to inflation on the balance sheet, see Chapter II, Section L, *supra*.

[4] For a discussion of estimations of depreciation, see Chapter II, Section G, *supra*.

[5] For a discussion on estimating bad debts, see Chapter II, Section I, *supra*.

[6] For a discussion of the methods of inventory valuation, see Chapter II, Section H, *supra*.

[7] For a discussion of when goodwill is recorded and when it is not, see Chapter II, Section K, *supra*.

[8] For a discussion of the principle of conservatism, see Chapter IV, Section B, *supra*.

[9] For a discussion of contingent liabilities, see Chapter II, Section D, *supra*.

[10] For example. the 1983 Annual Report of The Firestone Tire & Rubber Company reported in a note to its financial statements the following, under the heading "Contingent Liabilities":

Various legal actions, proceedings, and claims are pending or may be instituted against the Company, including those arising out of alleged defects in tires, multi-piece rims, and other products produced or sold by the Company. Certain of these pending legal actions are, or purport to be, class actions. Some of the foregoing involve or may involve compensatory, punitive, or other damages in substantial amounts.

Litigation is subject to many uncertainties and it is reasonably possible that some of the legal actions, proceedings, or claims referred to above could be decided unfavorably to the Company. Although the amount of liability on October 31, 1983 with respect to these matters could not be ascertained, the Company believes that any resulting liability should not materially affect the Company's financial position.

[11] Financial Accounting Standards Board, Statement of Financial Accounting Standards No. 106 (adopted December 1990, to be effective for fiscal years beginning after December 15, 1992).

Furthermore, in some instances, corporate managers have derived a number of methods, consistent with generally accepted accounting principles, for keeping debt obligations from appearing on the balance sheet ("off-balance sheet" financing). Since the financial health of a corporation is frequently evaluated in light of the corporation's debt-to-equity ratio,[12] managers have an incentive to keep the amount of debt appearing on the balance sheet as low as possible.

Perhaps the most common method for removing debt from a balance sheet is the "sale-leaseback" arrangement. An example would be Company A owning an expensive piece of equipment which it uses in its operations, the purchase of which equipment Company A financed through the sale of debt instruments. Rather than reflect this debt on its balance sheet, Company A sells the equipment to Company B and proceeds to lease the equipment back from Company B. Company A uses the proceeds of the sale of the equipment to Company B to retire the debt Company A had incurred to purchase the equipment. Generally accepted accounting principles require that obligations under long-term leases, which leases must meet certain specifications, be carried as liabilities on a company's balance sheet.[13] Leases can, however, be structured in such a manner as to avoid this reporting requirement and the obligations would appear only in the footnotes to the financial statements.

In the above example, let us assume that Company A's lease with Company B for the equipment is structured so as to avoid being reported as a liability on the balance sheet. The result then of these financial maneuvers would be that Company A still has the use of the equipment but without carrying the debt for its purchase, following the sale of the equipment to Company B. Instead of paying interest and principal on its debt instruments, Company A pays rent to Company B. Company A's debt-to-equity ratio has been lowered. Company A's operations, however, remain constant.

In summary, the balance sheet lists most assets and liabilities of a business and records their book values. Some assets and liabilities, however, the measurement of which is quite uncertain, are not recorded on the balance sheet. In addition, some sophisticated financing structures are often utilized that allow liabilities to be removed from the balance sheet. As a consequence, some might argue that, in certain instances, the balance sheet does not fully reflect the financial position of a business.

C. BALANCE SHEET FORM AND SUPPLEMENTAL INFORMATION

How Do We Know One When We See One?

The balance sheets of both merchandising and manufacturing firms distinguish between current and noncurrent assets and current and noncurrent liabilities.[14] This classification allows bankers and other creditors to more readily determine the ability of a business to repay loans and credits. In industries where there is no regular operating cycle,[15] such as banking, finance, real estate, and life insurance, the current/noncurrent classification has little relevance and is not followed.

In addition to assets and liabilities, the balance sheet also presents the equity interests in a business. The equity interest in a business is the ownership interest which is computed by subtracting the liabilities of the business from its assets.

1. Formats. There are two primary formats in which the balance sheet will typically be presented and a third format which is infrequently employed. The choice of format is not of major significance, but law students and lawyers should be familiar with the varying appearances of balance sheets.

At one time, the most common presentation of information on the balance sheet was the *account form*. Assets are listed on the left side and liabilities and shareholders' equity on the right. This form is illustrated in Exhibit 5.1. Some believe that the account form makes it simpler to visualize the relationship between

---

[12] For a discussion of ratio analysis, see Chapter VIII, *infra.*

[13] Financial Accounting Standards Board, Statement of Financial Accounting Standards No. 13 (Nov. 1976).

[14] For a discussion of the distinction between current and noncurrent assets and liabilities, see Chapter II, Section B, *supra.*

[15] For an explanation of the operating cycle, see Chapter II, Section B, *supra.*

the assets of a business, which appear on one side of the balance sheet, and the claims against these assets, which appear on the other side of the balance sheet.

The same data can be arranged vertically in a *report form*. This arrangement, illustrated in Exhibit 5.2, is tantamount to cutting the account form in two and placing the right side (liabilities and equities) beneath the left side (assets). The major benefit of the report form appears to be the economy it offers in printing. It more readily fits onto a single page than does the account form. It is important to emphasize that identical information appears in these two different forms. In recent years, the report form has been the preferred format.

EXHIBIT 5.1

Account Form Balance Sheet

The Prime Company

Balance Sheet

December 31, 19_____

Assets		Liabilities and Shareholders' Equity	
Current assets		Current liabilities	
Cash	$ 50	Notes payable	$ 50
Accounts receivable	150	Accounts payable	110
Inventories	100	Other	40
Total current assets	300	Total current liabilities	200
Long term investments	100	Mortgage payable	300
Plant assets	500	Total liabilities	500
		Shareholders' equity	
		Capital stock	100
		Other paid-in capital	100
		Retained earnings	200
		Total shareholders' equity	400
		Total liabilities	
Total assets	$900	and shareholders' equity	$900

EXHIBIT 5.2

Report Form Balance Sheet
The Prime Company
Balance Sheet
December 31, 19_____

Assets
  Current assets

Cash	$ 50
Accounts receivable	150
Inventories	100
Total current assets	300
Long term investments	100
Plant assets	500
Total assets	900

Liabilities
  Current liabilities

Notes payable	50
Accounts payable	110
Other	40
Total current liabilities	200
Mortgage payable	300
Total liabilities	500

Shareholders' equity

Capital stock	100
Other paid-in capital	100
Retained earnings	200
Total shareholders' equity	400
Total liabilities and shareholders' equity	$ 900

There is another balance sheet form, referred to as the *financial position form*, the arrangement of which emphasizes the working capital situation of a business. This form will only infrequently be encountered. We need not explore its features other than to indicate that even though this form focuses on the working capital of a business, it too uses the same data as found in the other two forms.

  2. Comparative Financial Statements. The usefulness of balance sheets, as of all financial statements, is enhanced by comparison with prior statements. By such comparisons a reader may more readily perceive changes or trends. For example, from the comparative income statement, the reader can discern whether revenues from sales are increasing or if earnings are better in one year than in another. From the comparative balance sheet, the reader can discern whether the working capital position of a company is more or less secure. To facilitate such comparisons, it is accepted practice for the same statement to contain data for the current year and usually the two preceding years (in the instance of the Income Statement).

  In addition, some reports will include comparative selected financial items for a five-year, or longer, period. As an example, see the financial statements of the H.J. Heinz Company in Appendix B. Regulations of the Securities and Exchange Commission prescribe the type of comparative information that is required of publicly reporting companies.

  3. Supplemental Information. The information on the balance sheet, as in the case of the other financial statements, is supplemented through the use of parenthetical notations, footnotes, and supporting schedules. Parenthetical comments permit the preparer of the balance sheet to qualify, on the face of the balance sheet, the data presented thereupon. For example, short-term investments presented on a balance sheet when carried at cost[16] might be qualified in a parenthetical comment, which would also provide the market value of such investments. Notice on the balance sheet of the H.J. Heinz Company, in Appendix B, that there is a qualifying explanation, set off by a comma, indicating that the short-term investments are carried "at cost which approximates market." One might also find a particular feature of issued stock highlighted in a footnote. For example, the liquidation value of preferred stock might be presented in a parenthetical phrase.

Lengthier qualifications would appear in footnotes. The footnotes do not distract from the flow of the balance sheet, but they nonetheless can contain information vital to understanding of the balance sheet (as well as to the other financial statements). The footnotes might be used to disclose or expand upon a variety of matters, such as the amount and nature of contingent liabilities, the nature of an extraordinary gain or loss, or the nature of a company's capital stock.

The first footnote (or at times a separate summary preceding the footnotes) will usually be devoted to an explanation of significant accounting policies.[17] This summary will typically contain disclosures with respect to depreciation methods, inventory valuation, amortization of intangibles, and other matters. Disclosure is recommended in those situations in which a selection from among acceptable alternatives has been made, the company is part of an industry with peculiar accounting principles and methods, or the company employs innovative applications of generally accepted accounting principles.

Supporting schedules are used to provide information in greater detail about a specific balance sheet item than appears on the balance sheet itself. As an example, a separate schedule might be used to further explain the nature of and the depreciation allowed for various plant assets. Notice Note 5 to the financial statements of the H.J. Heinz Company in Appendix B. The schedule contained in this note provides more detailed information on the Company's income taxes than is found in the balance sheet.

It cannot be too strongly emphasized that these parentheticals, footnotes, and supporting schedules are an integral part of the balance sheet and the other financial statements. In order to understand the financial statements, they must be read in conjunction with these qualifying materials. The reader of the balance sheet who ignores the supplementary materials might never realize that earnings for a particular year were high because of an unexpected sale or that a company's future earnings are in doubt because of an uncertain contingent liability.

4. Auditor's Report. Another tool that is available to evaluate the information in the balance sheet as well as in the other financial statements is the "auditor's report." Management has primary responsibility for establishing sound accounting practices and preparing the financial statements. However, to insure the reliability of the financial statements, management will engage the services of an independent public accountant to "audit" or examine the financial data developed by a business and present an opinion on the reliability of the financial statement in the auditor's report. Typically, the auditor's opinion immediately precedes the financial statements or follows at the end of the footnotes. The report briefly indicates the scope of the examination that the auditor conducted and provides the auditor's opinion of the fairness of the information presented. The concept of fairness includes a determination that the financial statements are presented in accordance with generally accepted accounting principles, that the principles have been applied in a manner consistent with the previous year, and that adequate disclosure has been made of material financial information. If these standards are met, the auditor issues an "unqualified" opinion.

The auditor can also issue various reports that provide other than an unqualified opinion. The auditor might be concerned that: 1) the examination he or she conducted was in some way limited; 2) the statements do not fairly represent the financial position of the business; 3) accounting principles are not consistently

---

[16] Recall that short-term investments that are classified as "Held-to-maturity" are carried at amortized cost. See Chapter II, Section J, *supra*.

[17] This disclosure is mandated by generally accepted accounting principles. See American Institute of Certified Public Accountants, Accounting Principles Board Opinion No. 22 (April 1972) For an example of such a summary, see the Notes to the financial statements of the H.J. Heinz Company in Appendix B.

applied; or 4) there are uncertainties about future developments, the impact of which cannot be satisfactorily estimated. If the auditor has one of these concerns, his or her opinion must be "qualified."

If the exceptions to the auditor's standards of fairness are substantial and pervasive, the auditor must issue an "adverse opinion." This is rarely done, since most businesses prefer to change their accounting practices to accommodate the auditor's concerns.

Finally, an auditor can issue a disclaimer of opinion if he feels he was seriously limited in the scope of his examination or that there are major items about which he is uncertain. Again, disclaimers of opinions are rare occurrences.

Auditors' opinions that are other than unqualified are caution signals to the reader of the financial statements. They warn the reader that the standard assumptions as to reliability of the financial statements cannot be applied across the board. The auditor's opinion will identify those concerns that the auditor has, allowing the reader to know to what extent he or she may or may not rely upon the financial statements.

D. CONSOLIDATED FINANCIAL STATEMENTS

With Corporate Affiliates, How Do You Show the Whole Instead of the Separate Parts

As we have explored the financial statements of corporations, we have referred to the specific company that is the subject of the financial statements as if it were a single entity. In reality, many of the larger, nationally recognized corporations consist of several separate corporations. These separate corporations are frequently related by a parent-subsidiary relationship. The parent company will own a substantial portion (usually 51% or more) of one or more subsidiaries. Despite the parent corporation's ownership of a substantial portion of stock in a subsidiary corporation (or in several subsidiary corporations), the parent and subsidiary remain separate legal entities. They also remain separate accounting entities and financial statements will be prepared for both the parent and subsidiary corporation.

Although separate entities, the several corporations, together, often constitute what amounts to a single business enterprise.[18] Since there is an intertwining of management as well as financial operations between a parent and subsidiary, creditors and investors are interested in financial information about the collective business enterprise. Consequently, in addition to the separate financial statements prepared for both the parent and subsidiary corporation, a consolidated financial statement is prepared, combining the statements of the parent and its subsidiary(ies).

The consolidated financial statements include consolidated versions of all the financial statements which a company might prepare — the balance sheet, income statement, statement of retained earnings and statement of cash flows. The financial statements which you might have read in the annual reports of most of the household name corporations were consolidated statements. The financial statements of the H.J. Heinz Company in Appendix B are consolidated.

Our concern at present is with understanding the consolidated balance sheet, but we will examine the consolidated income statement as well. The principles of consolidation for the balance sheet dictate that like assets and like liabilities of the several companies be combined. Similarly, like revenues and expenses of the several companies are combined in a consolidated income statement. To avoid duplication, however, intercompany transactions and balances must be eliminated. For example, in the case of the income statement, if one company of a consolidated group has made sales to another company within that group, the combined revenues derived from sales of the consolidated group must be reduced by the amount of the intercompany sales. In addition, the expense of the cost of sales for the consolidated group must be reduced by the cost of sales made between members of the group. If these reductions were not effected, the combined amount of sales would reflect the revenues generated when the first company in the group sold certain goods to the second company in the group, as well as the revenues generated when the second

---

[18] For example, a large manufacturing corporation might own a corporation that manufactures packages in which the manufacturing corporation sells its products. The parent corporation might also own a transportation company that ships the manufactured goods. Taken together, these three corporations can be regarded as comprising a single business entity.

company in the group sold the same goods to a party outside the group. Two sales of the same goods would be reflected in the total sales revenues of the combined group. Similarly, if a reduction were not made from expenses for the cost of sales, then the expense of cost of sales for the combined group would reflect the cost of two sales of the same goods.

The issues involved in consolidating the balance sheets of a parent and subsidiary are more complicated. At first blush, one might assume that all that is necessary is to add the assets and the liabilities on the balance sheet of the subsidiary to the assets and liabilities on the balance sheet of the parent and to eliminate intercompany receivables and payables. In effect, this would be adding the net assets of the subsidiary onto the balance sheet of the parent corporation. The problem which arises is that the balance sheet of the parent corporation already reflects the parent corporation's investment in the capital stock of the subsidiary. The investment account of the parent company shows the parent corporation's investment in the ownership equity of the subsidiary. Since ownership equity is equal to net assets, the net assets of the subsidiary are reflected on the parent corporation's balance sheet even before consolidation. To show on the consolidated balance sheet both the parent's investment in the subsidiary's capital stock, as well as the subsidiary's assets and liabilities (effectively, its net assets), is to duplicate the net assets of the subsidiary.

In consolidating the balance sheet of the parent and subsidiary, the accountant wants to eliminate, as an asset, the parent company's investment in the stock of the subsidiary. With the removal from the consolidated balance sheet of this investment in the subsidiary's capital stock, the capital stock of the subsidiary must also be eliminated from the shareholder's equity on the right hand side of the consolidated balance sheet. Again, this makes sense because what then remains on the consolidated balance sheet is a single representation of the assets and liabilities of the subsidiary and a single representation of the claim of equity holders[19] against those net assets. This is the claim of the equity holders of the parent corporation.

Although this all might sound complicated enough, we still have not addressed the real sticking point. We spoke as though the accountant can simply eliminate the potential duplication of the subsidiary's net assets on the consolidated balance sheet by removing the parents' investment in the subsidiary's capital stock. However, it is a rare situation in which the cost of the parent company's investment in the subsidiary will equal the book value of the net assets of the subsidiary. The price of the capital stock of a company is not dictated by the book value of the underlying assets less liabilities. Thus, the accountant cannot merely eliminate the parent's investment in the subsidiary's capital stock in order to avoid duplication. Certain adjustments must also be made in different instances in the subsidiary's various equity surplus, asset, or liabilities accounts, as well as in the parent's goodwill account. There are various methods of adjustment depending upon which consolidating approach is employed, whether the subsidiary is wholly owned or the parent has a sizeable minority interest, whether the subsidiary has or has not had an operating history, and whether the cost of the capital stock of the subsidiary is equal to, greater or less than the book value of its net assets. The detailed treatment of how to consolidate financial statements is the primary subject matter of textbooks on advanced accounting. Consolidation principles can safely be considered beyond the scope of the law student or lawyer seeking an introduction to accounting.

Consolidated statements are generally prepared when the parent company's interest in the subsidiary exceeds 50%, except when the operations of the subsidiary are dissimilar to those of the consolidated group. Thus, the operations of a financial subsidiary would not be consolidated with those of a merchandising or manufacturing parent.

Consolidated statements generally are more meaningful to the shareholders of the parent corporation than are its own unconsolidated statements. The consolidated balance sheet includes the resources and obligations of the entire group of consolidated companies, all under the control of the parent corporation. The consolidated income statement reflects the aggregate revenues and expenses of the group. However, creditors or minority shareholders of subsidiary companies may find consolidated statements less useful than the separate statement of the particular subsidiary.

---

[19] This is the case except where there is also a representation for a minority interest.

CHAPTER VI

A FURTHER EXAMINATION OF THE INCOME STATEMENT

A. SIGNIFICANCE OF THE INCOME STATEMENT

Did the Business Make or Lose Money?

The income statement, or statement of earnings, measures the success of a business in achieving an excess of revenues over expenses. The income statement reports on the income-related transactions that occur during a given period, providing an itemization of the revenues and expenses of the business during that time. Balancing revenues against expenses, it shows the net income or net loss for the period.[1]

To many investors and creditors, the income statement is considered more important than the balance sheet in portraying the financial health of a business. As a practical matter, both statements are critical in making a meaningful investigation of the financial health of a business. The income statement reports on past earnings, and the balance sheet measures the resources available to continue to maintain or to improve upon past earnings. It is worth emphasizing that while the balance sheet describes the financial position of a business at a specific point in time, the income statement measures net income over a period of time (the period of time between two balance sheets).

B. DEFINITIONS

Revenue, Expenses, Gains, and Losses

The income statement summarizes the revenues and expenses of an enterprise's transactions for a specific fiscal period. Before we explore the structure of the income statement, it is necessary to understand the basic categories that appear on this statement.

The revenues that are recorded during the year are comprised of any inflows of assets (without an offsetting outflow of assets) or settlements (payments) of liabilities, or both, that arise in the course of a business entity's primary operations. Revenues primarily arise from sales of merchandise or services.

When net assets are increased by transactions which are peripheral or incidental to the primary business of an entity, we refer to these increases as "gains." Distinguishing between revenues and gains depends upon discerning the typical activities of an enterprise. Were a large manufacturing firm to sell one of its plants, the sale price less book value would constitute gain since manufacturing firms do not typically sell their manufacturing facilities.[2]

The expenses that are recorded during the year consist of outflows of assets (without an offsetting inflow of assets) or incurrence of liabilities, or both, arising from the carrying out of the primary activities of a business. Expenses are more varied than revenues. Expenses include cost of merchandise (goods) sold,[3]

---

[1] Another way of phrasing this is that the income statement measures profits. However, because the term "profits" has its own particular meaning to the layperson, the accountant avoids that term and instead speaks of "net income" in discussing what the general public would describe as "profits."

[2] A further distinction can be drawn between gains which are extraordinary and those which are not. See Section D of this Chapter, *infra.*

[3] Bear in mind that the cost of goods sold is rarely identical with the cost of goods purchased to be sold during a period. The cost of goods sold is computed by adding the inventory at the beginning of a period to the purchases made during that period and subtracting from that sum the inventory at the end of the period. Those goods that are not sold appear on the balance sheet among the current assets.

salaries and wages, supplies consumed, rent, electricity, telephone, fuel, various taxes, interest, insurance, advertising and depreciation on buildings, equipment, furniture and fixtures.

In a merchandising firm, various related expenses are at times categorized under a number of major sub-headings. In addition to "cost of goods sold," examples of sub-headings that might be found on a typical income statement are "selling expenses" and "administrative expenses." (See Exhibit 6.2, *infra*.) Included within selling expenses would be items such as sales salaries, advertising expenses, delivery expenses and depreciation of sales equipment. One might also include an aliquot portion of the rent, the depreciation on buildings, and utility and maintenance costs attributable to sales. "Administrative expenses" is a catch-all category which would include salaries of management, rent or depreciation costs not attributable to sales, and expenses arising from bad debts.

An additional expense category that is sometimes shown on an income statement is "financial expenses." The most frequently appearing item under this category would be interest costs. If interest costs are not very large, they might also be carried under administrative expenses.

Just as gains appear on income statements, there is frequently an item called "losses." Losses are decreases in net assets that result from transactions which are incidental to the ordinary business of an entity.[4]

A manufacturing operation will have some expense items that are significantly different from the expense items of a merchandising firm. These expenses of the manufacturing firm must also be reflected on the income statement. In the manufacturing process, labor is applied to convert raw materials into finished products. In addition, there are a number of indirect (or overhead) costs that go into the manufacturing process. Only the cost of the finished goods sold appears on the income statement as the cost of sales. But a manufacturing firm might summarize on a supplementary schedule the cost of direct materials, direct labor, and manufacturing overhead (a catch-all category including indirect labor, supplies, plant depreciation, insurance, taxes, and other costs). For an example of such a supplementary statement, see Exhibit 6.1, *infra*. These costs are transferred into work in process and constitute the cost of manufacturing.

As goods are completed, there is a transfer out of work in process and into the finished goods inventory. The amount of the transfer is demonstrated below in Exhibit 6.1, a Schedule of Cost of Goods Manufactured and Sold. To the manufacturer's costs incurred during the year ($147,000) is added the beginning inventory of work in process ($25,000), to arrive at total work in process costs for the year ($172,000). Most of the goods (units), however, have been completed and transferred to finished goods. This is demonstrated by subtracting the cost of goods still in process at the end of the year ($20,000) to arrive at a cost of finished goods completed ($152,000).

Addition of the beginning inventory of finished goods ($40,000) provides a total of goods available for sale ($192,000). However, $30,000 of these goods were on hand at the end of the year, constituting the inventory of finished goods. Thus, the cost of goods sold is computed as $162,000 ($192,000 − $30,000).

This figure of $162,000 reflects all relevant manufacturing costs applicable to the goods sold during the period. The Schedule of Cost of Goods Manufactured and Sold details how the cost of goods sold is calculated. The amount shown as Cost of Goods Sold is the same amount that appears as the Cost of Goods Sold on the income statement. (See Exhibit 6.2, *infra*.)

The cost of inventories of raw materials still on hand at the end of the period for which the income statement has been prepared, as well as the cost of inventories of goods in process and finished goods not yet sold, are not expenses. These costs have not resulted in a decrease in net assets. Rather, when the raw materials were acquired, the business exchanged some of its asset cash for an equal amount of the asset raw materials. Similarly, when goods in process were created, the business exchanged an amount of its asset raw materials (plus labor and other costs) for the asset goods in process. This exchange neither increased nor decreased net assets.

Since the costs of raw materials, goods in process, and finished goods still held by the business are not expenses, they are not reflected on the income statement. These costs can be found on the balance sheet

---

[4] A further distinction can be made between losses which are extraordinary and those which are not. See Section E of this Chapter, *infra*.

as current assets. Only when the finished products are delivered to the customer in the context of a sale and are thus no longer available for the production of future revenue are the costs of these inventories shown as expenses on the income statement. For at that point, there is a decrease in net assets.[5]

EXHIBIT 6.1

(A schedule of cost of goods manufactured and sold for a manufacturing firm)

The Illustrative Company, Inc.

Schedule of Cost of Goods Manufactured and Sold
For The Year Ended December 31, 1993

Direct materials		$ 40,000
Direct labor		80,000
Manufacturing Overhead		
Indirect labor	$15,000	
Factory supplies	2,000	
Building depreciation	5,000	
Utilities	3,000	
Insurance	1,000	
Property taxes	1,000	27,000
Total cost to manufacture charged to work in process		147,000
Add: Work in process inventory January 1, 1993		25,000
Total work in process costs		172,000
Deduct: Work in process inventory December 31, 1993		20,000
Cost of goods manufactured (finished goods completed)		152,000
Add: Finished goods January 1, 1993		40,000
Total cost of goods available for sale		192,000
Deduct: Finished Goods December 31, 1993		30,000
Cost of goods sold		$162,000

---

[5] One might ask why it is said that assets are decreased when a business sells goods. From at least one vantage point, a sale of goods looks like an exchange of finished goods of the seller for cash or accounts receivable delivered from the buyer. This exchange, at first blush, does not much differ from the exchange of cash for raw materials in the manufacturing process, an exchange which we identified as not an expense.

We can say, however, that virtually by definition, a sale is an activity the purpose of which is typically to generate income. All income-generating activities are comprised of two elements — a revenue element and, charged against the revenue element, an expense element. The revenue element increases net assets and is balanced, in the fundamental equation, by an increase in net worth, the expense element decreases assets and is balanced, in the fundamental equations, by a decrease in net worth. Businesses typically strive to have the revenues from a sale exceed the expenses. When they succeed in this endeavor, the net effect on the business of the revenue and expense elements will be a net increase in assets and a net increase in net worth.

Frequently, for the sake of simplicity, the expense and revenue elements of a sale are collapsed into one step and we analyze a sale only in terms of the net result of the expense and revenue elements, that is a decrease in inventory counterbalanced by an increase in cash or accounts receivable (from the sale of the inventory). In fact, in the first Chapter, when we wanted to be quite elementary in our analysis of accounting activities, we examined sales in terms of this one-step analysis. (See Transaction Group 4, Chapter 1, *infra.*) But, as we have seen, each sale, in actuality, is comprised of two steps — one composed of the expense element and one composed of the revenue element. In the step comprising the expense element, we can see that assets are indeed decreased as is consistent with our definition of expense.

C. THE INCOME STATEMENT IN THE CONTEXT OF OTHER FINANCIAL STATEMENTS

Fitting What We Are Learning Together With What We Have Already Learned

Certain information which is found on the income statement might be best understood if we attempt to integrate this new information with what we have already explored about assets and liabilities on the balance sheet. In general, the revenues that appear on an income statement increase the net assets of the balance sheet, while expenses decrease net assets. We have already seen a number of instances of this relationship. For example, as we saw in our discussion of inventory in a merchandising firm,[6] when the asset inventory is consumed as sales are made, the business incurs an expense on the income statement, which is identified as the cost of goods sold. The smaller the amount of inventory on a balance sheet at the end of a financial period (in comparison to the beginning of the period) the greater is the expense cost of goods sold on the income statement.

In another instance, we saw that, as fixed assets are utilized and the book value of the asset on the balance sheet is reduced, the cost of the asset so utilized is allocated to depreciation expenses on the income statement.[7] That amount which is added to the depreciation allowance on the balance sheet during a specific time period (and which thereby reduces the net book value of the asset on the balance sheet from the beginning to the end of a financial period) must equal the depreciation expense for that period. As a final example, we also saw in our discussion of assets that prepaid services and supplies will be carried as current assets on the balance sheet.[8] As these services and supplies are utilized, the current asset prepaid expense on the balance sheet is reduced, and the expense on the income statement for that service or supply is correspondingly increased. For example, insurance premiums are typically prepaid. As the policy period progresses, the prepayment is transformed from an asset to an expense.

Another way to characterize the relationship between the assets on a balance sheet and the expenses on an income statement is to say that assets are prepaid expenses. As we saw in the examples above, as assets are consumed, the business incurs an expense. We essentially identified this relationship already in Section B of this Chapter when we explained that the cost of inventory becomes an expense only when the inventory is sold. Only then are net assets decreased (resulting in an expense). The concept is difficult to fully appreciate. If it is not immediately clear, reread the discussion in Section B, *supra*, mull it over a bit, and come back to it again after you have completed this Chapter.

The income statement and balance sheet are also linked through the statement of retained earnings. The net income for a period that appears at the bottom of the income statement is entered onto the statement of retained earnings. After an appropriate subtraction is made for dividends declared, that net income figure is added on to the retained earnings of the business. The balance sheet will also show the retained earnings as of the date of the balance sheet. Needless to say, the ending balance of retained earnings on the statement of retained earnings will be identical to the amount of retained earnings on the balance sheet of the same date.

D. FORMS OF THE INCOME STATEMENT

Single Step or Multiple Step

The format of the income statement in terms of classification and arrangement of revenue, expenses, gains and losses is less standardized than that of the balance sheet. Despite numerous variations, however, there are essentially two basic approaches — the *single-step* and the *multiple-step*.

1. Single-Step Format. The single-step format is so named because there is essentially but one subtraction of expenses from revenues that is required. The total of all expenses is deducted from the total of all revenues to arrive at a net income figure. However, even with a single-step form, income taxes

---

[6] See Chapter II, Section H, *supra*.

[7] See Chapter II, Section G, *supra*.

[8] See Chapter II, Section B, *supra*.

frequently will be reported as a separate item that also will need to be subtracted from "net income before taxes" to produce "net income." Gains and losses are included with revenues and expenses. At times, however, they may be shown separately as additions or deductions (for an example of the single-step method, see Exhibit 6.2, *infra*).

The obvious advantage of the single-step method is that it provides a simple mechanism for determining income and it avoids any implication that one type of revenue or expense is more significant than any other.

EXHIBIT 6.2

(A single-step income statement)
The Illustrative Company, Inc.

Income Statement
For The Year Ended December 31, 1993

Revenues:		
Net sales		$261,000
Other revenues (dividends and interest)		11,000
Total revenues		272,000
Expenses:		
Cost of goods sold	$162,000	
Selling expense	34,000	
Administrative expense	16,000	
Interest expense	6,000	
Other expenses (loss on sale of investments)	3,000	
Total expenses		221,000
Income before taxes		51,000
Income taxes		20,000
Net income		$ 31,000

2. Multiple-Step Format. The multiple-step format provides several intermediate balances before arriving at a figure for net income. In the multiple-step format, the cost of sales is deducted from sales revenue to arrive at gross margin (profit). From gross margin are subtracted selling and administrative expenses to arrive at income from operations. Additions and subtractions are then made for any non-operational revenues and expenses, such as interest expenses, extraordinary gains and losses and income taxes. The multiple-step format matches specific expenditures with specific revenues and provides a division between revenue and expenses arising both from operations and other sources.

In addition, the multiple-step format presents intermediate income figures which allow a reader to readily compute performance ratios between various items on the income statement. For example, one of the analytic measures employed to evaluate the profitability of an enterprise is the ratio of gross margin to cost of sales. (*See* Chapter VIII, *infra*.) This ratio expresses the percentage that goods have been marked up for sale in order to cover selling and administrative costs and to allow the seller a profit.

We can see how the same information that was presented in a single-step income statement (Exhibit 6.2) would be presented in a multiple-step income statement (Exhibit 6.3).

EXHIBIT 6.3

(A multiple-step income statement)
The Illustrative Company, Inc.

Income Statement
For The Year Ended December 31, 1993

Net sales		$261,000
Cost of goods sold		162,000
Gross margin		99,000
Selling expense	$34,000	
Administrative expense	16,000	50,000
Income from operations		49,000
Other revenues (dividends and interest)		11,000
		60,000
Other expenses		
Interest	6,000	
Loss on sale of investments	3,000	9,000
Income before taxes		51,000
Income taxes		20,000
Net income		$ 31,000

E. EXTRAORDINARY ITEMS AND ADJUSTMENTS

To Include or Not to Include

Normal, recurring revenues and expenses for a given period are included in the income statement. Gains and losses from peripheral operations of a business are also included in the income statement, though often as items separate from the general expense and revenue categories.

Problems arise, however, in determining how to treat gains and losses which are extraordinary. It is one matter to include in an income statement gains and losses which arise from peripheral operations of a business. Examples of such gains or losses from peripheral operations might include the sale at a gain of land which was acquired for once-intended expansion or the sale at a loss of equipment which has become obsolete.

But how should the accountant handle gains and losses which are both *unusual in nature* and *infrequent in occurrence*? Should losses resulting from an act of nature, such as an earthquake, be included in the income statement? Contrariwise, should gains resulting from the discovery of oil on land held by a business for disposing of refuse be included in the income statement? Does the inclusion of these extraordinary gains and losses allow the reader of the financial statements to evaluate the profitability of a business during a normal fiscal period?

There have been two schools of thought on how to treat extraordinary gains and losses. Accountants who argue that the income statement should reflect only *current operating performance*, believe that net income should be derived only from regular, recurring earnings of a business. They would prefer to report extraordinary items on the statement of retained earnings (as additions to or subtractions from retained earnings). They feel that to include extraordinary items in an income statement would mislead readers as to the future earnings potential of an enterprise.

Proponents of the *all-inclusive income statement* argue that extraordinary items should be included in the income statement, since such items, even though unusual, impact on the profitability of an enterprise. Furthermore, if extraordinary items did not have to appear on the income statement, businesses might choose to manipulate their individual interpretations of "extraordinary" in such a manner as to artificially boost income (*i.e.*, by typically defining losses as extraordinary and gains as ordinary).

Generally accepted accounting principles today are in conformance with the all-inclusive approach.[9] Extraordinary items are required to be reported on the income statement but as items separate from other revenues and expenses. Whether an event is "extraordinary" turns on the nature of the event (usual or unusual) and the frequency of its occurrence. The evaluation must take into consideration the environment in which an entity operates. Thus, losses for a Florida citrus grower resulting from frost are not extraordinary, because such losses occur every three to four years. On the other hand, the loss resulting when a hurricane destroys the oil refinery of an oil producer is extraordinary. The hurricane loss would appear on the income statement, but it would be identified as extraordinary and segregated from both other losses as well as normal expenses.

Gains or losses which are not extraordinary because they are either unusual or infrequent, but not both, are also reported on the income statement as a component of income separate from normal operations.[10] As an example, gains or losses from currency exchanges, which are not unusual in nature but which are infrequent for a particular company, would not be carried as an extraordinary item. However, such gains or losses would still be distinguished from items arising out of normal operations. Thus, one could find on a given income statement (i) expenses and revenues, (ii) gains and losses which are not extraordinary and (iii) extraordinary gains and losses.

Another example of a loss which is not extraordinary would be write-downs or write-offs of operational assets, such as plants or equipment which have lost operational value. Generally accepted accounting principles dictate that operational assets not be carried at a book value in excess of their economic value in use. Thus, if a hula hoop manufacturing machine owned by a toy manufacturer becomes obsolete because the demand for hula hoops declines, the book value of the machine must be written down to reflect the fact that the machine will not be providing service to the toy manufacturer who will no longer produce hula hoops. This write-down in asset value will be accompanied by a recognition of loss for the amount of the write-down.[11] This write-down loss will not be extraordinary, because it is not an unusual occurrence in business, in its nature and perhaps in frequency. When circumstances require, a business will also write down such assets as receivables, inventories and intangible assets, among others.

Questions of inclusion or exclusion in the income statement also arise when treating adjustments of prior period statements. Such adjustments might arise because an error had earlier been made, an estimate had proved wrong (e.g., the estimated useful life of an asset) or because an accounting principle is changed (e.g., a switch from FIFO to LIFO) or for other reasons. Generally, these adjustments are reflected on the income statement. However, adjustments resulting from the correction of prior period errors should be reflected only on the statement of retained earnings.[12]

There would be limited rewards for most attorneys or law students in committing to memory the dictates of the generally accepted accounting principles regarding the inclusion and exclusion of extraordinary items and prior period adjustments from the income statement. Not only is it the accountant's responsibility to make the decision as to treatment of extraordinary items and adjustments, but the accepted treatment of extraordinary items and adjustments has varied over time.

It is important, however, for the attorney, when reviewing the financial statements of a business, to recognize that the bottom line of the income statement — the amount of net income — might well be reflecting events other than those arising in the normal operations of a business. Past net income might prove an inappropriate basis for predicting future earnings if extraordinary items and adjustments have impacted upon the income figures. The existence of these unusual and extraordinary items should be readily ascertainable by examining the entries on the income statement. It is also essential to examine the statement

[9] See American Institute of Certified Public Accountants, Accounting Principles Board Opinion No. 9 (Dec. 1966). Also see Accounting Principles Board Opinion No. 30 (June 1973).

[10] See American Institute of Certified Public Accountants, Accounting Principles Board Opinion No. 30, par. 26 (June 1973).

[11] The basic accounting equation will thus remain in balance. The loss will reduce the net worth of the manufacturer. However, this reduction in net worth will be offset by a reduction in the book value of the equipment asset.

[12] See American Institute of Certified Public Accountants, Accounting Principles Board Opinion No. 9 (Dec. 1966) and No. 20 (July 1971) and Financial Accounting Standards Board, Statement of Financial Accounting Standards No. 16 (June 1977).

of retained earnings for possible similar entries. A further explanation of these extraordinary items will typically be found in the footnotes to the financial statements.[13]

F. THE TIME PERIOD FOR REFLECTING EXPENSES AND REVENUES

Accruals and Deferrals

If all expenses incurred by a business were paid for at the time they were incurred, and the business in turn was paid for services it rendered at the time such services were rendered, expenses and revenues would automatically be allocated to the appropriate fiscal period. Such simplicity of payment procedures, however, is not the typical mode of business operations. Most commonly, a business will deliver goods or provide services to a purchaser at one point in time for which payment will not be received until a later point in time. In other instances, a business will pay for a service, such as insurance protection, perhaps a year in advance and will only receive the service purchased through these payments (the insurance protection) as the year progresses.

How does a business account for these transactions? Should the business that sold goods or provided services on credit recognize in its accounting records the income arising from its credit sales at the time that the sales are made or at the time payment is received? Should the business that pays for insurance in advance recognize in its accounting records the full insurance expense at the time that the insurance premium is paid or at the time that the insurance protection is actually provided?

1. **Cash Basis.** One simple solution to the timing of financial record entries is to record increases in income only at the time when cash is received for services or goods sold and to record decreases in income only when disbursements of cash are made for expenses incurred. This is the "cash basis" method of accounting. Cash basis accounting is typically used by individuals, and professional and other service organizations. There is a tax advantage which results from the ability of the business to record expenses as they are incurred but to defer the recording of income until payment is actually collected from the customer. The recognition of income and the related income tax are thereby deferred. For example, consider a law firm which had annual expenses (largely salary) of $250,000, all of which were paid. During the same year, the firm billed its customers for services amounting to $450,000. Assume also that because some of the services were only provided toward the end of the year, not all of the customers had paid their bills by year's end. In fact, of the $450,000 billed by the law firm, only $350,000 had been paid to the firm by the close of the year. Since net income under the cash basis method of accounting would be the difference between cash inflow as compared to cash outflow, the firm would report earnings of only $100,000, even though it had earned a contractual right to an additional $100,000 for which it had not yet received payment.

Law Firm Income (Cash Basis)

Income from services performed	$350,000.00
Less costs incurred	250,000.00
Net income before taxes	$100,000.00

Under generally accepted accounting principles, the cash basis of accounting is an unacceptable accounting method for companies with publicly published financial statements. The cash basis method is inconsistent with the principle that expenses should be matched with corresponding revenues. Because cash basis accounting does not always match revenues and expenses, it permits a business to distort its income during a fiscal period.

2. **Accrual Basis.** The almost universal method by which businesses account for income is the "accrual basis." Under this method, income is recognized at the point at which it is earned and not at the time of collection, as under cash basis accounting. Contrariwise, expenses are recognized as they are incurred and

---

[13] For a discussion of the footnotes to the financial statements, see Chapter V, Section C, *supra.*

not when they are paid. Under the accrual method, salaries that an employer owes his employees for work done are recorded as expenses even if the salaries have not yet been paid. For example, assume a business pays its employees on a calendar weekly basis, but the end of the fiscal year, December 31, falls on Thursday. By the end of the fiscal year, the business will have incurred an expense for four days of salary, although the salary will not yet have been paid. Similarly, if the same employer has an interest-bearing bank account which has earned a certain amount of interest by the end of the fiscal period, that interest would be recognized as income even though the funds have not yet been paid to the business nor even credited to the bank account.

The advantage of the accrual basis of accounting for income is that it more accurately matches expenses with revenues during the appropriate period than does the cash basis. On an accrual basis, the distortion of the income of the hypothetical law firm that we saw under the cash basis would not exist. Although the firm was not paid its full fees during its fiscal period, those fees were earned and consequently would be recognized. Earnings for the period would reflect not merely costs incurred but revenues earned. Under the accrual basis, earnings for the firm would be $200,000.00.

Law Firm Income (Accrual Basis)

Income from services performed	$450,000.00
Less cost incurred	250,000.00
Net income before taxes	$200,000.00

The difficulty with the accrual method is that an income statement cannot be prepared solely on the basis of cash receipts and disbursements. For example, consider the situation in which manufacturing Firm A is paid in advance for work to be done. On a cash basis income statement the receipt of this advance payment from the customer would be treated as revenue. Under the accrual method, however, it may not be recorded as revenue until earned.

Similarly, consider Firm B which pays interest on a loan every six months. Assume that the firm's fiscal period ends three months before a specific interest payment is due. Although the firm has not yet paid the interest due up until the end of its fiscal period, under the accrual method, it must record the interest expense incurred, although as yet unpaid.

Essentially then, the accrual method requires that businesses make adjustments to the actual amount of income received or expenses paid before recording the income and expenses on the income statement. These adjustments are called "accruals" and "deferrals." An "accrual" is the recognition of an expense or revenue in an accounting period prior to the time that payment is made or cash received. A "deferral" is the recognition of an expense or revenue in an accounting period after payment is made or cash is received. There are four situations in which accrual or deferral adjustments must be made.

a. **Accrued expenses.** When a business has incurred expenses but has not paid these expenses by the end of the fiscal period, these accrued expenses should be reflected on the income statement, together with the expenses that have been paid. In the example given above of the business firm that pays interest on a loan every six months, but which has incurred three months' worth of interest expense by the end of its fiscal period, the three months of interest would be included on the income statement as part of the total interest expense for the period.

This accrued expense will decrease the business firm's net income for the particular fiscal period and, consequently, its net worth as of the end of the period. However, as of the close of the fiscal period, there will be no corresponding decline in assets to offset the firm's decline in net worth, since the interest payment will not as yet have been paid. To insure that the basic equation remains in balance, the accountant will record an increase in the liability "interest payable" to reflect the interest obligation that has been incurred and not yet paid. Thus, the decrease in net worth reflected in the recognition of the accrued expense will be offset by the increase in liability reflected in the interest payable obligation. When the interest is finally paid, the liability "interest payable" will decrease, and the asset cash will correspondingly decrease. Thus, the fundamental equation will remain in balance throughout the recording of the expense as well as its payment.

b. Accrued income. Accrued income items on an income statement are the counterpart of accrued expenses. If a firm has earned income but has not collected this income by the end of a fiscal period, it will reflect the income earned as accrued income among the current assets on its income statement. For example, the bank which made the loan to Firm B above will have earned three months' interest on its loan but will not yet have received payment. This accrued interest income will be included on its income statement as part of the total interest earned for the period.

This accrued income would increase the net income of the bank for the particular fiscal period and its net worth at the end of the period. To maintain the balance of the fundamental equation, the accountant would set up a corresponding amount for the asset "accrued interest receivable" (or just "interest receivable"). When the bank collects the amounts owing to it, it will decrease its asset "accrued interest receivable" and increase its asset "cash."

c. Deferred expenses. In situations in which a business has paid in advance for services ("prepaid expenses"), there also is a problem in matching expenses with revenues. Here, the problem is not one of recognizing an expense prior to actual expenditure of cash. With prepaid expenses, the cash has already been paid, but the services for which the expenditure has been made have not yet been received. The principle of matching income with appropriate expenses dictates that only that portion of the prepaid expense for which services have been received be recognized as a current expense. So, if a business pays $3,000 for a three-year insurance premium, after one year has passed, the firm will only recognize, on an accrual basis, $1,000 worth of insurance expenses. This recognized expense will reduce net worth by $1,000. However, the firm has already reduced its asset cash by the full $3,000 which was paid out a year earlier. In order to maintain the balance of the fundamental equation, the firm will also carry as an asset $2,000 of "prepaid insurance" on the balance sheet. As the next two years pass and the time periods covered by the premiums expire, the asset of prepaid expense will be reduced as the net worth of the firm is reduced by the recognition of additional insurance expense.

d. Deferred income. Finally, in situations in which a business has been paid in advance for goods or services, it must allocate this prepaid income to the appropriate subsequent fiscal periods in which the income is actually earned. Again, the principle of matching income with appropriate expenses dictates that the income received not be recognized on the income statement until that income is actually earned. Thus, if a magazine publisher is paid $45 in advance for a three-year magazine subscription, during the first year of the subscription, the publisher will recognize as income only one-third of the subscription price, or $15. This recognized income will increase net worth by only $15. To insure that the fundamental equation stays in balance, the publisher will reflect the unearned portion of the prepaid subscription on the balance sheet as the liability "unearned (or deferred) subscription income," because the publisher will owe subscription services in that amount to the subscriber. As the subscription is delivered over the next two years, the publisher will annually record a subscription income of $15 and will correspondingly decrease the deferred subscription item by an equivalent amount.

In each instance, the accrual method provides a business with a more accurate reflection of this real net income during any particular fiscal period. Although additional accounting entries are required to coordinate income and expenses on the financial statements, these entries insure that the financial statements more accurately reflect the results of operations (on the income statement) and the financial position (on the balance sheet) of the business.

CHAPTER VII

THE STATEMENT OF CASH FLOWS

A. WHAT IS THIS STATEMENT ALL ABOUT?

Aren't the Other Financial Statements Adequate?

We have seen that the balance sheet reports on the total assets, liabilities, and ownership equity at specific points in time. It does not report upon changes in any of these items during a specified period. The income statement reports on earnings during a period of time. The statement of retained earnings (and, when necessary, a statement of changes in shareholder equity) explains the net change in ownership equity. However, none of these statements provides a picture of the flow of cash or cash equivalents during a particular period of time. In addition, these statements indicate neither the sources of a company's cash or cash equivalents nor upon what they were expended. It is only the Statement of Cash Flows which examines these issues.[1]

This relatively innocuous introductory statement raises a host of crucial questions. While we can pretty much figure out what "cash" is, what are "cash equivalents"? Why do we want to know about the flow of cash and cash equivalents? Why can we not figure out everything we need to know about the flow of cash and cash equivalents from the other financial statements which we have examined? Does the Statement of Cash Flows really explain the sources from which cash is derived and the uses made of cash resources? Just how do we go about constructing a Statement of Cash Flows?

Let us take these questions one at a time.

Firms may maintain a certain amount of cash in the form of currency on hand or demand deposits from which the cash may be withdrawn without notice or penalty. Both currency on hand and cash kept in demand deposits are considered "cash." At times, a firm's cash may exceed its immediate needs, but the cash might be required for needs which could arise in the foreseeable future. In such instances, a firm may seek to place its excess cash in short-term, highly liquid investment vehicles. "Short-term," in this instance, is defined as ninety days or less. Such investment vehicles would include money market accounts, commercial paper and U.S. Treasury bills. These short-term, liquid investment vehicles may be referred to as cash equivalents. Cash equivalent investments allow a firm to earn interest on its cash until such time as the cash is required. Because of the liquid nature of cash equivalents, these investments may be liquidated into cash on relatively short notice. Because cash equivalents are so close in nature to cash, we analyze cash equivalents as well as cash when we are examining a firm's overall management of its cash position in the Statement of Cash Flows. In addition, a transfer between a firm's cash account and any of its cash equivalent accounts is not treated as receipt of cash or payment of cash. In order to be considered a "cash equivalent," an investment must be 1) readily convertible to known amounts of cash; and 2) so close to maturity that the market value of the investment will not be affected by interest rate fluctuations.[2]

---

[1] In 1971, the Accounting Principles Board directed that a financial statement referred to as a "Statement of Changes in Financial Positions" ("SCFP") be considered a basic financial statement. American Institute of Certified Public Accountants, Opinions of the Accounting Principles Board, No. 19 (Mar. 1971). This SCFP was a forerunner of the Statement of Cash Flows. In November 1987, the Financial Accounting Standards Board adopted the Statement of Cash Flows as a replacement for the SCFP, effective for fiscal years ending after July 15, 1988. Statement of Financial Accounting Standards No. 95, "Statement of Cash Flows" (Financial Accounting Standards Boards, 1987). The Statement of Cash Flows must be included in the financial statements of a company for each period for which results of operation are provided.

[2] Statement of Financial Accounting Standards No. 95, "Statement of Cash Flows" (Financial Accounting Standards Board, 1987).

Broadly speaking, the purpose of the Statement of Cash Flows ("SCF") is to provide a firm with information about its cash receipts and cash payments during a specified period of time. More specifically, the SCF helps investors, creditors, and other interested persons to evaluate the ability of a firm to (1) generate cash flow, (2) meet its financial obligations as they become due, (3) pay dividends, and (4) maintain operations at current levels or expand them. The SCF also assists a reader in determining a firm's ability to respond to unexpected needs for cash and to take advantage of unanticipated opportunities. The greater the ability of a firm to generate cash, the greater is its ability to absorb declines in business and to accept sudden opportunities. In addition, the SCF can be useful in assessing a firm's need for external financing and in explaining differences between a firm's net income and related cash payments and receipts.

Understanding why it is important to be able to analyze cash flows does not explain why information identical to that provided in the SCF cannot be obtained directly from the Income Statement, the Balance Sheet, and the Statement of Retained Earnings. To understand the benefits of the SCF, we need to recall what we have discussed regarding these other financial statements. When we discussed the Income Statement in Chapter VI, we noted that the "accrual basis" is the almost universal method by which businesses account for income. This means that income is recognized when it is earned (as opposed to when it is received) and expenses are recognized when incurred (as opposed to when funds are disbursed). In other words, the fact that a firm's income statement indicates significant earnings does not necessarily mean that cash or cash equivalents reflecting those earnings have yet been received by the firm.

For example, a firm that sells goods or services to its customers would typically report income for its sales close in time to when those sales were actually made. As a practical matter, however, although customers may owe funds to the firm as soon as they are billed for the goods or services received, customers do not necessarily remit payment as soon as a bill is received. Consequently, a firm might well report income (reflecting sales) in excess of cash received for those sales (reflecting payment made). In addition, even once a firm receives payments for goods or services sold, the income statement does not reveal whether such payment has been retained by the firm in a relatively liquid form. Cash that is received may be transferred into another asset such as inventory, a building, or a long-term investment. The Income Statement reveals whether a firm has been profitable, it does not convey information regarding how its profits have been utilized.

The Balance Sheet is similarly an inadequate substitute for the SCF. As was discussed in Chapter V, the Balance Sheet provides a snapshot of the financial position of a business at a specific point in time. The Statement of Cash Flows, on the other hand, indicates changes in cash positions. The SCF also can be used to determine the nature of the business activity which either generates or uses up the cash assets of the firm. The Balance Sheet does not provide information regarding either the derivation of the cash on hand or the uses made of previous cash assets.

Finally, the Statement of Retained Earnings provides information only regarding the accumulated surplus (or deficit) of a firm and does not serve as a substitute for the SCF.

Prior to 1988, information similar to that found in the Statement of Cash Flows was provided by the Statement of Changes in Financial Position (SCFP). The SCFP focused on the inflow and outflow of "funds" which were defined as either cash or working capital. By the time the SCF was approved as the relevant substitute financial document, most businesses were using the cash format of the SCFP. This cash format was similar to the current SCF. Accordingly, the transition to the SCF as the approved financial document was not difficult to achieve.

B.   WHAT DOES THE STATEMENT OF CASH FLOWS TELL US ABOUT SOURCES AND USES OF CASH?

We Want to Know Not Just What's There, But How It Got There and Where It Goes

How does the SCF identify the sources from which cash resources are generated and the uses made of such resources? Within the SCF, both payments and receipts of cash payments are classified into three categories — operating activities, investing activities, and financing activities. By analyzing cash flows in terms of these three activities, the SCF provides an indication of the impact that each of the major activities of a firm has on cash resources of that firm. The net change in cash and cash equivalents for a specified period is determined by adding together the effect on cash of each of the activities.

Operating activities are those activities that are typically associated with a firm's producing and providing goods and services. Cash flows from operating activities are generally the cash effects of transactions and other events that would be considered in computing net income. By definition of the Financial Accounting Standards Board, operating activities include "all transactions and other events that are not defined as investing or financing activities."[3] Typical cash inflows from operating activities include cash receipts from sales of goods or services. Among such cash receipts would be receipts from the collection of accounts and receipts of interest or dividends. Also included would be any other cash receipt that does not stem from investing or financing transactions. Proceeds received in settlement of lawsuits or insurance claims relating to operations would be cash inflows from operating activities. Cash outflows from operating activities typically include: payments to suppliers and workers; payments of interest and taxes; and all other payments not related to investing or financing activities. Accordingly, payments to settle suits and payments to charities would be included with operating activities cash outflows.

Investing activities are activities relating to making and collecting loans, purchasing or selling (not issuing) debt or equity securities, and acquiring or disposing of long-term assets used in the production of goods or services such as property, plant, and equipment. Cash flows from investing activities will include receipts from sales of long-term assets, marketable securities, and the collection of loans. Cash outflows associated with investing activities include payments to purchase long-term assets used in production, payments made to purchase marketable securities, and cash loaned to borrowers.

Financing activities are understood to include obtaining resources from owners and providing owners with a return on and a return of their investment, borrowing, and repaying resources to creditors. Cash inflows related to financing activities include proceeds from issuing stock, from issuing bonds and other debt instruments, and from other short or long-term borrowing. Cash outflows related to financing activities include payment of dividends and other distributions to owners (including reacquisition of equity instruments), repayments of amounts borrowed, and other long-term payments to creditors.

C. NONCASH TRANSACTIONS

How Do We Record those Noncash Events That Impact on the Firm's Cash Position?

There are some significant financing and investing activities which are entirely noncash in nature but which may nevertheless impact upon the future cash position of a firm. Since the Statement of Cash Flows is designed to reflect the cash position of a business, it is important to, in some manner, record these noncash transactions which may impact upon the cash position of the business. These noncash transactions are recorded in a separate schedule that may follow the Statement of Cash Flows or may appear in the notes to the financial statements.

What kind of noncash transactions can have a future impact on cash flows? Exchanging common stock for a series of long-term bonds has no immediate impact on cash during the period of time in which the transaction occurs. However, in the future, there will no longer be a need to expend cash to pay interest on the bonds or to pay cash to retire those instruments. (Note that the increase in common stock outstanding might result in a greater amount of cash outflow for dividends.) Similarly, the assumption of a long-term debt in exchange for the acquisition of a new building or equipment does not affect the cash position of a firm. Nonetheless, the long-term debt has cash implications for the future since interest will need to be paid. Awareness of these transactions will assist readers of the financial statements to anticipate the firm's future cash flow.

---

[3] Statement of Financial Accounting Standards No. 95, "Statement of Cash Flows," par. 21, "Cash Flows from Operating Activities" (Financial Accounting Standards Board, 1987).

D. METHODS OF PREPARING THE STATEMENT OF CASH FLOWS

Direct v. Indirect

The cash flows which occur most frequently and are most significant to a business are those that arise from operating activities. There are two approved methods for reporting cash flows from operating activities — the direct and the indirect. The direct method shows the major categories of operating cash receipts and cash payments. The major category of cash receipts is cash received from customers. Categories of cash payments include cash paid to suppliers of goods and services, cash paid to workers for wages, and cash paid for such items as interest and taxes. The difference between the operating cash receipts and operating cash payments represents the net cash flows from operating activities. If the direct method of reporting net cash flow from operating activities is used, a reconciliation of net income and net cash flows from operating activities must be provided in a separate schedule.

The indirect (or reconciliation) method for preparing the SCF is a presentation which relies upon a readjustment of the net income reported in the income statement. Since the income identified on the income statement is reported on an accrual basis, it is necessary to adjust this presentation to compensate for the effects of deferrals of past cash receipts and accruals of anticipated cash receipts. For example, the income statement reports sales revenue of the current period, regardless of whether collection was made for such sales. The SCF would include in cash inflows from sales, amounts received during the current period reflecting collections on outstanding receivables applicable to a prior period. The SCF would also need to reduce cash inflows from sales to reflect current sales not yet collected.

In addition, the amount of net income reported in the income statement reflects the impact on revenues of the depreciation expense. Accordingly, in the SCF, an amount must be added back to net income to eliminate this reduction since the depreciation expense does not involve an outflow of cash.

The advantage of the direct method is that it gives the reader a clear picture of the major categories of cash flows. The advantage of the indirect method, on the other hand, is that it allows the reader to understand the differences between the income statement and the cash flows arising from operating activities. Also, the data needed for the indirect method is typically more readily available than the data needed for the direct method.

When the current version of the Statement of Cash Flows was adopted in 1987 as a part of the basic set of financial statements,[4] The Financial Accounting Standards Board (FASB), the accounting board which promulgated the guidelines for the SCF, advised that either the direct or the indirect method may be used for reporting cash flows associated with operating activities. The FASB "encouraged" businesses to use the direct method. However, since the promulgation of the new guidelines for the SCF, the vast majority of businesses have chosen to use the indirect method.[5]

E. ACTUALLY PREPARING THE SCF

For Other than the Casual Reader

It would be instructive to construct a Statement of Cash Flows. This section will identify the information that is necessary to prepare the Statement and will examine how the Statement is prepared. For the faint of heart, who desire only a passing familiarity with the SCF, a close reading of this section is not essential. For those hearty readers with sufficient courage to plow forward, there are two examples presented on how to construct a SCF. The first example is intended to be quite simple to follow since it incorporates relatively little information. The second example is of greater substance. In both instances, both the indirect and the direct method are illustrated.

---

[4] Statement of Financial Accounting Standards, No. 95, "Statement of Cash Flows" (Financial Accounting Standards Board, 1987).

[5] American Institute of Certified Public Accountants, "Accounting Trends & Techniques" 461, Table 5-3 (1996).

1. Simplified SCF Indirect Method. Let us examine how we would construct a Statement of Cash Flows for the Illustrative Company, using the indirect method. Much of the information that is required to prepare the SCF can be obtained from a comparison of the balance sheets of the Illustrative Company at the beginning and the end of the period covered by the SCF (see Exhibit 7.1, *infra*) and from the current income statement (see Exhibit 7.2, *infra*). The information obtained from these two financial statements will be supplemented with information from the Statement of Retained Earnings concerning dividends paid. Finally, some information which we will require may be available only from the financial books of the company.

EXHIBIT 7.1

Illustrative Company
Comparative Balance Sheets

	End of Year	Beginning of Year
Cash	$ 45,000	$ 20,000
Accounts receivable	28,000	40,000
Plant assets	100,000	100,000
Less Accumulated depreciation	(33,000)	(27,000)
Land	32,000	25,000
	172,000	158,000
Accounts payable	21,000	23,000
Capital stock	80,000	80,000
Retained earnings	71,000	55,000
	$172,000	$158,000

EXHIBIT 7.2

Illustrative Company
Income Statement
Relevant Year

Sales Revenue		$216,000
Operating expenses		
Depreciation	6,000	
Other	184,000	190,000
Income before taxes		26,000
Income tax		5,000
Net Income		$ 21,000

In addition to the information provided in the above financial statements, the financial books of the Illustrative Company reveal that the Company paid cash of $7,000 for the land it acquired and paid dividends amounting to $5,000. Based upon the above financial statements and this additional information, how do we derive the indirect method SCF found below in Exhibit 7.3?

a. Operating Activities. We should recall that the figure for cash flows from operating activities is derived by making adjustments to the income statement. Initially, we should note that the net income for the period was $21,000. Adjustments need to be made to that income figure to reflect the fact that: 1) not all revenues and expenditures represent actual cash flows; and 2) some changes that appear in the balance sheet are the result of cash flows which are not reflected in the income statement. Within the first category of adjustments, we need to note that, although depreciation reduced the Illustrative Company's income by $6,000, this expenditure did not represent an outflow of cash. If there were no charge for depreciation, net income would be $6,000 greater. Accordingly, the $21,000 of net income needs to be increased by $6,000 in order to obtain the net cash provided by operating activities.

Within the second category of adjustments, we should note that the balance sheet indicates that accounts receivable were reduced by $12,000 during the period. This difference in amount arises from an inflow of cash from customers who owed money to the company at the end of the preceding period. This cash inflow needs to be reflected on the SCF and it is done by adding $12,000 to the net income of the income statement. Similarly, to the extent that accounts payable were reduced by $2,000, the company made an expenditure of cash greater than the $184,000 of other operating expenses reported in the income statement. This additional outflow of cash needs to be reflected on the SCF.

b. Investing Activities. Since land is a long-term asset used in the production of goods or services, the acquisition of land is treated as a financing activity in the SCF. The only financing activity conducted by the Illustrative Company during the period was the acquisition of land, which is reflected in the balance sheet by the $7,000 increased value of the asset land. The financial records of the Company indicate that cash was used to purchase this land. This purchase of land thus represents a cash outflow of $7,000 which is to be reflected on the SCF under Cash Flows from Investing Activities.

c. Financing Activities. Returning resources to owners and receiving resources from owners both constitute "financing activities." The payment of $5,000 of dividends to shareholders is viewed as a financing activity. This dividend payment represents an outflow of cash from the company and is so recorded on the SCF.

d. Netting Cash Flows. The total cash flows from the three activities are netted together to produce either a net increase or a net decrease in cash during the period of the SCF. This net change is then added to or subtracted from the cash on hand at the beginning of the period to produce a new figure for the cash available at the end of the year.

EXHIBIT 7.3

Illustrative Company
Statement of Cash Flows (Indirect)
Relevant Year

CASH FLOWS FROM OPERATING ACTIVITIES		
Net income		$21,000
Adjustments for differences between income and cash flows from operating activities		
Depreciation	6,000	
Decrease in Accounts receivable	12,000	
Decrease in Accounts payable	(2,000)	16,000
Net cash provided by operating activities		37,000
CASH FLOWS FROM INVESTING ACTIVITES		
Cash used to purchase land		(7,000)
CASH FLOWS FROM FINANCING ACTIVITIES		
Payment of dividends		(5,000)
Net increase in cash		25,000
Cash at beginning of year		20,000
Cash at end of year		$45,000

Direct Method. In constructing an SCF for the Illustrative Company using the direct method (see Exhibit 7.4, *infra*), we utilize the identical information and headings for reporting cash flows from investing activities and cash from financing activities. In the category of cash flows from operating activities, we employ a different approach. With the direct method, we are essentially creating a cash basis income statement. To determine the net cash flow provided by operating activities of the Illustrative Company, we first identify the cash received from customers. This figure equals the sales revenues plus the decrease in accounts receivable. Cash received from customers must be reduced by the cash paid for expenses (supplies, wages, and other costs of operation) as well as the cash paid for income taxes. The remainder of these calculations reveals the net cash provided by operating activities.

The direct method SCF also calls for a separate schedule to reconcile cash from operating activities (as it appears on the direct method SCF) with the income statement. This reconciliation schedule would be the same as the first section of the SCF prepared by the indirect method.

EXHIBIT 7.4

Illustrative Company
Statement of Cash Flows (Direct)

CASH FLOWS FROM OPERATING ACTIVITIES	
Cash received from customers	$228,000
Cash paid for expenses	(186,000)
Income Taxes paid	(5,000)
Net cash provided by operating activities	37,000
CASH FLOW FROM INVESTING ACTIVITIES	
Cash used to purchase land	(7,000)
CASH FLOW FROM FINANCING ACTIVITIES	
Payment of dividends	(5,000)
Net increase in cash	25,000
Cash at beginning of year	20,000
Cash at end of year	$ 45,000

2. More Complex SCF. The same process that was employed above may be used to produce a sophisticated SCF involving more detailed information. Let us construct an SCF for the Hypothetical Corporation based upon comparative balance sheets for the Corporation (Exhibit 7.5), the income statement (Exhibit 7.6), and the additional financial information provided below.

EXHIBIT 7.5

Hypothetical Corporation
Comparative Balance Sheets and Analysis of
Increases and Decreases

	Ending Balance Sheet	Beginning Balance Sheet	Increases in Assets and Decreases in Equities	Decreases in Assets and Increases in Equities
Assets				
Cash	$ 25,000	$ 10,000	$ 15,000	
Temporary investments	30,000	40,000		$ 10,000
Accounts receivable	64,000	58,000	6,000	
Inventories	61,000	50,000	11,000	
Prepaid expenses	5,000	7,000		2,000
Land	10,000	20,000		10,000
Buildings	130,000	30,000	100,000	
Equipment	96,000	31,000	65,000	
Allowance for depreciation	(26,700)	(21,000)		5,700
Goodwill	19,400	20,000		600
	$413,700	$245,000		
Accounts payable	$ 70,000	$ 55,000		$ 15,000
Notes payable	27,000	5,000		22,000
Income taxes payable	4,000	6,000	2,000	
Accrued interest expense	1,500	1,500		
Other accrued expenses	1,600	4,600	3,000	
Mortgage payable	74,800	- 0 -		74,800
Equity				
Capital stock	145,000	100,000		45,000
Premium on capital stock	33,900	13,900		20,000
Retained earnings	74,000	59,000		15,000
Treasury stock, cost	(18,100)	- 0 -	18,100	
	$413,700	$245,000	$220,100	$220,100

EXHIBIT 7.6

Hypothetical Corporation
Income Statement
Relevant Year

Revenues		
Sales		$259,000
Expenses		
Cost of goods sold	163,000	
Depreciation & amortization	6,300	
Wages and operating expenses	58,700	
Interest expense	6,000	
Total expenses		234,000
Income before taxes		25,000
Income taxes		7,000
Net income before extraordinary items		18,000
Gain on sale of land, net of applicable income tax		4,000
Net income		$ 22,000

In addition to the information contained in the comparative balance sheets and the income statement, we should note the following facts. The Hypothetical Corporation paid out $7,000 in dividends. It bought a factory building for $100,000 at the beginning of the year by paying $20,000 in cash and taking out an $80,000 mortgage. Within the year, Hypothetical made a $5,200 principal payment on its mortgage, leaving only $74,800 due at the end of the year. It acquired factory equipment for $65,000 to put in its building. It paid for the equipment by issuing $65,000 of capital stock at a premium. The Corporation also sold land costing $10,000 out of the $20,000 worth of land it owned. The proceeds of this sale, after applicable income tax on the gain, netted the Corporation $14,000. Thus, the sale resulted in an extraordinary gain after taxes of $4,000. Finally, Hypothetical bought some treasury stock for $18,100 cash.

Indirect Method. From the information provided, we can now construct the SCF for the Hypothetical Corporation by the indirect method, as follows in Exhibit 7.7.

EXHIBIT 7.7

Hypothetical Corporation
Statement of Cash Flows (Indirect)
Relevant Year

CASH FLOWS FROM OPERATION ACTIVITIES			
Net Income			$22,000
Adjustments for differences between income and cash flows from operating activities			
Depreciation and amortization		6,300	
Gain on sale of land, net of applicable income tax		(4,000)	
Increase in accounts receivable		(6,000)	
Increase in inventories		(11,000)	
Decrease in prepaid expenses		2,000	
Increase in accounts payable		15,000	
Decrease in income taxes payable		(2,000)	
Decrease in accrued expenses		(3,000)	(2,700)
Net cash provided by operating activities			19,300
CASH FLOWS FROM INVESTING ACTIVITIES			
Purchase of building			
Cost	100,000		
Mortgage payable	80,000		
Cash outlay		(20,000)	
Sale of land, net of income tax on gain		14,000	
Net cash used in investing activities			(6,000)
CASH FLOWS FROM FINANCING ACTIVITIES			
Borrowing on note payable		22,000	
Principle payment on mortgage		(5,200)	
Purchase of treasury stock		(18,100)	
Payment of dividends		(7,000)	
Net cash used in financing activities			(8,300)
Net increase in cash and temporary investments			5,000
Cash and temporary investment at beginning of year			50,000
Cash and temporary investments at end of year			$55,000

Notice that, when reviewing cash flows from operating activities, while the Hypothetical Corporation had net income for the period of $22,000, its cash and temporary investments increased by only $5,000 for the year. In computing cash flows from operating activities, net income for the year is increased by the decrease in prepaid expenses and by the increase in accounts payable. Contrariwise, the initial amount of net income is decreased by increases in accounts receivable and inventory, and by decreases in accrued expenses and income tax payable. As we have previously seen, depreciation and amortization must be added back into net income since those expenses did not represent outflows of cash. In addition, the gain from the sale of land is subtracted from net income since that gain will be accounted for in cash flows from investing activities where the funds received for the sale of lands are recorded.

When examining the cash flows from investing activities, notice that, while cash was reduced by $100,000 in order to purchase a factory building, $80,000 of that payment was covered by a mortgage. Thus, the net effect of the transaction was an outflow of only $20,000 of cash.

The outflows of cash from financing activities are relatively predictable. A borrowing on a note payable increased the cash flow, while principal payments on a mortgage, purchase of treasury stock, and payment of dividends all reduced the cash flow from financing activities.

Finally, those investing and financing activities which did not affect cash flows are reported on a separate schedule. Accordingly, the issuance of capital stock in payment of a $65,000 building is reported on the Schedule of Investing and Financing Activities Not Affecting Cash (Exhibit 7.8).

EXHIBIT 7.8

Schedule of Investing and Financing
Activities Not Affecting Cash

Issue of capital stock in exchange for equipment —	
Par value	$45,000
Premium on capital stock	20,000
	$65,000

Direct Method. Based upon the financial information above, we also have the ability to construct the SCF for the Hypothetical Corporation using the direct method. Let us remember that differences between the direct and indirect methods will be reflected only in the portion of the SCF which reports upon cash flows from operating activities. Both the direct and the indirect methods will report on the net cash flow of the business. Under the direct method, we will record the major classes of operating cash receipts and operating cash payments. The difference between the amounts reported in these two categories is the net cash flow from operating activities (Exhibit 7.9).

EXHIBIT 7.9

Hypothetical Corporation
Statement of Cash Flows (Direct)
Relevant Year

CASH FLOWS FROM OPERATING ACTIVITIES

Cash Receipts		
Collections from customers		$253,000
Cash Payments		
For merchandise	159,000	
For wages and other		
operating expenses	59,700	
For interest	6,000	
For income taxes	9,000	233,700
Net cash provided by		
operating activities		$ 19,300

Notice that the Collections from Customers figure is arrived at by deducting the net increase in the accounts receivable from the amount reported as Sales" on the income statement. We decrease sales by this amount because those sales which result only in an increase of receivables will not have as yet increased the cash flows. Similarly, when we compute the cash outlay for merchandise, we decrease the amount found in the income statement by the increase in accounts payable (since such increase in accounts payable has not yet resulted in an outflow of cash). In addition, we add on to the cost of goods sold the increase in inventory.

To determine the amount of wages and other operating expenses, we add to the figure already appearing in the income statement the decrease in accrued expenses and we subtract the decrease in prepaid expenses. (We add the decrease in accrued expenses because cash was paid out to decrease such accruals. Adding the decrease to expenses will accordingly increase the cash outflow, thus reducing the final amount of cash. We subtract the decrease in prepaid expenses because less cash had to be paid out for expenses. By subtracting this decrease from expenses, we are accordingly increasing the final amount of cash.)

Because the balance sheet shows neither an increase nor a decrease in accrued interest expense, there is no need to alter the interest expense that appears in the income statement. Had there been a change in the accrued interest expense, an increase in such accrual would be deducted from the interest expense for the period. (Cash would not yet have been expended for such accrued expense and, accordingly, the interest expense reported on the income statement would be greater than the actual cash outlay for the period.) A decrease in such accrued interest expense would be added to the interest expense for the period. Similarly, the decrease in income taxes payable reported on the comparative balance sheet is added to the amount reported in the income statement in order to determine the cash payments for income taxes paid. (The decrease in income taxes payable means that cash was paid out to reduce that balance sheet liability and this cash must be reported on the statement of cash flows, along with the cash paid out during that period as an expense item.)

To complete the presentation of the direct method Operating Activities portion of the Statement of Cash Flows, it is necessary to also prepare a schedule to explain the difference between the net income reported in the income statement and the cash flows from operating activities provided in the direct method. This schedule is identical to the operating activities section of the Statement of Cash Flows prepared by the indirect method. The remainder of the direct method Statement of Cash Flows, i.e., the portions dealing with financing activities and investing activities, is identical to those portions of the indirect method Statement of Cash Flows.

F.   WHAT THE SCF REVEALS

What Is It that this SCF Tells Us, Anyhow?

Having constructed a typical SCF in Section E above, it is useful to examine what it is that we can now learn from this statement. Since there is more information involved in the financial statements for the Hypothetical Corporation (Exhibits 7.5 to 7.9), we will use these statements for our studies.

It may be observed that the Hypothetical Corporation generated $19,300 of net cash from operating activities. This net cash flow is a sizeable percentage of the net income of $22,000. However, the largest single contribution to that net cash flow came from an increase in accounts payable. This increase in net cash will not lead to significant financing flexibility in the future since the accounts payable must ultimately be paid. Essentially, the Hypothetical Corporation has delayed making payments which are owing to suppliers and to other parties. The increase in net cash which arose from the depreciation expense, $6,300, is a meaningful increase in net cash, since the depreciation expense did not result in any outlay of cash and will not result in an outlay of cash until that time when it is necessary to replace the equipment being depreciated.

Hypothetical also decreased its net cash flow from operating activities by increasing its inventory by $11,000. Unless, the company had previously been short on inventory, it might want to examine whether it is necessary to carry this much additional inventory. Although the expanded inventory would hopefully eventually be used, this increased inventory has reduced the flexibility that would otherwise inure to the company from a greater amount of net cash.

In terms of financing activities, the cash flow from operations easily covers the $7,000 of dividends paid out by the Corporation as well as the principal payment that needed to be made on the mortgage. While the operating activities cash flow would not have been sufficient to also cover the purchase of treasury stock, that act of capital restructuring was essentially financed by borrowing with a note payable.

The Hypothetical Corporation's expansion resulting from the purchase of a $100,000 building was financed in part by the Corporation's taking out an $80,000 mortgage and in part by the Corporation's sale of land. The net decrease in cash flows from financing and investing activities reduced the increase in cash flows from operating activities to a mere $5,000. This increase left the Corporation with a total of $55,000 of cash and temporary investments, which is about one quarter of the cash that the Corporation expends during the year for operating activities. Presumably, the cash on hand that is expended as expenses arise will be replaced by subsequent earnings from operations.

CHAPTER VIII

FINANCIAL ANALYSIS

A. EVALUATING THE ACCOUNTING ENTITY

Methods to Predict Future Performance and to Measure Results of Operations

Until this point, we have primarily directed our energies toward understanding the accounting process and to examining the preparation and utility of the financial statements. In this Chapter, we want to engage our newly acquired knowledge to develop mechanisms to evaluate the current performance of specific businesses and to help predict the future financial condition of these firms. Accountants have devised methods to help make these evaluations and predictions based upon the financial statements of a business. We will examine the methods they have devised.

Information about current operations and the future condition of a business is of interest to creditors, investors and managers, and others. Among other matters, investors seek information regarding present return on investment and what the percentage of profit will be in comparison with the investment made. Creditors want to know about the ability of a business to pay its obligations as they mature. Management is interested in information regarding present efficiency of operation or the liquidity position of the business, as well as other matters.

As law students and lawyers, we are interested in understanding the mechanisms of financial analysis to help us evaluate certain legal questions. Evaluative information regarding solvency, capital structure, liquidity, and other matters is critical to legal issues that arise in corporate, tax, securities, and partnership law, as well as other areas. For example, the debt-to-equity ratio is an analytical tool that is critical in determining whether or not newly issued bonds might be viewed as equity instruments by the Internal Revenue Service. The Securities and Exchange Commission requires that disclosure be made in registration statements regarding the dilution impact of newly issued equity securities. Solvency analysis is central in many jurisdictions in determining when corporations can issue dividends. These are but a few of the legal matters that require a grasp of financial analysis techniques.

Individual figures in financial statements have only limited significance in and of themselves. Individual figures, however, acquire significance when compared with other figures: the similar figure for the same company for a prior year; similar figures for other companies in the same industry; or another figure in the same company's set of financial statements. Each comparison can be expressed as a percentage or a ratio. For example, if earnings for Company A for Year One are $20,000 and earnings for Year Two are $30,000, then the earnings of Year Two are 150% of the earnings of Year One and the ratio of earnings of Year Two to Year One is 3:2. A further comparison can be made between the increases in earnings of Company A and similarly situated Company B. This inter-company comparison might indicate whether this 150% increase in earnings for Company A was typical for the industry or reflective of special events or operations which impacted solely upon Company A.

Comparisons need not be made only between two figures. Comparisons can also be made between individual figures and totals of individual figures. As an illustration, if Company A has $100,000 worth of current assets and of that figure, $20,000 is in cash, then cash would represent 20% of Company A's current assets. Alternatively, cash to current assets would create a ratio of 1:5. Again, a further comparison might be made between the cash to current asset position of similarly situated Company B.

Percentage and ratio analysis are two basic tools used to analyze the data found in financial statements in order to evaluate the financial condition of a business. We will examine the utility of these methods in the following section.

B. METHODS OF ANALYSIS

Percentage and Ratio Analysis

1. **Horizontal Analysis.** A common method for analyzing the financial condition of a business is to compare financial statements from a prior period with statements from a current period. Comparisons of items in prior period financial statements is sometimes referred to as "horizontal analysis." The comparison can be made both in terms of a dollar amount of increase or decrease, as well as a percentage change. Comparisons can be made between the financial statements of just two periods or for the financial statements of several periods. As more periods are compared, the reader of these comparative statements may well be able to discern trends of varying significance.

To illustrate the utility of horizontal analysis, one can examine the comparative balance sheet of Company A below (Exhibit 8.1) which has columns indicating both dollar amount and percentage changes in various balance sheet items. The comparative statements reveal sizeable increases in plant and other assets, together with a decrease in current liabilities. These changes are offset by increases in long-term liabilities and shareholders' equity and a decrease in current assets.

EXHIBIT 8.1
(Horizontal Analysis)
Company A.

Comparative Balance Sheet
December 31, Year 2 and Year 1

Assets	Year 2	Year 1	Increase (Decrease)	Percent Change
	(in Thousands)			
Current assets	$ 175	$ 200	(25)	(12.5)
Plant assets	95	66	29	43.9
Other assets	29	9	20	145.0
Total assets	299	275	24	8.7
Liabilities				
Current liabilities	108	125	(17)	(13.6)
Long-term liabilities	66	32	34	106.3
Total liabilities	174	157	17	10.8
Shareholders' Equity				
Common stock, $10 par	60	60	-	-
Retained earnings	65	58	7	12.1
Total shareholders' equity	125	118	7	5.9
Total liabilities and shareholders' equity	$ 299	$ 275	24	8.7

Income statements can also be analyzed to reveal increases and decreases in expense, revenue and income items. Exhibit 8.2 presents such an analysis. Review of the figures permits certain observations but also gives rise to questions that cannot be answered without more information. For example, we see that there has been a decrease in sales, but we do not know why. (Were fewer goods sold? Was there a decline in the unit selling price charged by Company A?) We also do not know why the cost of sales did not decline in the same proportion. (Was there an increase in the unit cost of goods sold?) The increase in depreciation presumably is due to the sizeable increase in plant assets. Similarly, the increase in interest expense is related to the doubling of long-term liabilities. Why, however, is there an increase in selling and administrative expenses?

EXHIBIT 8.2
(Horizontal Analysis)
Company A.

Comparative Income Statements
Calendar Year 2 and Year 1

	Year 2	Year 1	Increase (Decrease)	Percent Change
	(in Thousands)			
Sales	$ 494	$506	(12)	(2.4)
Deduct:				
Cost of sales excluding depreciation	413	418	(5)	(1.2)
Depreciation	7	5	2	40.0
Selling and administrative expense	56	51	5	9.8
Interest expense	5	3	2	66.7
Total costs and expenses	481	477	4	0.84
Earnings before income taxes	13	29	(16)	(55.2)
Deduct: Taxes on income	4	13	(9)	(69.2)
Net income	$ 9	$ 16	(7)	(43.8)

To appreciate the significance of the changes in the items on the income statement, one might want to compare Company A's performance with that of another company in a similar business, or with average figures for the industry of which Company A is a part. However, when making inter-company comparisons, dollar amount differentials might have limited relevance. For example, assume a comparison of Company A with Company B, whose net income decreased by only $2,000 for the year in question. At first blush, Company B's performance might appear to outshine that of Company A, since Company A's net income declined by $7,000. However, if Company B's net income decreased from $4,000 a year to $2,000, Company B's $2,000 decline in income represents a 50% decrease in earnings. Company A's $7,000 decline, on the other hand. represents only a 43.8% decrease in earnings.

To facilitate comparisons between income and other financial statements of various companies, the changes in items are frequently expressed in percentages, rather than in absolute dollar amounts. By using percentages, all data are reduced to a common size base of 100%. Thus, meaningful comparison of similar items can be made between companies of significantly different size. Financial statements which present data in percentages are referred to as "common-size" statements.

2. Vertical Analysis. Another analytic tool is a percentage calculation of the component items within a given financial statement. This analysis, referred to as "vertical analysis," establishes one item of a financial statement as the base of 100% and compares other items on the financial statement to that first item as percentages of the base. To illustrate, in Exhibit 8.3, vertically analyzed balance sheets for Company A have been prepared based upon the same figures that we used for Company A in Exhibit 8.1. Notice that each Asset item is compared as a percentage of total assets. Also, each Liability item and Equity item is compared as a percentage of Total Liabilities and Shareholders' Equity. For example, at the end of Year Two, plant assets represented 31.8% of the total assets of Company A.

Vertical analysis can be combined with horizontal analysis and a comparison can be made between prior year financial statements and current financial statements to discern changes or trends. Thus, again in Exhibit 8.3, when we compare the balance sheet of Company A at the end of Year One with the balance sheet of Company A at the end of Year Two, we can see that current assets, which a year earlier represented

72.7% of total assets, at the end of Year Two represented only 58.5% of total assets. That change reflects a decrease in the liquidity (ability to be converted into cash) of the assets of Company A. The two balance sheets together also alert the reader to the fact that the equity of long-term creditors as a percentage of total assets increased in Year Two to 22.1% from 11.6% in Year One. (Since Total Liabilities and Shareholders' Equity equal Total Assets, the ratio of Long-term Liabilities to Total Liabilities and Shareholders' Equity will equal the ratio of Long-term Liabilities to Total Assets.) This change means that Company A has a greater debt obligation per dollar of assets at the end of Year Two to service than it had at the end of Year One.

EXHIBIT 8.3

(Comparative Vertical Analysis)

Company A

Comparative Balance Sheets
December 31, Year 2 and Year 1

	Year 2		Year 1	
Assets	(In Thousands)	Percents	(In Thousands)	Percents
Current assets	$ 175	58.5	$ 200	72.7
Plant assets	95	31.8	66	24.0
Other assets	29	9.7	9	3.3
Total assets	299	100.0	275	100.0
Liabilities				
Current liabilities	108	36.1	125	45.5
Long-term liabilities	66	22.1	32	11.6
Total liabilities	174	58.2	157	57.1
Shareholders' Equity				
Common stock $10 par	60	20.0	60	21.8
Retained earnings	65	21.8	58	21.1
Total shareholders' equity	125	41.8	118	42.9
Total liabilities and shareholders' equity	$ 299	100.0	$ 275	100.0

A similar vertical analysis can be prepared for the income statement of Company A. With the income statement, each item is stated as a percentage of sales. (Notice that all expenses plus earnings before taxes equal the revenues from sales.) From Exhibit 8.4, using the same amounts found in Exhibit 8.2, we discover that selling and administrative expenses in Year Two represented 11.3% of the cost of sales, and this was up from 10.1% in the preceding year. Earnings before taxes amounted to 2.6% of total revenues in Year Two, down significantly from the 5.7% in Year One. Essentially, the Company's profit margin on its sales has fallen off.

EXHIBIT 8.4

(Comparative Vertical Analysis)

Company A

Comparative Income Statements
Calendar Year 2 and Year 1

	Year 2		Year 1	
Assets	(In Thousands)	Percents	(In Thousands)	Percents
Sales	$ 494	100.0	$506	100.0
Deduct:				
Cost of sales, excluding depreciation	413	83.6	418	82.6
Depreciation	7	1.4	5	1.0
Selling and administrative expense	56	11.4	51	10.1
Interest expense	5	1.0	3	.6
Total costs and expenses	481	97.4	477	94.3
Earnings before income taxes	13	2.6	29	5.7
Deduct: Taxes on income	4	.8	13	2.6
Net income	$ 9	1.8	$ 16	3.1

3. Standard Ratios. In addition to horizontal and vertical percentage analysis, there are numerous relationships between items on financial statements that analysts will express as ratios. These ratios are central to an examination of the financial health of a business. The relationship experienced as a ratio might be between two items on the same financial statement (as in a debt-to-equity ratio derived from the balance sheet) or, between one item from one financial statement and another item from a different financial statement (as in earnings-to-equity ratios prepared from the income statement in conjunction with the balance sheet).

For different parties related to a business, the utility of specific ratios will vary. For example, short-term creditors might be most interested in liquidity ratios which can help predict the ability of a business to repay loans which the creditor is considering extending. Investors, on the other hand, might be most interested in ratios which analyze the profitability of a business. Managers might want to examine certain ratios that help analyze the efficiency of the operations of a business. For convenience of study, we can categorize analytic ratios into four categories: (a) liquidity; (b) long-term solvency and capital structure; (c) efficiency; and (d) profitability. We will examine a number of common ratios to see how they are prepared and what information they can provide. The data employed will be taken from the balance sheet and income statement of Company A (Exhibits 8.1 and 8.2) and from the vertically compared income statements (Exhibit 8.4).

Company A of course, is a textbook illustration. It contains no unusual items. In the real business world, however, companies encounter and report upon usual items — for example, a non-recurring gain or a non-recurring expense or loss. In such cases, the comparability of ratios involving net income may be improved by adjustment to eliminate the unusual elements.

As the reader proceeds through this Section, he or she will find it instructive to refer to Appendix B and to seek to compute the relevant ratios for the H.J. Heinz Company. Note, however, the restructuring charges reported in the fiscal year ended April 30, 1997 in note 4 of the consolidated financial statements.

a. Liquidity ratios

i. Current ratio. The liquidity ratios are designed in general to measure a business's ability to meet its current obligations as they mature. The "current ratio" or "working capital" ratio expresses the proportion between current assets and current liabilities. This proportion provides a measure of the percentage by which current assets can decline in relation to current liabilities during a financially difficult time (perhaps caused by a business downturn or an unexpected loss) without the business losing its ability to pay its debts. As a crude rule of thumb, businesses and creditors find comfort in a current ratio of 2:1. This generalization will, however, vary among different industries and also based upon the composition of the various current assets. For example, current assets primarily comprised of inventory are less liquid than current assets primarily comprised of cash and accounts receivable. In the former instance, creditor comfort might require a higher current ratio than in the latter instance.

The current ratio for Company A at the end of Year Two (*see* Exhibit 8.1) was 175 ÷ 108 or 1.62:1. This, obviously, is less than 2:1. On the other hand, it is a slight improvement over the working capital position of the prior year when the ratio was 200 ÷ 125 or 1.60:1. In a given case, one might be more impressed by a steadily improving (or declining) trend in the current ratio than by the ratio at a given moment in time.

As we have noted earlier, current assets less current liabilities measures working capital. And working capital in turn also is a measure of the margin of safety that a firm possesses to be able to pay its debts. Because working capital provides an absolute amount, as opposed to a relationship between two figures, it is in some ways a less meaningful measure of the margin of safety than is the current ratio. For example, to say that two firms in the same industry have an identical amount of net working capital, say $50,000, might tell analysts very little about the relative health of the two businesses. If it is discovered that the first business has current assets of $1,000,000 and the second business has current assets of $100,000, then we see that the second business has a satisfactory current ratio of 2:1 ($100,000 ÷ 50,000). The first firm, however, has a current ratio of 1.05:1 ($1,000,000 ÷ 950,000).

It is also possible that working capital can decrease (or increase) while the current ratio increases (or decreases). The working capital for Company A, you might notice (see Exhibit 8.1, *supra*), went from $75,000 to $67,000 between Years One and Two. At the same time, the current ratio, as we have seen, went from 1.60:1 to 1.62:1. Thus, as indicators of financial health, working capital and the current ratio can be at loggerheads. Both matters must be analyzed for a complete picture of the health of a business.

ii. Acid-test ratio. The "acid-test ratio" or "quick ratio" is a measurement of a business' ability to convert its current assets quickly into cash to pay its current liabilities. While the current ratio compares all of the current assets of a business — cash, marketable securities, accounts receivable, inventory, and prepaid expenses — to its current liabilities, the acid-test ratio compares only the first three current assets. Neither inventory nor prepaid expenses are quickly convertible into cash and so are not included in the acid-test ratio. Inventory has to first be sold and then the resulting accounts receivable have to be collected before a business receives cash for its inventory. Prepaid expenses are not current assets which will generate cash. Rather, prepaid expenses represent a savings of a future cash expenditure.

A crude rule of thumb would require a business to have an acid-test ratio of 1:1. Such a 1:1 ratio would suggest that a business would be able to pay all of its current liabilities relatively quickly. We do not presently have adequate information about the composition of Company A's current assets to compute the acid-test ratio.

b. Long-term solvency and capital structure. Long-term solvency ratios are used to predict a business' ability to pay its long-term creditors. At the same time, they are useful in providing information regarding interest payment demands on a company's earnings that, but for the interest obligations, would go to the equity holders.

i. Debt-to-equity ratio. The debt-to-total-equity ratio compares a company's debt to its total liabilities plus owner's equity. Since total equity equals total assets, the debt to equity ratio expresses a ratio of a firm's debts as compared to its assets. The ratio is useful for creditors in determining the protection they might receive in case of insolvency. An acceptable ratio differs from industry to industry. For Company A, we can compute from Exhibit 8.1 (or as shown in Exhibit 8.3) that the ratio at the end of Year Two was 174,000 divided by 299,000 or 58.2%.

Other expressions of this ratio are debt-to-equity (owner's equity exclusive of liabilities) or the ratio of owner's equity to the total of liabilities plus equity. In each instance, the ratio derived is informative of the protection provided creditors. The ratio also provides some limited information regarding the drain on earnings that the interest payment commitment represents to the firm.

ii. Times-interest-earned ratio. A more direct comparison of earnings and interest is the "times-interest-earned" ratio. This ratio compares earnings before interest charges and taxes to interest charges alone. This ratio indicates the coverage that bondholders have from earnings to insure payment of interest on the debt obligations they hold. For Company A, as can be computed from Exhibit 8.2, during Year Two, the times-interest-earned ratio would be

$$\frac{(interest\ expense + earnings\ before\ taxes)}{interest\ expense} = \frac{5,000 + 13,000}{5,000} \quad or \quad \frac{18,000}{5,000} = 3.6.$$

iii. Book value per share. This frequently used ratio provides a measurement of the amount of net assets backing each share of common stock. It is a theoretical measurement of what the common stockholders of a corporation would receive after corporate assets were liquidated and all liabilities paid off. It is theoretical since the determination of asset value is made solely on the basis of balance sheet book value. It is unlikely that assets sold in liquidation would precisely equal book value. Although book value is considered of interest to shareholders and potential investors as a measurement of the value of their stock in a corporation, it is only a crude measurement in light of the arbitrary nature of the conventional accounting procedures used to measure asset value.

For a corporation with no preferred stock, book value is computed by dividing shareholders' equity by the number of common shares outstanding. As can be determined from Exhibit 8.1, at the end of Year Two, Company A had total Shareholders' Equity of $125,000 and 6,000 shares outstanding. Thus, book value was equal to $125,000 divided by 6,000 or $20.83 per share.

c. Efficiency ratios

i. Accounts receivable turnover. Ratio analysis can be utilized to assist in assessing the efficiency with which management utilizes the resources available to the company. The accounts receivable turnover ratio indicates the number of times receivables are turned into cash each year. It is computed by dividing total credit sales by the average receivables balance. The ratio provides a sense of the quality of the accounts receivable and also of the speed of management in collecting its accounts receivable. The higher the turnover ratio, the more liquid the company's accounts receivable can be considered.

Because the balance sheet in Exhibit 8.1 was somewhat simplified, it did not include a breakdown of current assets. This breakdown is necessary to calculate the accounts receivable turnover. Let us assume the details of current assets are as shown below in Exhibit 8.5.

EXHIBIT 8.5

Company A

Current Assets

December 31, Year 2 and Year 1

	Year 2	Year 1
Cash and short-term investments	$ 12	$ 16
Accounts receivable, net	48	55
Inventories	113	127
Other	2	2
Total current assets	$175	$200

Utilizing data from Exhibits 8.2 and 8.5, *supra*, in terms of thousands, we can calculate accounts receivable turnover as follows:

$$\frac{\text{Sales for Year 2}}{\text{Average Accounts Receivable}} = \frac{494}{\frac{48 + 55}{2}} = \frac{494}{51.5} = 9.6$$

Notice that we compute the Average Accounts Receivable by taking the average of the beginning and ending balance of accounts receivable. Also, notice that we are assuming that substantially all sales were on credit. In cases where cash sales comprise a significant percentage of total sales, the numerator should include credit sales only.

The efficiency of accounts receivable collections can be measured in another way, in terms of the "average age of accounts receivable," *i.e.*, the average number of days it takes to collect from trade debtors. This figure can be computed for Company A by dividing 365 by 9.6 (the turnover ratio), giving 38 days as the average period of time accounts receivable were outstanding during Year Two. The lower the number of days accounts receivable are outstanding, the more efficient are the collections.

ii. Inventory turnover. This ratio measures how quickly inventory is sold. Generally, the higher the inventory turnover ratio, the more efficiently a business is operating. A higher ratio means that a greater volume of sales is being generated for a given investment in inventory than would be suggested by a lower ratio. A low ratio might suggest that some inventory is obsolete or overpriced. Also, too high an inventory turnover ratio might suggest that a firm is frequently out of stock and losing customers' sales as a consequence. Each industry will have its own acceptable range of turnover ratios.

Inventory turnover is computed by dividing the cost of goods sold by the average inventory. Average inventory is computed by taking the average of the beginning and ending inventory. Utilizing information from Exhibits 8.2 and 8.5 in terms of thousands we can calculate inventory turnover as follows:

$$\frac{\text{Cost of Goods Sold}}{\text{Average Inventory}} = \frac{413}{\frac{113 + 127}{2}} = \frac{413}{120} = 3.4$$

iii. Asset turnover ratio. This ratio measures sales against average total assets. It is designed to indicate how efficiently a company uses its assets. It shows the amount of sales generated by a specific amount of assets. One has to determine whether to exclude from the asset base of this ratio long-term investments or other assets not devoted to the regular manufacturing or merchandising activities of the enterprise. Average total assets are computed by taking the average of the total assets at the beginning and the end of the period.

Based upon data found in Exhibits 8.1 and 8.2, *supra*, we can calculate the asset turnover ratio of Company A for Year Two as follows:

$$\frac{\text{Sales}}{\text{Average Total Assets}} = \frac{494}{\frac{299 + 275}{2}} = \frac{494}{287} = 1.72$$

d. Profitability ratios. Profitability ratios, in a sense, measure overall success. They are perhaps the most significant ratios for investors, since they express a "rate of return." The profitability ratios we will examine are "earnings per share," "price earnings ratio," "return on total assets," "return on investment," and "profit margin on sales."

i. Earnings per share. This well might be the most commonly used financial analysis ratio. When there is only one class of stock, "earnings per share" are computed by dividing the net income for the period by the average number of shares outstanding. To illustrate, utilizing the data from Exhibits 8.1 and 8.2, the income for Company A during Year Two was $9,000 and there were 6,000 (60,000 divided by $10 par) shares outstanding throughout the year. The earnings per share for Year Two were $1.50.

"Earnings per share" refers only to earnings per share of common stock. When there are preferred shares as well as common, the dividend applicable to the preferred stock is subtracted from net income and the resulting net amount is divided by the average number of common shares outstanding.

The earnings per share figure is usually prominently displayed in financial reports. However, it carries significance only in comparison with prior periods or when utilized to compute the price-earnings ratio (see *infra*) or to compute the ratio of dividends per share to earnings per share.

When there has been extraordinary income, the earnings per share figures are computed for ordinary net income, the extraordinary income and the final net income.

With more complex capital structures there may be securities outstanding convertible into common stock. or there may be options, warrants, or rights, which could be exercised to obtain common stocks. In such cases, the calculation of earnings per share can be quite complex. It must take into account the dilution effect on earnings per share of the possible conversions and exercise of rights. As an example, assume that, in addition to its 6,000 shares of common stock, Company A had 50 bonds outstanding which were convertible into common stock on a basis of 40 shares of common stock for each bond. To compute the fully diluted earnings per share figure, one would divide earnings of $9,000 by 6,000 (common) plus 2,000 (common upon conversion of the bonds). Fully diluted earnings per share would thus be 9,000 divided by 8,000 or $1.13 per share.[1]

ii. Price-earnings ratio. This ratio is expressed as a multiple — *i.e.*, the number of times by which the per share earnings must be multiplied to arrive at the current market price of the stock. A high multiple would tend to indicate that investors believe future earnings will be greater than present earnings and/or that the stock has growth potential. With a market price of $40 per share for Company X and earnings for the past year of $4.00 a share, the price-earnings ratio, or multiple, would be 10. If the price were $30, the multiple would be 7½. Price-earnings ratios or P/E ratios are often provided with the trading prices of securities found in newspapers.

iii. Return on total assets. This is a general measure of profitability and managerial efficiency. The theory behind this ratio is that a business' assets generate its income. The rate of return may be computed before or after income taxes. It is also a common practice to add onto earnings the interest expense before computing the ratio. The rationale is that assets are provided not only by shareholders but also by creditors.

---

[1] Actually, correctional computations would have to be made to increase the earnings figure by the amount of interest payments that had otherwise gone to the bondholders.

Therefore, the return on assets should include the interest paid to creditors, as well as the income allocable to shareholders.

Referring to Company A, the return before income taxes for Year Two would be the $13,000 earnings before income taxes (see Exhibit 8.2) plus the interest expense of $5,000 (see Exhibit 8.2), a total of $18,000. From Exhibit 8.1, we may compute average assets as $287,000 (275,000 plus 299,000, divided by 2), the average of the total assets at the beginning and end of the year.

The rate of return is 6.3% (18,000 divided by 287,000).

Looking again at Exhibits 8.1 and 8.2, we can compute the rate of return on total assets after taxes. In the numerator, we would add $9,000 of earnings plus $5,000 of interest expense[2] and divide by the same denominator of $287,000 of average assets. We arrive at an after-tax rate of return of 4.9 (14,000 divided by 287,000.

iv.   **Rate of return on investment.** Contrasted with the rate of return on total assets, shareholders may be more interested in the rate of return on shareholders' equity. This ratio can be computed by dividing the after-tax earnings (found in Exhibit 8.2) of $9,000 by the average shareholders' equity (computed from Exhibit 8.1). This return for Year Two for Company A is 7.4% (9,000 divided by 118,000 plus 125,000, divided by 2).

Note that the rate of return on shareholders' equity (computed after taxes) for Year Two in the case of Company A exceeds the rate of return on total assets after income taxes which we computed in paragraph (iii) above. (7.4% contrasted with 4.9%.) This illustrates what is termed the factor of "leverage." The total interest cost of $5,000 applicable to the average total funds provided by creditors of $165,500 (computed by dividing by 2 the sum of 174,000 plus 157,000) is only 3%. This is significantly less than the return of 6.3% before taxes earned on total assets. Essentially, the equity owners reap the benefits of a rate of return on the borrowed money that exceeds the cost (interest) of borrowing those funds. [Note that, although interest is paid on long-term liabilities and on short-term bank loans, accounts payable which also constitute creditors' funds normally do not carry any interest cost. This latter fact reduces the average cost of total liabilities.]

When borrowings can provide assets at an interest cost less than the rate of return that can be achieved on those additional assets, there is a favorable leverage situation and the return on shareholders' equity is increased. There is a risk involved, however. If the rate of return on assets falls below the cost of borrowed funds, there then is a negative impact on the rate of return on shareholders' equity.

v.   **Profit margin on sales.** There are two different items which may be applied as ratios of sales to measure profitability: net income (net profit) and gross margin (gross profit).

a.   **Ratio of net income to sales.** The ratio of net income to sales is stated as a percentage of sales. For Company A, this measure is shown for both Year Two and Year One in the vertically analyzed comparative income statement presented in Exhibit 8.4. For Year Two, the rate of return was 1.8% and for Year One, it was 3.1%. There are decided industry differences in the average rate of net profit, and these are related to the rate of inventory turnover. Food processing companies and grocery chains, for example, have rapid inventory turnover and low ratios of net income to sales. Companies with slower moving inventories, such as jewelry stores or stores selling musical instruments, would be expected to show higher rates of return on sales.

b.   **Gross profit ratio and inventory mark-up.** The gross profit (gross margin) ratio is also computed as a percentage of sales. Although it can be computed for both manufacturing and merchandising enterprises, it is generally of greater interest in the merchandising field.

Although the gross margin does not always appear as a separate figure in an income statement, it can be computed by subtracting cost of sales from sales. For example, with sales of $300 and cost of sales of $200, the gross margin would be $100. The gross profit rate, then, is 100 divided by 300, or 33 1/3%.

---

[2] Additional adjustments need to be made to reflect tax consequences.

(Matthew Bender & Co., Inc.)

Particularly in a merchandising enterprise, one encounters the term "mark-up," which will usually be stated as a percentage. If an item in inventory costing $60 is priced for sale at $100, the mark-up or prospective gross margin is $40. In computing the mark-up percentage, one can relate the gross margin to the selling price or to the cost. Based on the selling price, the mark-up is 40% (40 divided by 100); based on the cost of the merchandise, it is 66 ⅔% (40 divided by 60). To avoid misunderstanding when referring to mark-up, it is important to know whether the percentage is based on cost or on selling price.

The gross profit percentage based on sales is equivalent to the average mark-up based on selling price.

c. Caveat on the utility of ratios. Ratios have their limitations. Although they appear to be scientific in nature, they should be used with caution. Ultimately, many ratios are based upon historical costs, the arbitrary measurement of which can lead to distortions. For example, return on asset ratios of two companies, with very similar assets and very similar earnings, might be dramatically different if the assets of one company were fully depreciated and the assets of the other had just begun to be depreciated.

Ratio comparisons among firms can be very misleading if the businesses use different accounting techniques. During a period of inflation, a LIFO valuation of inventory would reduce both net income and total assets and could result in a different return on investment ratios when compared with a firm employing a FIFO valuation method.

Even when ratios are used as a means of tracking trends within a single business, there are other factors that well might influence the analysis of a company's performance. Industry trends as well as general economic factors might be more relevant to a business performance than internally generated factors.

Finally, ratio analysis, like all of accounting, requires the employment of a certain amount of common sense. If one is examining the debt structure of a corporation, then one has to know when a debtor/lender relationship exists and when it does not. If Corporation A sells Corporation B assets XYZ, the monies Corporation A receives from Corporation B for the assets would typically not be considered borrowed monies. Assume, however, in the sale documents, that Corporation B was given an unconditional right to sell assets XYZ back to Corporation A after six months and to receive interest on the sale monies for the time that such monies were held by Corporation A. Then the sale begins to look more like a loan from, B to A, collateralized by assets XYZ. Regardless of the treatment by accountants, the financial analyst would have to determine whether to include the potential loan in his calculation of the debt-to-equity ratio. The conclusion reached by the analyst is arrived at by common sense.

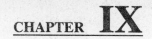

PUTTING THE ACCOUNTING PROCESS TO WORK TO ASSIST IN MAKING LEGAL DECISIONS ABOUT DISTRIBUTIONS

A. ACCOUNTING AND CORPORATE DISTRIBUTIONS TO SHAREHOLDERS

How Accounting Affects What the Corporation Can Give Its Owners

While the accounting process and the resulting statements provide the attorney (as well as others) with a means to evaluate the financial condition of a corporation, they also provide a mechanism to determine whether the corporation is in compliance with various state statutory restrictions regarding corporate distributions and share repurchases.

In this Chapter, we want to explore how the accounting process, in conjunction with state corporate laws, impacts upon corporate distributions and share repurchases (which, essentially, are a form of distribution). We will discover that state statutes restrict the ability of a corporation to make distributions not only in terms of the relative amount of the corporation's assets and liabilities, but, in some instances, based on the allocation of equity among the various sub-categories of equity.[1]

B. TYPES OF CORPORATE DISTRIBUTIONS

What are They, How Does the Accountant Deal with Them? When are They Made?

A corporate distribution can be defined in terms of its impact upon the accounting equation as a transfer of assets from the corporation to its shareholders that results in a decrease in net assets and a corresponding decrease in stockholder equity. Conventional corporate distributions can be classified into two types — dividends and stock repurchases.

1. **Cash Dividends.** Dividends are essentially a distribution to the shareholders of the income earned or the gains made by the corporation. They represent to the shareholders a return on their investment (equity). Dividends are declared by the board of directors. Ordinary dividends are generally paid in cash though they can be paid in other assets, such as property, as well as in acknowledgment of indebtedness. Such payments affect the accounting equation by reducing the asset cash (or other assets distributed) and by reducing the retained earnings element of shareholders' equity. The equity account of retained earnings is reduced because ordinary dividends represent an outflow of earnings and it is the retained earnings account that measures the accumulated earnings of a corporation. The ordinary cash dividend has no effect on paid-in capital.

2. **Stock Dividends.** It needs mentioning that dividends are, at times, paid in the form of stock of the corporation. When dividends are paid in stock, each shareholder is issued a *pro rata* portion of new shares based upon present stock holdings. In essence, this is only a paper transaction in which the amount of equity of the corporation remains constant, but becomes divided among a greater number of shares. Although this share issuance is referred to as a "stock dividend," it is not really a distribution since no assets leave the corporation, the total amount of equity remains unchanged, and each shareholder's proportionate interest

---

[1] For a discussion of the sub-categories of equity, see Chapter III, *supra*.

remains constant. Share dividends permit the corporation to retain its profits while giving shareholders some sense of an investment return (albeit, not a realistic sense).

Although stock dividends do not alter the total shareholders' equity of the corporation, as stated, they do increase the number of shares outstanding. Since stated capital is a function of the number of shares outstanding (multiplied either by par or stated value) and since stock dividends increase this number (and do not affect par or stated value), then stock dividends must increase a corporation's stated capital. However, accountants cannot fabricate stated capital out of thin air. To accommodate this increase in stated capital, accountants decrease retained earnings by a comparable amount.

The amount by which stated capital is increased, and retained earnings are decreased, depends upon the size of the stock dividend. Shareholders tend to look upon stock dividends as effecting a distribution of corporate earnings (which they do not), as opposed to effecting a reduction of the proportion of corporate equity represented by each share (which they do). This misperception is often shared by the investing community as a whole. Consequently, if the stock dividend is small enough that it does not significantly augment the total number of shares outstanding, the fair market value of the corporation's stock may remain constant (even though the ownership interest represented by each share is diminished). In essence then, although a shareholder's proportionate interest in the corporation remains constant, the market price of his total holdings (his original shares plus the stock dividend shares) may increase.

To reflect the perception of many shareholders that the stock dividend constitutes a real distribution, the accountant decreases retained earnings by an amount equal to the fair market value of the shares issued as a dividend.[2] If the reduction in retained earnings exceeds the increase in stated capital, the differential is applied to capital surplus. Using fair market value as the amount by which retained earnings is decreased gives recognition to the benefit experienced by the shareholder-recipient of the stock dividends.

As an illustration of the effect stock dividends would have on a balance sheet, assume that the shareholders' equity portion of the balance sheet of the Illustrative Corporation on December 31, 1993 appears as follows:

ILLUSTRATIVE CORPORATION

Shareholders' Equity
December 31, Year 1

Capital Stock:	
Common stock ($1 par value; 20,000 shares authorized; 10,000 shares issued)	$10,000
Retained earnings	25,000
Total shareholders' equity	$35,000

Assume that on the following January 15, when the fair market value of its common stock is $5 per share, the Illustrative Corporation issues a 1-for-10 stock dividend. For every 10 shares held by a shareholder, an additional one share is distributed. Since this distribution is less than 25% of the outstanding shares (it is 10% of the outstanding shares), the reduction in retained earnings is computed to equal the fair market value of the shares times the number of shares issued. There are 1,000 shares issued. Thus retained earnings will be reduced by $5,000. On the other hand, the newly issued shares will increase stated capital by $1,000 ($1 par value times 1,000 shares) and will create $4,000 worth of capital surplus ($4 premium per share times 1,000 shares). Total shareholders' equity remains constant.

The shareholders' equity portion of the Illustrative Corporation's balance sheet (assuming all else remained equal) would appear as follows on January 31, Year 2.

---

[2] This approach is used only if the dividend represents less than 25% of the outstanding shares of the corporation. If the dividend is greater than that amount, there is a presumption that the fair market value of the shares will decrease exactly as the proportionate interest in the corporation's equity represented by each share has decreased. In that case, retained earnings are reduced by the par value or the stated value of the newly issued shares multiplied by the total number of shares issued. See American Institute of Certified Public Accountants, Accounting Research Bulletin No. 43, ch. 7 (June 1953).

ILLUSTRATIVE CORPORATION

Shareholders' Equity
January 31, Year 2

Capital Stock:

Common stock ($1 par value; 20,000 shares authorized, 11,000 shares issued)	$11,000
Capital in excess of par	4,000
	$15,000
Retained earnings:	20,000
Total shareholders' equity	$35,000

As a final caveat, stock dividends should be distinguished from stock splits. With splits, the par or stated value is reduced and a proportionate number of new shares is issued. For example, assuming a two-for-one split, the total number of shares outstanding after the split will double and the par value of each share will be halved. Such splits are often effected to increase the marketability of shares by decreasing the per share price. Although splits require a change in the certificate of incorporation, there is no alteration made in any of the equity accounts. Thus, no transfers need be made out of retained earnings, as was required with the stock dividend.

3. Stock Repurchases. On certain occasions, a corporation will repurchase some of the outstanding stock held by its shareholders. It may do this for numerous reasons, including a desire to increase the earnings per share of the other shares not so reacquired. At other times, shares may be repurchased to prevent shares of a closely held corporation from being transferred to other than specified shareholders. Shares may also be repurchased for reissue to officers as bonuses. Regardless of the reason for the repurchase, all repurchases involve a flow of assets out of the corporation and into the hands of the shareholders. The corporation is reacquiring its shares and, in exchange, the shareholders are receiving corporate assets. Thus, we can categorize repurchases as distributions. Like other distributions, the corporation is limited in the amount of shares it can repurchase.

When shares are repurchased, even though they are held by the corporation, they are rarely included as assets on the corporation's books. This is not surprising, since these repurchased shares or "treasury shares" cannot be voted by the corporation nor do they give the corporation any rights to dividends nor any preemptive rights. Treasury shares possess no greater similarity to assets than do the authorized shares of a corporation which have never been issued. The fact that treasury shares were once outstanding does not alter their nature as treasury shares. The corporation can do nothing more with its treasury shares than it can do with excess authorized shares which it has not yet issued.

It is also philosophically unsound to include a corporation's own shares among its assets, since such an accounting practice would suggest that a corporation could own itself and also that it could measure its own wealth by its very self-ownership. Since treasury shares are generally not carried as assets, when a repurchase is made, the asset side of the balance sheet is reduced by the outflow of corporate assets necessary to repurchase the shares and there is no counterbalancing increase of assets.

On the shareholders' equity side of the balance sheet, however, the repurchased shares, even though *not* outstanding,[3] are still authorized and issued until canceled or "retired."[4] Treasury shares continue to exist

---

[3] "Outstanding" shares are authorized and issued shares still in the hands of the shareholders. By definition, treasury shares, which are held by the corporation, are not outstanding.

[4] When shares are retired, the authorized number of shares in the certificate of incorporation must be reduced. Retired shares, essentially, no longer exist. For retired shares to be reissued, there again must be an authorization made by the shareholders and an amendment filed to the certificate of incorporation.

and they can even be resold or otherwise redistributed without the need for any amendment to the certificate of incorporation. The continued existence of these shares should be reflected under the corporation's capital stock account. Since the amount of issued securities has not decreased, it would be considered erroneous under many state statutes to reduce the capital stock by an amount representing the repurchased shares.

The accountant is thus confronted with a quandary. Although corporate assets have been reduced, it is not clear where a corresponding reduction can be made in shareholders' equity to preserve the basic equality of the balance sheet. While it is not clear which equity account should be reduced to reflect the reacquisition, it is clear that corporate funds have been expended as if a dividend had been paid and shareholders' equity has, in some manner, been depleted. If we can somehow reduce shareholders' equity in general, then our sense of accounting procedure will be maintained, and the balance sheet will stay balanced.

This rather delicate accounting problem presented by a corporation's acquisition of treasury stocks is recorded by the accountant in a number of ways. The most accepted, and perhaps most clever, is to ignore which specific element of shareholders' equity the share repurchase reduces. Instead, the accountant shows the cost of the repurchased shares as a general charge against equity. At the same time, retained earnings or earned surplus is generally restricted by the same amount. This restriction reflects the fact that retained earnings have been utilized and the same amount cannot be expended again until the restriction is removed.[5] Thus, a corporation with $10,000 worth of capital stock, a paid-in surplus of $5,000, and earned surplus of $8,000, which has just reacquired $3,000 worth of stock to hold as treasury shares, would have a balance sheet for which the shareholders' equity section would appear as follows:

Shareholders' Equity

Paid in capital:			
Capital stock		$10,000	
Paid-in surplus		5,000	
			$15,000
Retained earnings:			
Restricted		3,000	
Non-restricted		5,000	
			8,000
			23,000
Less total cost of treasury stock			3,000
Total shareholders' equity			$20,000

4. Caveats. It is important to note that not all outflows of corporate assets are classified as corporate distributions. Payment of corporate liabilities, such as payments of accounts payable or payments to purchase equipment are not distributions. Similarly, not all decreases in shareholders' equity constitute distributions. A loss, for example, reduces shareholders' equity, but it is not a distribution.

It should be noted that the concept of treasury shares has been eliminated in the Revised Model Business Corporation Act. Shares reacquired by the corporation are treated as authorized but unissued shares.[6]

5. When Does the Corporation Decide to Make Distributions? There are a variety of business factors involved in determining a corporation's distribution policy. Considerations might include available cash resources, projected earnings, anticipated cash flows, projected operating and/or expansion costs, impact

---

[5] We will discover in Section C of this Chapter that the repurchase of shares is at times limited by statute to the amount of the corporation's retained earnings. Consequently, the amount expended to repurchase shares must be recorded as a restriction against retained earnings to prevent the same retained earnings from being applied against further share reacquisitions or other distributions.

[6] RMBCA § 6.31.

of distributions on the market price of stock, interest in courting shareholders' approval, possible contractual restraints, inflationary cost needs, contingency needs and other factors. However, overriding these business concerns are the limitations that might be placed upon distributions by state law. That is the subject of our next section.

C. RESTRICTIONS ON DISTRIBUTIONS

Various Statutory Limitations on a Corporation's Ability to Make Distributions

Even though corporations are privately owned and essentially autonomous, state corporate laws, through a variety of restrictions, limit the amount of distributions that can be made by the corporation to its owners, the shareholders. A number of justifications are offered to explain this anomaly. Initially, the restrictions can be explained as the *quid pro quo* for the limited liability provided shareholders under the statutory scheme. In other words, since only the corporation itself and not its shareholders is ultimately liable to creditors for corporate debts, distribution-restriction statutes seek to maintain within the corporation a certain minimum amount of assets which would be available to pay off creditors' claims in the event of bankruptcy. These assets are metaphorically referred to as a "cushion" for the protection of creditors.

Thus, the distribution-restriction statutes seek to insure that a certain amount of the corporation's net assets cannot be distributed to shareholders but must remain within the corporation for the protection of creditors. These net assets incidentally insure operating capital for the corporation. In some jurisdictions, the amount of net assets that must remain in the corporation equals the stated capital of the corporation. Such net assets are at times referred to as the "capital" of the corporation. Another way of saying that net assets equal to stated capital may not be distributed, is that the corporation's capital may not be "impaired." A subsidiary benefit of insuring a cushion for creditors is that shareholders are protected in their investment, since the same funds that must be retained in the corporation for creditors are also available for ordinary corporate purposes during normal business operations.

State statutes take two basic approaches to limit dividends and other distributions to shareholders. One approach focuses upon the surplus accounts in shareholders' equity. It requires the existence, prior to distribution, of earned surplus or, under a more liberal test, capital surplus. This approach is intended to insure that the amount of net assets which are at least equal to paid-in capital (or, under the more liberal test, stated capital) be retained within the corporation to meet the claims of creditors. The other approach imposes a solvency test upon the corporation. The solvency test requires that the corporation not be insolvent prior to the payment of the dividend and that it not be rendered insolvent by such payment.

There are statutory variations in each of these two central approaches to restricting distributions. The statutory restrictions are applied to distributions both by cash dividend and by share reacquisition. At times, these various distribution restrictions are also applied to stock dividends. In discussing the various distribution restriction methods below, we will analyze the methods, first in the context of the cash or property dividends, and then in the context of distributions by share reacquisition and distributions by stock dividends. Finally, we will look at some practical limitations to the distribution restriction statutes and some recent legislative approaches in dealing with these limitations.

1. Earned Surplus Test. The most commonly employed surplus test is the earned surplus test. This test permits the payment of dividends out of the assets of the corporation only to the extent of the amount of the corporation's earned surplus (retained earnings). As we have discussed, when a cash dividend is distributed, the asset account of cash is reduced by the amount of the distribution, and a corresponding decrease occurs in the equity account of earned surplus (retained earnings). What the earned surplus test permits is a distribution of assets only up to the point where the earned surplus (retained earnings) of the corporation is eliminated by the payment. The earned surplus test thus limits the amount of dividends that can be paid to that portion of the equity that represents undistributed net profits and gains accumulated since the corporation was organized.

2. Balance Sheet or Capital Surplus Test. A more permissive surplus test is the "balance sheet," "capital surplus," or, merely, "surplus," test, which permits distributions out of capital surplus as well as earned surplus. Under this test, earned surplus, along with that portion of paid-in capital that exceeds the stated capital of the corporation, can be utilized for distribution to shareholders. In other words, under the capital surplus test, distributions are not limited to a return of the profits of a corporation, but may also include portions of contributed capital that represented consideration for the purchase of shares. Distributions may be made under this test even if the corporation has accumulated no earned surplus.[7] Under the capital surplus test, however, the stated capital or legal capital must remain within the corporation.

The advantages of using low par stock (or no par stock with a low stated value) become apparent in the context of the capital surplus test. The lower the par value in relation to the issuance price, the greater the capital surplus available to the corporation for distribution to its shareholders. Thus, merely by establishing an arbitrarily low figure for par when issuing securities, the corporation can gain flexibility in distributing corporate funds to shareholders, out of contributed capital.

Note: When discussing the various surplus tests (both earned and capital), one frequently describes a distribution as having been made "from" or "out of" a surplus account. The funds distributed do not, of course, come from the surplus accounts. The funds come from the assets of the corporation. Counterbalancing the decrease in assets resulting from the distribution, however, there is an equivalent decrease in one or more surplus accounts. What the terminology implies is that payment of those assets is permitted to an amount not in excess of the amount in the particular surplus account.

3. Nimble-Dividend or Current Earnings Test. The nimble-dividend test might be considered the most permissive of the distribution restriction statutes which are functionally linked to shareholders' equity. Under this standard, dividends may be distributed even if the stated capital of the corporation is impaired,[8] so long as there are current profits for the limited period of time upon which the dividend period is based (*e.g.*, the current fiscal year). This test was presumably named to reflect the haste with which directors must act in declaring a dividend prior to the termination of the relevant time period. Under this test, even a corporation with no capital surplus and only an accumulated net deficit from its operations would still be able to pay a dividend for a year in which it has shown some earnings. Thus, a hypothetical corporation might show in its balance sheet an impairment of stated capital as follows:[9]

Stated capital	$1,000
Retained earnings (deficit)	(500)
Total Shareholders' equity	$ 500

Nevertheless, if there are subsequent current earnings of any amount, the corporation could make a distribution of those earnings under the nimble-dividend test, leaving its stated capital impaired.

The function of a nimble-dividend test is to permit a corporation which has been unable to make distributions for a period of time because of repeated deficits, to pay dividends to its shareholders during that year when it finally has been able to improve its financial position to some degree. The corporation's deficit condition continues, to the detriment of its creditors, but the corporation is able to make its shares more attractive to its current shareholders and to new investors through the distribution of dividends.[10]

---

[7] Capital surplus test statutes have not always been clear as to whether distributions can be made just from the capital surplus account, even in a situation where earned surplus exists.

[8] A corporation's capital is impaired if the total assets are less than total liabilities plus stated capital — that is, if all the corporation's assets were applied to pay off all of the corporation's creditors, the net assets that remain would not equal stated capital. The protection upon which creditors supposedly rely would not exist in the corporation.

[9] We would say that the capital of the corporation in this example was impaired prior to the distribution, because the net assets in the corporation were not equal to the stated capital of the corporation. We know this because net assets equal shareholders' equity. Shareholders' equity was less than stated capital, since part of the shareholders' equity was reduced by the accumulated deficit.

[10] It is often the financially unhealthy corporation which, unable to attract new financing from creditors, must turn to equity financing from new investors. The nimble-dividend statute allows such corporations to hold out to new investors the promise of present dividends even in light of an accumulated deficit. See B. Manning and J. Hanks, Legal Capital 83 (3d ed. 1990).

4. Insolvency Tests. The insolvency tests are a totally distinct set of tests from those which rely upon one or another category of shareholders' equity. The insolvency tests look to the relative amount of the corporation's actual assets and liabilities to determine whether dividends can be paid. Under the insolvency tests, distribution may not be made when a corporation is insolvent or when payment of the distribution would render the corporation insolvent.

There are two types of insolvency test — the "equity" insolvency test and the "bankruptcy" insolvency test. Under the equity test, a corporation is deemed insolvent if it is unable to pay its debts as they become due. Under the bankruptcy test, a corporation is insolvent when its total liabilities are greater than its total assets. In other words, the equity test measures both the ability of a corporation to convert its assets into cash and the amount of those easily convertible assets. When a corporation's assets can be readily converted into cash, those assets are said to be "liquid." A corporation might have great wealth, far exceeding its total obligations, tied up in land or buildings without being able to readily convert this wealth into cash to pay corporate obligations as they mature.

The bankruptcy test investigates the liquidation value of a corporation. In other words, the bankruptcy insolvency test asks what creditors would receive if all of the corporation's assets were sold and applied against all of its liabilities.

A corporation can be insolvent under one test but solvent under the other. A corporation might have an adequate cash flow to pay off its debts as they come due (equity solvency) but insufficient aggregate assets to pay off all liabilities were they to become due at once (bankruptcy insolvency) or vice versa.

It also frequently happens that a corporation which is insolvent in one sense is insolvent in the other sense as well. Thus, it is common for a corporation which has insufficient cash to pay its debts as they become due to also have total assets which do not equal total liabilities.

Under the Revised Model Business Corporation Act, both insolvency tests, equity and bankruptcy, are used together to restrict corporate distributions.[11] Elsewhere, the insolvency tests are frequently used in conjunction with other statutory limitations or restrictions which rely upon equity accounts. For example, under the Model Business Corporation Act that existed prior to 1979 (the "Old" MBCA),[12] dividends could only be paid out of earned surplus and only to the extent that the corporation was not insolvent and would not be rendered insolvent by such payments. Although the earned surplus test by itself insures that the corporation has sufficient past earnings to warrant a dividend, the insolvency test adds the additional protection of insuring that the assets of the corporation are sufficiently liquid to allow the corporation to pay off its obligations as they arise.

5. Restrictions on Share Reacquisition. Often, the same tests that are employed to limit cash dividend distributions are also imposed upon a corporation when it seeks to distribute its assets through the repurchase of its shares. At times, however, these restrictions are not identical. When the two tests diverge, the tests imposed upon share repurchases tend to be more permissive. This distinction can be rationalized by the fact that share reacquisitions, unlike dividends, do not necessarily permanently reduce surplus. As discussed in Section B of this Chapter, the purchase of treasury shares results in a restriction of earned surplus. Treasury shares, however, can be resold. Upon resale, the restriction that was placed upon a corporation's earned surplus is removed.[13]

[11] RMBCA § 6.40. The language of this section, at first blush, may appear to permit a distribution if either insolvency test is satisfied. The conjunctive nature of the restrictions, however, becomes apparent upon reading the introductory phrase to paragraph (c) which directs that "No distribution may be made" if either of the insolvency tests is not met.

[12] Model Business Corporation Act (as amended through 1978) § 45(a) (dividends) and § 2(n) ("insolvency" definition). For a comparison of the Old MBCA and the post-1979 version of the MBCA, now incorporated in the Revised Model Business Corporation Act (the "RMBCA"), see paragraph 9, "The Solutions Offered by the RMBCA," below. The approaches of both the Old MBCA and the RMBCA are used by a considerable number of states. Accordingly, it is important to be familiar with both approaches to limiting dividend payments.

[13] The RMBCA eliminated the concept of treasury shares. § 6.31. The RMBCA also does not provide a different restriction for repurchasing shares as opposed to issuing dividends. Both transactions are defined as "distributions" pursuant to § 1.40(6) and all distributions are restricted by § 6.40.

An example of differential treatment of dividends and repurchases can be found in the Old MBCA. Under that version of the Model Code, dividends in cash and property can be paid only out of unrestricted and unreserved earned surplus of the corporation.[14] An insolvency test is also imposed upon the payment of dividends. On the other hand, the provisions restricting repurchases are more permissive. Although repurchases are also generally restricted to earned surplus (in conjunction with an insolvency test), the Code allows repurchases from capital surplus as well as by a majority vote of shareholders or by specific permission in the articles of incorporation.[15]

A number of jurisdictions permit the repurchase of shares from stated capital in the case of certain types of securities. For example, the New York corporation statute permits the repurchase of redeemable shares[16] out of stated capital.[17] Some commentators have explained this exception as a reflection of the temporary character of redeemable shares.[18] The suggestion implied in this explanation is that the capital represented by the redeemable share is only being loaned to the corporation and can be repaid out of stated capital since the preservation of stated capital is intended for the welfare of creditors and the owner of redeemable shares is, in essence, a creditor.

Other situations in which shares may be repurchased out of stated capital as an exception to the general rule include the payment of dissenting shareholders and the elimination of fractional shares. No exception from the general rule is permitted, however, if the corporation is insolvent or would be rendered insolvent by the repurchase.

6. Restrictions on Stock Dividends. Perhaps because stock dividends are not really a distribution of assets, a number of states place no restrictions on their issuance. In those jurisdictions in which an attempt is made to restrict share dividends, the statutes typically allow share dividends to be made so long as an amount equal to the par thereof is transferred from surplus (whether capital or earned) to stated capital (if the shares are previously unissued shares).[19] This transfer reflects the augmentation of stated capital that occurs with the increased number of issued and outstanding shares. If the dividend is made from treasury shares, no transfer need be made into stated capital since such shares, having been already issued, are represented in the stated capital.[20]

7. Distributions by Wasting Asset Corporations. An exception to the general rule that distributions shall not be made from the stated capital of the corporations is often provided for "wasting asset corporations." These corporations are organized to exploit a specific asset and are intended to deplete[21] the value of that asset during the life of the corporation. Examples of such assets would include mines, timberlands, oil fields, and perhaps a patent or lease of limited duration. Since, upon termination of these corporations, the liquidation value of their assets would be nominal, their investors expect during the life of the corporation not merely to make a profit on their investment but to receive back their capital contribution as well. The capital contribution is returned to the investors by allowing payment of dividends out of all receipts of the corporation less only the costs of production, marketing and overhead. No deductions need be made from general receipts for depletion of the basic asset.

Pursuant to normal accounting practices, deductions for depletion reduce earnings as well as net assets and, consequently, limit distributions that can be made by a corporation pursuant to an earned surplus test or a bankruptcy insolvency test. Under a wasting asset corporation distribution statute, however, depletion

---

[14] Old MBCA § 45(a).

[15] Old MBCA § 6.

[16] Shares which a corporation has a contractual right or obligation to repurchase are sometimes referred to as "redeemables."

[17] N.Y.Bus. Corp. Law § 513(c) (McKinney 1985) (hereinafter "N.Y. Bus. Corp. Law").

[18] H. Ballantine, Ballantine on Corporations 620 (rev. ed. 1946).

[19] Old MBCA § 45(d).

[20] Old MBCA § 45(c).

[21] The term "depletion" refers to the depreciation of wasting assets. For a full discussion of depreciation and depletion, see Chapter II, Section G, *supra.*

(Matthew Bender & Co., Inc.)

does not reduce the amount of earnings available for distribution.[22] This exception for dividend treatment of wasting asset corporations allows the shareholder to recoup his or her original investment during the operating life of the corporation as that asset is actually consumed. Were these reductions of earnings to be recognized, then the total earned surplus after distribution of dividends might actually be a deficit. Allowing distributions during this time can result in an impairment of stated capital but would still be permitted.

Some wasting asset corporation type statutes specifically permit payment of dividends out of accounting reserves set aside for depletion.[23] Other statutes simply direct that dividends may be paid out of net proceeds, without taking into consideration the depletion of the corporation's assets.[24]

8. Inadequacies of the Distribution Restriction Statutes

a. Reducing stated capital. There is a striking inconsistency in the theory of creditor protection underlying those distribution restriction statutes which rely upon categories of equity. Although most of these statutes rely upon the retention of stated capital within the corporation, it is actually quite simple for the stated capital to be reduced. In fact, corporate statutes typically provide one or more methods for allowing the corporation to reduce its stated capital. Thus, stated capital, an initially arbitrary measurement device, which is intended to insure that an equal amount of net assets are not distributed out from the corporation, can be unilaterally reduced.

Corporations may seek to reduce stated capital in a number of situations. A corporation that has incurred losses resulting in a deficit which would prevent the issuance of dividends might find it attractive to reduce its stated capital and apply the corresponding surplus that is created to the elimination of the deficit.[25] In other situations, a corporation which finds that it has more capital invested in the corporation than it needs, might want to reduce stated capital through one of a number of capital-reduction techniques and then distribute the surplus created to the shareholders. So, reduction of capital can be used to eliminate a deficit, thus allowing future earnings to be distributed, or it can be used to allow immediate distributions. In either situation, the net result is to decrease the stated capital upon which creditors theoretically rely and increase the equity surplus available for distribution to shareholders.

Stated capital may be reduced in a number of ways. Many state statutes permit a reduction of capital by a charter amendment reducing the par value of those authorized shares that have a par value.[26] Other statutes authorize stated capital to be reduced by a simple resolution of the board of directors[27] and perhaps also with the approval of the shareholders.[28] Such provisions are useful for corporations with no-par stock where the stated value was initially determined by resolution of the directors.[29] Such reduction-of-capital provisions may also be employed where the premium paid for securities has been carried as stated capital rather than as capital surplus.

Capital can also be reduced in a *pro rata* exchange of stock in which the total par value of the newly created securities is less than the total par value of the securities that were received in exchange.[30] An

---

[22] See, for example, Old MBCA § 45(b).

[23] See, for example, Old MBCA § 45(b).

[24] See, for example, Del. Code Ann. Title 8 § 170(b) (1983) (hereinafter "Del. Gen. Corp. Law").

[25] Technically, what is involved here is a two-step process. In the first step, the corporation reduces stated capital and creates capital surplus. For example, see N.Y. Bus. Corp. Law § 517(a)(3), which labels the resulting surplus "capital surplus." In the second step, the capital surplus is applied to reduce the deficit. See N.Y. Bus. Corp. Law § 517(a)(4), which permits capital surplus to be used to eliminate a deficit in the earned surplus account.

The combined transactions are frequently referred to as a "quasi-reorganization."

[26] For example, see Ohio Rev. Code Ann. § 1701.69(B)(6) and (8) (Page's 1992) (hereinafter "Ohio Gen. Corp. Law").

Some statutes which permit a reduction of par by amendment are unclear as to the impact of the amendment on stated capital. For example, see Old MBCA § 58(e).

[27] For example, see N.Y. Bus. Corp. Law § 516.

[28] For example, see Old MBCA § 69.

[29] For a discussion of the setting of stated value with no par stock, see Chapter III, Section B, *supra*.

[30] See Del. Gen. Corp. Law § 244(3).

example might be a one-for-one exchange of common $10 par stock for preferred $100 par stock, with a resulting $90 per share reduction of stated capital.

A last method for reducing capital is the cancellation of reacquired shares. When repurchased shares, which are held as treasury shares, are retired, the restriction that was placed upon earned surplus is removed and an aliquot portion of stated capital is eliminated.[31] Although, in this instance, the distribution to the shareholders occurred when the shares were repurchased, the actual reduction of capital occurs only upon the retirement of the shares. As with other reductions of capital, the retirement of shares leading to a reduction of capital frequently will require the filing of a certificate with the Secretary of State of the appropriate jurisdiction to provide notice of the reduced capital to those who might deal with the corporation.[32]

Although these avenues for writing down stated capital significantly reduce the protection that the stated capital account can provide creditors of the corporations, there are some minimum safeguards that remain for the creditors. Statutes that permit the write-down of stated capital through the filing of a certificate of capital reduction will frequently prohibit the reduction of capital below various computable sums. A good example of one such minimum figure would be the aggregate liquidation preference of all shares with any such preference rights plus the aggregate par value of any par stock without such preferences.[33] Protection under such a provision would inure to the preferred shareholders as well as to the creditors. Other states may limit the reduction of stated capital to a specific dollar amount.

Some states limit the impact of reducing capital by limiting the kind of distributions that can be made from the resulting reduction surplus. Under the Old MBCA, the resulting reduction surplus is defined as capital surplus.[34] Capital surplus is not available for ordinary dividends.[35] It is, however, available for elimination of an accumulated deficit.[36] This latter application would then permit the corporation to issue dividends from any newly earned profits.

Additional protection from capital reduction is provided by statutes requiring shareholder approval for reductions of stated capital and for amendments to the charter affecting par value.[37]

Of course, creditors can protect themselves beyond the statutory safeguards through contractual arrangements with the corporation. As an example, a creditor might choose to draft a loan agreement with a covenant prohibiting the borrower from making distributions to its shareholders or repurchasing its own shares unless, after such distributions, a specified amount of net earnings remained in the corporation. Alternatively, the agreement might forbid the taking of any corporate action resulting in the reduction of capital. In some instances, a creditor might seek to have the corporation issue to the creditor the majority of the shares of a distinct class of securities, approval from which would have to be obtained before the corporation made any distributions.

Although creditor-protection mechanisms exist, it is apparent that, in the absence of non-statutory protection, the protection afforded creditors through the legal capital system is largely illusory.

b. Nimble-dividend distribution. As discussed above,[38] states which have adopted nimble-dividend provisions essentially permit distributions to be made even while the stated capital of a corporation is impaired. Under such provisions, although the net assets of a corporation might be less than stated capital, new earnings may be distributed to shareholders and need not be retained in the corporation for the purpose of insuring creditors the protection implicitly promised by the stated capital carried on the books of the corporation.

---

[31] See discussion of treasury shares and accounting for their retirement in Section B of this Chapter, *supra.*

[32] See Old MBCA § 69.

[33] For example, see Old MBCA § 69 and N.Y. Bus. Corp. Law 516(b).

[34] Old MBCA § 70.

[35] Old MBCA § 45. But compare § 46.

[36] Old MBCA § 70.

[37] See discussion above in this Chapter.

[38] See par. 3 of this Section, *supra.*

(Matthew Bender & Co., Inc.)

c.   Low-par and no-par shares. Distribution restriction provisions based upon shareholder equity concepts can also be criticized because of their arbitrary operation which can be entirely divorced from the reality of a corporation's financial health. The issuance of shares with either a low par in relation to the sale price or with no par and a low stated value increases the ability of a corporation to make distributions. The excess paid in above par or above the stated value, as discussed,[39] becomes capital surplus, which under some statutes is available for distribution both through share repurchases and direct distributions. Essentially then, an arbitrarily low par value will permit a corporation to make distributions from contributed capital, regardless of whether the corporation has experienced profits.

The figures chosen for par could place two otherwise similar corporations in vastly different positions regarding their respective abilities to make shareholder distributions. Two corporations with identical capital paid in by investors and identical histories of earnings could have totally different abilities to make distributions solely in terms of what numbers they chose to use for par or stated value. There are neither statutory restraints nor compelling guidelines as to what figure should be used for par. The only forces impacting upon corporations are concerns with image and perhaps whatever influence can be exerted by creditors.

d.   Writing-up assets. Finally, distribution restriction provisions which rely upon a bankruptcy insolvency test as well as those which rely upon the availability of surplus can be manipulated by a corporation's "writing-up" of its assets. Although accountants urge that assets be carried at historical cost,[40] at times when inflation has driven up the value of a corporation's assets, companies might choose to reflect that augmented value on their balance sheet by carrying the assets at their new inflated value instead of at their historical cost. This increases shareholders' equity. Since it is not "earned" surplus, it would be carried as capital surplus or revaluation surplus or unrealized appreciation surplus. A corporation with increased assets and increased surplus would be able to make additional distributions to shareholders pursuant to the bankruptcy insolvency test as well as some of the surplus tests.

The New York courts have permitted dividends to be paid out of the surplus created by writing up a corporation's assets. *Randall v. Bailey*, 23 N.Y.S.2d 143 (Sup. Ct. 1940), *aff'd*, 288 N.Y. 280, 43 N.E.2d 43 (1942). However, few other jurisdictions have examined this issue, and *Randall v. Bailey* has not been widely followed.

In those instances in which a jurisdiction does permit a corporation to write up its assets, a corporation can distribute additional dividends to its shareholders without any new capital flowing into the corporation. This, of course, reduces the protection afforded creditors by allowing distribution based upon the anticipated value of assets prior to the time that value is realized.[41] In instances of widely fluctuating markets, reliance upon unrealized appreciated value in fixing distributions could constitute a serious threat to the security of creditors.

9.   The Solutions Offered by the RMBCA. Responding to many of the inadequacies of the distribution restriction statutes, the re-drafters of the MBCA attempted to craft a distribution statute which would avoid some of the pitfalls discussed above.[42] The RMBCA does away entirely with the concept of par and stated

---

[39] See par. 2 of this Section, *supra.*

[40] See Chapter II, Section F, *supra.*

[41] Some jurisdictions prevent the distribution of surplus arising from unrealized appreciation in assets by relegating such revaluation surplus to a surplus category from which dividends cannot be made. Previously, Pa. Stat. Ann. tit. 15 § 1002(3) (repealed 1988) (hereinafter "Pa. Bus. Corp. Law") restricted revaluation surplus by identifying such surplus as capital surplus. Under Pa. Bus. Corp. Law § 1702 (repealed 1989), customary dividends were payable out of earned surplus not capital surplus. (Liquidation distributions out of capital surplus were permitted under Pa. Bus. Corp. Law § 1703 (repealed 1989), only if several restrictive limitations were met.)

[42] See American Bar Association, Section on Corporation, Banking and Business Law, Committee on Corporate Laws, "Changes in the Model Business Corporation Act — Amendments to Financial Provisions; A Report of the Committee on Corporate Laws" 34 Bus. Lawyer 1867 (1979) (hereinafter "Changes in the MBCA").

capital and looks to the ability of a corporation to pay its debts as they become due as the primary measurement of its ability to make distributions. The RMBCA deals with all distributions — whether dividends, repurchases of stock, or capital distributions — in the same manner.[43] The new version permits distribution so long as, after the distribution is complete, the corporation can satisfy both an equity and a bankruptcy insolvency test. Included in the bankruptcy insolvency test as potential charges against assets are all liabilities plus the liquidation rights of all shares with liquidation preferences. Thus, the RMBCA provides a measure of protection for preferred shareholders as well as for creditors. In rejecting the statutory system that relied upon stated capital and par, the re-drafters of the MBCA noted that the stated capital system could be misleading in appearing to provide protection for creditors and senior security holders.[44]

Under the RMBCA, it is conceivable that a corporation with assets of sufficient size and liquidity could make distributions that would impair the corporation's stated capital but not threaten insolvency. An example would be a corporation with the following hypothetical balance sheet seeking to make a distribution of $100.

Assets		Liabilities and Shareholders' Equity	
Cash	$200.00	Note obligation due in 3 months	$ 50.00
		Stated capital	150.00
Total assets	$200.00	Total liabilities and shareholders' equity	$200.00

After the payment of the full $100 distribution, the corporation would still be solvent, both in an equity as well as a bankruptcy sense. However, its stated capital would be impaired.

Contrariwise, under the RMBCA, a corporation could have significant earned surplus but might be unable to make any distributions. For example, a corporation which has invested its retained earnings in fixed assets, such as land and buildings, and was relatively cash-shy might not have sufficiently liquid assets to allow it to make a distribution and still satisfy the equity insolvency test.

Many commentators have expressed satisfaction with the RMBCA. However, many jurisdictions continue to rely upon par and stated capital to determine when distributions may be made.

---

[43] See RMBCA definitional § 1.40(6), in conjunction with § 6.40.

[44] See "Changes in MBCA," *supra*.

CHAPTER X

SHARE ISSUANCE AND CAPITAL CONTRIBUTION REQUIREMENTS

A. PROTECTION AFFORDED BY EQUITY ISSUANCE STATUTES

Concern for the Creditor; Concern for the Shareholder

Many of the concepts discussed in the previous Chapter that underline statutory restrictions on corporate distributions are also relevant when analyzing statutes regulating the corporation's issuance of stock. The basic goal of statutes regulating corporate distributions is to preserve the stated capital of a corporation in order to protect creditors. Similarly, statutes regulating the issuance of equity securities seek to insure that the aliquot portion of stated capital, represented by each issued share, is indeed paid into the corporation at the time the shares are issued.[1]

Corporate statutes regulating the issuance of equity securities are intended to provide comfort for creditors by insuring that when a corporation is organized or when it expands through a subsequent issuance of stock, a cushion of capital upon which creditors can rely is initially paid into the corporation. The message to creditors which is carried by this cushion essentially would read: "Do not be concerned about lending money to this corporation since even if our business does poorly, there is capital in this corporation, contributed by shareholders, which will be available to help insure that your loan is repaid when due." The cushion is computed by multiplying the number of shares outstanding by the par value of each share.

At the same time that equity issuance statutes protect creditors, they also serve to protect shareholders' interests. Each shareholder is assured, by operation of these statutes, that every other shareholder has paid in at least par value times the number of shares to acquire the shares owned. If shareholder A bought twice as many shares from a corporation as did Shareholder B, then (assuming B did not pay a premium for his shares) A paid at least twice as much capital into the corporation to acquire the ownership position as did Shareholder B. Thus, the equity issuance statutes provide an element of fairness to the shareholders of a corporation.

B. OPERATION OF EQUITY ISSUANCE STATUTES

Shareholder Liability for Par Value

The issue of whether the stated capital of a corporation has been paid in by investors, of course, does not generally arise unless the corporation has become insolvent.[2] When that happens, the question of what was transferred to the corporation in exchange for the shares issued can be critical should the corporation not possess sufficient assets to meet its obligations to its creditors.

In a situation in which the assets are not adequate to pay all creditors, modern corporation statutes hold shareholders liable for "the full consideration" for which its shares were issued.[3] (Such liability also extends

---

[1] The aliquot portion of stated capital represented by each issued share is the par value of such shares. Both Old MBCA § 18 and Del. Gen. Corp. Law § 153 require that shares with a par value be issued for such consideration at least equal to the par value.

[2] Insolvency is not a prerequisite for holding shareholders liable for the par value of shares they have acquired from the corporation. See, for example, *Maclary v. Pleasant Hills*, 109 A.2d 830 (Del. Ch. 1954) (in this derivative action, by an ongoing corporation, against shareholders/directors who had not paid full consideration, defendants were given the election to either pay the deficiency owing on the shares or to have the shares canceled).

[3] See, for example, Old MBCA § 25. Also, see Del. Gen. Corp. Law § 162.

to knowing assignees.) Full consideration for shares is generally further defined as at least equal to the par value of the shares issued.[4] As a practical matter, courts have not held shareholders liable for more than the par value of shares, even if the supposed consideration for which the shares were issued was in excess of par.[5] What these provisions mean in terms of protection of creditors is that shareholders can be compelled to pay to the corporation consideration at least equal to the corporation's stated value. If shares were indeed issued for other than full consideration (*i.e.*, if they were "watered"), then should the corporation's assets not cover its debts, shareholders would be personally liable to the corporation or to its creditors for the differential between the par value per share and the value paid to the corporation per share.

C. WHY LOW PAR AND NO PAR STOCK

Advantages When Issuing Stock

The potential imposition of liability under the equity issuance statutes, as well as the method for calculating surplus under the shareholder distribution statutes, make it attractive for corporations to issue equity securities with low par value or at no par. The advantages of low par and no par stock are analyzed below.

1. **Watered Stock.** If shares are issued for money, it is, of course, simple to determine whether at least par has been paid into the corporation for each share issued and whether there might be existing contingent shareholder liability. Shares are frequently issued, however, for assets other than money. A corporation's shares may be used to purchase an on-going business enterprise by exchanging stock for ownership rights in the tangible and intangible assets of the business. Shares may be also used to acquire property or equipment or to pay for services.

Where shares are issued in payment for non-money assets, a risk exists that an over-valuation of the assets received by the corporation as consideration can lead to "watered stock" (*i.e.*, stock which has been issued for inadequate consideration) and potential shareholder liability. The use of low par stock or no par stock with a low stated value can reduce those risks, since the actual value of the acquired assets or services need only meet the aggregate par value or stated value of the shares issued. For example, assume a corporation acquires an operating factory which the corporation has assessed as being worth $100,000 in value. A more accurate assessment would place the true value of the factory at $50,000. If the corporation issues, in exchange for the factory, 1,000 shares, each with a par of $100, then, indeed, the stock will be watered, since the full par value will not have been paid in. The corporation's exchange of shares with an aggregate par value of $100,000 for property with a value of $50,000 raises the potential of shareholder liability for the remaining $50,000. If, instead, the 1,000 shares exchanged for the factory have a par value of $1 or are "no-par" shares but are given a stated value of $1, then obviously the consideration exchanged for the shares at least equals par. In the latter example, the corporation will have exchanged shares with an aggregate par value or stated value of $1,000 for property worth $50,000. In this instance, the shares will have been fully paid, and there will be no potential shareholder liability.

Of course, any discussion of the "true value" of an acquired business assumes that there are uniformly accepted means of determining the worth of different non-money assets. This, however, is not the case. The value of an operation or a piece of equipment to two different businesses may vary greatly. For example, the true in-use value of a used bulldozer would predictably be greater for a construction company than for a law firm. Even when one focuses upon the needs of a single type of business, there are no certain answers as to how to value acquired property or business operations. In any instance, there would be different

---

[4] See, for example, Old MBCA § 18 and Del. Gen. Corp. Law § 153.

[5] Cary & Eisenberg, Cases and Materials on Corporations 1060 (1980). Also, see Israels, *Problems of Par and No Par Shares: A Reappraisal*, 47 Colum. L. Rev. 1279 at 1298 (1947) ("no case has yet arisen where [shareholders'] liability was sought to be imposed for inflation reflected in surplus rather than in stated capital"). Israels at 129 suggests that case law might develop where shareholders, indeed, are held liable for, in the words of Old MBCA § 18, "the full consideration for which [the corporation's] shares were issued" rather than merely par value. However, both authors indicate that such holdings had not yet arisen.

opinions about how the value of an acquired business should be ascertained — whether by looking at the net asset value of the business, its market value, some multiple of earnings, or a combination of factors.

If one chooses to look at earnings, are past earnings or projected earnings the relevant earning figures? Further, what multiplier should be used in regard to earnings? Because of the uncertainties in assessing the value of acquired assets, courts and statutes have tended to adopt a "good faith" rule in determining whether the value set for acquired assets is honestly established.[6] Thus, today, in the absence of gross overvaluation and knowledge of such overvaluation by the board of directors, creditors are generally unable to hold shareholders liable for "water" in shares held by the hareholders.

2. Subsequent Stock Issuance. The use of low par and no par stock can have benefits for a corporation which plans to make more than one issuance from a single authorization of shares. When the authorized shares of a corporation have a specified par value, as we have seen, statutes regulating the issuance of equity shares dictate that any issuance of such securities be made for value at least equal to par. In instances where a corporation's earlier issued shares are trading at a market price which is less than par, the corporation will have a problem with subsequent issuance of the originally authorized shares. In these circumstances, investors will only be willing to pay the market price for securities since, by definition, that is the price at which they could obtain the corporation's securities from earlier purchasers of the securities who now want to sell their shares. However, such consideration will not satisfy corporate statutes, which require that at least par be paid for issued shares. To get around this problem, the corporation would have to amend the corporate charter to authorize new shares with either a par value equal to or less than the current market price or no par shares with a stated value equal to or less than the current market price.

Were the originally issued shares to have been authorized with low par or no par, then the above problem would be avoided. The market price would have to fall below the low-par value to create a concern about complying with the share issuance statutes.[7]

As an example, assume that the corporate charter authorizes the issuance of 2,000 shares of $10 par stock. At t_1, the corporation issues 1,000 shares and sells them for $10 per share. Thereafter, a market develops for the corporation's securities. At t_2, when the corporation seeks to sell an additional 1,000 shares, the market price has fallen to $5 per share. Were the corporation to sell the new issue at the t_2 market price, it would not be receiving consideration at least equal to par for the t_2 issuance. However, were the par value of the originally authorized shares set at $1 or were there no par value set but rather a low stated value, then at t_2, adequate consideration could be obtained by selling the t_2 issuance at the t_2 market price.

3. Allocation of Shareholder Control in Disproportion to Capital Contributions. On occasion, investors in a corporation seek to allocate control among themselves in a manner disproportionate to the capital that each investor contributed to the corporation. For example, Investor A and Investor B may seek to organize a corporation in which Investor A will invest $1,000, and Investor B will invest $10,000, and which will be managed by Investor A alone. In recognition of the expectation that Investor A will be the primary contributor of services to the corporation and that these services will be as valuable to the corporation as Investor B's greater capital contribution, the investors might desire to distribute the corporation's 2000 shares equally between themselves. Should the par value be set so that the aggregate par value of the 1000 shares sold to investor B be equal to his purchase price (*i.e.*, par of $10 per share), then, obviously, investor A would not be able to buy more than 100 shares, since A has but $1,000 to invest and statutes regulating the issuance of shares require that consideration at least equal to par be contributed in exchange for the shares.[8]

---

[6] Many modern statutes hold that if directors act without fraud in assessing the value of the assets received, the judgment of the directors as to the value of such assets will be conclusive. See Old MBCA § 19 and Del. Gen. Corp. Law § 152.

[7] At common law, there was limited judicial precedent permitting the issuance of par stock at less than par if it could be shown that the consideration paid for the shares was all that the market was willing to pay for such securities. *Handley v. Stutz*, 139 U.S. 417 (1891).

[8] Furthermore, A cannot use his commitment to work for the corporation as partial payment for the shares, since most corporate statutes provide that the promise of future services will not constitute payment for the issuance of shares. Old MBCA § 19 and Del. Gen. Corp. Law § 152.

On the other hand, were the 2,000 shares issued at a low par value of $1 per share, then investor A's $1,000 would constitute full payment for his shares. Investor B's $10,000 contribution would add $1,000 to the stated capital of the corporation and $9,000 to its capital surplus.

Thus, the setting of a low par value for the corporation's shares would allow the two investors to achieve the control relationship they seek without requiring either one to diminish or increase his or her respective capital contribution.

4. Flexibility for Distributions. As discussed above,[9] the use of low par and no par stock when issuing shares provides a corporation with a certain degree of flexibility in making distributions to its shareholders. Many corporate distribution statutes limit the amount of distributions that can be made to shareholders to the size of the surplus account (including both capital and earned surplus) included in shareholders' equity.[10] The issuance of stock with a par value which is lower than the issuance price of the stock provides the corporation with an immediate capital surplus account. Thus, a corporation seeking the statutory freedom to make distributions even in the absence of any record of earnings would find it desirable to issue low par stock.[11]

D. THE RMBCA HAS ELIMINATED THE CONCEPT OF PAR

It Makes Sense But Will It Sell in Peoria?

As with that portion of the RMBCA which restricts distributions,[12] the portions of the RMBCA which regulate the issuance of new shares also completely avoid the concept of par and stated capital. The corporation's capitalization is no longer measured in terms of whether par value is paid in. Section 6.21 now permits directors to "authorize shares to be issued for consideration consisting of any tangible or intangible property or benefit to the corporation . . ." without any requirement that such price be at least equal to par.

Similarly, Section 21 of the Old MBCA which established which portion of paid-in capital would equal stated capital and which portion would equal capital surplus, was deleted altogether.

The re-drafters of the MBCA recognized that par was a totally arbitrary term which bore no relation to the financial health of a corporation.[13] Under a statutory regime based upon par and stated capital, two corporations with identical paid-in capital and an identical record of earnings would be able to distribute entirely different amounts to their shareholders based solely upon what figure was chosen to represent par for the corporation's shares.[14] In addition, the figure set as par is amendable and, accordingly, the protection thought to be offered to creditors by the existence of a stated capital "cushion"[15] is misleading. Furthermore, even when par has been paid in upon the issuance of securities, if a corporation, at a later point, has experienced a net loss from operations, its stated capital might be impaired and serve as no cushion whatsoever to creditors. For example, consider the corporation which at t_1, issued 1,000 shares, with par of $1, at a purchase price of $2 per share. Immediately after issuance, the shareholders' equity in the corporation would consist of $1,000 of stated capital and $1,000 of capital surplus. If, by t_1 plus two years, the corporation has suffered a net loss of $1,500, the stated capital of the corporation would be impaired. Thus, although par had been paid in, there would be no cushion upon which creditors might rely.

---

[9] *See* Chapter IX, Section C, par. (2) *supra*, discussing the Balance Sheet Test.

[10] *See, for example*, Old MBCA § 46 and Del. Gen. Corp. Law § 170.

[11] A similar result can be achieved through the issuance of no-par stock. Under statutes such as the Old MBCA § 21 and Del. Gen. Corp. Law § 154, if the board of directors, within a requisite period of time (*e.g.*, 60 days), sets the stated value at a price less than the paid consideration, then the excess of the aggregate consideration paid in over the stated value becomes surplus.

[12] *See* Chapter IX, Section C, par. 9, *supra*, dealing with financial provisions of the RMBCA.

[13] *See* American Bar Association, Section on Corporation, Banking and Business Law, Committee on Corporate Laws, "Changes in the Model Business Corporation Act — Amendments to Financial Provisions; A Report of the Committee on Corporate Laws" 34 Bus. Law 1867 (1979).

[14] *See* Chapter IX, Section C, par. 8(c), *supra*.

[15] *See* Chapter IX, Section C, par. 8(a), *supra*.

Instead of looking to the shareholders' equity accounts for protecting creditors, the RMBCA looks to a corporation's ability to pay its debts after distributions are made.[16] Creditors are protected through prohibitions against distributions which would leave the corporation insolvent either in a bankruptcy sense or in an equity (cash-flow) sense.[17]

Although the share issuance and distribution-regulating scheme of the RMBCA makes good sense, many state corporate statutes still operate under the traditional concepts of par and stated capital. Thus, while recognizing the logic of the RMBCA system, it is imperative to be familiar with the operation of the statutes which presently exist to regulate share issuance.

---

[16] See Chapter IX, Section C, par. 9, *supra*.

[17] RMBCA § 6.40.

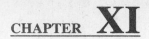

ACCOUNTING FOR SOLE PROPRIETORSHIPS AND PARTNERSHIPS

A. INTRODUCTION: DIFFERENCES FROM OTHER BUSINESS FORMS

It's Pretty Much the Same, But . . .

When the accounting process was introduced in Chapter I of this manual, it was noted that the business form upon which the manual would primarily focus would be the corporation. The reader was also advised, however, that "most of the accounting functions that are relevant to the corporation are generic in nature and will have an application to all business enterprises." Accordingly, when we examined the application of the fundamental accounting equation to various transactions that occurred within a corporate form of business, we were also learning how the fundamental equation would apply to other business forms. While the guidance provided in the first chapter continues to be relevant, it should be noted that there are some distinctions between the financial statements of the corporation and those of other forms of business. In this Chapter, we will explore the nature of the financial statements of two other forms of business which the attorney might encounter — the sole proprietorship and the partnership.

The distinctions between the financial statements of the corporation and these other forms of business relate primarily to the capital accounts (*i.e.*, accounts representing the interest(s) of the owner(s)) and matters related to the capital accounts. Although the business form to which the lawyer will most frequently be exposed is the corporation, there are certainly instances where familiarity with the sole proprietorship and the partnership will also be essential. Accordingly, it is valuable to investigate the unique features of the financial statements of these two alternative forms of business. In a subsequent Chapter, we will also explore the financial statements of the not-for-profit corporation. These financial statements differ more markedly from the statements of the for-profit corporation.

B. FINANCIAL STATEMENTS OF THE SOLE PROPRIETORSHIP

One Owner, One Capital Account

When the balance sheet of the corporation was discussed in the first Chapter, the ownership interest of the shareholders was referred to as "Shareholders' Equity." Subsequently, this capital account of "Shareholders' Equity" was further divided into accounts called "Stated Capital," "Capital Surplus," and "Earned Surplus." In a sole proprietorship, there is obviously only a single owner. The entire net worth of a sole proprietorship is represented by the capital account of the owner which reflects the owner's original investment plus retained earnings (or less net losses), less any withdrawals. Unlike the corporation, however, the capital account of the sole proprietorship does not distinguish between net worth that reflects initial investment as opposed to net worth that reflects retained earnings. The dollar amount of the capital account represents the owner's rights in the assets of the business after all liabilities are paid off. In other words, owner's net worth is equal to the net book value of those assets minus liabilities that would be distributed to the owner in the event of a liquidation. A creditor of a sole proprietorship will look to the capital account of the owner as a "cushion" to insure that the book assets of the sole proprietorship would actually cover the liabilities of the business in the event the business had to be liquidated.[1] Usually the capital account

---

[1] Of course, the book value of assets may vary greatly from the value of the assets that will be derived ("realized") at a liquidation sale. Accordingly, there is no guarantee that, just because assets equal or exceed liabilities on a balance sheet, creditors will have

of a sole proprietorship is identified by the actual name of the owner. The use of the owner's name to identify the capital account can be thought of as a reminder that the owner is generally liable for the obligations of the business, even when such liabilities exceed the total assets of the business.

The Balance Sheet of a typical sole proprietorship, Joseph Reader, bookseller, might appear as shown in Exhibit 11.1.

EXHIBIT 11.1

The Unusual Bookshop
Joseph Reader, proprietor

Balance Sheet
December 31, 20_____

ASSETS		LIABILITIES AND CAPITAL	
Cash	$ 3,200	Accrued expenses	$ 1,800
Accounts receivable	700	Accounts payable	3,100
Merchandise inventory	14,300		
Fixtures and Equipment (less accumulated depreciation of $3,000	11,000	Total liabilities	4,900
		Joseph Reader, capital	24,300
Total assets	$29,200	Total liabilities and capital	$29,200

The financial operations of a sole proprietorship will be reflected in an income statement similar to the income statement of a corporation (see *supra*, Exhibit 1.3). However, instead of a reference to "Earnings per Share," the owner's earnings would be identified as "Net Income" or "Net Profit." A simplified version of an income statement for a sole proprietorship appears below as Exhibit 11.2.

EXHIBIT 11.2

The Unusual Bookshop
Joseph Reader, Proprietor

Income Statement
Twelve months ended December 31, 20_____

Net Sales		$240,000
Cost of books sold		100,000
Gross Margin		140,000
Rent	$28,000	
Salaries	65,000	
Advertising	5,000	
Total Expenses		98,000
Net Income		$ 42,000

the protection they need in a liquidation situation. All things being equal, however, the greater the amount by which assets exceed liabilities (and consequently, the greater the owner's equity), the greater the likelihood that creditors will be paid off in the event of liquidation. For a discussion of the inconsistencies between book value and market price, see, *supra*, Chapter II, Section L, "Historical Cost and Its Deficiencies."

Note 1: Since a sole proprietorship is not a separate legal entity, the business will not be separately taxed on the net income which it earns. Instead, the net income is attributed to the owner who must include it in his personal tax return as part of his taxable income.

Note 2: Some states and municipalities may impose a tax on an unincorporated enterprise based on its income.

The ownership equity of a sole proprietor is reflected as a line in the balance sheet of the business (see Exhibit 11.1 above). The sole proprietor's ownership equity is also separately recorded in a Statement of Capital (*see* Exhibit 11.3 below). A Statement of Capital is similar, though not identical, to the Corporation's Statement of Retained Earnings (*see* Exhibit 1.4, above, in Chapter I). A Statement of Retained Earnings shows changes in the earned surplus of a corporation during a given period. The sole proprietor's Statement of Capital shows net earnings (or losses) during a given period, but, it also shows how these earnings (or losses) impact upon the owner's capital position as of the beginning of the period.

Before earnings are added to the proprietor's beginning capital, however, it is common practice to apply against earnings any withdrawals made by the owner during the period to arrive at a net increase or decrease in capital. Of course, if the business suffered losses during the relevant period, these losses are further augmented by withdrawals made by the owner during this period. A sole proprietor does not draw any salary nor receive any dividends from his business. Instead, an owner may withdraw cash for personal use, from time to time, as he or she finds necessary. Such withdrawals are commonly referred to as "drawings." In summary, the Statement of Capital of a sole proprietorship will show the owner's capital as of the beginning of the relevant period, increases or decreases to that capital resulting from earnings (losses) and withdrawals, and, finally, the owner's capital at the end of the relevant period.

We know that the Unusual Bookshop earned $42,000 for the 12-month period reflected in the Income Statement found in Exhibit 11.2 above. If Joseph Reader, the owner of The Unusual Bookshop, withdrew $39,000 during the year, the net effect of earnings and drawings on his Statement of Capital might be shown as in Exhibit 11.3 below.

EXHIBIT 11.3

The Unusual Bookshop
Statement of Capital
Calendar Year 20_____

Joseph Reader, capital 1/1/20_____		$21,300
Net Income for the period	$42,000	
Deduct drawings	39,000	
Net increase in capital		3,000
Joseph Reader, capital 12/31/20_____		24,300

Note 1: A sole proprietor might also pay *personal* expenses through the business bank account or from the business petty cash fund. Such payments do not represent expenses of the business and properly should be charged to the drawing account.

Note 2: The Statement of Capital would also disclose any infusion of capital made during the period.

C. FINANCIAL STATEMENTS OF THE PARTNERSHIP

Multiple Owners, Multiple Capital Accounts

The only significant difference between the balance sheet of a partnership and the balance sheet of a comparable corporation is that the ownership interest of each partner will be reflected in a separate capital account. Unlike the corporation, the capital account of each partner will not be further divided into stated capital, capital surplus, and earned surplus accounts. The balance in each partner's capital account is derived from the contributions that the partner made to the partnership, plus his or her share of partnership income earned over time (or less losses suffered), less those sums withdrawn by the partner over time. The Balance Sheet of the Plastics Laminating Company, a partnership of Lawrence Green and Jack Kane is illustrated below in Exhibit 11.4.

EXHIBIT 11.4

Plastics Laminating Company

Balance Sheet
December 31, 20_____

ASSETS		LIABILITIES AND CAPITAL		
Cash	$ 17,200	Accrued expenses		$ 6,300
Accounts receivable	40,100	Accounts payable		21,900
Inventories	25,000	Total liabilities		28,200
Fixtures and Equipment				
(less accumulated		L. Green, capital	53,322	
depreciation of $23,400)	60,700			
		J. Kane, capital	61,748	
		Total capital		114,800
Total assets	$143,000	Total liabilities and capital		$143,000

The ownership equity of the partners is reflected in the Statement of Capital. Usually, each partner's equity will be represented by three different items of equity: the partner's capital at the beginning of the period, the partner's share of profits for the year, and the partner's withdrawals for the year. Cumulatively, the balances of these three amounts will make apparent the changes within the partners' capital positions from the beginning to the end of the year. After a period of partnership operation, a partner's capital position will reflect partnership contributions made by the partner, cumulative earnings (and losses) allocated to such partner, and cumulative withdrawals made by such partner. A Statement of Capital for a partnership could also be arranged to merely show the difference between the partners' beginning and ending capital. Such a format would not explain the basis of the change in a particular partner's capital position.

The Statement of Capital for the partners of the Plastics Laminating Company, the balance sheet for which was examined above, appears below in Exhibit 11.5.

EXHIBIT 11.5

Plastics Laminating Company
Statement of Capital
Calender Year 20_____

	L. Green	J. Kane	Total
Capital balances, January 1	$50,800	$57,500	$108,300
Add: Net Income	45,422	35,978	81,400
	96,222	93,478	189,700
Deduct: Drawings	42,900	32,000	74,900
Capital balances, December 31	$53,322	$61,478	$114,800

Note: If capital contributions were made during the year, they would also be reflected in the Statement of Capital as additions to capital balances.

D. SHARING OF NET INCOME

Share Equally Unless Otherwise Agreed

You may have noticed, when examining the Statement of Capital, that the net income of the Plastics Laminating Company was not shared equally by the two partners, Green and Kane. Perhaps this appeared at odds with what you have previously learned about partnerships. Indeed, the Uniform Partnership Act ("UPA")[2] specifies that partners shall share profits (and losses) equally. However, the UPA permits partnership rights to an equal sharing of profits to be altered by agreement among the partners.[3] . Apparently, Green and Kane have agreed to share profits between themselves in other than an equal distribution.

How do partners share profits other than on an equal basis and how is this distribution reflected in a partnership financial statement? Partners may, by agreement, distribute profits in proportion to a fixed ratio. That ratio may be created to reflect the relative capital contributions made by the partners, the relative talents or reputations the individual partners bring to the firm, or in anticipation of the relative services that the partners intend to provide the firm. Profits may also be distributed in proportion to a variable ratio which can be designed to reflect the relative balances in the partners' capital accounts at a particular point in time or the actual hours "billed" by the respective partners over a defined period of time. It should be emphasized that in the absence of an agreement to the contrary, profits will be divided equally even if partners have made unequal capital contributions or if they expend unequal amounts of service for the partnership.

Partners may choose to withdraw their profits in the form of a "salary," if they are working for the partnership, or as interest earned on their capital contribution. Withdrawals may be made in such form even though partners, who are owners, are not technically employees or creditors.[4] The salary or interest earned is essentially a means of allocating profits. The right of a partner to withdraw profits in the form of salary or interest must be agreed upon ahead of time by the partnership. Such salary or interest withdrawals would in part or in whole determine how partnership profits are to be distributed. Residual profits, if any, after funds are allocated for partners' salary or interest, would then be distributed in proportion to either a previously agreed ratio or equally among the partners.

Obviously, profit distribution agreements can combine a number of approaches described above and they can be quite complicated. From an accounting perspective, an interesting question that may arise in describing the distribution mechanism formula is whether salary or interest distributions to partners should be considered expenses of operating the firm or distribution of profits. The differences that can result from these two different approaches are discussed below more fully in Section E.

As an illustration of a specific income-sharing agreement, consider the Plastics Laminating Company, the balance sheet and statement of capital of which we examined above. Let us assume that the partnership agreement for the firm calls for:

a. interest at the rate of 10% per annum on the capital balances at the beginning of the year;

b. partners' "salaries" of $22,000 for Green and $18,000 for Kane; and

c. distribution of the remainder in the ratio of 60% to Green and 40% to Kane.

To meet these specifications for distribution of profits, the net income for the year should be apportioned as shown in the Allocation of Profit schedule found below in Exhibit 11.6. Such an Allocation of Profit schedule could serve as a supporting document to a firm's income statement or it could be incorporated

---

[2] The Uniform Partnership Act of 1914 (the "UPA") is the statute which governs the existence and operation of partnerships in most states. Section 18(a) of the UPA provides that each partner shall share equally in the profits of the partnership. The Uniform Partnership Act of 1994 (the "RUPA") maintains the same principle of sharing profits. RUPA § 807.

[3] The introduction to Section 18 of the UPA advises that the rights and duties specified within that section are subject "to any agreement" between the partners. Also see RUPA § 103

[4] Partners can make loans to their partnerships and become actual creditors. As creditors, pursuant to UPA § 40, partners would have priority over other partners with respect to capital upon dissolution. UPA § 40(b)(II). However, other non-partner creditors would have priority over partner-creditors. UPA § 40(b)(I). Also see RUPA § 103.

into the actual income statement of the firm. Note, that, after interest and partners' salaries are distributed to the partners, the partnership might have suffered a net loss. In that instance, the loss will have to be absorbed by the partners as agreed upon in the partnership agreement (or equally, in the absence of an agreement).

EXHIBIT 11.6

Plastics Laminating Company
Allocation of Profit
Calendar Year 20_____

	Green	Kane	Total
Interest at 10% on capital balance at January 1	$ 5,080	$ 5,750	$10,830
Salaries	22,000	18,000	40,000
Share of remainder 60%	18,342		
40%		12,228	30,570
Totals	$45,422	$35,978	$81,400

The allocation of profit agreed to by Green and Kane allows the two partners to be compensated in a manner that reflects their respective contributions to the partnership. For example, Kane has a greater capital balance than Green as of the beginning of the calendar year and thus receives more than Green in the form of interest on capital. However, Green assumedly provides the partnership with greater or more valuable services than Kane and consequently receives a higher salary than Kane.

E. PARTNERS' SALARIES AND INTEREST ON CAPITAL

Expenses or Allocations of Profit?

When partners, as part of their partnership agreement, arrange for a regular drawing (typically on a weekly or monthly basis), they may refer to these drawings as "salaries." Since partners are owners of their business, it may be argued that partnership salaries are more appropriately classified as allocations of profits rather than as operational expenses. In contrast, salaries of employees clearly are to be identified as operational expenses of the business.

When partner salaries are provided for in partnership agreements, they may be reported as an element on the Allocation of Profit schedule (see Exhibit 11.6 above) or among the expenses identified in the Income Statement (see Exhibit 11.7, Method B, below). One would expect partners' salaries to be shown separately on the Income Statement and designated as "partners' salaries" to distinguish them from salaries to employees. If partners' salaries are included in the Income Statement as an expense, then the amount remaining to be allocated to partners as profit would be "profit after salaries to partners."

Treating partners' salaries as an expense item, rather than as an allocation of profits can help partners better understand how their firm is performing. Were a person, other than a partner, to perform the services for which a partner is paid his partnership salary, that person would receive a salary equivalent to the partner's salary. This non-partner salary would clearly be considered an expense of doing business and would reduce net income. To augment profits by failing to deduct an expense item that would otherwise be a legitimate cost of doing business artificially inflates the return on the partners' investment that is reflected in the income statement. Treating partners' salaries as expense items for accounting purposes allows partners to more realistically assess business performance and to better compare their compensation as "employees."

The Income Statement for the Plastics Laminating Company, found below in Exhibit 11.7, has been prepared in two alternative formats. In Method A, the partners' salaries are not accounted for as an expense item and net income is reported prior to a deduction for such salaries (the partners' salaries will appear as an element on the Allocation of Profit schedule). In Method B, the partners' salaries are accounted for as an expense item. Notice that the Net Income reported in Method B is less than the Net Income reported in Method A by an amount that is equal to the partners' salaries.

EXHIBIT 11.7

Plastics Laminating Company
Income Statement
Twelve Months ended December 31, 20_____

	Method A	Method B
Sales	$300,000	$300,000
Cost of Sales		
Materials	60,000	60,000
Factory payroll	55,000	55,000
Factory expenses	30,000	30,000
Total cost of sales	145,000	145,000
Gross Margin	155,000	155,000
Expenses		
Partner's salaries		40,000
Office salaries	36,000	36,000
Rent and office expenses	17,000	17,000
Other expenses	20,600	20,600
Total expenses	73,600	113,600
Net income (before partners' salaries)	$ 81,400	
Net income (after partners' salaries)		$ 41,400

NOTE: In Method A, partners' salaries do not appear on the income statement since they are being treated as distributions of profits. In Method B, partners' salaries are treated as a business expense.

Another issue that may arise in regard to partners' salaries is whether such salaries should be treated as a portion of the profits that are to be allocated to the partners. Alternatively, the salaries could be treated independently of profits and the allocation of profits could be computed from the net income remaining after salaries are distributed. Which treatment is used can affect the total income distributed to a specific partner. These two different treatments do not actually reflect different accounting approaches, but rather varying profit distribution agreements among the partners.

How these alternative treatments can impact on total distributions to different partners can be explained as follows: In a typical partnership, partnership salaries will not be exactly proportional to partners' rights to profits. For example, in the Plastics Laminating Company, discussed above, the ratio of Green's salary to Kane's salary was $22,000:$18,000 or 11:9. However, the ratio of Green's share of profits to Kane's share of profits was 60%:40% or 3:2. In other words, Green's salary was about 22% greater than Kane's; but Green's share of the profits was 50% greater than Kane's. Whenever this disproportionality exists between partners' salaries and partners' rights to profits, the total distribution of profits to a particular partner will vary depending upon whether salaries are treated as a portion of the profits that are allocated to the partners or whether profits are instead computed from the net income remaining after salaries are distributed.

The impact that this difference in treatment of partnership salaries could have in a particular partnership can be illustrated if we examine how partners Green and Kane of the Plastics Laminating Company would individually fare under the two different approaches. In Section D above, we discovered that the partnership agreement between Green and Kane directed that residual profits be distributed only after partners' salaries and interest had been deducted from net income. Pursuant to that treatment, Green received a total of $45,422 in salary, interest, and profit and Kane received a total of $35,978 in salary, interest, and profit. If the partnership agreement between Kane and Green instead directed that salaries be treated as a draw on the profits that are allocated to partners, then Green would have received 60% of the net income before partners' salaries. And Kane would have received 40% of the net income before partners' salaries. In Exhibit 11.7, we discovered that net income before partners' salaries and interest was $81,400. Accordingly, under this latter approach, Green would receive $48,840 (approximately $3,400 more than under the alternative method) and Kane would receive $32,560 (approximately $3,400 less than under the alternative method).

It becomes apparent that it is important for the partnership agreement to specify whether partners' salaries are to be treated as draws on profits or if profits are to be calculated only after net income is reduced by the amount to be paid in salary. This matter can be easily handled in the partnership agreement by language that might read: 1) "partners' salaries are to be calculated and profits are to be distributed from the net income remaining after such salaries are paid," or, alternatively, 2) "profits are to be allocated from net income prior to the payment of partners' salaries and such salaries are to be treated as 'draws' against allocated profits."

The same questions raised regarding the treatment of partners' salaries arise regarding the treatment of payment to partners of interest on their capital accounts. Interest payments to partners may be treated as an element of allocation of profit or they may be included in the income statement as one of the expenses. If treated as an expense, interest to partners should be separated out from other interest paid by the business and should be labelled "interest to partners" or with an equivalent title. As in the instance of salaries, these different treatments can impact on the total distribution received by individual partners. If a partnership agreement provides for both interest on capital and salaries to partners, either both items should be shown as elements in allocation of income or both should be included among the expenses and clearly distinguished from other forms of interest and from salaries to employees.

Similarly, pursuant to the partnership agreement, interest-to-partner expenses may be treated, as an element of the profit allocation. Alternatively, profits may be computed only after interest to partners expenses are deducted from net income. As with salaries, these different treatments can impact on the total distribution received by individual partners.

F. PARTNERSHIP LIQUIDATION

When It's Over, How Does It End?

When a partnership liquidates its business, it will typically sell its assets, pay off its creditors and distribute the residual assets to the partners (or collect funds from partners to pay off creditors or to pay the interest of other partners). This liquidation process is referred to as "winding-up." When the winding-up of the partnership is completed, the partnership is "terminated." Winding-up may be caused by "dissolution," which is defined by the Uniform Partnership Act as "the change in the relation of the partners caused by any partner ceasing to be associated in the carrying on as distinguished from the winding-up of the business."[5]

A partner may cease to be associated with a partnership because of death or withdrawal or termination of a pre-specified term. Winding-up and termination may also be brought about merely when the partners decide to end the business of the partnership even in the absence of any other change in partnership relations. To restate the relationship among these terms, one might say that dissolution of a partnership may lead to winding-up which can lead to termination. The process of winding-up in conjunction with termination can also be referred to as "liquidation."

The winding-up process encompasses several elements. One important element is the sale of assets, which typically leads to a realization of cash. It is unlikely that the cash realized from the sale of a partnership's assets will precisely equal the value at which those assets were carried on the books of the partnership.

---

[5] UPA § 29. The relationship between dissolution, termination, and winding-up is described in § 30 of the UPA as follows: On dissolution the partnership is not terminated, but continues until the winding-up of partnership affairs is completed. Under the RUPA, "a partnership continues afterdissolution only for the purpose of winding up its business. The partnership is terminated when the winding up of its business is completed." RUPA § 802.

The difference between the amount of cash realized upon the sale of partnership assets and the value of those assets on the books of the partnership will usually result in either a gain or a loss for the partnership. Such gain or loss must be carried over to the capital accounts of the individual partners.

The winding-up process also requires the payment of creditors and the distribution of residual assets to partners (or the collection from partners of additional cash to pay creditors or other partners). The impact on the individual partners of winding-up and termination will be markedly different depending upon whether or not the residual assets are sufficient to satisfy the capital accounts of the individual partners.

In attempting to understand the winding-up process, it is helpful to focus upon several different financial scenarios that may occur at the end of the life of a partnership. It is useful to explore what occurs when there is a differential between the amount realized on the sale of assets and the book value of those assets. It is also useful to explore what happens to the residual assets, after payment of creditors, with regard to satisfying the capital accounts of the partners.

Realization of assets unequal to book value. When the assets of a partnership are liquidated during winding-up, the cash realized upon the sale of the liquidated assets in essence becomes the partnership's new assets. Should the cash realized from the sale of the liquidated assets exceed the book value at which the liquidated assets were carried, then the partnership would have experienced gain on the sale which gain should be allocated to the partners and recorded in their respective capital accounts. Likewise, if the cash realized from the liquidated assets is less than the book value at which the liquidated assets were carried, the partnership would have experienced a loss on the sale which loss should be allocated to the partners and recorded in their respective capital accounts.

For example, let us assume that the ABC partnership is made up of Andrews, Baker, and Cohen, who share partnership profits and losses on a 3:2:1 basis, and that, prior to liquidation, the total partnership assets were carried on the partnership books at $120,000. If those partnership assets are sold on liquidation for $120,000, there is no change in the partnership capital accounts as a result of such sale. If, however, the assets are sold for only $108,000, then the partners have to absorb a $12,000 loss on a 3:2:1 basis. Accordingly, Andrews' capital account would be reduced by $6,000, Baker's account would be reduced by $4,000, and Cohen's account would be reduced by $2,000. On the other hand, if the assets were sold for $126,000, then the partnership will have experienced a $6,000 gain and the capital accounts of the three partners would be increased as follows: Andrews, $3,000; Baker, $2,000; Cohen, $1,000.

Residual assets and their impact upon capital accounts. As a practical matter, liquidations are generally conducted in installments. It typically is not until the end of the liquidation process that the final distribution owing to, or payment required from, partners can be determined. For simplicity's sake, however, we will deal with liquidation below as if it were a process that occurs at a single point of time.

To illustrate, let us examine a situation in which all gains and losses realized on the conversion of assets to cash have been distributed to the partners and recorded in their respective capital accounts and that, after this process is completed, all capital accounts have credit balances. We know that, to satisfy the Uniform Partnership Act, liquidation must be conducted in a manner that insures that the payment of funds to creditors takes priority over payment of funds to partners whether for their partnership loans, capital accounts, or profits.[6] Let us further assume, that our illustrative partnership is still comprised of three persons, Partners A, B, and C, who split profits and losses on a 3:2:1 basis and whose capital accounts, totaling $41,000, appear as follows:

---

[6] Section 40 of the UPA provides guidance regarding the priority of the claims of various parties to the assets of the partnership upon liquidation. Partnership liabilities are to be paid off in the following order.

I. Those owing to creditors other than partners.

II. Those owing to partners other than for capital and profits.

III. Those owing to partners in respect of capital.

IV. Those owing to partners in respect of profits.

See also RUPA § 807.

Partner A	$ 9,000
Partner B	$18,000
Partner C	$14,000

If, after all liabilities to creditors are repaid, the partnership has residual cash which exceeds the sum of the capital accounts, then the partnership would pay out to the individual partners their respective capital accounts and then would split the rest of the cash, as gain, on a 3:2:1 basis. For example, if, after all creditors are paid, the partnership retained $53,000 in cash, then Partners A, B, and C would receive a total of $41,000 for their capital accounts and the remaining $12,000 would be distributed to the partners as follows: A, $6,000; B, $4,000; C, $2,000.

What happens, however, if, after creditors are paid off, residual cash does not equal the sum of the partners' capital accounts but is sufficient for all partners to receive partial payment on their capital accounts? Assume that cash on hand after all liabilities are paid equals $35,000. This amount of cash is $6,000 less than what is needed to distribute to each partner the full amount of his or her capital account. This shortfall represents a loss and must be distributed on a 3:2:1 basis. In other words, A's capital account is reduced by $3,000 and accordingly A receives $6,000. B's capital account is reduced by $2,000 and B receives $16,000. C's capital account is reduced by $1,000 and C receives $13,000.

Finally, we should explore what happens when the residual cash, after all liabilities are paid off, is insufficient to insure that all partners will receive even partial payment of their capital account. Let us assume that, after the debts are paid, only $17,000 in cash is held by the partnership. Since the sum of the partners' accounts equals $41,000, the partnership has suffered a loss of $24,000 which must be absorbed by the partners on a 3:2:1 basis. Accordingly, A must absorb $12,000, B must absorb $8,000, and C must absorb $4,000. Since A had only $9,000 in his or her capital account, A must pay in an additional $3,000. B then receives $10,000 ($18,000 less $8,000) and C receives $10,000 ($14,000 less $4,000). It is important to observe that partner A had to pay in additional capital in order to make certain that A's partners received their proper distributions. Thus, even when a partnership has sufficient assets to pay off all creditors, additional capital can be required from some of the partners to insure that other partners receive their appropriate capital account distribution.

What if Partner A can not make up the $3,000 deficiency? Then this deficiency has to be absorbed by Partners B and C in their relative profit-and-loss sharing ratios — i.e., 2:1. As a consequence, Partner B's capital is charged with two-thirds of the deficiency or $2,000. Partner C is charged with one-third of the deficiency or $1,000. The final distribution of the $17,000 will be $9,000 to Partner B and $8,000 to Partner C.

As indicated at the beginning of this discussion, liquidations are usually conducted in installments. In such cases, calculation of distributions can be more involved. One must avoid distribution of an amount which, at the end of liquidation, would result in a capital deficiency in any partner's account. For further discussion regarding installment liquidation and distribution, the reader is referred to the problems in the Appendix.

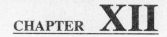

CHAPTER **XII**

ACCOUNTING FOR NON-PROFIT ORGANIZATIONS

A. INTRODUCTION: BASIC UNDERSTANDING

Non-Profit Doesn't Mean It Has to Lose Money

Attorneys frequently need to interact with organizations that provide a benefit to society and also operate on a non-profit basis. These organizations include, without limitation, educational institutions, hospitals, charities, cultural institutions such as libraries and museums, religious groups, trade associations, and other affinity groups. Lawyers may be called upon to provide such organizations with legal opinions, to assist in creating or rearranging their business structure, to help protect such organizations from liability risks, to insure that the organizations operate within externally imposed operating guidelines for charities, to facilitate commercial operations of these organizations, as well as numerous other purposes. In performing these functions, it well may be necessary for an attorney to review and understand the financial statements of the organization. The need for lawyers to understand the financial statements of non-profits has intensified as many non-profit organizations have come to engage in activities formerly conducted exclusively by for-profit companies. While the financial statements of non-profit organizations bear similarities to the statements of "for-profit organizations," they are by no means identical.

The term "non-profit" or "not-for-profit" should not be read as suggesting that the organization is a "for-profit" enterprise that is operating at a loss. Instead, the terms describe an organization whose owners do not expect a return of profits from the operations of the enterprise. Rather than producing a profit for the owners, not-for-profit organizations provide socially desirable services to society or to members of the non-profit corporation itself.

There are two accounting models that may be used to reflect the assets and liabilities of non-profit organizations. *Fund Accounting* segregates assets and liabilities into groups associated with a particular program or with restrictions imposed by contributors or by the board of directors upon the assets of a non-profit organization. Fund accounting applies to the internal accounting of a non-profit organizations and, until 1994, also governed the structure of the external reporting to the general public. However, as discussed below in the paragraph entitled "Financial Statements," in 1993, the FASB in its *Statement of Financial Accounting Standards No. 117*, established a new formulation for external reporting in terms of classes of net assets. This new formulation is referred to, herein, as the *Net Asset Class Model*.

Despite the new formulation for external reporting, the Fund Accounting model, by that or any other name, is necessary so that an organization can properly exercise its stewardship and determine whether various obligations and commitments have been fulfilled and whether restrictions or limitations have been observed. Reporting by funds is most appropriate for internal use. As noted, the Net Asset Class model replaces Fund Accounting for external reporting.[1] To a certain extent, it is a change in nomenclature. The Net Asset Class model will be discussed in this Chapter in the sections on financial statements.

---

[1] For example, the financial statements of the American Friends Service Committee for the year ended September 30, 1996, contains the following note:

FUND ACCOUNTING

Though the Committee has adopted SFAS No. 117 for external reporting purposes, it has not altered the way in which it administers its internal accounting in order to ensure observation of limitations and restrictions placed on the use of resources available to the Committee. The accounts of the Committee are maintained in accordance with the principles of "fund accounting." This is the procedure by which resources for various purposes are classified for accounting purposes into funds that are in accordance with specified activities or objectives. Separate accounts are maintained for each fund.

Since Fund Accounting best explains the restrictions or limitations upon the use of certain funds, it remains critical for the attorney to understand Fund Accounting. Only by understanding of the Fund Accounting model, may the attorney be able to evaluate whether the administrators of a non-profit organization have met certain of their fiduciary and/or legal obligations.

B. FUND ACCOUNTING

If There are No Owners, Then What Happens to Owners' Equity?

Financial statements of not-for-profit organizations, whether prepared by the Fund Accounting method or the Net Asset Class method, are similar to the statements of "for profit" organizations. They reflect the organization's assets and liabilities, and its revenues and expenses. These statements are prepared from accounting records similar to those utilized by profit-seeking enterprises. There is, however, one significant difference between accounting for profit-seeking business enterprises and accounting for non-profit organizations. That difference is the equity interest. When the fundamental equation for a profit-seeking enterprise was discussed in Chapter I, it was explained that:

$$\text{Assets} - \text{Liabilities} = \text{Ownership Equity.}$$

For a profit-seeking corporation, ownership equity is represented by shareholders' equity. For a sole-proprietorship or a partnership, ownership equity is represented by proprietor's or partners' capital. The not-for-profit organization, however, is not owned. There are trustees or directors or similar persons, affiliated with a not-for-profit enterprise, who are selected to serve the enterprise as fiduciaries and who have accepted the responsibilities that such position imposes. These selected fiduciaries are obligated to preserve the assets of the not-for-profit enterprise and to utilize them in a manner that insures that the purposes of the enterprise are fulfilled. These fiduciaries, however, are not owners.

Since there are no owners of a not-for-profit enterprise, there are no ownership interests. Accordingly, when we examine the fundamental equation in the context of a not-for-profit enterprise, it does not make sense to say that assets less liabilities equals owners' equity. However, assets less liabilities does show the resources of the enterprise that have not been spent or obligated and which therefore are available for the use of the enterprise. In other words, assets less liabilities reflects the resources that a not-for-profit has available to provide its services to society. Since a not-for-profit organization does not seek to make a profit but, rather, to provide socially desirable services, it is useful to devise an accounting approach that will identify the value of the resources available to achieve the socially desirable functions of the non-profit organization.

At any given point in time, a specific aggregation of assets and related liabilities dedicated to a specific purpose constitutes a "fund." The assets and liabilities of any given non-profit organization generally include more than a single fund. A "fund" as used in fund accounting is not to be thought of only as cash or other assets readily convertible into cash. In addition to cash and securities, fund assets may include receivables, inventory, land, buildings, and equipment as well as other assets. Each fund has a balance. This fund balance reflects the unobligated resources of the enterprise available for the use of the enterprise. In essence, the fund balance replaces "owners' equity" in the fundamental equation. The fundamental accounting equation applicable to a not-for-profit enterprise can thus be expressed for each fund as:

$$\text{Assets} - \text{Liabilities} = \text{Total Fund Balance.}$$

For the entire enterprise:

$$\text{Total Assets} - \text{Total Liabilities} = \text{Total Fund Balances}$$

Stated differently, assets equal liabilities plus the fund balance(s).

C. CATEGORIES OF FUNDS

One Organization, But Multiple Funds

As discussed above, not-for-profit organizations may have several categories of funds. The categories identify the different purposes to which the assets within those funds have been committed or different restrictions placed upon the assets within the fund. Different types of not-for-profit organizations (e.g., Health and Welfare, Colleges and Universities, Hospitals, and Professional Societies) will have different categories of funds. Some categories of funds are common to most not-for-profit organizations.

1.   **Restricted Funds.** A restricted fund is created when resources are donated to the organization for a specific purpose which is less broad in scope than the overall purpose of the organization. Accordingly, all funds of a not-for-profit organization are either restricted or unrestricted. An example of a restricted fund might include a donation made to a law school to develop the library's Securities Law collection or a grant made to a hospital to operate a clinic for pre-natal care. Restricted donations that are similar in nature may be combined into a single fund. Thus, all gifts given to a law school to build or acquire a new building may be placed into a fund restricted for the acquisition or construction of a new building.

Contributions may be restricted for a specific purpose or for a period of time. All of the restrictions listed above are *purpose restrictions*. A contribution of a sum of money, restricted by the donor for expenditures in a future period, is *time restricted*.

2.   **Unrestricted Funds.** All not-for-profit organizations function with at least one unrestricted fund which might also be called an "operating fund" or perhaps, a "general fund." A General Fund accounts for all of the resources of the organization not otherwise restricted by the donor or grantor for specified purposes. Assets of the General Fund are derived from unrestricted donations as well as revenues that may arise out of operations. The assets of the Unrestricted Fund are to be expended for the purpose of achieving the primary objectives of the organization. Other funds identified on the balance sheet under separate headings, such as a Plant and Building Fund and a Board-Designated Fund, may also be unrestricted in the sense that assets in those funds were not contributed for specific purposes designated by the donor or grantor.

3.   **Endowment Funds.** An Endowment Fund is a fund whose assets are to be preserved indefinitely by the organization. The income produced by these assets, however, may be expended for general purposes. If so designated by the donor of the assets, the income from an Endowment Fund may be allocated to a specific purpose, in which case the income is transferred to a restricted fund.

4.   **Board-Designated Funds.** Resources that were once unrestricted may be designated for a specific purpose by the board of directors of the not-for-profit organization. They then become Board-Designated Funds. The ends for which the board may designate these funds may include the construction of a new building, the funding of a special program, the expansion of a current operation, or other purposes. Since the resources in a board-designated fund are not restricted by the donor or grantor, such funds should be grouped under unrestricted funds. Board-designated funds may be utilized in the manner of an Endowment Fund in which case only the income produced by the resources within the fund would be spent. Board-Designated Funds may also be utilized by drawing upon the principal of the fund. Unspent resources in a Board-Designated Fund may be returned by the board to an unrestricted fund. At that point, that Board-Designated Fund would no longer appear on a balance sheet.

5.   **Plant and Building Funds.** The resources included in these funds are the fixed assets of the organization that are used in day-to-day operations, including buildings, land, equipment, furniture, and fixtures. Unexpended funds designated for activities such as building acquisition or construction will also be included within the category of Plant and Building Funds. Depreciation will be recorded on the fixed assets in these funds. Liabilities related to the assets in the funds, such as mortgages and other loans, are taken into account in computing the balance of the Plant and Building Funds.

D. FINANCIAL STATEMENTS

What Are The Basics

Historically financial statements of not-for profit organizations were displayed in a variety of patterns governed by various AICPA pronouncements[2] and industry manuals[3] so that there were considerable differences among the presentations of the different types of not-for-profit organizations.

In June, 1993, after years of study and preparations, the Financial Accounting Standards Board issued its *Statement of Financial Accounting Standards No.117, Financial Statements of Not-for-Profit Organizations.*[4] Statement No. 117 establishes a Net Asset Class Model and the minimum requirements for all not-for-profit organizations for a complete set of financial statements for public reporting. What is required is:

1. a Statement of Financial Position (Balance Sheet),[5]

2. a Statement of Activities (Revenues and Expenses), and

3. a Statement of Cash Flows.

The focus in these statements is on the whole entity, not on fund groups. When dealing with Health and Welfare organizations, FASB requires a fourth statement in addition to the three required for all other not-for-profits. The fourth statement is a Functional Allocation of Expenses.

The term "fund balance" is not used in this set of statements required by FASB. Instead, the resultant of assets minus related liabilities is termed "net assets." Total net assets are divided into three net asset classes based on donor imposed restrictions. These classes are permanently restricted, temporarily restricted and unrestricted.

It might appear that fund balance and net assets are equal to one another, but this is true only of certain "totals" that appear on each of these models. While the total of fund balance is equal to the total of net asset classes, a given fund does not necessarily correspond to any specific net asset class. For example, a plant fund may include: land to be held in perpetuity and to be treated in the net asset class model as part of permanently restricted net assets; a building erected from prior unrestricted contributions to be included as part of unrestricted net assets; and cash contributed for construction of an addition to the building. In the Fund Accounting Model, you could examine the plant fund and immediately determine the nature and the amount of all three components. The same information would be more difficult to obtain from the Net Asset class model. Illustrative examples patterned after those in Statement No. 117 appear in the exhibits found in the following discussions. It is apparent that, in actual practice, there are variations in these formats. Development of appropriate variations is encouraged by the FASB.

E. THE BALANCE SHEET

Broken Down By Restrictions

Similar to the form found in the presentation found in not-for-profit organizations, assets and liabilities are arrayed in terms of relative liquidity. However, as illustrated in Exhibit 12.1, cash and contributions

---

[2] *Audits of Colleges and Universities*, 1973; *Audits of Voluntary Health and Welfare Organizations*, 1974; *Statement of Position 78-10 Accounting Principles and Reporting Practices for Certain Nonprofit Organizations*, 1978; *Audits of Providers of Health Care Services*, 1990.

[3] For example: *Standards of Accounting and Financial Reporting for Voluntary Health and Welfare Organizations*: National Health Council, Inc. The National Assembly of National Voluntary Health and Social Welfare Organizations, Inc. and the United Way of America. (Because of the color of its binding, this manual is commonly referred to as the "black book."); *College and University Business Administration*, The National Association of College and University Business Officers; *Museum Accounting Handbook*, the American Association of Museums.

[4] Statement No. 117 became effective for annual financial statements for fiscal years beginning after December 15,1994, except that for organizations with less than $5 million in total assets and less than $1 million in annual expenses, the effective date was one year later.

[5] A comment on language: The FASB directs the use of title "Statement of Financial Position," not "Balance Sheet." However, it is interesting to note, of the 600 for profit companies surveyed in Accounting Trends and Techniques, 1996, 562 use the term Balance Sheet, 32 use Statement of Financial Positions, and 6 use Statement of Financial Condition.

receivable , restricted by donors for investment in plant, should be listed with plant assets rather than with cash and cash equivalents or with contributions receivable.

The balance sheet or accompanying notes, is also to include a break-down of net assets into the three classes: unrestricted, temporarily restricted, and permanently restricted.

Actual Balance Sheets and Statements of Position illustrating fund accounting and net asset class models are shown in the following appendices:

American Accounting Association Annual Report: Independent Auditors' Report:

Appendix C -1996 (net asset class model)

Appendix D -1991 (fund accounting model)

National Charities Information Bureau, a welfare not-for-profit organization

Appendix E -1996 (net asset class model)

Appendix F -1991 (fund accounting model)

EXHIBIT 12.1

Philanthropic Welfare Agency

Statements of Financial Position
December 31, 20X1 and 20X0

ASSETS	20X1	20X0
Cash	$ 60,000	$ 70,000
Accrued Interest Receivable	15,000	14,000
Pledges Receivable	20,000	30,000
Inventory of Publications	13,000	11,000
Assets restricted to investments in land, buildings, & equipment	25,000	20,000
Land, buildings, & equipment, net of depreciation	150,000	130,000
Long-term investments	180,000	170,000
Total Assets	463,000	445,000
LIABILITIES		
Accrued Expenses	11,000	9,000
Accounts Payable	23,000	25,000
Notes Payable	19,000	18,000
Mortgage Payable	60,000	70,000
Total Liabilities	113,000	122,000
NET ASSETS		
Unrestricted	85,000	73,000
Temporarily restricted	45,000	40,000
Permanently restricted	220,000	210,000
Total Net Assets	350,000	323,000
Total Liabilities/Net Assets	463,000	445,000

F. STATEMENT OF ACTIVITIES

What was received. What was spent.

A Statement of Activities is similar to the income statement of a for profit organization. It reports on the revenue and support of a non-profit organization and its expenses for a stated period of time. The statement should show the increase or decrease in each class of net assets; the net assets at the beginning of the period and the net assets at the end. Statement No. 117 presents three different formats. The illustration in exhibit 12.2 appears to be the format most commonly followed.

One should note that all expenses are to be assigned to unrestricted net assets. As a consequence, it is necessary to make a transfer from temporarily unrestricted net assets to unrestricted net assets for restrictions that have been fulfilled.

Actual Statements of Activities are presented in Appendices C through F as follows:

American Accounting Association:

   Appendix C -1996 (Statement of Activities)

   Appendix D -1991 (Statements of Support and Revenue, Expenses and Changes in Fund Balances)

National Charities Informations Bureau

   Appendix E -1996 (Statement of Activities)

   Appendix F -1991 (Statement of Public Support, Revenue and Expenses and Changes in Fund Balances)

EXHIBIT 12.2

Philanthropic Welfare Agency
Statement of Activities
Year Ended December 31, 20X1

Revenues and Support	Unrestricted	Temporarily Restricted	Currently Restricted	Total
Contributions	$422,000		$ 10,000	$432,000
Grants	30,000	70,000		100,000
Income on investments	10,000	8,000		18,000
Sale of Publications	50,000			50,000
Net assets released from restrictions	73,000	(73,000)		
Total revenue and support	**585,000**	**5,000**	**10,000**	**600,000**

EXPENSES

Program A	334,000			
Program B	157,000			
Management and general	61,000			
Fund raising	21,000			
Total Expenses	**573,000**			**573,000**
Change in Net Assets	12,000	5,000	10,000	27,000
Net Assets at begin. of year	73,000	40,000	210,000	323,000
Net Assets at end of year	**85,000**	**45,000**	**220,000**	**350,000**

G. STATEMENT OF CASH FLOWS

The Focus Here is on Cash and Equivalents

Prior to the issuance of Statement No. 117, Statements of Cash Flows were not required for either colleges or universities or voluntary health and welfare organizations. A cash flow statement is now required in the reports of all non-profit organizations. Similar to business entities, the statement of cash flows may be presented by either the direct or indirect method. The vast majority of business organizations use the indirect method, as presented in Exhibit 12.3.

Both the American Accounting Association (Appendix C) and the National Charities Information Bureau (Appendix E) utilized the indirect method.

EXHIBIT 12.3

Philanthropic Welfare Agency
Statement of Cash Flows
Year Ended December 31, 20X1

Cash Flows from Operating Activities

Increase in Net Assets		$27,000
Adjustments to reconcile increase in net assets to net cash used by operating activities		
Depreciation	$26,000	
Increase in accrued interest receivable	(1,000)	
Decrease in pledges receivable	10,000	
Increase in inventory of publication	(2,000)	
Increase in accrued expenses	2,000	
Decrease in accounts payable	(2,000)	33,000
Cash flows from investing activities		
Purchase of equipment	(46,000)	
Purchase of investments net	(10,000)	
Increase in assets restricted to investment in land, bldgs., & equip.	(5,000)	(61,000)
Cash flows from financing activities		
Increase in notes payable	1,000	
Repayment on mortgage	(10,000)	(9,000)
Net decrease in cash		$(10,000)
Cash at beginning of year		70,000
Cash at end of year		60,000

H. STATEMENT OF FUNCTIONAL ALLOCATION OF EXPENSES

Okay, Those are the Expenses, But on What Were They Spent?

Contributors to and supervisors of not-for-profit organizations are interested not only in how the organization spends money in terms of broad administrative categories (program services, management in general and fund raising), but also in a more specific sense. At one time or another, it might be important to know what portion of the funds spent on program services is expended on items such as salary, rent, staff travel, supplies, etc. The Statement of Functional Allocation of Expenses provides this more particularized breakdown of expenses.[6]

Exhibit 12.4. The total of all expenses in the Statement of Functional Allocation of Expenses should be equal to the

same total of expenses for all funds in the Statement of Activities. Compare Exhibit 12.2 with Exhibit 12.4.

---

[6] The National Charities Information Bureau (NCIB), a not-for-profit organization which evaluates charities, calls for charities to supply a Statement of Functional Allocation of Expenses in addition to such statements required by Generally Accepted Accounting Principles. In June 1993, the Financial Accounting Standards Board issued Statement No. 117, which requires voluntary health and welfare organizations to provide a Statement of Functional Allocation of Expenses.

Exhibit 12.4
Philanthropic Welfare Agency
Statement of Functional Allocation of Expenses
Year Ended December 31, 20XX

| | Program Services | | Supporting Services Management | Fund | |
	A	B	and General	Raising	Total
Salaries	$168,000	$142,000	$63,000	$32,000	$405,000
Building maintenance	25,000	21,000	9,200	4,800	60,000
Mail Services	3,000	2,700	1,100	1,700	8,500
Printing	8,500	6,000	3,000	5,000	22,500
Postage	8,800	7,200	3,100	4,900	24,000
Telephone	3,200	2,400	1,600	800	8,000
Travel	2,400	2,000	1,100	7,00	6,200
Supplies	1,200	1,000	600	300	3,100
Miscellaneous	3,800	2,400	2,300	1,200	9,700
Total Expenses before Depreciation	223,900	186,700	85,000	51,400	547,000
Depreciation	10,600	9,100	4,200	2,100	26,000
Total Expenses	**234,500**	**195,800**	**89,200**	**53,500**	**573,000**

APPENDIX A

THE MECHANICS OF ACCOUNTING

For Those Who Need to Know What Makes Things Tick

1. INTRODUCTION

In this text, the authors have presented and defined the significant accounting terms appearing in financial statements. With regard to the mechanics of accounting, however, there has been a conscious effort to avoid discussing the underlying technical aspects of the process. The authors felt safe in adopting this approach, since it is primarily the financial statements which are utilized by the attorney in his work. The mechanical aspects of accounting are not crucial for working with the financial statements.

At times, however, the attorney might require an understanding of how financial data is recorded, summarized, and then reported on in the financial statements. At these instances, an understanding of what might be referred to as the "accounting mechanism," can prove useful. In this Appendix, the accounting mechanism is explained under topics such as "Accounts," "Ledgers," "Debits and Credits," "Real and nominal accounts," "Originating documents," "Journals," "Trial balances," "Controlling accounts," "Merchandising accounts," and the "Preparation of interim statements."

As explained in Chapter I, the accounting process rests upon the fundamental equation of assets, liabilities, and equity. Every business transaction affects two or more elements in the fundamental equation so that the equation always remains in balance. This was demonstrated in an illustrative series of transactions entered into a tabular analysis. See Exhibit 1.1, *supra*. Theoretically, such a tabular arrangement in a greatly expanded form could be used to keep track of the much greater volume of transactions encountered in even a small business enterprise. Quite obviously, however, such a tabular arrangement would become much too cumbersome.

The modern accounting mechanism is much more efficient and can cope, when necessary, with the thousands of transactions that take place in a modest business in the course of a year, or, in some larger enterprises, in the course of a single day. For example, every sale to a customer constitutes a transaction, and in some larger merchandising establishments there might occur thousands of sales transactions in the course of an hour, not to mention all of the other transactions with regard to purchases of materials, supplies, and services and to payment of accounts payable and of wages and salaries and all the other expenses of doing business.

2. MANUAL AND COMPUTER RECORDING

Before proceeding further, it is appropriate to explain how accounting entries are made and accounting records maintained. Until the advent some years ago of bookkeeping machines, then of punched card recording devices, and currently of modern electronic computers, all accounting records were handwritten. Even today, some small businesses may maintain manual accounting records. On the other hand, when a very large number of transactions are involved, an electronic data processing system (also referred to as a computerized system) is faster, more efficient, and less prone to error.

One might expect then the following exposition to be phrased in terms of a computerized accounting system. Even though electronic accounting systems parallel manual accounting systems, however, it is believed easier to understand the accounting mechanism and the relationships between debits and credits and between accounts and financial statements in terms of the visible notations found in handwritten records.

Where appropriate, references will be made to parallel computer procedures.

3. ACCOUNTS

Each column in the tabular analysis in Exhibit 1.1 constitutes an "account," although not in conventional form. In essence, an account is a collection center into which are entered in money amounts all increases and decreases in a specific asset or a specific liability or a specific element of ownership equity.

Thus, in terms of the small set of transactions employed for the tabular analysis in the first chapter, there were accounts for each of the three assets — cash, accounts receivable, and merchandise, for the single liability — accounts payable, and for each of the two items of ownership equity — capital stock and retained earnings. With these accounts (columns in the tabular analysis) we were able to prepare a balance sheet merely from the balances in the accounts at the balance sheet date. Reference to the specific increases and decreases which were entered during the fiscal period into each account was not necessary. Only the balances in the accounts appear on the balance sheet. The income statement, however, could not be prepared in the same manner.

a.   Real and Nominal Accounts. To prepare the income statement, reference to the final balance in retained earnings was not sufficient. To ascertain the details of the revenues earned and the expenses incurred, it was also necessary to refer to the entries made in the retained earnings account (column) during the period. The tabular illustration in Chapter I was extremely condensed and contained only one entry for revenues and one entry for expenses. In almost all business enterprises. however, there may be several different categories of revenues and many different categories of expenses. Each type of revenue transaction and each type of expense transaction may occur many times in the course of the year.

If all of these transactions were entered directly into retained earnings, it would be a Herculean task to analyze and sort all of the revenue and expense transactions which had taken place during the year. Such analysis would be necessary in order to prepare an income statement. Therefore, to more readily obtain the information as to revenues and expenses, "nominal" or temporary accounts are utilized during the fiscal period in which to enter the various categories of increases or decreases in retained earnings. These nominal accounts constitute temporary subdivisions of ownership equity. In the case of a corporation, they represent temporary subdivisions of retained earnings.[1] Thus, during the fiscal period, there will exist separate accounts for each category of expense and each category of revenue. At the end of the period, these nominal accounts will be "closed" by transferring the balances to a "profit and loss summary" account. (Alternative titles for the profit and loss summary include "profit and loss account," "income and expense summary," and "revenue and expense summary.")

In turn, the profit and loss account will be closed and its balance transferred to the retained earnings account. If these temporary accounts were not closed each year, the balances would continue to increase so that at the end of Year 2, the account balances would include the amounts entered in Year 1. The nominal accounts are opened (or reopened) at the beginning of each successive fiscal year and closed by transfer to the profit and loss summary at the end of each fiscal year. This technique of utilizing nominal accounts simplifies the categorization of increases and decreases in ownership equity that occur during the year. The closing of the nominal accounts at the end of each year so as to start with a zero balance segregates revenues and expenses for each successive year.

In contrast to the term "nominal" or "temporary," the accounts which appear on the balance sheet are termed "real" or "permanent" accounts. Real accounts are not closed but they are "balanced" at the end of each fiscal year. The ending balance is carried forward and becomes the beginning balance of the next period.

4. LEDGER

All of the accounts together constitute the "ledger.". In this handwritten system, each account is likely to be recorded on a separate page. These pages may lie within a bound volume. More commonly, for greater flexibility, the accounts are written on loose-leaf pages which are kept in a binder. The bound

---

[1] The applicable ownership equity account in a sole proprietorship would be the owner's capital account. In a partnership, it would be the several partners' capital accounts.

volume or the binder containing all of these accounts is referred to as the "general ledger." (There are also "subsidiary ledgers" which will be explained further on in this Appendix.)

In an electronic data processing system entries are made into the computer by pressing keys on a keyboard. These entries are not visible unless the computer is instructed to show them on a screen or to provide a print-out. Generally, print-outs can be obtained of any or all accounts in a ledger.

5. FORM OF ACCOUNT

There are various formats for handwritten accounts. All will have at least two money columns, one for increases and one for decreases in the account. Some formats provide a third money column in which to enter the balance of the account. In addition to money columns, there are also several columns in which to enter the dates of the transactions, cross-references and miscellaneous informational notations.

The most common form of account in a manual system resembles a "T" with the title of the account written across the top. Below the title on one side of the vertical dividing line are listed all of the increases in the account and on the other side are listed all of the decreases. The left-hand side of the account is for "debits," and the right-hand side for "credits." Omitting the miscellaneous columns for dates, cross-references, and notations, a sketch of an account is shown below. (Exhibit App. 1)

EXHIBIT APP. 1

Title of Account

Debits	Credits

Although not as complete as the account form that would be used in a formal set of accounts, this simplified format is useful in explaining accounting concepts and often is employed in accounting analyses.

Accounts in a computerized system, although not in a clear "T" format, generally list debits and credits in separate columns with the debit column to the left of the credit column. There would also be columns for dates, cross-references and informational notations.

Illustrations of the use of a set of accounts with a variety of both debit and credit entries will be given in a later section of this Appendix.

6. DEBITS AND CREDITS: DOUBLE ENTRY ACCOUNTING

The accounting mechanism is ingeniously constructed, although this is not immediately evident. One might consider self-evident the concept of the basic equation — that assets are equal to equities. One might also consider that the concept of a separate account for each element in the basic equation is a logical development. The utilization of two separate columns, however, one for increases and one for decreases, is not quite so obviously a necessary development. After all, one might have tried to keep the records in a columnar analysis, such as in the First Chapter, with increases and decreases for a given asset or equity being entered in the same single column. However, accepting the use of two columns, it is not an unreasonable development that they were placed side by side, so that we may refer to them as the left-hand (or left-side) column and the right-hand (or right-side) column. Obviously, one side is to gather increases in the account, and the other is for decreases.

The real ingenuity, however, was to set a rigid pattern for the increases so that, *for each and every transaction,* the left-side entries would be equal to the right-side entries. Selecting the left-side for increases in assets may have been entirely arbitrary, but this selection automatically establishes the remainder of the pattern. In order for left-side and right-side entries to offset each other, with the left-side assigned for increases in assets, it follows, in utilizing the basic equation, that increases in equities must be entered on the right-side. Further, since increases in assets are to be recorded on the left-side, decreases in assets must be recorded on the right-side. Similarly, since increases in equities are to be recorded on the right-side, decreases in equities must be recorded on the left-side.

Although entries into accounts can be referred to simply as "left-side" or "right-side" entries, accountants for many years have employed the terms "debit" for the left-side and "credit" for the right-side. Whether an account is for an asset or for an equity, the left-side is a debit, and the right-side is a credit. (A debit may also be referred to as a "charge," but there is no similar substitute for a credit.)

The rule of debit and credit as developed above may be summarized as follows:

DEBIT (left-side) to increase an asset or decrease an element of equity.

CREDIT (right-side) to decrease an asset or increase an element of equity.

Most transactions affect only two accounts, with one account debited and the other credited. Some transactions, however, are more complex and affect more than two accounts. But even in complex transactions, the nature of the fundamental equation and the rule of debit and credit enforces an equality of debits and credits. In any transaction, the debit(s) arising out of the transaction must be equal to the credit(s) arising out of the transaction or the fundamental equation will no longer balance. The fact that two or more accounts are involved with the entry for any transaction, and that there is a counterbalancing of debits and credits provides the basis for the term "double entry" accounting. For any given transaction, one does not make an entry into one account only. There has to be a counterbalancing entry into some other account(s).

Before proceeding further, a word is in order about the term "entry." The term may refer to a debit entry or to a credit entry. However, at times the combination of the debit entry (or entries) arising from a given transaction and the credit entry (or entries) arising from the same transaction may be referred to collectively as the "entry for the transaction."

Although debits and credits are counterbalanced in the entry for each transaction, as for the individual accounts themselves, there will always be either an excess of debits or an excess of credits or the debits and the credits will be equal. Asset accounts normally carry debit (left-side) balances, because the left-side entries (debit) to the account, representing increases in the asset, will exceed the right-side (credit) entries to the account for decreases in the asset.

In similar fashion, equity accounts normally carry credit (right-side) balances. Since every one of the entries for the various transactions is balanced in terms of debits and credits, the aggregate of the balances of all of the accounts in the ledger will balance. That is, the total of all of the balances in the accounts with debit balances will be equal to the total of all of the balances in the accounts with credit balances. If the total of the debit balances is not equal to the total of the credit balances, then some error has been made. For example, there may have been an imbalance in one of the original entries or a debit entry might have been placed in error on the credit side of an account. There may even have been an error somewhere along the line in the additions and subtractions involved in arriving at the various account balances.

Computer programs generally do not accept entries out of balance.

The fact that the totals of balances are in agreement is not proof, however, that no error exists. For example, there may have been an entry into the wrong account. If that is so, two account balances will be incorrect, but the errors offset one another so the totals of the account balances remain in agreement.

The debit and credit analysis can be amplified further by dividing equities into their two general components — liabilities and ownership equity. This has been done in the following table. To emphasize the left-side and right-side aspects of entries into accounts, the types of accounts are listed in the center of this table and the debit and credit effects are listed on either side, the debits on the left and the credits on the right.

DEBIT (left-side)	TYPE OF ACCOUNT	CREDIT (right-side)
Increase	Asset	Decrease
Decrease	Liability	Increase
Decrease	Ownership equity	Increase

Illustrative transactions, real accounts only

At this point, illustrative transactions would be in order. For the present, however, we will work in terms of real accounts only. Limiting ourselves to simple transactions with a single debit and a single credit, there are nine possible combinations of increases and decreases in the three categories of accounts, assets, liabilities, and ownership equity. Nine illustrative transactions follow:

DEBIT (left-side)	TRANSACTION	CREDIT (right-side)
Increase asset, cash	1. Issue capital stock at par for cash	Increase ownership equity account, capital stock
Increase asset, cash	2. Borrow money on a bank loan	Increase liability, loan payable
Increase asset, office equipment	3. Purchase office equipment for cash	Decrease asset, cash
Decrease shareholder equity account, retained earnings	4. Issue a stock dividend[2]	Increase shareholder equity account, capital stock
Decrease shareholder liability, equity account, preferred capital stock	5. Redeem preferred stock by issuance of notes payable	Increase notes payable
Decrease shareholder equity account, retained earnings	6. Pay a cash dividend[3]	Decrease asset, cash
Decrease liability, bonds payable	7. Convertible bonds converted to capital stock[2]	Increase shareholder equity account, capital stock
Decrease liability, accounts payable	8. Issue a note payable to settle an account payable	Increase liability, notes payable
Decrease liability, accounts payable	9. Pay cash on an account payable	Decrease asset, cash

Note that all the nine possible debit and credit combinations have been covered. The first three transactions involve debit (left-side) entries increasing an asset account. The next three (4, 5 and 6) involve debit (left-side) entries decreasing a shareholders' equity account. The last three (7, 8 and 9) require debit (left-side) entries decreasing liability accounts. In each of these three sets of three entries, the debits have been paired

[2] It has been assumed that no capital surplus was created in transactions 4 and 7. Such could well be true if the capital stock were without either par or stated value. Were that capital stock to have either a par or a stated value, a portion of the total credit in the transaction would go to stated capital and the remainder to capital surplus.

[3] In principle, a liability is created when a cash dividend is declared, and the liability is settled by the cash payment of the dividend. Thus, transaction 6 combines what in some cases is treated as two transactions. The declaration of the dividend results in a decrease in retained earnings and an increase in the liability, dividend payable. The subsequent payment decreases the liability, dividend payable, and decreases cash. In combining the two transactions., the increase and decrease of the liability, dividend payable, offset one another, and the net result is a decrease in retained earnings and a decrease in the asset, cash.

[2] It has been assumed that no capital surplus was created in transactions 4 and 7. Such could well be true if the capital stock were without either par or stated value. Were that capital stock to have either a par or a stated value, a portion of the total credit in the transaction would go to stated capital and the remainder to capital surplus.

with credits (right-side) to a shareholders' equity account, a liability account, and an asset account, respectively. Thus, illustration of the three possible entries involving credit (right-side) entries increasing a shareholders' equity account are found in transactions 1, 4 and 7. Transactions involving a credit (right-side) entry increasing a liability account are illustrated in entries 2, 5 and 8. Finally, the three possible pairs of entries involving a credit (right-side) entry decreasing an asset are demonstrated in transactions 3, 6 and 9.

Rationale and illustrative transactions involving nominal accounts

To this point, the discussion has been in terms of real accounts. There are, however, the revenue and expense accounts to be considered. As already indicated (see "Real and nominal accounts," *supra*), the revenue and expense (or nominal) accounts are temporary subdivisions of ownership equity. The rule of debit and credit can now be amplified to cover all of the categories into which equities have been divided.

There is more than one way to explain the rationale of debit and credit as applied to nominal accounts. However, regardless of which rationale one prefers, the selection of debit and credit is identical and the outcome of the entries is the same.

Inasmuch as revenue and expense accounts are temporary accounts, they are closed at the end of the annual fiscal period. That is, their balances are transferred to a profit and loss summary account. The balance in the profit and loss account after this transfer is, in turn, transferred to an ownership equity account which will appear on the balance sheet. If the business entity is a corporation, the ownership equity account would be retained earnings. In a sole partnership, the account would be the owner's capital account. In a partnership, the transfer would be divided in some manner among the several partners' capital accounts. Consequently, an entry into a revenue or an expense account is to be viewed as an entry into an equity account. Some illustrations may be in order and are provided in the following transactions.

Transaction 1. A law firm bills a client for services rendered and sets up an account receivable for the amount of the billing. The entry will be to debit (left-side) an account receivable to show the increase in the asset and to credit (right-side) a revenue account for "fees earned." The credit (right-side) entry to the account for fees earned increases the ownership equity and will find its way to the partners' capital accounts when the nominal accounts are closed and balances transferred at the end of the fiscal year. Recording of revenue always gives rise to credit (right-side) entries. The only debit (left-side) entries to a revenue account would be when the account is closed at the end of the year and the balance transferred or, only infrequently, as a result of some correction or adjustment.

Transaction 2. A service enterprise pays employees' salaries. There will be a debit (left-side) entry to a "salaries expense" account to decrease ownership equity, and an offsetting credit (right-side) entry to cash to decrease the asset cash. Expenses always give rise to debit (left-side) entries to expense accounts. The only credit (right-side) entries to expense accounts would occur when the account is closed at the end of the fiscal year and the balance transferred, or as a result of some correction or adjustment.

Note that a debit (left-side) entry to the salaries expense account decreases ownership equity. One generally expects an ownership equity account to build up a credit (right-side) balance, but the salaries expense account builds up a debit (left-side) balance. The reason for this is that although it is an element of ownership equity, an expense account is really a *negative* element of ownership equity. By increasing the balance of the expense account (understand that this is a debit, left-side, balance), one is making a greater reduction of ownership equity.

Rather than regularly analyzing an income account as a positive element of ownership equity and an expense account as a negative element, some prefer to view them as separate categories of accounts. A reformulation in tabular form of the debit and credit consequences on the different types of accounts follows with categories for the nominal accounts.

(Matthew Bender & Co., Inc.)

DEBIT (left-side)	TYPE OF ACCOUNT	CREDIT (right-side)
	Real Accounts	
Increase	Asset	Decrease
Decrease	Liability	Increase
Decrease	Ownership equity	Increase
	Nominal Accounts	
Decrease	Revenue	Increase
Increase[4]	Expense	Decrease

Typical account balances

The reader is reminded that one expects both debit and credit entries to be made to most real accounts but only credit entries to income accounts (except for corrections, adjustments, and final transfer of balance) and only debit entries to expense accounts (except for corrections, adjustments, and final transfer).

It has already been stated that asset accounts normally carry debit (left-side) balances and that liability and ownership equity accounts (not including nominal accounts) normally carry credit (right-side) balances. Taking the nominal accounts into consideration as well, one finds debit (left-side) balances in asset and expense accounts and credit (right-side) balances in liability, ownership equity, and income accounts. There are, of course, some non-typical situations. For instance, a cash overdraft would result in a credit (right-side) balance in the cash account which, at that point, would constitute a liability in the amount of the overdraft. Another instance arises when there is a deficit in retained earnings. The retained earnings account would then show a debit (left-side) balance.

Mixed accounts

There are some accounts which may be termed "mixed accounts," because they contain elements of two categories of accounts. An illustration of this would be an account which has been charged (debited) with the cost of insurance premiums. This account may be treated as an asset account, in which case one might expect to find a title, such as "prepaid insurance." On the other hand, it may be treated as an expense account, in which case the title is likely to be "insurance expense." In either case, the proper entry when an insurance premium is paid is to debit (left-side) this account. Regardless of title, however, it is neither entirely an asset nor entirely an expense, for premiums are normally paid in advance and represent assets when paid, but become expenses as the insurance policy matures. Accounts such as these may be adjusted on a periodic basis during the fiscal year, such as monthly or quarterly, or only at the end of the year.

If the account has been viewed as an asset, the adjustment involves the removal of the expense element. This adjustment may be made periodically during the course of the year (such as monthly or quarterly) or only annually.

If the account is adjusted monthly (or quarterly), the removal of the expense would be accomplished by monthly (or quarterly) transfer to an insurance expense account. The transferring entry would be a debit (left-side) entry to the expense account to increase the insurance expense and a credit (right-side) entry to the prepaid insurance account to reduce the asset.

If the adjustment of the prepaid insurance account is made only at the end of the fiscal year, the debit (left-side) entry might be made to an expense account. Or it might be made directly to the profit and loss summary account, since an insurance expense account would then immediately be closed and its balance transferred to the profit and loss summary account.

If, on the other hand, the original payments for insurance premiums were charged to an insurance expense account, monthly adjustments would not be feasible.[5] However, at the end of the year, before the insurance

---

[4] One is reminded that the debit (left-side) entry to an expense account which records an increase in an expense has the effect of decreasing ownership equity. And the credit (right-side) entry recording a decrease in an expense has the effect of increasing ownership equity.

[5] As indicated later in this Appendix, interim statements can be prepared by means of certain working paper techniques. Appropriate adjustment would be made on the workpapers to separate the asset and expense elements of the insurance expense account.

expense account was closed, it would be necessary to remove the asset element from the account. This would be accomplished by setting up a prepaid insurance account and debiting (left-side) it for the portion of the premiums that were unexpired. The offsetting credit (right-side) would be to the insurance expense account to reduce its balance by the amount of the unexpired premiums, so that the account would now be a pure expense account. The insurance expense account would then be closed to the profit and loss summary along with all the other expense accounts.

To restore the ledger to the pattern regularly followed, the amount transferred to unexpired insurance as an adjustment at the end of the year would, after the ledger had been closed, be transferred back to the insurance expense account. This would then conform to the pattern that all costs for insurance premiums would be accumulated during the year in the insurance expense account.

In the illustrative "T" account ledger (see Exhibit App. 2, *infra*) the "plumbing supplies" account is a mixed account (similar to prepaid insurance) and is included with the asset accounts in the ledger. In entry 14 (see Exhibit App. 4), the expense element was extracted from the account and transferred to the plumbing supplies expense account. The plumbing supplies expense was then closed in entry 20, and its entire balance was transferred to the profit and loss summary account.

7. ILLUSTRATIVE "T" ACCOUNT LEDGER

Before proceeding further, the reader would probably like to see an illustrative set of accounts comprising a ledger. Accordingly, a series of transactions have been detailed below and entered directly into a set of informal "T" accounts of the AB Plumbers, Inc. (see Exhibit App. 2.) Instead of dates, the transactions (or entries) have been numbered. These numbers have also been entered into the "T" accounts to serve as cross references.

1. *A* contributes a truck at an agreed valuation of $5,000 and receives in exchange 500 shares of no-par capital stock of AB Plumbers, Inc.

To record this transaction, the asset account, truck, is debited (left-side) for the increase and capital stock is credited (right-side) to reflect the increase in ownership equity.

2. *B* contributes $5,000 in cash and receives 500 shares of capital stock.

Cash is debited (left-side) for the increase in the asset, and capital stock is credited (right-side) for the increase in ownership equity.

3. Rent is paid, $500.

The rent expense account is debited (left-side) increasing the expense and the cash account is credited (right-side) to decrease the asset. Inasmuch as rent expense is a nominal account, a temporary subdivision of ownership equity, the debit can also be analyzed as a decrease in ownership equity.

4. Plumbing supplies are purchased for cash, $600.

The plumbing supplies account is being treated as an asset and is debited (left-side) to record the increase in supplies. Actually, the plumbing supplies account is a mixed account similar to prepaid insurance (discussed earlier in this Appendix) and it will be adjusted at the end of the period. The credit (right-side) entry records the reduction of the asset cash.

EXHIBIT APP. 2

"T" Account Ledger

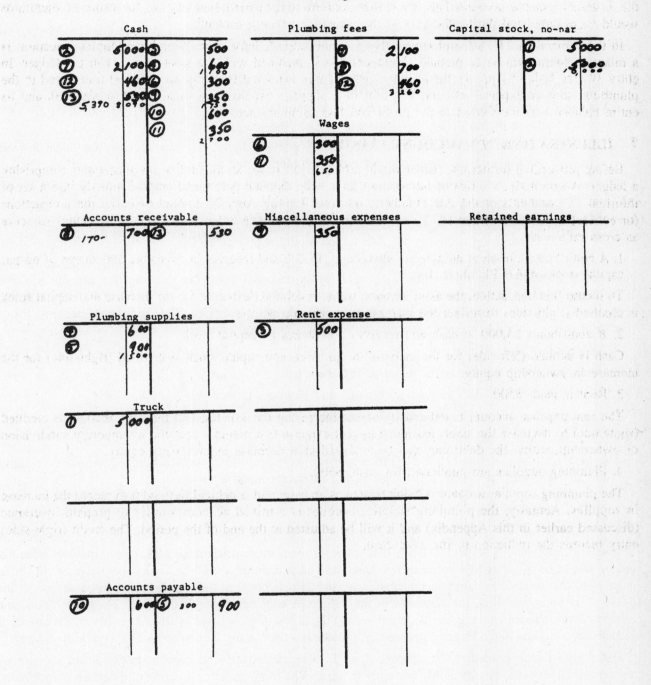

5. Plumbing supplies are purchased on credit, $900.

The debit entry is the same as in entry 4. The credit (right-side) entry to accounts payable records the increase in the liability.

6. Wages are paid, $300.

The debit (left-side) entry to wages records an expense and the credit (right-side) entry reflects the decrease in the asset, cash. As explained in entry 3, the debit to the expense account can be analyzed as a decrease in ownership equity.

7. Plumbing services are provided to clients, and payment is received in cash, $2,100.

Cash is debited (left-side) for the increase in the asset, and plumbing fees are credited (right-side) to record the revenue earned. The plumbing fees account is a nominal account, and the credit (right-side) entry can also be analyzed as an increase in ownership equity.

8. Bills are rendered to clients for plumbing services provided, $700.

A debit (left-side) is made to accounts receivable to record the increase in this asset. The credit (right-side entry is the same as in entry 7).

9. Bills for miscellaneous expenses are paid, $350. (For simplicity, this one account has been utilized to represent a variety of expense accounts normally encountered.)

This entry records the increase in expenses by a debit (left-side) to miscellaneous expenses. The credit (right-side) to cash reflects the decrease in this asset. The analysis of this transaction is similar to that for entries 3 and 6.

10. Payment is made on accounts payable for plumbing supplies, $600.

The debit (left-side) is made to accounts payable to record the decrease in the liability because of this payment. The credit (right-side) records the decrease in the asset cash. The fact that the account payable arose from the purchase of plumbing supplies does not make this entry any different than if the liability being paid had arisen from the purchase of equipment or office supplies. The significant elements are a reduction of the liability, accounts payable, offset by a reduction of the asset cash.

11. Wages are paid, $350.

The analysis for this entry is the same as for entry 6.

12. Plumbing services are provided to clients, and payment is received in cash, $460.

The analysis for this entry is the same as for entry 7.

13. Accounts receivable are collected, $530.

The cash account is debited (left-side) to record the increase in the asset, cash, and accounts receivable is credited (right-side) to record a decrease in the asset, accounts receivable.

8. TRIAL BALANCES

Even though all the accounts in this illustrative "T" account ledger are on a single page, the account balances are not readily apparent. Such perception is even more difficult in a real life situation where a ledger would have a larger number of accounts, and each account would be on a separate page. In order to provide this overview of the account balances and also to confirm that the ledger is in balance, a "trial balance" is taken of all of the accounts in the ledger. A trial balance is a listing of all of the debit and credit account balances in a ledger. In order to do this, a "footing" is taken where necessary of the columns in each account, and balances are computed. A footing is a total at the foot or bottom of a column of figures.

Refer now to the preceding illustration of a "T" account ledger. The regular entries in an account in a handwritten ledger are made in ink, one entry to a line. The footings for calculation of balances are normally written in pencil. They do not constitute entries, and the figures are written in smaller size and do not interfere with the next regular entry which may be made in the account. Such pencil footings have been illustrated on the credit side (right-side) of the cash account. Note the "1,100" after entry 4 representing the total of the credits to that point and "1,750" representing the total of the credits in the cash account through entry 9. For the trial balance to be taken after entry 13, the debit (left-side) footing (total) of the cash account is 8,090 and the credit (right-side) footing is 2,700. There is a debit balance in the cash account of 5,390. That is, the debit total of 8,090 exceeds the credit total of 2,700 by 5,390. This balance is also noted in small pencil figures to the left of the debit column.

The accounts receivable account also has both debit and credit entries, and the debit balance of 170 has been written on the left side. The only other account in this illustrative ledger with both debit and credit entries is accounts payable. The credits in this case exceed the debits so there is a credit (right-side) balance in the account of 300 which has been written in small figures in the open area to the left of the credit money column.

In the accounts for plumbing supplies and for wages, there were debit entries only. The debit (left-side) footings obviously constitute the debit balances, so no further notation was made in these accounts. The accounts for plumbing fees and for capital stock have credit entries only, and in these accounts the credit footings constitute the credit balances.

A trial balance presents a concise overview of the ledger and confirms that the ledger is in balance. The fact that the trial balance debit and credit totals are equal, however, does not confirm that no error has been made. For example, a transaction may have been entirely omitted, or a debit may have been entered as a debit but into the wrong account. A similar error could have been made with a credit entry. None of these errors would have thrown the ledger out of balance. A trial balance normally carries a date, not the date the trial balance is actually written, but the date through which the entries have been recorded. Most commonly, the dates of trial balances are the last days of each month.

The trial balance of the illustrative ledger after entry 13 follows, as Exhibit App. 3.

EXHIBIT APP. 3

Trial Balance

(Date)

Account Title	Debit Balance	Credit Balance
Cash	5,390	
Accounts receivable	170	
Plumbing supplies	1,500	
Truck	5,000	
Accounts payable		300
Plumbing fees		3,260
Wages (expense)	650	
Miscellaneous expenses	350	
Rent expense	500	
Capital stock		10,000
Totals	13,560	13,560

9. ADJUSTING AND CLOSING ENTRIES

At the end of the fiscal year, the ledger will be "adjusted" and then "closed." Adjustments involve formal recording of deferrals and accruals as of the end of the year as well as provision for depreciation and bad debts. Such adjustments have been discussed in Chapter VI. In the simple illustrative ledger for AB Plumbers, there are only the following two adjustments. The entries for these adjustments have been numbered 14 and 15, to follow the sequence of the entries already recorded.

14. The account for plumbing supplies shows a debit (left-side) balance of $1,500. However, a physical inventory of supplies on hand reveals that only $575 of supplies remain on hand.

Subtracting the ending inventory of supplies, $575, from the total of $1,500 of supplies available during the year, leaves $925 as the cost of supplies consumed during the year, which $925 represents an expense. In entry #14, a plumbing supplies expense account has been debited (left-side) to reflect the $925 expense incurred and plumbing supplies, an account treated as an asset, has been credited (right-side) for the decrease in the asset (see Exhibit App. 4). The plumbing supplies account was really a mixed account during the fiscal year, containing both asset and expense. This entry #14 separates the expense from the asset.

15. The cost of the truck has to be allocated over its expected useful life. This is accomplished by setting up depreciation expense for the period. The concept of depreciation has been discussed in Chapter II and the methods of calculation were also discussed in that Chapter. Let us assume that the appropriate amount to be provided for depreciation is $700.

A debit (left-side) for $700 is entered into the account for depreciation expense (see Exhibit App. 4). One might assume that the credit (right-side) should be entered into the account for the asset, truck, to decrease the book value of the asset. However, in order to preserve a clear record of the original cost of this depreciable asset, the credit (right-side) is not entered directly into the account for the truck but is entered into a separate "contra account"[6] or "valuation account" entitled "allowance for depreciation" (or "accumulated depreciation"). The balance in an asset valuation account is applied against the cost of the asset to arrive at remaining asset value. Thus, in the truck account, the record has been preserved of the original $5,000 cost of the truck to AB Plumbers. And, in the allowance for depreciation account, one finds the portion of the asset amount which has been charged off as depreciation. At the end of the first year, the accumulated depreciation is $700, and the book value of the truck is $4,300 (5,000 − 700.)

The depreciation expense account is a nominal account, the balance of which will be transferred to the profit and loss summary when the books are closed. The allowance for depreciation account, however, is a real account with a credit (right-side) balance which is to be used to arrive at the book value of the truck. If another $700 is set up as depreciation for the second year, the allowance for depreciation would then increase to $1,400, and the remaining book value would then be $3,600 (5,000 − 1,400).

The "T" account ledger after entries 14 and 15 appears in Exhibit App. 4.

---

[6] For a brief discussion of contra accounts, see Chapter II, Section G, *supra*.

EXHIBIT APP. 4

"T" Account Legder

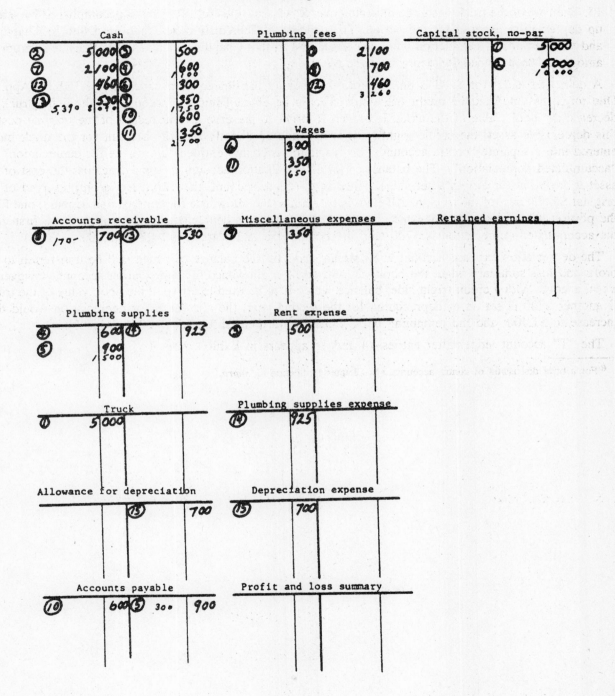

The closing entries involve the transfer of the balances in the various nominal accounts to the profit and loss summary and are illustrated in Exhibit App. 5. The revenue from plumbing fees is transferred in entry #16. The plumbing fees account carries a credit (right-side) balance. To accomplish the transfer, this revenue account is debited (left-side) for the full balance of the account and the profit and loss summary is credited (right-side). The revenue element has now been transferred to the profit and loss summary, and the balance in the plumbing fees account has been reduced to zero.

There are five expense accounts. The balances are transferred in entries 17 through 21. In entry 22, the $135 net income for the period is transferred to the retained earnings account. Lines are then drawn ("rulings") where there is more than one entry in an account. In the case of a nominal account, the rulings indicate that it has been closed. In the case of a real account, the rulings indicate that it has been balanced. Where there is more than a single debit or more than a single credit, the formal ruling and balancing process includes insertions of totals. In the case of real accounts, the ending balances are inserted on one side to bring the debit and credit totals into equality and then are inserted on the opposite side, after the totals have been inserted to be carried forward into the next fiscal year. The insertion of totals and of balances, it should be noted, does not constitute making entries. It is merely part of the formal closing of the books.

The "T" account ledger after all formal rulings appears in Exhibit App. 5.

EXHIBIT APP. 5

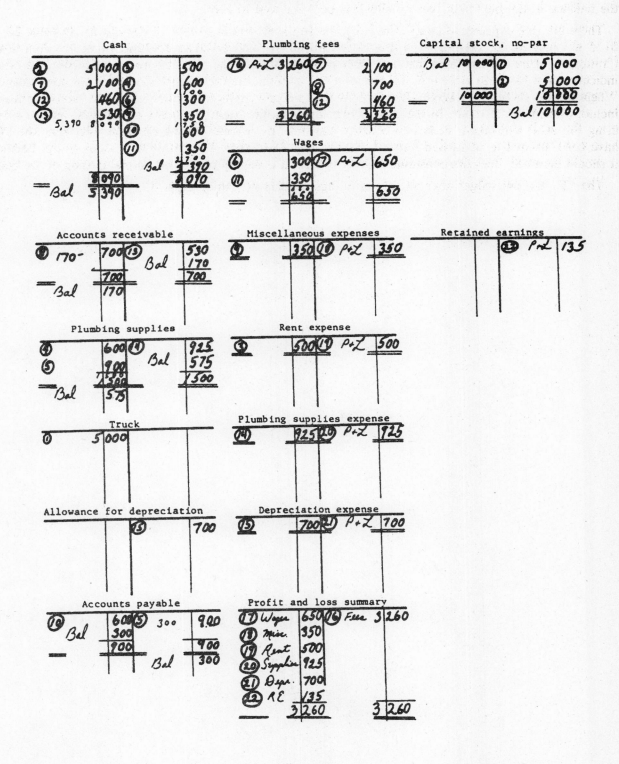

A "post closing trial balance," that is a trial balance of the ledger after the books have been closed, appears as Exhibit App. 6.

EXHIBIT APP. 6

Post Closing

Trial Balance
(date)

Account Title	Debit Balance	Credit Balance
Cash	5,390	
Accounts receivable	170	
Plumbing supplies	575	
Truck	5,000	
Allowance for depreciation		700
Accounts payable		300
Capital stock		10,000
Retained earnings		135
Totals	11,135	11,135

In a computerized system it is necessary to prepare and post closing journal entries. Upon instruction, the computer will transfer all nominal account balances to the retained earnings account. It should be noted, however, that before the closing transfers are made, the financial statements will have been printed by the computer.

10. SUMMARY OF THE ACCOUNTING SEQUENCE

Discussion to this point has been in terms of accounts, ledgers, and debits and credits. There are, however, other significant elements involved in the accounting mechanism. Data for entry of transactions is derived from various basic documents. This data provides the basis for the debit and credit consequences of the transaction.

The sequence of procedures involved in the accounting mechanism is that an entry based upon this data is made into a journal. Subsequently, the entries made in the journal are "posted" or transferred to the ledger. From time to time, a "trial balance" will be taken of the ledger to confirm that it is in balance and also to provide an overview of the account balances. Interim statements can be prepared during the year utilizing a trial balance as a starting point. At the end of the year, the ledger will be closed. That is, the nominal accounts will be closed and the real accounts balanced. Commonly this is referred to as "closing the books." Entries for the following year can then be made in the same ledger, although many businesses prefer to start a fresh ledger every year.

The various items in the foregoing summary have already been or will be explained in the following pages. Explanation will also be provided about additional items, such as merchandising accounts, controlling accounts and subsidiary ledgers.

11. BASIC DOCUMENTS

Transactions are evidenced by a variety of records and documents which provide the basic data for the accounting entries. These source documents include purchase invoices, sales invoices, cash register tapes, checks received, deposit slips, record of checks paid, various memoranda and sometimes legal documents, such as a contract or a statement of closing. As a rule, these documents are filed in some systematic manner and are retained for various lengths of time, sometimes for many years.

12. JOURNALS

Entries are not, as a rule, made directly from the source documents to the ledger.[7] As already stated, documents are filed and are saved for varying periods of time. However, they are sometimes quite voluminous. Purchase invoices, for example, may have attached copies of purchase orders as well as originals of receiving tallies and inspection reports. Documents also come in a variety of sizes, shapes and formats and would not generally serve as a reliable "book of original entry."

The book of original entry is the "journal." Although a business with only a small number of entries in the course of a year could function with only a single journal, modern businesses, in order to operate efficiently, require a number of different and specialized journals, each of which constitutes a book of original entry.

Transactions are entered chronologically into a journal in a format which establishes the debits and credits arising out of the transaction. There are specialized or "special" journals, each with a different format, designed specifically to record cash receipts, cash disbursements, purchases, and sales. These special journals are often referred to as the "cash receipts book," the "cash disbursements (or cash payments) book," the "purchases book," and the "sales book." Entries that cannot be made in a special journal are made in the "general journal."

A computerized system may utilize three programs: accounts receivable, accounts payable, and general ledger. Both sales and cash receipts would be entered through the accounts receivable program. Purchases and cash disbursements would be recorded by means of the accounts payable program. General journal entries would be recorded within the general ledger program.

Illustration of general journal format

A common format of the general journal is presented below with several illustrative entries. Bear in mind, however, that in an actual business all of these illustrative entries, except perhaps the opening entry at the inception of the business, would have been made in special journals. The format of a general journal entry, however, is often utilized in accounting analyses, and is illustrated in Exhibit App. 7.

---

[7] In some sophisticated electronic accounting systems, however, the punching of a cash register could conceivably actuate an entry into an electronic ledger. Another variation can be cited, applicable to a handwritten system, in which a posting may be made directly from a carbon copy of a sales invoice to an account in a subsidiary accounts receivable ledger.

EXHIBIT APP. 7

General Journal

	Debit	Credit
Cash	2,000	
Smart, capital		1,000
Smith, capital		1,000

      To record capital investments
of A. Smart and B. Smith to the firm
of Smart and Smith, Attorneys.

	Debit	Credit
Rent expense	400	
Cash		400

      To record payment of office
rent. (This entry, but in different
format, would have been made in the
cash disbursements journal.)

	Debit	Credit
Cash	700	
Income from fees		700

      To record fee received from
W. Jones for services rendered.
(This entry would actually have been
made in the cash receipts journal.)

Special journals and posting

The original accounting entry is recorded in chronological order into one of several journals. These entries have to be entered in or "posted" to the ledger. The special journals are arranged in various specific formats designed to reduce the time involved in making repetitive original entries and in posting these entries to the ledger. There are likely to be several columns in a special journal, so that a journal entry can be made entirely on a single line. Rather than posting each entry separately, the columns in the special journal will be totaled monthly, and the postings will be made from these column totals. The selection and order of the various columns in a special journal depend on such factors as the nature of the business, the types of transactions encountered, and the volume of activity.

A cash disbursements journal has been illustrated in Exhibit App. 8. Notice the column for check numbers. The first number is 741 and the last is 916. Almost two hundred checks were drawn in the month but only eight have been illustrated in the Exhibit. For convenience the first column of this journal is for credits (right-side) to the cash account, even though it is the left-hand column in this journal. All the other money columns are for debit (left-side) entries to various accounts.

Presumably, there are many checks made during the month for accounts payable and office supplies, as well as several payments for salaries, and special columns have been set up for these payments. Payments not falling into one of the special columns are extended to (entered in) the "sundry" column.

EXHIBIT APP. 8

CASH DISBURSEMENT'S JOURNAL.

Date	Check #	Payee	Amount of check (Cr)	√	Account Payable (Dr)	Payroll (Dr)	Office Supplies (Dr)	Sundry accounts (Dr) Title	Amount
Feb 1	741	Realty Corp.	700					Rent 46	700
	742	Jones Co.	357	√	357				
	743	Cash	510			510			
2	744	Ward's Statnry	95				95		
	745	X Telephone Co.	219					Tel. Exp 47	219
	746	Green Corp	1,516	√	1,516				
8	790	Cash	515			515			
28	916	Goldsmith Bros	49				49		1,927
			15,316		10,559	2,410	420		
			1		21	41	43		

Totaling of the columns permits a great saving in the number of postings. Instead of posting almost 200 separate credits to decrease the cash account for each of the checks drawn during the month (notice the check numbers go from 741 to 916), a single posting can be made for the $15,316 total for all the checks drawn during the month. The notation beneath the total indicates that this $15,316 was posted to account number 1, the cash account.

The many payments during the month on accounts payable totaled $10,559 and were posted in total as a debit to account 21, the accounts payable controlling account, decreasing the liability. (Controlling accounts are explained in the next section of this Appendix. In this connection, the function of the small column containing check marks () and located next to the amounts in the account payable column will be explained.) Similarly, totals for payroll and for office supplies have been posted to these expense accounts as debits (left-side), increasing the respective expenses. The items in the sundry column are each posted separately as debits to the expense accounts indicated. If no errors have been made, the totals of all the debit columns in this journal will be exactly equal to the single credit column. Consequently, the total debit postings to the ledger will be equal to the single credit posting to the cash account.

13. CONTROLLING ACCOUNTS AND SUBSIDIARY LEDGERS

Earlier references in this text to the account in the ledger for accounts receivable and to the account for accounts payable did not take cognizance of the number of different customers or vendors for whom separate accounts receivable or accounts payable would have to be maintained. Generally, a business will deal with a number of different vendors, sometimes only a dozen but, in other cases, well over a hundred. As for customers to whom a business sells on credit, again there may be only a dozen, but most commonly there are many more, sometimes several thousand or even more. Separate accounts are required for each customer and vendor.[8]

It is not feasible to work with a general ledger containing very many accounts. The larger the number of accounts, the more difficult and time-consuming it is, as a rule, to locate an error when a ledger proves to be out of balance. With a large number of postings required for a large number of accounts, it may not be possible for a single individual to perform all of the required work to post all of the entries and to summarize the account balances.

Accordingly, the accounting mechanism is designed so that the number of accounts in a general ledger can be reduced by use of "controlling accounts." A controlling account summarizes all of the entries made to a group of accounts of the same type. Entries for accounts receivable, for example, will be posted to the individual account records maintained for each customer. These individual accounts, collectively, constitute a "subsidiary ledger." This subsidiary ledger is "controlled" (represented) by the single account in the general ledger, generally entitled "accounts receivable," although a more complete title would be "accounts receivable control."

During the course of a month, each sales invoice is posted from the sales journal as a debit (left-side) to a specific customer's account in the subsidiary accounts receivable ledger. At the end of the month, a total is drawn from the sales journal of all such individual postings, and this total is posted as a single figure for the month to the accounts receivable control in the general ledger. Thus, all of the individual debit entries for sales during the month posted to the different customer accounts in the subsidiary accounts receivable ledger are duplicated in summary by the single debit to the accounts receivable control in the general ledger.

---

[8] In some accounting systems, a voucher system is employed for the payables". In such case, there would not be an account for each vendor. Instead, each purchase invoice would be treated as a separate liability, and the records would be maintained to reveal which invoices had been paid and which remained unpaid. With a voucher system, the purchases journal is replaced by a voucher register and the cash disbursements journal is usually reduced to a listing of checks issued in payment of vouchers already recorded.

Computer accounting programs generally include a voucher register.

A similar technique is applied to cash receipts listed in the cash receipts journal. Receipts are posted in detail as credits (right-side) to accounts receivable in the subsidiary ledger and in total for the month to the accounts receivable control in the general ledger.

For the most part, accounts payable are also handled through a controlling account in the general ledger supported by an accounts payable subsidiary ledger. Postings to the subsidiary ledger for purchases would be made as credits (right-side) to the various vendors' accounts. The source of these individual credits would be the individual entries in the purchases journal. At the end of the month, a summary posting would be made as a credit (right-side) to the accounts payable control in the general ledger.

Postings for payments on accounts payable would be made from the cash disbursements journal. Referring back to the sketch of a cash disbursements journal in the preceding section of this Appendix (Exhibit App. 8), the total debited (left-side) to the accounts payable control (account 21) for the month came to $10,559. Payments to vendors were individually posted during the month to the separate accounts maintained for each vendor in the subsidiary accounts payable ledger. Accounts in handwritten accounts payable and accounts receivable subsidiary ledgers are usually maintained in alphabetical order and are not assigned page or account numbers.[9] The check marks in the small column to the left of the amount in the accounts payable column indicates that these individual postings to appropriate ledger accounts were made.

In a large enterprise, it is likely that a sizeable proportion of the accounts in the general ledger will actually be controlling accounts, each one supported by a separate subsidiary ledger. With a large number of different pieces of equipment, for example, the detailed records would constitute a subsidiary ledger (sometimes termed "equipment register") while the single "equipment" account in the general ledger would constitute a control. The capital stock account also is a controlling account, supported by the detail in a stockholder's ledger. Even the cash account might be a controlling account in a general ledger of an enterprise with a number of different bank accounts.

14. MERCHANDISING ACCOUNTS

Periodic contrasted with perpetual inventory

To simplify the presentation of the basic accounting concepts, the illustrative transactions in Chapter I of purchases and sales of merchandise were presented on the assumption that "perpetual inventories" were maintained — that is, records were maintained to keep track on a continuous basis of the number of units of merchandise received and the cost of these units, the units and cost of merchandise sold, and the units and cost of merchandise remaining on hand. As we discussed in Chapter II, Section H, that type of record keeping is not always possible, especially when large numbers of inventory units are involved. Commonly, entries will be made only periodically to reflect cost of sales and dollar amounts of inventory. Such entries can be made only annually but may be made quarterly or even monthly.

Records may be kept on a continuous basis in terms of physical units only, with dollar entries made only periodically.

When inventories are entered on a periodic basis, the merchandise inventory account represents the amount of inventory at the beginning of the period. It does not take into account subsequent increases and decreases during the period. In contrast, under a perpetual inventory system, increases and decreases in inventory during the period are entered directly into the merchandise inventory account.

Merchandising accounts and illustrative entries

Merchandising accounts include accounts that record inventory, purchases, sales, and cost of sales. The entries in the merchandising accounts are different under the periodic inventory method from the entries under the perpetual inventory method. These differences are explained by means of the following series of illustrative transactions, together with entries into comparative sets of "T" accounts (Exhibit App. 9).

Beginning inventory. Assume there are two companies with identical merchandising transactions. The company employing the periodic inventory methods we will call the Periodic Company. The other company,

---

[9] In electronic systems, customers and vendors may be assigned account numbers rather than being listed in alphabetical order.

(Matthew Bender & Co., Inc.)

employing a perpetual inventory method, we will call the Perpetual Company. At the beginning of the fiscal period, the only account in the group of merchandising accounts carrying a balance is the merchandise inventory account. At this beginning point, both of the inventory accounts carry an identical debit (left-side) balance, which we will assume is $20,000. To simplify reference to the entries into the "T" accounts, this beginning inventory has been identified as item number 1.

Purchases. Each company makes purchases of merchandise during the year. Three transactions suffice for illustrative purposes: $9,000, $6,300 and $8,500 identified as items 2, 3 and 4.) The Perpetual Company will debit (left-side) these entries to merchandise inventory to record increases in this asset account. The credits (right-side) would be to accounts payable to record the increases in the liabilities.

The Periodic Company, however, is not in a position to maintain a continuous record of the amount of merchandise inventory. Any entry at all in the inventory account during the year would be misleading. Accordingly, a separate temporary account is set up to record purchases. The three purchases are entered into the purchases account as debits (left-side). The purchases account does not constitute an asset account but it is a temporary account measuring additions to the asset merchandise inventory by purchases made in the course of the fiscal period. Accordingly, these entries can be viewed as increases in assets. Alternatively, inasmuch as the merchandise acquired through these purchases will probably in large measure be sold and delivered to customers and thus constitute part of the cost of sales, one may view the purchases account as something similar to an expense account representing a decrease in ownership equity. Combining both approaches, the purchases account can be perceived as a mixed account containing both asset and expense. Regardless of the analytical concept preferred, the three purchases are entered into the purchases account of the Periodic Company as debits (left-side). These debits (left-side) may be viewed as increases in assets or as expenses or as a combination of both. The credits (right-side) in this case, too, would be to accounts payable.

Sales. Again, three transactions will suffice. Assume that sales were made on credit for $6,000, $18,000, and $12,000 (identified as items 5, 6 and 7). For both companies there would be debit (left-side) entries for these transactions to record the increases in accounts receivable. Also, for both of these companies, there would be credit (right-side) entries to a sales account. The sales account is a temporary account to record the gross increases in ownership equity arising from sales. This account is separate from the offsetting decrease in ownership equity arising from the transfer of the merchandise to the customer. This cost aspect of a sale will be treated in the following section, Cost of sales.

It should be noted that the Perpetual Company, by virtue of its perpetual inventory records, can at the time of sale readily determine the cost of the sale. Thus, it could make an entry in the same pattern as illustrated in Chapter I. That is, the single debit (left-side) to accounts receivable could be offset by two credits (right-side), one to reduce inventory for the cost of the goods sold and the other to increase retained earnings, an element of ownership equity, for the gross margin on the sale. Such entry was utilized to emphasize the concept of the basic accounting equation but a more sophisticated approach is applied in actual practice.

Under the elementary conceptual approach, there was no account in which one could find the figure for total sales. In order then to be able to readily ascertain total sales, under the perpetual inventory method as well as under the periodic method, the customary treatment is to make the entire credit (right-side) to the sales account.

Cost of sales (cost of goods sold). While the Periodic Company, knowing its average percentage of mark-up, can estimate the cost of goods applicable to any given sale, it serves no useful purpose to make such estimate for each sale. The actual cost of sales will be determined as explained below when the physical inventory is taken.

The Perpetual Company, on the other hand, keeps track on a continuous basis of inventory on hand and can readily determine the inventory cost applicable to specific sales. Further, since the merchandise inventory account is expected to show the amount of inventory on a continuous basis throughout the fiscal period, it is essential that the cost of merchandise sold be removed from the inventory account.

To contrast the two methods, then, the Periodic Company makes no entry at the time of sale to set up the cost of sale. The Perpetual Company, however, debits (left-side) a cost of sales account to record the decrease in ownership equity because of the cost or expense of giving up the merchandise sold to the customer. The offsetting credit (right-side) reduces the asset merchandise inventory. In order to illustrate by specific entries in the illustrative set of "T" accounts, we will assume that the costs of the merchandise applicable to the three sales were $3,900, $11,800, and $8,300 (entries 8, 9 and 10.) These amounts are posted during the year to both the cost of sales account of the Perpetual Company and to its inventory account.

Comparative sets of "T" accounts with entries through number 10 are shown in Exhibit App. 9.

Exhibit App. 9

Periodic Company	Perpetual Company

Merchandise inventory (Periodic)

Ⓛ 20 000	

Merchandise inventory (Perpetual)

① 20 000	⑧ 3 900
② 9 000	⑨ 11 800
③ 6 300	⑩ 8 300
④ 8 500	24 000
19,800 43 800	

Purchases (of merchandise) (Periodic)

② 9 000	
③ 6 300	
④ 8 500	
23 800	

Sales (Periodic)

	⑤ 6 000
	⑥ 18 000
	⑦ 12 000
	36 000

Sales (Perpetual)

	⑤ 6 000
	⑥ 18 000
	⑦ 12 000
	36 000

Cost of sales (Perpetual)

⑧ 3 900	
⑨ 11 800	
⑩ 8 300	
24 000	

Profit and loss summary (Periodic)

Profit and loss summary (Perpetual)

Cost of sales for a company employing the periodic inventory method is developed in the adjusting and summarizing entries at the end of the fiscal period. This will be demonstrated in a later section. At this point, however, it is pertinent to point out that cost of sales under the periodic inventory method is determined by adding the purchases to the beginning inventory in order to arrive at the cost of goods available for sale. Then, by subtracting the final inventory, one arrives at the cost of the goods that were sold.

Physical inventory and inventory discrepancies. Under the periodic inventory method, inventories can be computed by estimating the cost of sales based on prior experience and rate of mark-up. However, there is one further aspect of merchandise costs to be considered, inventory discrepancies. Even where a perpetual inventory has been maintained, it is expected that, at least annually, a physical inventory will be taken to determine the validity of the book inventory. Rarely is there not some discrepancy.

Discrepancies arise from errors in entries, errors in calculation of dollar amounts, and errors in counting that may occur with respect to both receipts and issuance of merchandise. In these respects, there may be both overages and underages. However, there are also likely to be shortages arising from loss through thefts and, depending on the nature of the merchandise, from discard because of spoilage, breakage and defects. Further, in terms of monetary valuation, inventory values may be marked down because items become shopworn or otherwise unsalable at regular prices. Normally, one expects there to be a net shortage arising from these discrepancies and losses and reductions in value.

As a matter of fact, the physical count of inventory may, in itself, contain errors. Assuming, however, an inventory count and calculation that appear to be reasonably accurate, the perpetual inventory records have to be adjusted to recognize inventory shortages and overages.

Under the periodic inventory method, these inventory discrepancies do not show up separately. What we term cost of sales or cost of merchandise sold also generally includes losses from theft of merchandise, inventory writedowns, and the net effect of other shortages and overages of inventory.

Adjusting and summarizing entries. Let us assume that after the actual physical inventory at the end of the year has been counted and priced, we find the ending inventory totals $19,400.

Among the entries that are made at the end of the period to adjust and close the books, the Periodic Company transfers the beginning inventory to the cost of sales in entry 11. (Entries 11-14 are shown on Exhibit App. 10.) It then transfers the total cost of purchases to the cost of sales account, $23,800 (entry 12.) The cost of sales now shows a total cost of goods that were available for sale during the course of the year of $43,800. However, there is an ending inventory of $19,400 which was not sold and must be transferred back to the merchandise inventory account to set up the correct amount in this asset account as of the end of the current fiscal year and then must be carried over to the beginning of the following fiscal year. In entry 13, the merchandise inventory account is debited (left side) to reflect the amount of the asset, and the cost of sales is credited (right-side) to reduce the cost or expense to be shown for the current fiscal year. The cost of sales for Periodic Company now remains with a balance of $24,400, which will later be transferred to the profit and loss summary account.

As for the Perpetual Company, its merchandise inventory account shows a balance of $19,800, and its cost of sales totals $24,000. The physical inventory, however, discloses net shortages aggregating $400. Entry 14 debits (left-side) this amount to cost of sales to increase this cost or expense for the period and credits (right-side) $400 to inventory to reduce it to $19,400 as computed by actual physical inventory.

The comparative merchandising "T" accounts with entries through 14 are illustrated in Exhibit App. 10.

EXHIBIT APP. 10

Comparative Merchandising "T" Accounts

Periodic Company   Perpetual Company

Merchandise inventory

①	20,000	⑪	20,000
⑬	19,400		

Merchandise inventory

①	20,000	⑧	3,900
②	9,000	⑨	11,800
③	6,300	⑩	8,300
④	8,500	⑭	24,000
	19,400 43,900		24,400

Purchases (of merchandise)

②	9,000	⑫	23,800
③	6,300		
④	8,500		
	23,800		

Sales

		⑤	6,000
		⑥	18,000
		⑦	12,000
			36,000

Sales

		⑤	6,000
		⑥	18,000
		⑦	12,000
			36,000

Cost of sales

⑪	20,000	⑬	19,400
⑫	23,800		
	24,400 43,800		

Cost of sales

⑧	3,900		
⑨	11,800		
⑩	8,300		
⑭	24,000		
	24,400		

Profit and loss summary

Profit and loss summary

The entries to close the sales and cost of sales accounts and to transfer their balances to the profit and loss summary are identical for both companies (see Exhibit App. 11). The sales account is closed with entry #15, and the cost of sales account, with entry #16 (see Exhibit App. 11). The gross margin for each company is now reflected in the profit and loss summary as $11,600.

For completeness of presentation, the several temporary accounts have been totaled and ruled off when closed, and the inventory account has been balanced. The "T" accounts after closing and balancing are shown in Exhibit App. 11.

EXHIBIT APP. 11

Comparative Merchandising "T" Accounts

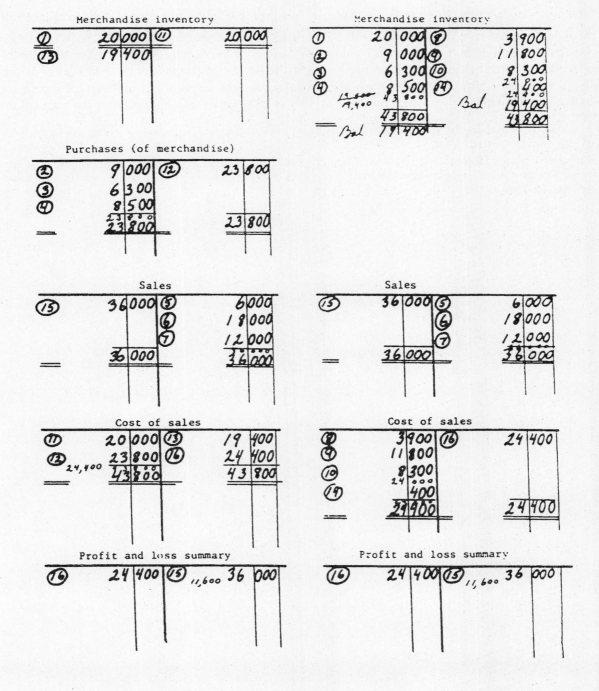

15. PREPARATION OF FINANCIAL STATEMENTS

Annual financial statements can be prepared from the data in the general ledger after the accounts have been adjusted. However, it usually is more convenient to prepare the financial statements by means of a work sheet procedure. Under this procedure, the trial balance at the end of the period is entered into a specially devised multi-column work sheet form. Adjustments are then also entered in this form. The figures of the trial balance and of the adjustments are then combined by addition or subtraction, as appropriate, to arrive at the account balances applicable to the financial statements. The balances of the real accounts provide the data for the balance sheet, and the balances of the nominal accounts provide the data for the income statement.

Interim statements, monthly or quarterly, for example, can be prepared by similar work sheet techniques.[10]

The accounting mechanism is concerned with the recording of financial transactions in such a manner as to provide the data required for financial statements. Although the accounting mechanism discussion has been presented in this Appendix, these mechanics, in some regards, represent the foundation of the accounting process, for it is by these means that the financial statements are prepared. However, to appreciate the superstructure of a building, one does not have to fully comprehend the composition of the foundation.

---

[10] Some accounting systems are designed to utilize monthly adjustments so that data for interim statements can routinely be obtained directly from the general ledger.

Computer programs greatly facilitate the preparation of financial statements. Although a work sheet format is available, it may not be utilized. With appropriate adjustments entered into the computer, monthly, quarterly or annual statements can be obtained as computer printouts.

APPENDIX B

PORTION OF FINANCIAL STATEMENTS FROM 1997 ANNUAL REPORT OF THE H.J. HEINZ COMPANY

CONSOLIDATED STATEMENTS OF INCOME AND RETAINED EARNINGS
H.J. Heinz Company and Subsidiaries

Fiscal Year Ended	April 30, 1997	May 1, 1996	May 3, 1995
(Dollars in thousands, except per share data)	(52 weeks)	(52 weeks)	(53 weeks)
CONSOLIDATED STATEMENTS OF INCOME:			
Sales	$9,357,007	$9,112,265	$8,086,794
Cost of products sold	6,385,091	5,775,357	5,119,597
Gross profit	2,971,916	3,336,908	2,967,197
Selling, general and administrative expenses	2,215,645	2,049,336	1,811,388
Operating income	756,271	1,287,572	1,155,809
Interest income	39,359	44,824	36,566
Interest expense	274,746	277,411	210,585
Other expense, net	41,820	31,324	43,783
Income before income taxes	479,064	1,023,661	938,007
Provision for income taxes	177,193	364,342	346,982
Net income	$ 301,871	$ 659,319	$ 591,025
CONSOLIDATED STATEMENTS OF RETAINED EARNINGS:			
Amount at beginning of year	$4,156,380	$3,878,988	$3,633,385
Net income	301,871	659,319	591,025
Cash dividends:			
Common stock	416,923	381,871	345,358
Preferred stock	43	56	64
Amount at end of year	$4,041,285	$4,156,380	$3,878,988
PER COMMON SHARE AMOUNTS:			
Net income	$ 0.81	$ 1.75	$ 1.59
Cash dividends	$ 1.13½	$ 1.03½	$ 0.94
Average shares for earnings per share	373,703,246	377,155,837	372,806,306

See Notes to Consolidated Financial Statements.

CONSOLIDATED BALANCE SHEETS

H.J. Heinz Company and Subsidiaries

Assets (Dollars in thousands)	April 30, 1997	May 1, 1996
CURRENT ASSETS:		
Cash and cash equivalents	$ 156,986	$ 90,064
Short-term investments, at cost which approximates market	31,451	18,316
Receivables (net of allowances: 1997 – $18,934 and 1996 – $17,298)	1,118,874	1,207,874
Inventories:		
Finished goods and work-in-process	1,040,104	1,115,367
Packaging material and ingredients	392,407	378,596
	1,432,511	1,493,963
Prepaid expenses	208,246	221,669
Other current assets	65,038	14,806
Total current assets	3,013,106	3,046,692
PROPERTY, PLANT AND EQUIPMENT:		
Land	55,992	62,243
Buildings and leasehold improvements	871,417	824,308
Equipment, furniture and other	3,453,189	3,333,493
	4,380,598	4,220,044
Less accumulated depreciation	1,901,378	1,603,216
Total property, plant and equipment, net	2,479,220	2,616,828
OTHER NON-CURRENT ASSETS:		
Goodwill (net of amortization: 1997 – $259,019 and 1996 – $211,693)	1,803,552	1,737,478
Other intangibles (net of amortization: 1997 – $163,232 and 1996 – $141,886)	627,096	649,048
Other non-current assets	514,813	573,645
Total other non-current assets	2,945,461	2,960,171
Total assets	$8,437,787	$8,623,691

See Notes to Consolidated Financial Statements.

Liabilities and Shareholders' Equity (Dollars in thousands)	April 30, 1997	May 1, 1996
CURRENT LIABILITIES:		
Short-term debt	$ 589,893	$ 994,586
Portion of long-term debt due within one year	573,549	87,583
Accounts payable	865,154	870,337
Salaries and wages	64,836	72,678
Accrued marketing	164,354	146,055
Accrued restructuring costs	210,804	–
Other accrued liabilities	315,662	368,182
Income taxes	96,163	175,701
Total current liabilities	2,880,415	2,715,122
LONG-TERM DEBT AND OTHER LIABILITIES:		
Long-term debt	2,283,993	2,281,659
Deferred income taxes	265,409	319,936
Non-pension postretirement benefits	211,500	209,994
Other	356,049	390,223
Total long-term debt and other liabilities	3,116,951	3,201,812
SHAREHOLDERS' EQUITY:		
Capital stock:		
Third cumulative preferred, $1.70 first series, $10 par value	241	271
Common stock, 431,096,485 shares issued, $.25 par value	107,774	107,774
	108,015	108,045
Additional capital	175,811	154,602
Retained earnings	4,041,285	4,156,380
Cumulative translation adjustments	(210,864)	(155,753)
	4,114,247	4,263,274
Less:		
Treasury shares, at cost (63,912,463 shares at April 30, 1997 and 62,498,417 shares at May 1, 1996)	1,629,501	1,500,866
Unfunded pension obligation	26,962	32,550
Unearned compensation relating to the ESOP	17,363	23,101
Total shareholders' equity	2,440,421	2,706,757
Total liabilities and shareholders' equity	$8,437,787	$8,623,691

CONSOLIDATED STATEMENTS OF CASH FLOWS

H.J. Heinz Company and Subsidiaries

Fiscal Year Ended (Dollars in thousands)	April 30, 1997 (52 weeks)	May 1, 1996 (52 weeks)	May 3, 1995 (53 weeks)
OPERATING ACTIVITIES:			
Net income	$ 301,871	$ 659,319	$ 591,025
Adjustments to reconcile net income to cash provided by operating activities:			
Depreciation	244,388	254,640	238,229
Amortization	96,102	89,169	77,038
Deferred tax (benefit) provision	(33,450)	135,235	134,304
Gain on sale of New Zealand ice cream business and U.K. real estate	(85,282)	–	–
Provision for restructuring	647,200	–	–
Other items, net	(42,527)	(82,198)	(43,680)
Changes in current assets and liabilities, excluding effects of acquisitions and divestitures:			
Receivables	74,445	(222,894)	(77,039)
Inventories	(5,329)	(102,269)	(87,580)
Prepaid expenses and other current assets	5,094	(14,361)	(27,634)
Accounts payable	18,003	126,596	111,361
Accrued liabilities	(182,555)	(114,015)	(72,644)
Income taxes	(162,962)	7,866	(90,874)
Cash provided by operating activities	874,998	737,088	752,506
INVESTING ACTIVITIES:			
Capital expenditures	(377,457)	(334,787)	(341,788)
Acquisitions, net of cash acquired	(208,383)	(156,006)	(1,178,819)
Proceeds from divestitures	165,555	82,061	52,497
Purchases of short-term investments	(1,223,884)	(982,824)	(1,808,327)
Sales and maturities of short-term investments	1,233,919	1,050,971	1,800,992
Investment in tax benefits	139	62,081	14,436
Other items, net	23,798	(11,637)	(12,819)
Cash (used for) investing activities	(386,313)	(290,141)	(1,473,828)
FINANCING ACTIVITIES:			
Proceeds from long-term debt	47,483	4,860	573,689
Payments on long-term debt	(99,176)	(46,791)	(10,209)
Proceeds from (payments on) commercial paper and short-term borrowings	133,732	(39,745)	630,310
Dividends	(416,966)	(381,927)	(345,422)
Purchase of treasury stock	(277,046)	(155,200)	(273,671)
Proceeds from minority interest	–	–	95,400
Exercise of stock options	135,082	95,853	44,263
Other items, net	47,131	52,149	19,047
Cash (used for) provided by financing activities	(429,760)	(470,801)	733,407
Effect of exchange rate changes on cash and cash equivalents	7,997	(10,420)	13,717
Net increase (decrease) in cash and cash equivalents	66,922	(34,274)	25,802
Cash and cash equivalents at beginning of year	90,064	124,338	98,536
Cash and cash equivalents at end of year	$ 156,986	$ 90,064	$ 124,338

See Notes to Consolidated Financial Statements.

NOTES TO CONSOLIDATED FINANCIAL STATEMENTS
H.J. Heinz Company and Subsidiaries

---

1. SIGNIFICANT ACCOUNTING POLICIES

Fiscal Year: H.J. Heinz Company (the "company") operates on a 52-'or 53-week fiscal year ending the Wednesday nearest April 30. However, certain foreign subsidiaries have earlier closing dates to facilitate timely reporting. Fiscal years for the financial statements included herein ended April 30, 1997, May 1, 1996 and May 3, 1995.

Principles of Consolidation: The consolidated financial statements include the accounts of the company and its subsidiaries. All intercompany accounts and transactions were eliminated. Certain prior-year amounts have been reclassified in order to conform with the 1997 presentation.

Use of Estimates: The preparation of financial statements, in conformity with generally accepted accounting principles, requires management to make estimates and assumptions that affect the reported amounts of assets and liabilities, the disclosure of contingent assets and liabilities at the date of the financial statements, and the reported amounts of revenues and expenses during the reporting period. Actual results could differ from these estimates.

Translation of Foreign Currencies: For all significant foreign operations, the functional currency is the local currency. Assets and liabilities of these operations are translated at the exchange rate in effect at each year-end. Income statement accounts are translated at the average rate of exchange prevailing during the year. Translation adjustments arising from the use of differing exchange rates from period to period are included as a component of shareholders' equity. Gains and losses from foreign currency transactions are included in net income for the period.

Cash Equivalents: Cash equivalents are defined as highly liquid investments with original maturities of 90 days or less.

Inventories: Inventories are stated at the lower of cost or market. Cost is determined principally under the average cost method.

Property, Plant and Equipment: Land, buildings and equipment are recorded at cost. For financial reporting purposes, depreciation is provided on the straight-line method over the estimated useful lives of the assets. Accelerated depreciation methods are generally used for income tax purposes. Expenditures for new facilities and improvements that substantially extend the capacity or useful life of an asset are capitalized. Ordinary repairs and maintenance are expensed as incurred. When property is retired or otherwise disposed, the cost and related depreciation are removed from the accounts and any related gains or losses are included in income.

Intangibles: Goodwill and other intangibles arising from acquisitions are being amortized on a straight-line basis over periods not exceeding 40 years. The company regularly reviews the individual components of the balances by evaluating the future cash flows of the businesses to determine the recoverability of the assets and recognizes, on a current basis, any diminution in value.

Long-Lived Assets: On May 2, 1996, the company adopted Statement of Financial Accounting Standard ("SFAS") No. 121, "Accounting for the Impairment of Long-Lived Assets and for Long-Lived Assets to Be Disposed Of." The implementation of this standard did not have a material effect on results of operations or financial position.

Revenue Recognition: The company generally recognizes revenue upon shipment of goods to customers or upon performance of services. However, in certain overseas countries, revenue is recognized upon receipt of the product by the customer.

Advertising Expenses: Advertising costs are generally expensed in the year in which the advertising first takes place.

Income Taxes: Deferred income taxes result primarily from temporary differences between financial and tax reporting. If it is more likely than not that some portion or all of a deferred tax asset will not be realized, a valuation allowance is recognized.

The company has not provided for possible U.S. taxes on the undistributed earnings of foreign subsidiaries that are considered to be reinvested indefinitely. Calculation of the unrecognized deferred tax liability for temporary differences related to these earnings is not practicable. Where it is contemplated that earnings will be remitted, credit for foreign taxes already paid generally will offset applicable U.S. income taxes. In cases where they will not offset U.S. income taxes, appropriate provisions are included in the Consolidated Statements of Income.

Net Income Per Common Share: Net income per common share has been computed by dividing income applicable to common shareholders by the weighted-average number of shares of common stock outstanding and common stock equivalents during the respective years. Fully diluted earnings per share are not significantly different from primary earnings per share and, accordingly, are not presented.

In February 1997, the FASB issued SFAS No. 128, "Earnings Per Share," effective for financial statements issued for periods ending after December 15, 1997. The new standard specifies the computation, presentation and disclosure requirements for earnings per share for entities with publicly held common stock. Since early adoption of the standard is prohibited, pro forma earnings per share amounts computed using the new standard are presented below.

	Fiscal Year Ended		
	1997	*1996*	*1995*
As presented	$0.81	$1.75	$1.59
Pro forma:			
Basic earnings per share	$0.82	$1.79	$1.61
Diluted earnings per share	$0.81	$1.75	$1.59

Stock-Based Employee Compensation Plans: Stock-based compensation is accounted for by using the intrinsic value-based method in accordance with Accounting Principles Board Opinion No. 25, "Accounting for Stock Issued to Employees."

Financial Instruments: The company uses derivative financial instruments for the purpose of hedging currency, price and interest rate exposures which exist as part of ongoing business operations. As a policy, the company does not engage in speculative or leveraged transactions, nor does the company hold or issue financial instruments for trading purposes.

□ *Interest Rate Swap Agreements:* The company may utilize interest rate swap agreements to lower funding costs, to diversify sources of funding or to alter interest rate exposure. Amounts paid or received on interest rate swap agreements are deferred and recognized as adjustments to interest expense. Gains and losses realized upon the settlement of such contracts are deferred and amortized to interest expense over the remaining term of the debt instrument or are recognized immediately if the underlying instrument is settled.

□ *Foreign Currency Contracts:* The company enters into forward, option and swap contracts to hedge transactions denominated in foreign currencies in order to reduce the currency risk associated with fluctuating exchange rates. Such contracts are used primarily to hedge purchases of certain raw materials and finished goods and payments arising from certain intercompany transactions with foreign subsidiaries. Gains and losses are deferred in the cost basis of the underlying transaction.

□ *Commodity Contracts:* In connection with purchasing certain commodities for future manufacturing requirements, the company enters into commodities futures and option contracts, as deemed appropriate, to reduce the effect of price fluctuations. Such contracts are accounted for as hedges, with gains and losses recognized as part of cost of products sold, and generally have a term of less than one year.

The cash flows related to the above financial instruments are classified in the Statements of Cash Flows in a manner consistent with those of the transactions being hedged.

Business Segment Information: Information concerning business segment and geographic data is in Management's Discussion and Analysis.

2. ACQUISITIONS

All of the following acquisitions have been accounted for as purchases and, accordingly, the respective purchase prices have been allocated to the respective assets and liabilities based upon their estimated fair values as of the acquisition date. Operating results of businesses acquired have been included in the Consolidated Statements of Income from the respective acquisition dates forward.

Fiscal 1997: The company acquired the following businesses for a total of $222.6 million, including notes to seller of $14.2 million. The preliminary allocations of the purchase price resulted in goodwill of $144.9 million and other intangible assets of $26.9 million, which will be amortized on a straight-line basis over periods not exceeding 40 years.

On November 4, 1996, the company acquired the assets of the canned beans and pasta business of Nestlé Canada Inc., together with a two-year license to use the Libby's brand. Under the agreement, the company also acquired the trademarks Deep-Browned Beans, Alpha-Getti and Zoodles, among others.

On September 23, 1996, the company acquired substantially all of the pet food businesses of Martin Feed Mills Limited of Elmira, Ontario. Martin produces and markets cat and dog food throughout Canada and also exports to Japan and Europe. Martin sells pet food under the Techni-Cal brand and markets products under the Medi-Cal label through veterinary offices and clinics.

On July 10, 1996, the company acquired Southern Country Foods Limited in Australia, one of the world's largest producers of canned corned beef and meals. During Fiscal 1997, the company also made other smaller acquisitions.

Pro forma results of the company, assuming the Fiscal 1997 acquisitions had been made at the beginning of each period presented, would not be materially different from the results reported.

Fiscal 1996: The company acquired the following businesses for a total of $193.4 million, including notes to sellers of $37.4 million. The allocations of purchase price resulted in goodwill of $128.1 million and other intangibles of $6.6 million, which is being amortized on a straight-line basis over periods not exceeding 40 years.

On March 28, 1996, the company acquired the Nature's Recipe business, which markets a brand of premium specialty pet foods.

On March 6, 1996, the company acquired Earth's Best, Inc., which produces a leading brand of premium, organic baby foods and will complement the company's range of infant cereals, juices and strained and junior foods.

The company acquired a majority interest in PMV/Zabreh, a producer of infant formulas and dairy products located in Zabreh, Moravia, Czech Republic.

The company increased its investment to 97% of Kecskeméti Konzervgyár RT, which produces jarred baby foods and canned vegetable products in Kecskemet, Hungary.

Other small acquisitions were also made during Fiscal 1996, including Fattoria Scaldasole S.p.A., which is a processor of organic foods in Italy; Alimentos Pilar S.A. of Argentina, a leading producer of pet and animal feed; the Craig's brand of jams and dressings in New Zealand; the Mareblu brand of canned tuna, which is sold exclusively in Italy; a majority interest in Indian Ocean Tuna Ltd., located in the Seychelles; and Britwest Ltd., which markets single-serve condiments, beverages and sauces in Britain and France.

Pro forma results of the company, assuming the Fiscal 1996 acquisitions had been made at the beginning of each period presented, would not be materially different from the results reported.

Fiscal 1995: On March 14, 1995, the company completed the acquisition of the North American pet food businesses of The Quaker Oats Company (the "Pet Food Business") for approximately $725 million. The acquisition has significantly strengthened the company's presence in the pet food industry. The funds used to acquire the Pet Food Business were provided primarily through the issuance of privately placed commercial paper.

The allocation of the purchase price has resulted in goodwill of $532.5 million and other intangible assets of $146.2 million. These items are being amortized on a straight-line basis over periods not exceeding 40 years.

The following pro forma information combines the consolidated results of operations as if the acquisition of the Pet Food Business had been consummated as of the beginning of

Fiscal 1995, after including the impact of certain adjustments. Adjustments include (i) the amortization of goodwill and other intangibles; (ii) interest expense related to the acquisition debt; (iii) depreciation on the restated values of property, plant and equipment; and (iv) the related income tax effects.

(Dollars in thousands, except per share amounts)	1995 (Unaudited)
Sales	$8,502,405
Net income	$ 585,803
Net income per share	$ 1.57

In connection with the acquisition of the Pet Food Business, the company established certain opening balance sheet accruals for employee severance and relocation costs (approximately $7 million) and facilities consolidation and closure costs (exit costs of approximately $24 million) based upon a preliminary assessment of such actions to be undertaken. The aforementioned amounts were included in "other accrued liabilities" as of May 3, 1995.

During 1996, management finalized integration plans and made minor adjustments to the opening balance sheet, while approximately $29 million was spent against the established accruals. As of May 1, 1996, remaining accruals were considered adequate for any severance, relocation or exit costs associated with the acquisition.

During 1995, the company also acquired the following other businesses (the "other 1995 acquisitions").

On December 2, 1994, the company acquired The All American Gourmet Company for a purchase price of approximately $200 million. The All American Gourmet Company produces The Budget Gourmet brand of frozen meals and side dishes.

On September 30, 1994, the company acquired the Family Products Division of Glaxo India, Ltd. for a purchase price of approximately $65 million. The Family Products Division, based in Bombay, India, produces a wide range of nutritional drinks, baby food and other consumer products.

On July 22, 1994, the company acquired the Farley's infant foods and adult nutrition business from The Boots Company PLC of Nottingham, England for a total purchase price of approximately $140 million.

On May 16, 1994, the company acquired the Borden Foodservice Group, a unit of Borden, Inc. The group's product range includes a single-serve line of condiments. Other acquisitions during 1995 included Dega, a foodservice products company located in Italy.

The allocation of the purchase prices of the other 1995 acquisitions (excluding the Pet Food Business) has resulted in goodwill of $142.0 million and other intangible assets of $168.3 million, which will be amortized on a straight-line basis over periods not exceeding 40 years.

The company established opening balance sheet accruals for the other 1995 acquisitions for employee severance and relocation costs (approximately $9 million) and facilities consolidation and closure costs (exit costs of approximately $37 million) based upon a preliminary assessment of such actions to be undertaken. These amounts were included in "other accrued liabilities" as of May 3, 1995.

During 1996, accruals for exit costs were reduced by approximately $23 million, resulting in a corresponding reduction to goodwill. This was primarily attributable to not pursuing a course of action that was anticipated at the acquisition date. Also during 1996, approximately $15 million was spent against the accruals established for employee severance and relocation costs, and exit costs. As of May 1, 1996, remaining accruals were considered adequate for any severance, relocation or exit costs associated with the other 1995 acquisitions.

On an unaudited pro forma basis, the sales of the company, as if the acquisition of the Pet Food Business and the other 1995 acquisitions were made as of the beginning of Fiscal 1995, would be $8.7 billion. The results of operations would not be materially different from those reported.

Pro forma results are not necessarily indicative of what actually would have occurred if the acquisitions had been in effect for all of Fiscal 1995. In addition, they are not intended to be a projection of future results and do not reflect any synergies that might be achieved from combined operations.

3. DIVESTITURES

During 1997 and 1996, the company sold several non-strategic businesses. Pro forma results of the company, assuming all of the divestitures had been made at the beginning of each period presented, would not be materially different from the results reported.

In the fourth quarter of Fiscal 1997, the company sold its New Zealand ice cream business to Peters & Brownes Limited of Perth, Australia for approximately $150 million. The pretax gain on the divestiture totaled $72.1 million, or $0.12 per share.

Fiscal 1996 divestitures included: an overseas sweetener business, the *Weight Watchers Magazine* and two regional dry pet food product lines. (See Note 13 to the Consolidated Financial Statements.)

4. RESTRUCTURING CHARGES

Charges related to the company's reorganization and restructuring program ("Project Millennia") were recorded in Fiscal 1997 and were recognized to reflect the closure or divestiture of approximately 25 facilities throughout the world, the net reduction of the global workforce by approximately 2,500 (excluding the businesses or facilities to be sold), and other initiatives involving the exit of certain underperforming businesses and product lines.

Restructuring and related costs recorded in Fiscal 1997 totaled $647.2 million pretax or $1.09 per share. Pretax charges of $477.8 million are classified as cost of products sold and $169.4 million as selling, general and administrative expenses.

The major components of the Fiscal 1997 charges and the remaining accrual balance as of April 30, 1997 were as follows:

(Dollars in millions)	Charge	Amounts Utilized	Accrued Restructuring Costs
Employee termination and severance costs	$164.5	$ (32.1)*	$132.4
Exit costs	158.4	(80.0)	78.4
Non-cash asset write-downs	324.3	(324.3)	–
	$647.2	$(436.4)	$210.8

* Includes $18.9 million in non-cash charges resulting from termination benefit programs.

Asset write-downs consist primarily of fixed asset and other long-term asset impairments that were recorded as a direct result of the company's decision to exit businesses or facilities ($206.8 million). Such assets were written down based on management's estimate of fair value. Write-downs were also recognized for estimated losses from disposals of inventories, packaging materials and other assets related to product line rationalizations and process changes as a direct result of the company's decision to exit businesses or facilities ($117.5 million).

5. INCOME TAXES

The following table summarizes the provision/(benefit) for U.S. federal and U.S. possessions, state and foreign taxes on income.

(Dollars in thousands)	1997	1996	1995
Current:			
U.S. federal and U.S. possessions	$ 67,274	$106,848	$114,819
State	6,458	11,475	19,106
Foreign	136,911	110,784	78,753
	210,643	229,107	212,678
Deferred:			
U.S. federal and U.S. possessions	(38,988)	87,239	47,676
State	(10,763)	10,408	6,897
Foreign	16,301	37,588	79,731
	(33,450)	135,235	134,304
Total tax provision	$177,193	$364,342	$346,982

The tax benefit resulting from adjustments to the beginning-of-the-year valuation allowance, due to a change in circumstances, to recognize the realizability of deferred tax assets in future years totaled $1.1 million in 1997, $12.5 million in 1996 and $3.1 million in 1995. The 1996 tax provision was reduced by $24.9 million due to the recognition of foreign tax losses. Tax expense resulting from allocating certain tax benefits directly to additional capital totaled $33.8 million in 1997 and $41.7 million in 1996.

The components of income before income taxes consist of the following:

(Dollars in thousands)	1997	1996	1995
Domestic	$ (47,219)	$ 500,034	$495,159
Foreign	526,283	523,627	442,848
	$479,064	$1,023,661	$938,007

The differences between the U.S. federal statutory tax rate and the company's consolidated effective tax rate are as follows:

	1997	1996	1995
U.S. federal statutory tax rate	35.0%	35.0%	35.0%
Tax on income of foreign subsidiaries	5.6	2.2	2.6
State income taxes (net of federal benefit)	(0.2)	1.8	2.1
Net valuation allowance	(0.7)	(1.3)	2.2
Tax credits	(2.1)	(0.2)	(2.7)
Earnings repatriation	5.5	1.3	(0.1)
Recognition of foreign tax losses	(0.7)	(2.4)	(0.1)
Tax on income of U.S. possessions subsidiaries	(2.8)	(1.7)	(1.4)
Other	(2.6)	0.9	(0.6)
Effective tax rate	37.0%	35.6%	37.0%

The deferred tax (assets) and deferred tax liabilities recorded on the balance sheets as of April 30, 1997 and May 1, 1996 are as follows:

(Dollars in thousands)	1997	1996
Depreciation/amortization	$ 448,327	$ 420,179
Benefit plans	73,081	69,040
Other	87,223	133,673
	608,631	622,892
Provision for estimated expenses	(188,220)	(45,910)
Operating loss carryforwards	(51,685)	(55,717)
Benefit plans	(100,327)	(122,448)
Tax credit carryforwards	(3,845)	(52,924)
Other	(112,607)	(142,609)
	(456,684)	(419,608)
Valuation allowance	5,459	35,594
Net deferred tax liabilities	$ 157,406	$ 238,878

At the end of 1997, net operating loss carryforwards totaled $121.5 million. Of that amount, $79.6 million expire between 1998 and 2010; the other $41.9 million do not expire. Foreign tax credit carryforwards total $3.8 million and expire through 2001.

The company's consolidated United States income tax returns have been audited by the Internal Revenue Service for all years through 1991.

Undistributed earnings of foreign subsidiaries considered to be reinvested permanently amounted to $2.35 billion at April 30, 1997.

The net change in the valuation allowance for deferred tax assets was a decrease of $30.1 million. The majority of this decrease, $27.0 million, partially offset the charge incurred for earnings repatriation due to the utilization of foreign tax credit carryforwards.

6. DEBT

Short-Term (Dollars in thousands)	1997	1996
Commercial paper	$ 97,008	$685,067
Bank and other borrowings	492,885	309,519
	$589,893	$994,586

On August 29, 1996, the company amended the line of credit agreements that support its domestic commercial paper programs, increasing availability and extending maturity dates. The amended terms provide for one agreement totaling $2.30 billion that expires in September 2001. The previous agreements provided for lines of credit totaling $2.00 billion, of which $1.20 billion was scheduled to expire in September 1996 and $800.0 million was scheduled to expire in September 2000.

At April 30, 1997, the company had $1.35 billion of domestic commercial paper outstanding. Due to the long-term nature of the amended credit agreement, all of the outstanding domestic commercial paper has been classified as long-term debt as of April 30, 1997. As of May 1, 1996, $1.48 billion of domestic commercial paper was outstanding, of which $800.0 million was classified as long-term debt due to the long-term nature of the supporting line of credit agreements. Aggregate domestic commercial paper had a weighted-average interest rate during 1997 of 5.4% and at year-end of 5.6%. In 1996, the weighted-average rate was 5.8% and the rate at year-end was 5.4%.

Total short-term debt had a weighted-average interest rate during 1997 of 7.6% and at year-end of 6.1%. The weighted-average interest rate on short-term debt during 1996 was 6.5% and at year-end was 6.2%.

The company had $850.3 million of other foreign lines of credit available at year-end, principally for overdraft protection.

Long-Term (Dollars in thousands)	Range of Interest	Maturity (Fiscal Year)	1997	1996
United States Dollars:				
Commercial paper	Variable	2002	$1,346,779	$ 800,000
Senior unsecured notes	5.50–6.88%	1998–2003	749,681	749,532
Eurodollar bonds	7.50–8.00	1998–2000	551,423	628,119
Revenue bonds	3.10–11.25	1999–2027	16,121	10,781
Promissory notes	4.00–10.00	1998–2005	49,220	60,154
Other	Variable	1998	7,072	6,797
			2,720,296	2,255,383
Foreign Currencies (U.S. Dollar Equivalents):				
Promissory notes:				
Pounds sterling	8.85%	1998–2006	41,260	51,100
Italian lire	8.50–12.55	1998–2004	28,209	34,487
Australian dollar	7.35	1998–2002	28,323	–
Other	6.95–14.90	1998–2022	39,454	28,272
			137,246	113,859
Total long-term debt			2,857,542	2,369,242
Less portion due within one year			573,549	87,583
			$2,283,993	$2,281,659

The amount of long-term debt that matures in each of the four years succeeding 1998 is: $30.3 million in 1999, $590.4 million in 2000, $19.0 million in 2001 and $1.37 billion in 2002.

On January 5, 1995, the company issued $300.0 million of three-year 8.0% notes in the international capital markets. The proceeds from the notes were utilized to repay domestic commercial paper. The company entered into an interest rate swap agreement that effectively converted the fixed interest rate associated with the notes to a variable rate based on LIBOR. Due to favorable market conditions, the company terminated the interest rate swap agreement and is amortizing the resulting gain over the remaining life of the notes, producing an effective borrowing rate of 7.3%.

In 1993, the company's United Kingdom affiliate privately placed with various banks £125.0 million ($197.0 million) aggregate principal of 8.85% notes due during 2013. In April 1993, an affiliated company paid £70.6 million ($111.3 million) for an interest in the notes. The notes are shown in the balance sheet as a net amount outstanding of £24.9 million ($40.3 million), which will be fully amortized in three years. The effective interest rate was 8.3% at April 30, 1997 and May 1, 1996.

7. SHAREHOLDERS' EQUITY

Capital Stock: The preferred stock outstanding is convertible at a rate of one share of preferred stock into 13.5 shares of common stock. The company can redeem the stock at $28.50 per share.

On April 30, 1997, there were authorized, but unissued, 2,200,000 shares of third cumulative preferred stock for which the series had not been designated.

Employee Stock Ownership Plan (ESOP): The company established an ESOP in 1990 to replace in full or in part the company's cash-matching contributions to the H.J. Heinz Company Employees Retirement and Savings Plan, a 401(k) plan for salaried employees. Matching contributions to the 401(k) plan are based on a percentage of the participants' contributions, subject to certain limitations.

To finance the plan, the ESOP borrowed $50.0 million directly from the company in 1990. The loan is in the form of a 15-year variable-rate interest-bearing note (an average of 5.6%, 5.5% and 5.6% for 1997, 1996 and 1995, respectively) and is included in the company's Consolidated Balance Sheets as unearned compensation. The proceeds of the note were used to purchase 2,366,862 shares of treasury stock from the company at approximately $21.13 per share.

The stock held by the ESOP is released for allocation to the participants' accounts over the term of the loan as company contributions to the ESOP are made. The company contributions are reported as compensation and interest expense. Compensation expense related to the ESOP for 1997, 1996 and 1995 was $3.0 million, $2.3 million and $3.7 million, respectively. Interest expense was $1.1 million, $1.5 million and $1.9 million for 1997, 1996 and 1995, respectively. The company's contributions to the ESOP and the dividends on the company stock held by the ESOP are used to repay loan interest and principal.

The dividends on the company stock held by the ESOP were $2.3 million, $2.1 million and $2.5 million in 1997, 1996 and 1995, respectively.

The ESOP shares outstanding at April 30, 1997 and May 1, 1996, respectively, were as follows: unallocated 711,725 and 958,141; committed-to-be-released 61,724 and 29,553; and allocated 1,156,236 and 1,036,904. Shares held by the ESOP are considered outstanding for purposes of calculating the company's net income per share.

Cumulative Translation Adjustments: Changes in the cumulative translation component of shareholders' equity result principally from translation of financial statements of foreign subsidiaries into U.S. dollars. The reduction in shareholders' equity related to the translation component increased $55.1 million in 1997, decreased $1.4 million in 1996 and decreased $107.0 million in 1995. During 1997, a gain of $13.8 million was transferred from the cumulative translation component of shareholders' equity and included in the determination of net income as a component of the $72.1 million gain recognized as a result of the liquidation of the company's investment in its New Zealand ice cream business. (See Note 3 to the Consolidated Financial Statements.)

Unfunded Pension Obligation: An adjustment for unfunded foreign pension obligations in excess of unamortized prior service costs was recorded, net of tax, as a reduction in shareholders' equity. (See Note 10 to the Consolidated Financial Statements.)

(Amounts in thousands)	Cumulative Preferred Stock Third, $1.70 First Series $10 Par Amount	Common Stock Issued Amount	Issued Shares	In Treasury Amount	In Treasury Shares	Additional Capital Amount
Balance April 27, 1994	$398	$107,774	431,096	$1,239,177	57,540	$134,255
Reacquired	–	–	–	273,671	11,456	–
Conversion of preferred into common stock	(40)	–	–	(976)	(54)	(937)
Stock options exercised, net of shares tendered for payment	–	–	–	(53,305)	(3,035)	(12,264)*
Other, net	–	–	–	(7,843)	(320)	237
Balance May 3, 1995	$358	$107,774	431,096	$1,450,724	65,587	$121,291
Reacquired	–	–	–	155,200	4,806	–
Conversion of preferred into common stock	(87)	–	–	(2,674)	(117)	(2,587)
Stock options exercised, net of shares tendered for payment	–	–	–	(101,751)	(7,747)	35,797*
Other, net	–	–	–	(633)	(31)	101
Balance May 1, 1996	$271	$107,774	431,096	$1,500,866	62,498	$154,602
Reacquired	–	–	–	277,046	7,939	–
Conversion of preferred into common stock	(30)	–	–	(963)	(41)	(932)
Stock options exercised, net of shares tendered for payment	–	–	–	(147,071)	(6,466)	21,946*
Other, net	–	–	–	(377)	(18)	195
Balance April 30, 1997	$241	$107,774	431,096	$1,629,501	63,912	$175,811
Authorized Shares—April 30, 1997	24		600,000			

* *Includes income tax benefit resulting from exercised stock options.*

8. SUPPLEMENTAL CASH FLOWS INFORMATION

(Dollars in thousands)	1997	1996	1995
Cash Paid During The Year For:			
Interest	$310,146	$308,564	$ 210,610
Income taxes	295,008	143,646	251,358
Details of Acquisitions:			
Fair value of assets	$264,560	$269,907	$1,359,028
Liabilities*	56,168	113,697	179,942
Cash paid	208,392	156,210	1,179,086
Less cash acquired	9	204	267
Net cash paid for acquisitions	$208,383	$156,006	$1,178,819

Includes notes to sellers of $14.2 million and $37.4 million in 1997 and 1996, respectively.

9. EMPLOYEES' STOCK OPTION PLANS AND MANAGEMENT INCENTIVE PLANS

Under the company's stock option plans, officers and other key employees may be granted options to purchase shares of the company's common stock. The option price on all outstanding options is equal to the fair market value of the stock at the date of grant. Generally, options are exercisable beginning from three years after date of grant and have a maximum term of 10 years.

The company has adopted the disclosure-only provisions of SFAS No. 123, "Accounting for Stock-Based Compensation." Accordingly, no compensation cost has been recognized for the company's stock option plans. If the company had elected to recognize compensation cost based on the fair value of the options granted at grant date as prescribed by SFAS No. 123, net income and earnings per share would have been reduced to the pro forma amounts indicated below:

(Dollars in thousands, except per share data)	1997	1996
Pro forma net income	$295,605	$658,798
Pro forma net income per common share	$ 0.79	$ 1.75

The pro forma effect on net income for 1997 and 1996 is not representative of the pro forma effect on net income in future years because it does not take into consideration pro forma compensation expense related to grants made prior to 1996.

The weighted-average fair value of options granted was $6.94 per share in 1997 and $6.27 per share in 1996.

The fair value of each option grant is estimated on the date of grant using the Black-Scholes option-pricing model with the following assumptions:

	1997	1996
Dividend yield	3.25%	3.28%
Volatility	17.46%	17.83%
Risk-free interest rate	6.33%	6.03%
Expected term (years)	5.5	5.5

Data regarding the company's stock option plans follows:

	Shares	Weighted-Average Exercise Price Per Share
Shares under option April 27, 1994	42,096,318	$20.55
Options granted	3,568,050	27.36
Options exercised	(3,038,937)	14.60
Options surrendered	(454,500)	24.27
Shares under option May 3, 1995	42,170,931	$21.52
Options granted	2,154,100	32.11
Options exercised	(11,713,653)	18.40
Options surrendered	(115,500)	25.26
Shares under option May 1, 1996	32,495,878	$23.33
Options granted	7,508,500	34.68
Options exercised	(6,466,030)	20.92
Options surrendered	(463,500)	25.87
Shares under option April 30, 1997	33,074,848	$26.34
Options exercisable at:		
May 3, 1995	17,754,381	$18.49
May 1, 1996	12,252,228	21.53
April 30, 1997	18,473,073	22.53

The following summarizes information about shares under option in the respective exercise price ranges at April 30, 1997:

Range of Exercise Price Per Share	Options Outstanding			Options Exercisable	
	Number Outstanding	Weighted-Average Remaining Life (Years)	Weighted-Average Exercise Price Per Share	Number Exercisable	Weighted-Average Exercise Price Per Share
$12.67–22.08	13,178,735	6.09	$21.33	11,905,235	$21.25
23.00–32.13	16,374,113	6.59	27.87	6,482,838	24.64
33.00–42.38	3,522,000	9.66	37.96	85,000	39.73
	33,074,848			18,473,073	

The shares authorized but not granted under the company's stock option plans were 11,316,235 at April 30, 1997 and 3,421,235 at May 1, 1996. Common stock reserved for options totaled 44,391,083 at April 30, 1997 and 35,917,113 at May 1, 1996.

Effective June 12, 1996, the Board of Directors adopted and the shareholders approved a new stock option plan providing for the grant of up to 15.0 million shares of common stock at any time over the next 10 years. In general, the terms of the 1996 plan are similar to the company's other stock option plans.

The company's management incentive plan covers officers and other key employees. Participants may elect to be paid on a current or deferred basis. The aggregate amount of all awards may not exceed certain limits in any year. Compensation under the management incentive plans was approximately $37 million in 1997, $37 million in 1996 and $24 million in 1995.

10. RETIREMENT PLANS

The company maintains retirement plans for the majority of its employees. Current defined benefit plans are provided primarily for domestic union and foreign employees. Benefits are based on years of service and compensation or stated amounts for each year of service. Plan assets are primarily invested in equities and fixed-income securities. The company's funding policy for domestic defined benefit plans is to contribute annually not less than the ERISA minimum funding standards nor more than the maximum amount which can be deducted for federal income tax purposes. Generally, foreign defined benefit plans are funded in amounts sufficient to comply with local regulations and ensure adequate funds to pay benefits to retirees as they become due.

Effective in 1993, the company discontinued future benefit accruals under the defined benefit plans for domestic non-union hourly and salaried employees and expanded its defined contribution plans for these same employees.

The company maintains defined contribution plans for the majority of its domestic non-union hourly and salaried employees. Defined contribution benefits are provided through company contributions that are a percentage of the participant's pay based on age, with the contribution rate increasing with age, and matching contributions based on a percentage of the participant's contributions to the 401(k) portion of the plan. (The company's matching contributions for salaried employees are provided under the ESOP. See Note 7 to the Consolidated Financial Statements.) In addition, certain non-union hourly employees receive supplemental contributions, which are paid at the discretion of the company.

Total pension cost consisted of the following:

(Dollars in thousands)	1997	1996	1995
Defined Benefit Plans:			
Benefits earned during the year	$ 15,583	$ 13,675	$ 14,648
Interest cost on projected benefit obligation	81,620	74,623	66,734
Actual return on plan assets	(149,513)	(200,592)	(26,254)
Net amortization and deferral	64,499	117,461	(56,285)
	12,189	5,167	(1,157)
Defined contribution plans (excluding the ESOP)	23,658	25,946	17,222
Total pension cost	$ 35,847	$ 31,113	$ 16,065

The following table sets forth the combined funded status of the company's principal defined benefit plans at April 30, 1997 and May 1, 1996.

(Dollars in thousands)	Plans for Which Assets Exceed Accumulated Benefits		Plans for Which Accumulated Benefits Exceed Assets	
	1997	1996	1997	1996
Actuarial present value of:				
Accumulated benefit obligation, primarily vested	$ 814,721	$737,026	$193,114	$187,275
Additional obligation for projected compensation increases	32,850	26,725	36,293	27,896
Projected benefit obligation	847,571	763,751	229,407	215,171
Plan assets, at fair value	1,079,148	962,510	149,868	138,505
Projected benefit obligation less than (in excess of) assets	231,577	198,759	(79,539)	(76,666)
Unamortized prior service cost	81,879	71,824	5,067	7,735
Unamortized actuarial (gains) losses, net	(70,324)	(60,439)	66,001	75,944
Unamortized net (assets) at date of adoption	(18,479)	(23,366)	(828)	(1,310)
Additional minimum liability	–	–	(44,870)	(54,472)
Prepaid (accrued) pension costs	$ 224,653	$186,778	$(54,169)	$(48,769)

The adjustment for unfunded foreign pension obligations in excess of the unamortized prior service costs was recorded, net of tax, as a reduction in shareholders' equity of $27.0 million and $32.6 million in 1997 and 1996, respectively. In 1997, the remaining portion of the unfunded obligation was recorded as other long-term assets and deferred taxes in the amounts of $2.1 million and $15.8 million, respectively. In 1996, the remaining portion of the unfunded obligation was recorded as other long-term assets and deferred taxes in the amounts of $2.8 million and $19.1 million, respectively.

The weighted-average rates used for the years ended April 30, 1997, May 1, 1996 and May 3, 1995 in determining the net pension costs and projected benefit obligations for defined benefit plans were as follows:

	1997	1996	1995
Expected rate of return on plan assets	9.6%	9.4%	10.0%
Discount rate	8.2%	8.4%	8.7%
Compensation increase rate	5.2%	5.3%	5.2%

Assumptions for foreign defined benefit plans are developed on a basis consistent with those for U.S. plans, adjusted for prevailing economic conditions.

11. POSTRETIREMENT BENEFITS OTHER THAN PENSIONS AND OTHER POSTEMPLOYMENT BENEFITS

The company and certain of its subsidiaries provide health care and life insurance benefits for retired employees and their eligible dependents. Certain of the company's U.S. and Canadian employees may become eligible for such benefits. In general, postretirement medical coverage is provided for eligible non-union hourly and salaried employees with at least 10 years of service rendered after the age of 45 and certain eligible union employees who retire with an immediate pension benefit. Effective May 1, 1996, retired employees share in the cost of the plan at a rate of 50%. The company currently does not fund these benefit arrangements and may modify plan provisions or terminate plans at its discretion.

Net postretirement costs consisted of the following:

(Dollars in thousands)	1997	1996	1995
Postretirement benefits earned during the year	$ 3,864	$ 2,736	$ 2,700
Interest cost on accumulated postretirement benefit obligation	11,694	13,350	13,249
Net amortization and deferral	(7,014)	(6,583)	(5,165)
Net postretirement benefit costs	$ 8,544	$ 9,503	$10,784

The following table sets forth the combined status of the company's postretirement benefit plans at April 30, 1997 and May 1, 1996.

(Dollars in thousands)	1997	1996
Accumulated postretirement benefit obligation:		
Retirees and spouses	$104,300	$109,006
Employees currently eligible to retire	14,790	21,756
Employees not yet eligible to retire	24,787	31,899
Total accumulated postretirement benefit obligation	143,877	162,661
Unamortized prior service cost	15,346	21,380
Unrecognized net gain	62,277	34,953
Accrued postretirement benefit obligation	221,500	218,994
Current portion, included in other accrued liabilities	10,000	9,000
Non-pension postretirement benefits	$211,500	$209,994

The weighted-average discount rate used in the calculation of the accumulated postretirement benefit obligation and the net postretirement benefit cost was 8.0% in 1997, 8.1% in 1996 and 8.4% in 1995. The assumed annual composite rate of increase in the per capita cost of company-provided health care benefits begins at 9.0% for 1998, gradually decreases to 5.2% by 2007, and remains at that level thereafter. A 1% increase in these health care cost trend rates would cause the accumulated postretirement obligation to increase by $16.9 million, and the aggregate of the service and interest components of 1997 net postretirement benefit costs to increase by $2.6 million.

12. FINANCIAL INSTRUMENTS

Foreign Currency Contracts: As of April 30, 1997 and May 1, 1996, the company held currency swap contracts with an aggregate notional amount of approximately $400 million. These contracts have maturity dates extending from 1998 through 2012. The company also had separate contracts to purchase certain foreign currencies as of April 30, 1997 and May 1, 1996 totaling $598.7 million and $444.8 million, respectively, and to sell certain foreign currencies totaling $62.2 million and $66.5 million, respectively, most of which mature within one year of the respective fiscal year-end. Net unrealized gains and losses associated with the company's foreign currency contracts as of April 30, 1997 and May 1, 1996 were not material.

Commodity Contracts: As of April 30, 1997 and May 1, 1996, the notional values and unrealized gains or losses related to commodity contracts held by the company were not material.

Fair Value of Financial Instruments: The company's significant financial instruments include cash and cash equivalents, short- and long-term investments, short- and long-term debt, interest rate swap agreements, currency exchange agreements and guarantees.

In evaluating the fair value of significant financial instruments, the company generally uses quoted market prices of the same or similar instruments or calculates an estimated fair value on a discounted cash flow basis using the rates available for instruments with the same remaining maturities. As of April 30, 1997 and May 1, 1996, the fair value of financial instruments held by the company approximated the recorded value.

Effective April 28, 1994, the company adopted SFAS No. 115, "Accounting for Certain Investments in Debt and Equity Securities." SFAS No. 115 requires that the carrying value of certain investments be adjusted to their fair value. The adoption of SFAS No. 115 had no effect on the company's financial position or results of operations. The company's investments are considered to be "available-for-sale" securities and are principally debt securities issued by foreign governments.

Concentrations of Credit Risk: Counterparties to currency exchange and interest rate derivatives consist of large major international financial institutions. The company continually monitors its positions and the credit ratings of the counterparties involved and, by policy, limits the amount of credit exposure to any one party. While the company may be exposed to potential losses due to the credit risk of non-performance by these counterparties, losses are not anticipated. Concentrations of credit risk with respect to accounts receivable are limited due to the large number of customers, generally short payment terms, and their dispersion across geographic areas.

13. QUARTERLY RESULTS (UNAUDITED)

(Dollars in thousands, except per share data)	1997 First	Second	Third	Fourth	Total
Sales	$2,208,760	$2,394,058	$2,307,538	$2,446,651	$9,357,007
Gross profit	795,639	847,504	848,289	480,484	2,971,916
Net income (loss)	179,530	177,520	174,387	(229,566)	301,871
Per Common Share Amounts:					
Net income (loss)	$0.48	$0.47	$0.47	$(0.61)	$0.81
Dividends	0.26½	0.29	0.29	0.29	1.13½

(Dollars in thousands, except per share data)	1996 First	Second	Third	Fourth	Total
Sales	$2,094,293	$2,288,277	$2,193,138	$2,536,557	$9,112,265
Gross profit	774,308	822,931	812,308	927,361	3,336,908
Net income	174,469	158,167	156,484	170,199	659,319
Per Common Share Amounts:					
Net income	$0.46	$0.42	$0.42	$0.45	$1.75
Dividends	0.24	0.26½	0.26½	0.26½	1.03½

Third-quarter 1997 results include restructuring and related costs ($0.03 per share), partially offset by a gain on the sale of real estate in the U.K. ($0.02 per share).

Fourth-quarter 1997 results include restructuring and related costs ($1.06 per share). (See Note 4 to the Consolidated Financial Statements.) These charges were partially offset by a gain on the sale of the New Zealand ice cream business ($0.12 per share). (See Note 3 to the Consolidated Financial Statements.)

Fourth-quarter 1996 results include gains related to the sale of the *Weight Watchers Magazine* ($0.02 per share) and the sale of two regional dry pet food product lines ($0.02 per share) and a charge for restructuring costs at certain overseas affiliates ($0.01 per share).

Fourth-quarter 1996 earnings also benefited from a lower effective tax rate resulting from the recognition of tax losses overseas and increased profits from operations in lower tax rate jurisdictions ($0.04 per share). (See Note 5 to the Consolidated Financial Statements.)

14. COMMITMENTS AND CONTINGENCIES

Legal Matters: On December 31, 1992, a food wholesale distributor filed suit against the company and its principal competitors in the U.S. baby food industry. Subsequent to that date, several similar lawsuits were filed in the same court and have been consolidated into a class action suit. The complaints, each of which seeks an injunction and unspecified treble money damages, allege a conspiracy to fix, maintain and stabilize the prices of baby food. Related suits have also been filed in Alabama and California state courts, seeking to represent a class of indirect purchasers of baby food in the respective states. The defendants have filed a motion for summary judgment to which the plaintiffs have filed a response. The company believes all of the suits are without merit and will defend itself vigorously against them. Certain other claims have been filed against the company or its subsidiaries and have not been finally adjudicated. The above-mentioned suits and claims, when finally concluded and determined, in the opinion of management, based upon the information that it presently possesses, will not have a material adverse effect on the company's consolidated financial position or results of operations.

Lease Commitments: Operating lease rentals for warehouse, production and office facilities and equipment amounted to approximately $93.2 million in 1997, $87.1 million in 1996 and $89.5 million in 1995. Future lease payments for non-cancellable operating leases as of April 30, 1997 totaled $276.7 million (1998–$55.6 million, 1999–$44.8 million, 2000–$37.3 million, 2001–$33.0 million, 2002–$26.9 million and thereafter–$79.1 million).

15. ADVERTISING COSTS

Advertising costs for fiscal years 1997, 1996 and 1995 were $346.8 million, $377.8 million and $314.8 million, respectively.

16. SUBSEQUENT EVENTS

On June 30, 1997, the company completed the sale of its frozen foodservice foods business to McCain Foods Limited of New Brunswick, Canada for approximately $500 million. The transaction included the sale of Heinz's Ore-Ida appetizer, pasta and potato foodservice business and the five Ore-Ida plants that manufacture the products. The Ore-Ida foodservice business contributed approximately $525 million in net sales for Fiscal 1997. The sale is not expected to have an adverse effect on the company's results of operations.

On June 30, 1997, the company acquired John West Foods Limited from Unilever. John West Foods Limited, with annual sales of more than $250 million, is the leading brand of canned tuna and fish in the United Kingdom. Based in Liverpool, John West Foods Limited sells its canned fish products throughout Continental Europe and in a number of other international markets. (John West operations in Australia, New Zealand and South Africa are not included in the transaction.)

RESPONSIBILITY STATEMENTS

RESPONSIBILITY FOR FINANCIAL STATEMENTS

Management of H.J. Heinz Company is responsible for the preparation of the financial statements and other information included in this annual report. The financial statements have been prepared in conformity with generally accepted accounting principles, incorporating management's best estimates and judgments, where applicable.

Management believes that the company's internal control systems provide reasonable assurance that assets are safeguarded, transactions are recorded and reported appropriately, and policies are followed. The concept of reasonable assurance recognizes that the cost of a control procedure should not exceed the expected benefits. Management believes that its systems provide this appropriate balance. An important element of the company's control systems is the ongoing program to promote control consciousness throughout the organization. Management's commitment to this program is emphasized through written policies and procedures (including a code of conduct), an effective internal audit function and a qualified financial staff.

The company engages independent public accountants who are responsible for performing an independent audit of the financial statements. Their report, which appears herein, is based on obtaining an understanding of the company's accounting systems and procedures and testing them as they deem necessary.

The company's Audit Committee is composed entirely of outside directors. The Audit Committee meets regularly, and when appropriate separately, with the independent public accountants, the internal auditors and financial management to review the work of each and to satisfy itself that each is discharging its responsibilities properly. Both the independent public accountants and the internal auditors have unrestricted access to the Audit Committee.

REPORT OF INDEPENDENT ACCOUNTANTS

To the Shareholders of
H.J. Heinz Company:

We have audited the accompanying Consolidated Balance Sheets of H.J. Heinz Company and Subsidiaries at April 30, 1997 and May 1, 1996, and the related Consolidated Statements of Income, Retained Earnings and Cash Flows for each of the three years in the period ended April 30, 1997. These financial statements are the responsibility of the company's management. Our responsibility is to express an opinion on these financial statements based on our audits.

We conducted our audits in accordance with generally accepted auditing standards. Those standards require that we plan and perform the audit to obtain reasonable assurance about whether the financial statements are free of material misstatement. An audit includes examining, on a test basis, evidence supporting the amounts and disclosures in the financial statements. An audit also includes assessing the accounting principles used and significant estimates made by management, as well as evaluating the overall financial statement presentation. We believe that our audits provide a reasonable basis for our opinion.

In our opinion, the financial statements referred to above present fairly, in all material respects, the consolidated financial position of H.J. Heinz Company and Subsidiaries at April 30, 1997 and May 1, 1996, and the consolidated results of their operations and their cash flows for each of the three years in the period ended April 30, 1997, in conformity with generally accepted accounting principles.

Coopers & Lybrand L.L.P.

600 Grant Street
Pittsburgh, Pennsylvania
June 17, 1997 except for Note 16,
as to which the date is June 30, 1997

ELEVEN-YEAR SUMMARY OF OPERATIONS AND OTHER RELATED DATA

H.J. Heinz Company and Subsidiaries

(Dollars in thousands, except per share data)	1997	1996	1995	1994
SUMMARY OF OPERATIONS:				
Sales	$9,357,007	$9,112,265	$8,086,794	$7,046,738
Cost of products sold	6,385,091	5,775,357	5,119,597	4,381,745
Interest expense	274,746	277,411	210,585	149,243
Provision for income taxes	177,193	364,342	346,982	319,442
Income before cumulative effect of accounting change	301,871	659,319	591,025	602,944
Cumulative effect of SFAS No. 106 adoption	–	–	–	–
Net income	301,871	659,319	591,025	602,944
Income per common share before cumulative effect				
of accounting change	0.81	1.75	1.59	1.57
Cumulative effect of SFAS No. 106 adoption	–	–	–	–
Net income per common share	0.81	1.75	1.59	1.57
OTHER RELATED DATA:				
Dividends paid:				
Common	416,923	381,871	345,358	325,887
per share	1.13½	1.03½	0.94	0.86
Preferred	43	56	64	71
Average shares for earnings per share	373,703,246	377,155,837	372,806,306	385,218,024
Number of employees	44,700	43,300	42,200	35,700
Capital expenditures	377,457	334,787	341,788	275,052
Depreciation and amortization expense	340,490	343,809	315,267	259,809
Total assets	8,437,787	8,623,691	8,247,188	6,381,146
Total debt	3,447,435	3,363,828	3,401,076	2,166,703
Shareholders' equity	2,440,421	2,706,757	2,472,869	2,338,551
Pretax return on average invested capital	12.6%	21.8%	22.1%	22.7%
Return on average shareholders' equity before				
cumulative effect of accounting change	11.7%	25.5%	24.6%	25.9%
Book value per common share	6.64	7.34	6.76	6.26
Price range of common stock:				
High	44⅞	36⅝	28⅜	26¾
Low	29¾	27⅝	21⅛	20½

The 1997 results include a pretax charge for restructuring and related costs of $647.2 million, offset by capital gains of $85.3 million from the sale of non-strategic assets in New Zealand and the U.K. The 1994 results include a pretax gain of $127.0 million relating to the divestiture of the confectionery and specialty rice businesses. The 1993 results include a pretax restructuring charge of $192.3 million. The 1992 results include a pretax gain of $221.5 million for the sale of The Hubinger Company, a pretax restructuring charge of $88.3 million and a pretax pension curtailment gain of $38.8 million.

	1993	1992	1991	1990	1989	1988	1987
	$7,103,374	$6,581,867	$6,647,118	$6,085,687	$5,800,877	$5,244,230	$4,639,486
	4,530,563	4,102,816	4,063,423	3,726,613	3,550,249	3,212,580	2,858,096
	146,491	134,948	137,592	108,542	77,694	73,995	50,978
	185,838	346,050	335,014	306,979	284,661	236,559	226,070
	529,943	638,295	567,999	504,451	440,230	386,014	338,506
	(133,630)	–	–	–	–	–	–
	396,313	638,295	567,999	504,451	440,230	386,014	338,506
	1.36	1.60	1.42	1.26	1.11	0.97	0.82
	(0.34)	–	–	–	–	–	–
	1.02	1.60	1.42	1.26	1.11	0.97	0.82
	297,009	270,512	239,212	207,387	178,340	154,418	132,278
	0.78	0.70	0.62	0.54	0.46⅓	0.40⅓	0.33
	78	86	91	113	134	155	177
	389,682,692	399,508,683	399,942,926	399,117,144	395,352,102	398,117,835	410,503,998
	37,700	35,500	34,100	37,300	36,200	39,000	37,500
	430,713	331,143	345,334	355,317	323,325	238,265	184,730
	234,935	211,786	196,138	168,523	148,104	133,348	109,868
	6,821,321	5,931,901	4,935,382	4,487,451	4,001,807	3,605,083	3,364,197
	2,613,736	1,902,483	1,226,694	1,256,607	962,321	780,330	876,620
	2,320,996	2,367,398	2,274,863	1,886,899	1,777,238	1,593,856	1,392,949
	18.7%	28.8%	31.3%	31.3%	31.4%	30.0%	29.5%
	22.0%	27.5%	27.3%	27.5%	26.1%	25.8%	24.6%
	6.08	6.21	5.84	4.96	4.61	4.16	3.60
	30⅜	32⅜	27⅜	23⅞	17⅛	17¼	16⅞
	23½	23⅜	19⅝	16⅜	12⅞	11⅛	12¼

APPENDIX C

AMERICAN ACCOUNTING ASSOCIATION ANNUAL REPORT (1996)

AMERICAN ACCOUNTING ASSOCIATION ANNUAL REPORT
INDEPENDENT AUDITORS' REPORT

Executive Committee of the American Accounting Association, Sarasota, Florida

We have audited the accompanying statements of financial position of the American Accounting Association (a not-for-profit organization) as of August 31, 1996 and 1995, and the related statements of activities, functional expenses, and cash flows for the years then ended. These financial statements are the responsibility of the Association's management. Our responsibility is to express an opinion on these financial statements based on our audit.

We conducted our audit in accordance with generally accepted auditing standards. Those standards require that we plan and perform the audit to obtain reasonable assurance about whether the financial statements are free of material misstatement. An audit includes examining, on a test basis, evidence supporting the amounts and disclosures in the financial statements. An audit also includes assessing the accounting principles used and significant estimates made by management, as well as evaluating the overall financial statement presentation. We believe that our audit provides a reasonable basis for our opinion.

In our opinion, the financial statements referred to above present fairly, in all material respects, the financial position of the American Accounting Association as of August 31, 1996 and 1995, and the changes in its net assets and its cash flows for the years then ended in conformity with generally accepted accounting principles.

PARENT, MARLAR, MODRAK & COMPANY
Certified Public Accountants

Bradenton, Florida
October 8, 1996

AMERICAN ACCOUNTING ASSOCIATION
STATEMENTS OF FINANCIAL POSITION
AUGUST 31, 1996 AND 1995

	1996	1995
ASSETS		
Cash and cash equivalents	$1,944,864	$1,371,632
Accounts receivable	116,366	478,210
Interest receivable	8,599	6,357
Pledges receivable—net	606,401	815,848
Publications inventory	74,494	46,385
Prepaids and other assets	23,584	20,960
Property and equipment, less accumulated depreciation	142,915	127,659
TOTAL ASSETS	$2,917,223	$2,867,051
LIABILITIES AND NET ASSETS		
LIABILITIES		
Accounts payable	$233,869	$126,331
Accrued liabilities	16,013	190
Deferred compensation payable	—	4,252
Deferred revenue—dues and subscriptions	608,117	507,522
Total liabilities	857,999	638,295
NET ASSETS		
Unrestricted	1,315,515	1,183,384
Temporarily restricted	743,709	1,045,372
Total net assets	2,059,224	2,228,756
TOTAL LIABILITIES AND NET ASSETS	$2,917,223	$2,867,051

See accompanying notes and Auditors' Report.

AMERICAN ACCOUNTING ASSOCIATION
STATEMENTS OF ACTIVITIES
FOR THE YEARS ENDED AUGUST 31, 1996 AND 1995

	Unrestricted	Temporarily Restricted	Total 1996	Total 1995
SUPPORT AND REVENUE				
Membership dues	$ 797,729	$ —	$ 797,729	$ 762,787
Subscriptions	293,308	—	293,308	316,746
Advertising	54,056	—	54,056	74,353
Publications	82,308	—	82,308	115,740
Contributions	493,222	78,700	571,922	1,544,031
Interest and dividend income	86,172	—	86,172	78,405
Annual meeting	572,646	—	572,646	524,694
Other revenue (primarily from programs and seminars)	519,229	—	519,229	581,299
Net assets released from restrictions	380,363	(380,363)	—	—
Total support and revenue	3,279,033	(301,663)	2,977,370	3,998,055
EXPENSES				
Program services				
Memberships and subscriptions	58,430	—	58,430	61,575
Seminars and conferences	508,121	—	508,121	526,694
Annual meeting	498,025	—	498,025	467,772
Regional meetings	249,964	—	249,964	232,545
Section meetings	191,186	—	191,186	166,761
General publications	490,428	—	490,428	463,714
Section publications	240,735	—	240,735	221,725
Committees and other programs	413,872	—	413,872	860,434
Support services				
Management and general	496,141	—	496,141	590,566
Total expenses	3,146,902	—	3,146,902	3,631,786
CHANGE IN NET ASSETS	132,131	(301,663)	(169,532)	366,269
NET ASSETS AT BEGINNING OF YEAR	1,183,384	1,045,372	2,228,756	1,982,000
PRIOR PERIOD ADJUSTMENTS (NOTE 7)				
Correction of net assets				
Dues	—	—	—	(45,271)
Contributions	—	—	—	(74,242)
NET ASSETS AT BEGINNING OF YEAR AS RESTATED	1,183,384	1,045,372	2,228,756	1,862,487
NET ASSETS AT END OF YEAR	$1,315,515	$ 743,709	$ 2,059,224	$ 2,228,756

See accompanying notes and Auditors' Report.

AMERICAN ACCOUNTING ASSOCIATION
STATEMENTS OF CASH FLOWS
FOR THE YEARS ENDED AUGUST 31, 1996 AND 1995

	1996	1995
CASH FLOWS FROM OPERATING ACTIVITIES		
Change in net assets	$ (169,532)	$ 366,269
Adjustments to reconcile change in net assets to net cash provided (used) by operating activities		
Depreciation	29,624	26,957
Effect of prior period adjustment	—	(74,242)
(Increase) decrease in:		
Pledges receivable	209,447	(121,910)
Accounts receivable	361,844	(12,827)
Interest receivable	(2,242)	(1,495)
Publications inventory	(28,109)	6,795
Prepaids and other assets	(2,624)	(3,126)
Increase (decrease) in:		
Accounts payable	107,538	(204,516)
Accrued liabilities	15,823	(6,042)
Deferred compensation payable	(4,252)	4,252
Deferred revenue—dues and subscriptions	100,595	17,963
Net cash provided (used) by operating activities	618,112	(1,922)
CASH FLOWS FROM INVESTING ACTIVITIES		
Purchase of equipment/furniture and fixtures	(44,880)	(16,972)
Net cash provided (used) by investing activities	(44,880)	(16,972)
NET INCREASE (DECREASE) IN CASH AND CASH EQUIVALENTS	573,232	(18,894)
CASH AND CASH EQUIVALENTS AT BEGINNING OF YEAR	1,371,632	1,390,526
CASH AND CASH EQUIVALENTS AT END OF YEAR	$1,944,864	$1,371,632

See accompanying notes and Auditors' Report.

NOTES TO FINANCIAL STATEMENTS
FOR THE YEARS ENDED AUGUST 31, 1996 AND 1995

NOTE 1—ORGANIZATION

The American Accounting Association (the Association) was founded in 1916 as a non-profit organization. The major objectives of the Association are to initiate and sponsor research in accounting, to publish the results of research and to advance accounting instruction and the development of accounting concepts and standards.

The Association achieves these objectives by publishing scholarly journals and by conducting meetings, consortia and conferences on a variety of pedagogical and research issues. It also publishes a newsletter and engages in other activities to enhance accounting teaching and research.

NOTE 2—SUMMARY OF SIGNIFICANT ACCOUNTING POLICIES

Basis of Accounting

The financial statements of the Association are prepared on the accrual basis of accounting in accordance with generally accepted accounting principles.

Promises to Give

Contributions are recognized when the donor makes a promise to give to the Association that is, in substance, unconditional. Contributions that are restricted by the donor are reported as increases in unrestricted net assets if the restrictions expire in the fiscal year in which the contributions are recognized. All other donor-restricted contributions are reported as increases in temporarily or permanently restricted net assets depending on the nature of the restrictions. When a restriction expires, temporarily restricted net assets are reclassified to unrestricted net assets.

Estimates

The preparation of financial statements in conformity with generally accepted accounting principles requires management to make estimates and assumptions that affect certain reported amounts and disclosures. Accordingly, actual results could differ from those estimates.

Financial Statement Presentation

The accompanying financial statements are prepared consistent with the Statement of Financial Accounting Standards No. 117 entitled "Financial Statements of Not-for-Profit Organizations" issued by the Financial Accounting Standards Board. Net assets and revenues, expenses, gains, and losses are classified based on the existence or absence of donor-imposed restrictions. Accordingly, net assets of the Association and changes therein are classified and reported as follows:

(Continued on page 14)

AMERICAN ACCOUNTING ASSOCIATION STATEMENT OF FUNCTIONAL EXPENSES FOR THE YEAR ENDED AUGUST 31, 1996

	Memberships and Subscriptions	Seminars and Conferences	Annual Meeting	Regional Meetings	Sections Meetings	General Publications	Sections Publications	Committees and Other Programs	Total Program Services	Management and General	Total Expenses
Salaries	$27,329	$13,162	$37,727	$9,644	$9,550	$44,732	$35,779	$2,450	$180,373	$159,954	$340,327
Employee benefits	4,662	2,245	6,435	1,645	1,629	7,630	6,103	418	30,767	27,284	58,051
Payroll taxes	2,238	1,078	3,090	790	782	3,664	2,931	201	14,774	13,102	27,876
Total salaries and related expenses	34,229	16,485	47,252	12,079	11,961	56,026	44,813	3,069	225,914	200,340	426,254
AECC	—	—	—	—	—	—	—	307,801	307,801	—	307,801
Awards	—	—	1,445	8,642	—	—	—	9,809	19,896	—	19,896
Bank fees	1,458	702	2,013	514	509	2,386	1,907	131	9,620	8,533	18,153
Beta Alpha Psi	—	—	—	—	—	—	—	—	—	63,785	63,785
CPE expenses	153	73	43,387	3,754	6,124	250	200	14	53,265	—	53,265
Dues and subscriptions	—	—	211	54	53	—	—	—	1,008	893	1,901
Editorial assistance	454	218	626	160	158	77,793	13,683	41	91,476	—	91,476
Equipment maintenance	—	—	—	—	—	742	594	—	2,993	2,654	5,647
Event coordinator	—	—	28,108	8,368	—	—	—	—	36,476	—	36,476
Hotel/food/beverage	253	283,383	222,111	152,855	125,036	642	614	8	783,385	16,459	799,844
Insurance	1,864	80	155	875	69	—	—	—	2,696	11,935	14,631
Miscellaneous	428	47,714	44,163	17,188	11,315	18,679	6,923	42,553	190,399	83,497	273,896
Office maintenance	1,928	99	99	99	99	1,275	1,275	—	3,374	16,025	19,399
Postage	260	2,224	11,289	1,642	8,582	135,035	41,104	2,111	203,915	9,441	213,356
Printing/copying	1,354	4,957	35,919	478	12,420	178,163	76,822	102	341,074	2,297	343,371
Professional fees	44	652	1,869	15	473	2,216	32,272	121	39,435	7,922	47,357
Publications	—	21	60	—	15	2,436	9,951	4	12,546	255	12,801
Registration/Exhibitor	—	—	28,835	4,039	—	—	—	—	32,874	—	32,874
Speakers	—	792	4,000	3,940	6,300	5,253	—	105	14,240	—	14,240
Supplies	11,645	104	13,449	415	411	1,083	1,539	—	33,609	7,164	40,773
Taxes	389	—	153	97	97	2,121	1,065	5	2,993	4,016	7,009
Telephone	936	2,120	1,292	515	327	826	1,225	84	8,620	5,703	14,323
Travel	472	147,507	9,174	1,018	8,457	1,356	1,765	47,772	214,991	35,125	250,116
Utilities	456	105	105	105	105	—	1,356	—	3,588	5,046	8,634
Total expenses before depreciation	56,323	507,236	495,715	249,283	190,511	486,282	237,108	413,730	2,636,188	481,090	3,117,278
Depreciation	2,107	885	2,310	681	675	4,146	3,627	142	14,573	15,051	29,624
TOTAL EXPENSES	$58,430	$508,121	$498,025	$249,964	$191,186	$490,428	$240,735	$413,872	$2,650,761	$496,141	$3,146,902

See accompanying notes and Auditors' Report.

AMERICAN ACCOUNTING ASSOCIATION STATEMENT OF FUNCTIONAL EXPENSES FOR THE YEAR ENDED AUGUST 31, 1995

	Memberships and Subscriptions	Seminars and Conferences	Annual Meeting	Regional Meetings	Sections Meetings	General Publications	Sections Publications	Committees and Other Programs	Total Program Services	Management and General	Total Expenses
Salaries	$27,473	$13,231	$37,925	$9,694	$9,600	$44,967	$35,967	$2,463	$181,320	$175,187	$356,507
Employee benefits	6,298	3,033	8,694	2,222	2,200	10,308	8,245	565	41,565	36,860	78,425
Payroll taxes	2,323	1,119	3,206	819	811	3,802	3,041	208	15,329	13,594	28,923
Total salaries and related expenses	36,094	17,383	49,825	12,735	12,611	59,077	47,253	3,236	238,214	225,641	463,855
AECC	—	—	—	—	—	—	—	685,096	685,096	—	685,096
Awards	96	46	876	10,112	—	158	—	19,284	30,272	10,852	41,124
Bank fees	1,506	725	2,079	34	526	2,465	1,971	9	636	564	1,200
Beta Alpha Psi	—	—	—	—	—	—	—	135	9,938	8,813	18,751
CPE expenses	22	10	43,653	6,131	12,657	—	—	—	62,441	36,034	98,475
Dues and subscriptions	—	—	30	7	7	36	28	2	142	127	269
Editorial assistance	544	262	751	192	190	35,000	17,805	—	52,805	—	52,805
Equipment maintenance	—	—	—	531	—	891	712	49	3,591	3,185	6,776
Event coordinator	—	—	20,500	15,991	—	—	—	—	36,491	—	36,491
Hotel/food/beverage	473	127,302	202,008	111,566	103,850	949	837	31	544,726	—	544,726
Insurance	—	195	503	151	150	—	—	—	3,289	3,451	6,740
Miscellaneous	6,183	296,648	58,954	53,179	6,929	80,793	28,545	150,859	682,090	184,046	866,136
Office maintenance	498	131	186	123	123	1,401	1,381	5	3,848	5,197	9,045
Postage	1,991	2,048	10,198	702	3,439	120,377	38,003	800	177,558	11,654	189,212
Printing/copying	744	7,454	31,598	11,203	8,607	171,924	75,847	538	307,171	—	307,171
Professional fees	—	358	1,027	263	260	1,218	974	67	4,911	4,355	9,266
Publications	—	—	—	—	—	—	—	—	—	—	—
Registration/Exhibitor	—	—	24,982	7,759	—	—	—	—	32,741	—	32,741
Speakers	—	—	11,129	77	3,592	1,665	1,331	91	14,798	—	14,798
Supplies	9,653	716	13,468	359	355	1,010	998	3	27,638	5,952	33,590
Taxes	357	92	126	87	87	1,243	—	—	2,760	3,750	6,510
Telephone	759	366	1,298	268	265	649	994	68	5,261	4,445	9,706
Travel	396	72,086	12,323	383	12,391	1,069	519	36	98,783	2,319	101,102
Utilities	359	83	83	83	—	—	1,069	—	2,829	3,974	6,803
Total expenses before depreciation	59,675	525,905	485,730	231,936	166,156	479,925	218,393	860,309	3,028,029	576,800	3,604,829
Depreciation	1,900	789	2,042	609	605	3,789	3,332	125	13,191	13,766	26,957
TOTAL EXPENSES	$61,575	$526,694	$487,772	$232,545	$166,761	$483,714	$221,725	$860,434	$3,041,220	$590,566	$3,631,786

See accompanying notes and Auditors' Report.

INDEPENDENT AUDITORS' REPORT ON ADDITIONAL INFORMATION

Executive Committee of the American Accounting Association, Sarasota, Florida

Our report on our audit of the basic financial statements of the American Accounting Association for the years ended August 31, 1996 and 1995 appears on Page [11]. We conducted our audit in accordance with generally accepted auditing standards for the purpose of forming an opinion on the basic financial statements taken as a whole. The supporting schedule on the statements of financial position as of August 31, 1996 and 1995, the supporting schedule on the statements of activities for the years ended August 31, 1996 and 1995, the supporting schedule of cash flows for the years ended August 31, 1996 and 1995 and the statement of major cash contributions received for the year ended August 31, 1996 are presented for the purposes of additional analysis and are not a required part of the basic financial statements. Such information has been subjected to the auditing procedures applied in the audit of the basic financial statements and, in our opinion, is fairly stated in all material respects in relation to the basic financial statements taken as a whole.

PARENT, MARLAR, MODRAK & COMPANY
Certified Public Accountants

Bradenton, Florida
October 8, 1996

AMERICAN ACCOUNTING ASSOCIATION
SUPPORTING SCHEDULE OF THE STATEMENTS OF FINANCIAL POSITION
AUGUST 31, 1996 AND 1995

	August 31, 1996					August 31, 1995
ASSETS	General Fund	Section Funds	Region Funds	Fellowship Fund	Total All Funds	Total All Funds
Cash and cash equivalents	$1,220,230	$497,675	$137,377	$89,582	$1,944,864	$1,371,632
Accounts receivable	116,366	—	—	—	116,366	478,210
Interest receivable	8,599	—	—	—	8,599	6,357
Pledges receivable—net	606,401	—	—	—	606,401	815,848
Publications inventory	74,494	—	—	—	74,494	46,385
Prepaids and other assets	23,584	—	—	—	23,584	20,960
Property and equipment, less accumulated depreciation	142,915	—	—	—	142,915	127,659
TOTAL ASSETS	$2,192,589	$497,675	$137,377	$89,582	$2,917,223	$2,867,051
LIABILITIES AND NET ASSETS						
LIABILITIES						
Accounts payable	$ 233,869	$ —	$ —	$ —	$ 233,869	$ 126,331
Accrued liabilities	16,013	—	—	—	16,013	190
Deferred compensation payable	—	—	—	—	—	4,252
Deferred revenue—dues and subscriptions	494,297	113,820	—	—	608,117	507,522
Total liabilities	744,179	113,820			857,999	638,295
NET ASSETS						
Unrestricted	794,283	383,855	137,377	—	1,315,515	1,183,384
Temporarily restricted	654,127	—	—	89,582	743,709	1,045,372
Total net assets	1,448,410	383,855	137,377	89,582	2,059,224	2,228,756
TOTAL LIABILITIES AND NET ASSETS	$2,192,589	$497,675	$137,377	$89,582	$2,917,223	$2,867,051

See accompanying notes and Auditors' Report.

AMERICAN ACCOUNTING ASSOCIATION
SUPPORTING SCHEDULE OF THE STATEMENTS OF ACTIVITIES
FOR THE YEARS ENDED AUGUST 31, 1996 AND 1995

	August 31, 1996					August 31, 1995
	General Fund	Section Funds	Region Funds	Fellowship Fund	Total All Funds	Total All Funds
SUPPORT AND REVENUE						
Membership dues	$ 601,832	$195,897	$ —	$ —	$ 797,729	$ 782,787
Subscriptions	264,298	29,010	—	—	293,308	316,746
Advertising	49,006	4,950	100	—	54,056	74,353
Publications	79,398	2,910	—	—	82,308	115,740
Contributions	462,849	49,753	49,896	9,424	571,922	1,544,031
Interest and dividend income	78,026	—	8,146	—	86,172	78,405
Annual meeting	572,646	—	—	—	572,646	524,694
Other revenue (primarily from programs and seminars)	178,071	154,602	186,556	—	519,229	581,299
Total support and revenue	2,286,126	437,122	244,698	9,424	2,977,370	3,998,055
EXPENSES						
Program services						
Membership and subscriptions	58,430	—	—	—	58,430	61,575
Seminars and conferences	508,121	—	—	—	508,121	526,694
Annual meeting	490,367	7,076	582	—	498,025	487,772
Regional meetings	16,693	—	233,271	—	249,964	232,545
Section meetings	16,534	174,652	—	—	191,186	166,761
General publications	490,089	—	339	—	490,428	483,714
Section publications	65,965	174,770	—	—	240,735	221,725
Committees and other programs	379,164	30,277	4,431	—	413,872	860,434
Support services						
Management and general	461,336	18,552	3,753	12,500	496,141	590,566
Total expenses	2,486,699	405,327	242,376	12,500	3,146,902	3,631,786
CHANGES IN NET ASSETS	(200,573)	31,795	2,322	(3,076)	(169,532)	366,269
NET ASSETS AT BEGINNING OF YEAR	1,648,983	352,060	135,055	92,658	2,228,756	1,982,000
PRIOR PERIOD ADJUSTMENTS (NOTE 7)						
Correction of net assets						
Dues	—	—	—	—	—	(45,271)
Contributions						(74,242)
NET ASSETS AT BEGINNING OF YEAR, AS RESTATED	1,648,983	352,060	135,055	92,658	2,228,756	1,862,487
NET ASSETS AT END OF YEAR	$1,448,410	$383,855	$137,377	$89,582	$2,059,224	$2,228,756

See accompanying notes and Auditors' Report.

AMERICAN ACCOUNTING ASSOCIATION
SUPPORTING SCHEDULE OF THE STATEMENTS OF CASH FLOWS
FOR THE YEARS ENDED AUGUST 31, 1996 and 1995

	August 31, 1996					August 31, 1995
	General Fund	Section Funds	Region Funds	Fellowship Fund	Total All Funds	Total All Funds
CASH FLOWS FROM OPERATING ACTIVITIES						
Change in net assets	$ (200,573)	$ 31,795	$ 2,322	$ (3,076)	$ (169,532)	$ 366,269
Adjustments to reconcile change in net assets to net cash provided (used) by operating activities						
Depreciation	29,624	—	—	—	29,624	26,957
Effect of prior period adjustment	—	—	—	—	—	(74,242)
(Increase) decrease in:						
Pledges receivable	209,447	—	—	—	209,447	(121,910)
Accounts receivable	361,844	—	—	—	361,844	(12,827)
Interest receivable	(2,242)	—	—	—	(2,242)	(1,495)
Publications inventory	(28,109)	—	—	—	(28,109)	6,795
Prepaids and other assets	(2,624)	—	—	—	(2,624)	(3,126)
Increase (decrease) in:						
Accounts payable	107,538	—	—	—	107,538	(204,516)
Accrued liabilities	15,823	—	—	—	15,823	(6,042)
Deferred compensation payable	(4,252)	—	—	—	(4,252)	4,252
Deferred revenue—dues and subscriptions	92,697	7,898	—	—	100,595	17,963
Net cash provided (used) by operating activities	579,173	39,693	2,322	(3,076)	618,112	(1,922)
CASH FLOWS FROM INVESTING ACTIVITIES						
Purchase of equipment	(44,880)	—	—	—	(44,880)	(16,972)
Net cash provided (used) by investing activities	(44,880)	—	—	—	(44,880)	(16,972)
NET INCREASE (DECREASE) IN CASH AND CASH EQUIVALENTS	534,293	39,693	2,322	(3,076)	573,232	(18,894)
CASH AND CASH EQUIVALENTS AT BEGINNING OF YEAR	685,937	457,982	135,055	92,658	1,371,632	1,390,526
CASH AND CASH EQUIVALENTS AT END OF YEAR	$1,220,230	$497,675	$137,377	$89,582	$1,944,864	$1,371,632

See accompanying notes and Auditors' Report.

Notes to Financial Statements
(Continued from page 11)

Unrestricted Net Assets:
Net assets that are not subject to donor-imposed or time restricted stipulations.

Temporarily Restricted Net Assets:
Net assets subject to donor-imposed stipulations that may or will be met either by actions of the Association and/or the passage of time. When a restriction expires, temporarily restricted net assets are reclassified to unrestricted net assets and reported in the statement of activities as net assets released from restrictions.

However, managed fund groups are still maintained for internal management reports.

Functional Expenses
Functional expenses are allocated based on direct and indirect expenses. Direct expenses are allocated to the Program or Supporting Service from which the expense arose. Indirect expenses are allocated by a square footage formula to those expenses identifiable to property and equipment and by a time study of days worked to all other indirect expenses.

Miscellaneous Expense
For the year ended August 31, 1995, miscellaneous expense included expenses from the following:

Seminars & Conferences
Corporate Accounting Policy Seminar
Financial Reporting Issues Conference
New Faculty Consortium
Trueblood Seminar
Professionalism and Ethics Seminar
Doctoral Consortium

Management & General
Executive Committee Expense
Council Expense
Officer Related Expenses
Contribution to Financial Accounting Foundation
Executive Director Search & Transition Expenses

For the year ended August 31, 1996, all hotel and travel related expenses were removed from the above categories and reclassed to the appropriate line item on the statement of functional expenses.

Net Assets Released from Restrictions
Expiration of time and program restrictions relate to contributions recognized as temporarily restricted support in prior years.

Publications Inventory
Publications inventory is stated at the lower of cost or market. Cost is determined using the first-in, first-out (FIFO) method.

Publication Revenue
Publication revenue is recognized when the related publications (books) are sold.

Fellowship Grants
Fellowship grants are expensed at the time the grant is approved by the Association.

Income Taxes
The Association is generally exempt from income taxes under Section 501(c)(3) of the Internal Revenue Code. The Association is required to pay income taxes on the excess of revenues derived from activities unrelated to the tax-exempt purpose of the organization over the related expenses. The Association had no liability for such taxes for the years ended August 31, 1996 and 1995.

NOTE 3—CASH AND CASH EQUIVALENTS
The Association considers all highly liquid investments purchased with an original maturity of three months or less to be cash equivalents. At August 31, cash and cash equivalents consist of the following:

	1996	1995
U.S. Treasury and Government Securities:	$1,944,864	$1,371,632
Cash and equivalents owned by the following managed fund groups		
General Operations	$1,220,230	$ 685,937
Fellowship	89,582	92,658
Sections	497,675	457,982
Regions	137,377	135,055
	$1,944,864	$1,371,632

The Association utilizes a cash management system which automatically transfers the excess balance above a predetermined target level into an investment fund. This fund is limited to securities which are guaranteed by the full faith and credit of the U.S. Government, and repurchase agreements collateralized by U.S. Government obligations.

NOTE 4—ACCOUNTS AND INTEREST RECEIVABLE
The allowance for uncollectible accounts receivable was estimated to be $–0– at August 31, 1996 and 1995.

NOTE 5—PLEDGES RECEIVABLE

	1996	1995
Pledges receivable—less than 1 year	$ 344,556	$ 294,000
Pledges receivable—1 to 5 years	279,185	575,924
Discount on pledges receivable	(17,340)	(54,076)
Pledges receivable—net	$ 606,401	$ 815,848

NOTE 6—PROPERTY AND EQUIPMENT
Property and equipment are stated at cost less accumulated depreciation. Equipment donated August, 1991 was recorded at catalog retail price at date of donation. Depreciation is computed using the straight-line method over the estimated useful lives of the assets which range from 5 to 20 years.

Property and equipment consisted of the following at August 31:

	1996	1995
Land	$ 29,748	$ 29,748
Land improvements	15,252	15,252
Building	174,666	174,666
Furniture and equipment	251,134	206,254
	470,800	425,920
Less accumulated depreciation	(327,885)	(298,261)
	$ 142,915	$ 127,659

Depreciation expense for fiscal years ending 1996 and 1995 is as follows:

	1996	1995
Assets carried at cost	$ 29,055	$ 25,818
Assets carried at catalog retail price	569	1,139
	$ 29,624	$ 26,957

(Continued on page 15)

CALL FOR PAPERS

University of Waterloo
1998 Auditing Symposium

The Center for Assurance Services at the University of Waterloo will hold a symposium at the university March 26–28, 1998. The Symposium is sponsored by the Ernst & Young Foundation (Canada) and co-sponsored by the Auditing Section of the American Accounting Association. Proceedings will be published as a supplement to *Auditing: A Journal of Practice & Theory,* subject to editorial review and approval by the Editor of the journal.

Theme

This symposium will focus on issues related to Assurance Services, broadly considered, with a particular interest in services beyond those involving an audit of historic financial statements.

Papers are invited from academe and practice. Submitted papers should be at an advanced stage of completion. Authors must adhere to the "Editorial Policy Publication of Auditing Symposium Papers" published in Volume 11, 1992, supplement to *Auditing: A Journal of Practice & Theory.* Copies of "Instructions to Authors" contained in this policy statement are published in each issue of *Auditing: A Journal of Practice & Theory* or are available, upon request, from the University of Waterloo.

Please send four copies of the paper, together with a submission fee of $50.00 (U.S.) payable to the American Accounting Association, by November 1, 1997 to:

W. Morley Lemon
Audit Symposium Chairperson
Center for Assurance Services
School of Accountancy
University of Waterloo
Waterloo, Ontario Canada N2L 3G1
Phone: (519) 888-4567 (ext. 3732)
Fax: (519) 888-7562

Notice of acceptance or rejection will be sent out by January 15, 1998. Revised papers must be received by February 20, 1998.

Notes to Financial Statements
(Continued from page 14)

NOTE 7—PRIOR PERIOD ADJUSTMENTS

Dues Income

The accounting for calendar year section dues not received as part of the annual conference registration was previously completely recognized as revenue in the subsequent fiscal year of the Association. The Association is now recognizing three quarters of income and deferring one quarter of the dues income to reflect the final quarter's publication obligation to members. The effect of the previous treatment was to overstate August 31, 1994 net assets and to understate the deferred revenue associated with these dues by $45,271.

Program Contributions

During the Association's fiscal years ending before August 31, 1990, certain funding amounts were recognized before the associated costs were incurred. Correction of this error reduced August 31, 1994 unrestricted net assets by $74,242.

NOTE 8—EMPLOYEE BENEFIT PLAN

The Association has a defined contribution, money purchase pension plan which covers substantially all employees. Employer contributions to the plan are 7% of qualifying employee compensation. The Association's contributions to the plan for 1996 and 1995 were $16,843 and $41,315, respectively. The Association also has adopted a 403(b) salary reduction plan for eligible employees. The Association has no obligation for employer contributions to this plan.

Discussion and Analysis AAA FY 1996 Audited Financial Statements *(Continued from page 10)*

During FY 1996, the Association published the work of 426 authors.

Committees and Awards

During FY 1996, there were six Association-wide standing committees and 27 committees appointed by the president. Two hundred sixty-five members participated on these committees.

A list of the Association awards and selection criteria is published each year in a fall issue of *Accounting Education News.* During FY 1996, there were six Association-wide awards (eight recipients).

Administration

At the end of FY 1996, the Sarasota administrative staff included ten full-time staff equivalents. These employees are responsible for tracking and billing Association members, record keeping and financial reporting, publications, and providing various levels of administrative service to members, regions, sections and committees.

Future Activities

The FY 1996 financial statements, as well as those of previous years, included the assets, revenues, support and expenses of the Accounting Education Change Commission (AECC). In August 1996, the AECC completed its scheduled activities and, as previously planned, turned over its leadership role and responsibility for dissemination of information gained through the AECC grant program to the Association. In keeping with the recommendations of the committee charged with planning for the transition and with the wishes of Council, the Association is undertaking a major faculty development initiative, which will include hiring a full-time director of faculty development. The faculty development initiative will provide the Association with the opportunity to significantly enhance member services, but also will make it more challenging to predict demands on the Sarasota office and the levels and variability of future costs.

American Accounting Association Finance Committee

AMERICAN ACCOUNTING ASSOCIATION
STATEMENT OF MAJOR CASH CONTRIBUTIONS RECEIVED
FOR THE YEAR ENDED AUGUST 31, 1996

	1996
GENERAL FUND	
Deloitte & Touche LLP/Foundation	$301,955
Ernst & Young Foundation	125,772
Arthur Andersen & Co. LLP/Foundation	211,770
Price Waterhouse LLP	130,423
Coopers & Lybrand Foundation	120,423
KPMG Peat Marwick Foundation	130,423
Richard D. Irwin	7,000
General Motors	3,000
Exxon Corporation	4,000
Institute of Management Accountants	4,000
Johnson & Johnson	5,000
IBM	8,000
Black & Decker	3,000
Corning, Inc.	3,000
FELLOWSHIP FUND	
Coopers & Lybrand Foundation	5,000
SECTION FUNDS	
KPMG Peat Marwick Foundation	20,099
CGA Research	4,258
Ernst & Young Foundation	3,500
REGION FUNDS	
Ernst & Young Foundation	7,800
N.Y. Society of CPAs	3,530

See accompanying notes and Auditors' Report.

AMERICAN ACCOUNTING ASSOCIATION ANNUAL REPORT: INDEPENDENT AUDITORS' REPORT (1991)

To the Executive Committee of the American Accounting Association

We have audited the accompanying balance sheet of the American Accounting Association (a non-profit organization) as of August 31, 1991, and the related statements of support, revenue, expenses, and changes in fund balance and cash flows for the year then ended. These financial statements are the responsibility of the Association's management. Our responsibility is to express an opinion on these financial statements based on our audit. The financial statements of the American Accounting Association as of August 31, 1990, were audited by other auditors whose report dated October 10, 1990, expressed an unqualified opinion on those statements.

We conducted our audit in accordance with generally accepted auditing standards. Those standards require that we plan and perform the audit to obtain reasonable assurance about whether the financial statements are free of material misstatement. An audit includes examining, on a test basis, evidence supporting the amounts and disclosures in the financial statements. An audit also includes assessing the accounting principles used and significant estimates made by management, as well as evaluating the overall financial statement presentation. We believe that our audit provides a reasonable basis for our opinion.

In our opinion, the financial statements referred to above present fairly, in all material respects, the financial position of the American Accounting Association as of August 31, 1991, and the results of its operations and the changes in its cash flows for the year then ended in conformity with generally accepted accounting principles.

Our audit was made for the purpose of forming an opinion on the basic financial statements taken as a whole. The Statements of Pledges Earned and Contributions Received on page 17 is presented for the purposes of additional analysis and is not a required part of the basic financial statements. Such information has been subjected to the auditing procedures applied in the audit of the basic financial statements and, in our opinion, is fairly stated in all material respects in relation to the basic financial statements taken as a whole.

VALDES, MCLAIN, PRATT & CO.
Certified Public Accountants

Bradenton, Florida
October 31, 1991

AMERICAN ACCOUNTING ASSOCIATION
BALANCE SHEETS
AUGUST 31, 1991 AND AUGUST 31, 1990

| | August 31, 1991 | | | | | August 31, 1990 | |
| | Designated | | | Restricted | | | |
ASSETS	General Fund	Sections Funds	Regions Funds	Fellowship Fund	Total All Funds	General Fund	Total All Funds
CURRENT ASSETS							
Cash and cash equivalents	$ 698,939	$251,502	$136,965	$11,219	$1,098,625	$ 160,767	$ 521,914
Investments	400,000	—	—	—	400,000	400,000	400,000
Current portion of Pledges receivable	292,750	—	—	—	292,750	345,442	345,442
Accounts and interest receivable	115,740	—	—	—	115,740	46,984	46,984
Publications inventory	34,489	—	—	—	34,489	36,782	36,782
Prepaids and other assets	40,879	390	70	—	41,339	2,646	4,562
Total current assets	1,582,797	251,892	137,035	11,219	1,982,943	992,621	1,355,684

| | August 31, 1991 | | | | | August 31, 1990 | |
| | | Designated | | Restricted | | | |
ASSETS	General Fund	Sections Funds	Regions Funds	Fellowship Fund	Total All Funds	General Fund	Total All Funds
OTHER ASSETS							
Pledges receivable, less current portion	209,565	—	—	—	209,565	301,818	301,818
Restricted assets, deferred compensation plan	167,471	—	—	—	167,471	88,500	88,500
Property and equipment, net	133,698	—	—	—	133,698	149,202	149,202
Total other assets	510,734				510,734	539,620	539,620
TOTAL ASSETS	$2,093,531	$251,892	$137,035	$11,219	$2,493,677	$1,532,141	$1,895,204
LIABILITIES AND FUND BALANCE							
CURRENT LIABILITIES							
Accounts payable and accrued liabilities	$ 195,328	$ 6,588	$ —	$ 5,000	$ 206,916	$ 174,932	$ 211,317
Current portion of deferred revenue	336,426	38,668	—	—	375,094	281,348	316,686
Current portion of deferred support	630,547	—	—	—	630,547	250,734	250,734
Total current liabilities	1,162,301	45,256	—	5,000	1,212,557	707,014	778,737
OTHER LIABILITIES							
Deferred compensation	167,471	—	—	—	167,471	88,500	88,500
Deferred revenue, less current portion	2,712	—	—	—	2,712	17,616	17,616
Deferred support, less current portion	148,965	—	—	—	148,965	306,965	306,965
Total other liabilities	319,148				319,148	413,081	413,081
TOTAL LIABILITIES	1,481,449	45,256		5,000	1,531,705	1,120,095	1,191,818
FUND BALANCE							
Unrestricted	612,082	—	—	—	612,082	412,046	412,046
Designated or restricted	—	206,636	137,035	6,219	349,890	—	291,340
Total fund balance	612,082	206,636	137,035	6,219	961,972	412,046	703,386
TOTAL LIABILITIES AND FUND BALANCE	$2,093,531	$251,892	$137,035	$11,219	$2,493,677	$1,532,141	$1,895,204

The accompanying notes are an integral part of the financial statements.

AMERICAN ACCOUNTING ASSOCIATION
STATEMENTS OF SUPPORT AND REVENUE, EXPENSES AND CHANGES IN FUND BALANCES
FOR THE YEAR ENDED AUGUST 31, 1991 AND AUGUST 31, 1990

| | August 31, 1991 | | | | | August 31,1990 | |
| | | Designated | | Restricted | | | |
	General Fund	Sections Funds	Regions Funds	Fellowship Fund	Total All Funds	General Fund	Total All Funds
SUPPORT AND REVENUE							
Membership dues	$ 520,906	$152,209	$ —	$ —	$ 673,115	$ 391,625	$ 516,436
Subscriptions	256,016	—	—	—	256,016	145,747	145,747
Advertising	144,428	3,150	26,393	—	173,971	139,428	153,878
Publications	97,343	24,451	—	—	121,794	104,250	131,275
Contributions	1,195,786	19,893	38,443	14,937	1,269,059	817,149	907,015
Interest and dividend income	54,467	—	754	—	55,221	48,312	49,032
Annual Convention	531,352	—	—	—	531,352	420,463	420,463
Other revenue(Primarily programs and seminars)	243,783	98,055	166,022	—	507,860	185,006	444,390
Total support and revenue	3,044,081	297,758	231,612	14,937	3,588,388	2,251,880	2,768,236
EXPENSES							
Cost of publications	470,114	98,031	—	—	568,145	529,49	637,940
Programs and seminars	1,229,226	74,168	—	—	1,303,393	782,456	848,298
Research and education	—	750	—	—	750	743	1,022
Committees	55,813	—	—	—	55,813	48,946	48,946
Officers meetings	48,749	—	—	—	48,749	44,756	44,756
Administration	534,726	92,529	38,814	—	666,069	506,721	835,015
Financial Accounting Foundation contribution	12,623	—	—	—	12,623	12,089	12,089
Fellowship grants	—	—	—	10,000	10,000	—	40,000
Annual convention	435,515	5,636	—	—	441,151	323,079	329,639
Other expenses	57,280	2	165,827	—	223,109	37,446	28,846
Total expenses	2,844,045	271,116	204,641	10,000	3,329,802	2,285,885	2,826,551
EXCESS (DEFICIENCY) OF SUPPORT AND REVENUE OVER (UNDER) EXPENSES	200,036	26,642	26,971	4,937	258,586	(34,005)	(58,315)
FUND BALANCES, BEGINNING OF YEAR	412,046	179,994	110,064	1,282	703,386	446,051	761,701
FUND BALANCES, END OF YEAR	$ 612,082	$206,636	$137,036	$ 6,219	$ 961,972	$ 412,046	$ 703,386

The accompanying notes are an integral part of the financial statements.

AMERICAN ACCOUNTING ASSOCIATION
STATEMENTS OF CASH FLOW
FOR THE YEARS ENDED AUGUST 31, 1991 AND AUGUST 31, 1990

| | August 31, 1991 | | | | | August 31, 1990 | |
| | | Designated | | Restricted | | | |
	General Fund	Sections Funds	Regions Funds	Fellowship Fund	Total All Funds	General Fund	Total All Funds
CASH FLOWS FROM OPERATING ACTIVITIES							
From operations:							
Excess (deficiency) of support and revenue over(under)expenses	$200,036	$ 26,642	$ 26,971	$ 4,937	$258,586	$ (34,005)	$ (58,315)
Charges (credits) not affecting cash in the current period:							
Depreciation	21,199	—	—	—	21,199	18,997	18,997
(Increase) decrease in:							
Investments	—	—	—	—	—	(300,000)	(300,000)
Pledges receivable-current and long-term	144,945	—	—	—	144,945	62,529	65,688
Accounts and interest receivable	(68,756)	—	—	—	(68,756)	12,049	12,049
Publications inventory	2,293	—	—	—	2,293	1,536	1,536
Prepaids and other assets	(38,234)	1,092	365	—	(36,777)	12,582	10,666
Increase (decrease) in:							
Accounts payable and accrued liabilities	20,396	452	(250)	(25,000)	(4,402)	93,858	88,742
Deferred revenue-current and long-term	40,174	3,330	—	—	43,504	100,880	118,187
Deferred support-current and long term	221,813	—	—	—	221,813	(95,227)	(96,227)
Deferred compensation	78,971	—	—	—	78,971	29,100	29,100
NET CASH PROVIDED IN OPERATING ACTIVITIES	622,837	31,516	27,086	(20,063)	661,376	(97,701)	(108,577)
CASH FLOWS FROM INVESTING ACTIVITIES							
Purchase of property, plant and equipment	(5,694)	—	—	—	(5,694)	(3,144)	(3,144)
Increase in restricted assets	(78,971)	—	—	—	(78,971)	(29,100)	(29,100)
NET CASH USED IN INVESTING ACTIVITIES	(84,665)	—	—	—	(84,665)	(32,244)	(32,244)
CASH FLOWS FROM FINANCING ACTIVITIES							
Transfer between funds	—	—	—	—	—	—	—
NET INCREASE IN CASH AND CASH EQUIVALENTS	538,172	31,516	27,086	(20,063)	576,711	(129,945)	(140,821)
CASH AND CASH EQUIVALENTS, BEGINNING OF YEAR	160,767	219,986	109,879	31,282	521,914	290,712	662,735
CASH AND CASH EQUIVALENTS, END OF YEAR	$698,939	$261,502	$ 136,965	$11,219	$1,098,625	$160,767	$521,914

The accompanying notes are an integral part of the financial statements.

NOTES TO FINANCIAL STATEMENTS

NOTE 1—SUMMARY OF SIGNIFICANT ACCOUNTING POLICIES:

Basis of Accounting

The financial statements of the American Accounting Association (the "Association" are prepared consistent with the Statement of position (SOP) 78-10 entitled "Accounting Principles and Reporting Practices for Certain Nonprofit Organizations" issued by the American Insitiue of Certified Public Accountants.

The financial statements include the general, sections, fellowship and regions funds of the Association. The general fund includes all activity related to the Accounting Education Change Commission (AECC)

Cash Equivalents and Investments

The Association considers all highly liquid investments purchased with an original maturity of three mnonths or less to be cash equivalents. The association considers all other investments to be investments and recordss them at cost which approximates market.

Pledges

Pledges are recorded as receivables in the year the pledge is made. Pledges for support of future periods are recorded as deferred amounts in the respective funds to which they apply. Support restricted by the donor for use in specified programs is recognized when the related program expenses are incurred. Non-restricted pledges, including pledges of publications are included in the general fund.

Publications Inventory

Publications inventory is stated at the lower of cost or market. Cost is determined using the first-in, first-out (FIFO) method.

Property and Equipment

Property and equipment are stated at cost less accumulated depreciation. Depreciation is computed using the straight-line method over the estimated useful lives of the assets which range from 5 to 20 years.

Membership Dues and Subscriptions

Membership dues and subscriptions are recognized as revenue ratably over the applicable membership and subscription period. Unearned receipts are reflected as deferred revenue.

Publication Revenue

Publication revenue is recognized when the related publications (books) are sold.

Fellowship Grants

Fellowship grants are expensed at the time the grant is approved by the Association.

Research Projects

Research project expenses relate to projects authorized by the Director of Research and Director of Education and are recorded in the year the projects are authorized. These projects are funded primarily through pledges of support. Unearned pledges are reflected as deferred support. Projects currently ongoing are the Senior Faculty Consortium, the New Faculty Consortium,. the Doctoral Consortium, the Seminar on Professionalism and Ethics, and the International Lecturer Program.

Income Taxes

Pursuant to a determination letter received form the Internal Revenue Service, the Association is generally exempt from Federal income tax under Section 501(c)(3) of the Internal Revenue Code, and accordingly, income taxes have not been provided in trhe accompanying financial statments.

NOTE 2—DESCRIPTION OF FUNDS

The assets, liabilites and fund balances of the Association are reported in four self balancing funds as follows:

General Fund

This fund is used to account for the operations of the Association as those operations and activities not aoccouted for in other established funds, including all activity of the AECC. All cash is managed and invested through the general fund. All investment earnings are recorded in the general fund and regions fund.

Sections Fund

This fund was established to account for the activities of the Association's special-interest membership groups, such as the auditing section and public sector section.

Fellowship Fund

This fund was established to record the operations of the Fellowship program. Fellowships are awarded using funds generated by contributions to this fund.

Regions

These funds are established to record the operations of regional groups. These groups represent geographic areas, the purpose of which is holding annual meetings for the presentation and discussion of subjects in accounting and allied fields of interest to members of the Association. Funds are generated by collections for these meeetings at the regional level.

NOTE 3—CASH AND CASH EQUIVALENTS

	August 31.	
	1991	1990
Cash and money market funds	$1,098,625	$221.914
Certificates of deposit	—	300.000
	$1,098,625	$521.914

NOTE 4—PROPERTY AND EQUIPMENT

	August 31.	
	1991	1990
Land	$ 29,748	$ 29,748
Land improvements	15,252	15,252
Building	173,271	173,271
Furniture and equipment	113,295	107,600
	331,566	325,871
Less accumulated depreciation	(197,868)	(176,669)
	$ 133,698	$149,202

Compute equipment was donated to the Association during the year ended August 31, 1991 and was recorded at catalog retail price of $5,965. Depreciation expense for the year was:

	August 31.	
	1991	1990
Assets carried at historical cost	$ 20,629	$ 18,997
Assets carried at catalog retail price	570	—
	$ 21,199	$ 18,997

NOTE 5—EMPLOYEE BENEFIT PLAN

The Association has a defined contribution, contributory money pourchase pension plan which covers substantially all employees. During fiscal years 1991 and 1990, contributions to the plan were based upon 15% of qualifyinhg employee conpensation, and approximated $41,278 and $36,190 respectively.

NOTE 6—EMPLOYMENT AGREEMENT

The Association entered into an employment agreement, effective September 1, 1985, requiring the payment of a minimum annual salary of $54,400 to its Executive Director. In additon, the agreement required that the Association set aside a minimum of $55,600 per year for retirement or termination of the Executive Director. At August 31, 1991 and 1990, $167,471 and $88,500, respecptively, were acrued for deferred compensation and were invested in securities designated for such purposes. The agreement expired on August 31, 1990. Per the Employment Addendum dated August 15, 1990, the term of employment has been extended to August 31, 1995 The Addendum provides for a pension contribution equal to 15% of total compensation annually and four weeks fo paid vacation annually. The Executive Committee determines the Executive Director's total salary annually. Total salary for fiscal year 1991 is $87,000.

NOTE 7—MAJOR PROGRAM-REVENUES AND EXPENSES

Revenues and expenses for the corporate A ting Policy Seminar, ProfessionaUsm/Ethics Seminar, Accounting Education Change Commission and the Trueblood Seminar were as follows for the year ended:

	August 31,1991			
	Corporate Accounting Policy Seminar	Professionalism and Ethics Seminar	Accounting Education Change Commission	Trueblood Seminar
Revenues	$55,890	$91,767	$633,684	$221,430
Expenses	55,8901	91,7671	633,6841	221,4301
Excess revenues over expenses	$ _	$ _	$ _	$ _

August 31,1991

Corporate Accounting Policy Seminar	Professionalism and Ethics Seminar	Accounting Education Change Commission	Trueblood Seminar

STATEMENTS OF PLEDGES EARNED AND CONTRIBUTIONS RECEIVED
FOR THE YEAR ENDED AUGUST 31, 1991 AND 1990

	For the Year Ended August 31, 1991	1990		For the Year Ended August 31, 1991	1990
GENERAL FUND			SECTIONS FUNDS		
Arthur Anderson & Co. Foundation	$183,436	$131,771	Arthur Anderson & Co. Foundation	2,324	—
Coopers & Lybrand Foundation	81,034	74,247	Coopers & Lybrand Foundation	3,000	—
Deloitte & Touche Foundation	381,942	253,191	Deloitte & Touche Foundation	1,250	—
Exxon Corporation	5,000	4,000	KPMG Foundation	12,681	—
Ford Motors	—	3,500	Other	638	9,531
Price Waterhouse Foundation	110,401	44,881		19,093	9,531
KPMG Foundation	194,785	127,064	FELLOWSHIP FUND		
Ernst & Young Foundation	162,068	148,495	American Accounting Association		
Boise Cascade Corporation	—	10,000	Members and Others	3,687	4,410
Hewlett-Packard Company	10,000	10,000	Coopers & Lybrand Foundation	5,000	5,000
Monsanto Company	20,000	10,000	Price Waterhouse Foundation	5,000	5,000
Other	47,120	—	Deloitte & Touche Foundation	1,250	—
	1,195,786	817,149		14,937	14,410
			REGIONS FUNDS		
			Other	38,443	65,925
			TOTAL	$1,269,059	$907,015

ACCOUNTING EDUCATION CHANGE COMMISSION HOLDS FALL MEETING

The Accounting Education Change Commission held its fall meeting near the Newark Airport, November 4-5, 1991. A broad array of Commission initiatives were considered.

Chairman Doyle Z. Williams reported that the move of the Commission's administrative offices from Bainbridge Island, Washington to Torrance, California had been completed. He also reported that *Issues Statement No. 2*, "AECC Urges Decoupling of Academic Studies and Professional Accounting Exanunation Preparation," had been printed and widely distributed. The AAA Annual Meeting Round-table Discussion led by Charles Nesson was video taped by Arthur Andersen & Co. Copies have been provided to accounting programs.

The Commission heard a report from James Blum, Director of Examinations of the American Institute of Certified Public Accountants on the results of the Practice Analysis of Certified Public Accountants in Public Accounting. The Practice Analysis was commissioned by the AICPA! SBoard of Examiners and serves as a driver for the content of the CPA Examination. Following a discussion of the presentation, the Comniission decided to address selected issues surrounding the future content of the CPA Examination.

Don Kieso reported on a conference of the Accreditation Board of Engineering and Technology programs (ABET). The Commission noted several parallels in the issues of accreditation and quality education between engineering and accounting.

The Commission agreed to recommend to the American Accounting Association that it explore the possibility of establishing a new award, patterned after the Distinguished In'temational Lecturer, but with an emphasis on pedagogy with a domestic itinerary. The Commission also agreed to pursue the possibility of arranging video taping of a session on teaching by Professors Tom Dyckman and Peter Wilson at the AAA New Faculty Consortium. Efforts win be made to also sponsor two half-day continuing education seminars immediately preceding the 1992 AAA Annual Meeting.

The Student Quality Task Force reported that it had distributed a survey to accounting programs administrators on student recruiting tactics. The Task Force continues to receive responses and welcomes ideas on effective recruiting strategies from WI accounting educators. The Comniission provided feedback to the task force's paper on "The First Course in Accounting."

APPENDIX E

NATIONAL CHARITIES INFORMATION BUREAU
1996 ANNUAL REPORT

PANETH, HABER & ZIMMERMAN LLP
CERTIFIED PUBLIC ACCOUNTANTS

600 Third Avenue
New York, NY 10016-1938
Telephone 212 503-8800
Facsimile 212 370-3759

The Board of Directors
National Charities Information Bureau, Inc.
New York, NY

INDEPENDENT AUDITORS' REPORT

To the Board of Directors:

We have audited the accompanying statement of financial position of National Charities Information Bureau, Inc. ("NCIB") as of December 31, 1996 and 1995 and the related statements of activities, functional expenses and cash flows for the years then ended. These financial statements are the responsibility of NCIB's management. Our responsibility is to express an opinion on these financial statements based on our audits.

We conducted our audits in accordance with generally accepted auditing standards. Those standards require that we plan and perform the audit to obtain reasonable assurance about whether the financial statements are free of material misstatement. An audit includes examining, on a test basis, evidence supporting the amounts and disclosures in the financial statements. An audit also includes assessing the accounting principles used and significant estimates made by management, as well as evaluating the overall financial statement presentation. We believe that our audits provide a reasonable basis for our opinion.

In our opinion, the financial statements referred to above present fairly, in all material respects, the financial position of National Charities Information Bureau, Inc. as of December 31, 1996 and 1995, and the changes in its net assets and its cash flows for the years then ended in conformity with generally accepted accounting principles.

Paneth, Haber & Zimmerman LLP

New York, NY
January 31, 1997

¶ Associated Worldwide with Jeffreys Henry International

NATIONAL CHARITIES INFORMATION BUREAU, INC.   EXHIBIT "A"
STATEMENT OF FINANCIAL POSITION
AS OF DECEMBER 31, 1996 AND 1995

	As of December 31, 1996	As of December 31, 1995
ASSETS		
Current Assets		
Cash (From Exhibit "C")	$ 115,709	$ 59,423
Pledges Receivable (Notes 2C and 3)	214,118	180,940
Other Current Assets	8,017	7,391
Total Current Assets	337,844	247,754
Property and Equipment (Note 2B)		
Office Furniture and Equipment—Less Accumulated Depreciation of $247,864 in 1996 and $217,768 in 1995	33,085	63,181
Leasehold Improvements—Less Accumulated Amortization of $262,557 in 1996 and $242,397 in 1995	39,865	60,025
Total Property and Equipment	72,950	123,206
Non-Current Assets		
Security Deposit	6,250	6,250
Pledges Receivable (Notes 2C and 3)	-	100,000
TOTAL ASSETS	$ 417,044	$ 477,210
LIABILITIES AND NET ASSETS		
Current Liabilities		
Accounts Payable	$ 19,956	$ 77,470
Accrued Salary, Payroll Taxes and Benefits	46,809	28,777
Bank Loan Payable (Note 9)	95,000	-
Other Current Liabilities	12,406	9,896
TOTAL LIABILITIES	174,171	116,143
Net Assets (From Exhibit "B")		
Unrestricted	227,573	167,567
Temporarily Restricted (Note 7)	15,300	193,500
TOTAL NET ASSETS	242,873	361,067
TOTAL LIABILITIES AND NET ASSETS	$ 417,044	$ 477,210

The accompanying notes are an integral part of these financial statements.

NATIONAL CHARITIES INFORMATION BUREAU, INC.
STATEMENT OF ACTIVITIES
FOR THE YEARS ENDED DECEMBER 31, 1996 AND 1995

EXHIBIT "8"

	Year Ended December 31, 1996			Year Ended December 31, 1995		
	Unrestricted	Temporarily Restricted	Total 1996	Unrestricted	Temporarily Restricted	Total 1995
REVENUE AND OTHER SUPPORT:						
Contributions and Grants (Note 2C)	$ 915,605	$ 75,000	$ 990,605	$ 944,053	$ 403,500	$ 1,347,553
Other	3,280	-	3,280	14,186	-	14,186
Net Assets Released from Restrictions:						
Satisfaction of Program and Time Restrictions						
(Note 6)	253,200	(253,200)	-	279,642	(279,642)	-
Total Revenue and Other Support	1,172,085	(178,200)	993,885	1,237,881	123,858	1,361,739
EXPENSES (From Exhibit "B-1"):						
Program Services	778,688	-	778,688	825,712	-	825,712
Management and General	150,873	-	150,873	112,522	-	112,522
Fund Raising	182,518	-	182,518	238,078	-	238,078
Total Expenses	1,112,079	-	1,112,079	1,176,312	-	1,176,312
INCREASE (DECREASE) IN NET ASSETS	60,006	(178,200)	(118,194)	61,569	123,858	185,427
NET ASSETS, BEGINNING OF YEAR	167,567	193,500	361,067	105,998	69,642	175,640
NET ASSETS, END OF YEAR	$ 227,573	$ 15,300	$ 242,873	$ 167,567	$ 193,500	$ 361,067

The accompanying notes are an integral part of these financial statements.

NATIONAL CHARITIES INFORMATION BUREAU, INC.
STATEMENT OF FUNCTIONAL EXPENSES
FOR THE YEARS ENDED DECEMBER 31, 1996 AND 1995

EXHIBIT "B-1"

| | Year Ended December 31, 1996 | | | | | |
| | | Supporting Services | | | | |
	Total Program Services	Management and General	Fund Raising	Total	Total Expenses 1996	1995
Salaries	$ 402,547	$ 51,765	$ 79,946	$ 131,711	$ 534,258	$ 504,753
Payroll Taxes and Employee Benefits (Note 4)	85,659	11,015	17,012	28,027	113,686	108,408
Total Salaries and Related Costs	488,206	62,780	96,958	159,738	647,944	613,161
Consulting Fees	58,608	25,000	-	25,000	83,608	83,935
Mail Service	5,755	-	9,134	9,134	14,889	33,727
Occupancy (Note 5)	81,503	16,301	18,629	34,930	116,433	111,437
Printing	14,652	4,760	25,679	30,439	45,091	93,600
Postage	27,400	10,922	10,406	21,328	48,728	60,737
Professional Fees (Note 2D)	-	15,716	-	15,716	15,716	56,026
Telephone	12,848	1,345	2,840	4,185	17,033	14,904
Equipment Rental (Note 5)	13,663	1,757	2,714	4,471	18,134	17,857
Insurance	9,504	1,222	1,888	3,110	12,614	11,436
Travel	8,883	1,142	1,764	2,906	11,789	9,004
Supplies	5,254	676	1,044	1,720	6,974	5,501
Miscellaneous	17,233	2,216	3,421	5,637	22,870	16,014
Total Expenses Before Depreciation and Amortization	743,509	143,837	174,477	318,314	1,061,823	1,127,339
Depreciation and Amortization	35,179	7,036	8,041	15,077	50,256	48,973
TOTAL EXPENSES (To Exhibit "B")	$ 778,688	$ 150,873	$ 182,518	$ 333,391	$ 1,112,079	$ 1,176,312

The accompanying notes are an integral part of these financial statements.

NATIONAL CHARITIES INFORMATION BUREAU, INC.
STATEMENT OF CASH FLOWS
FOR THE YEARS ENDED DECEMBER 31, 1996 AND 1995

EXHIBIT "C"

| | Year Ended December 31, | |
	1996	1995
CASH FLOWS FROM (USED BY) OPERATING ACTIVITIES:		
Increase (Decrease) in Net Assets (From Exhibit "B")	$(118,194)	$ 185,427
Adjustments to Reconcile Increase (Decrease) in Net Assets to Net Cash Provided by Operating Activities:		
Depreciation and Amortization	50,256	48,973
Sub-Total	(67,938)	234,400
Changes in Operating Assets and Liabilities:		
(Increase) Decrease in Assets:		
Pledges Receivable	66,822	(191,476)
Inventory		6,293
Other Current Assets	(626)	129
Increase (Decrease) in Liabilities:		
Accounts Payable	(57,514)	74
Accrued Salary, Payroll Taxes and Benefits	18,032	7,080
Security Deposit		(1,417)
Other Current Liabilities	2,510	(12,657)
Net Cash Provided (Used) by Operating Activities	(38,714)	42,426
CASH FLOWS FROM (USED BY) INVESTING ACTIVITIES:		
Property and Equipment Acquisitions	-	(12,888)
Net Cash Used by Investing Activities	-	(12,888)
CASH FLOWS FROM (USED BY) FINANCING ACTIVITIES:		
Repayment of Loan	-	(7,500)
Proceeds from Loan	95,000	-
Net Cash Provided (Used) by Financing Activities	95,000	(7,500)
Net Increase in Cash	56,286	22,038
CASH—Beginning of Year	59,423	37,385
CASH—End of Year (To Exhibit "A")	$ 115,709	$ 59,423

The accompanying notes are an integral part of these financial statements.

NATIONAL CHARITIES INFORMATION BUREAU, INC.
NOTES TO FINANCIAL STATEMENTS
FOR THE YEAR ENDED DECEMBER 31, 1996

NOTE 1—ORGANIZATION AND PURPOSE

The National Charities Information Bureau, Inc. ("NCIB") is a New York State Membership Not-for-Profit corporation organized in 1918, exempt from income taxes under Section 501(c)(3) of the United States Internal Revenue Service Code. Contributions by donors qualify for the maximum charitable deduction.

NCIB's primary program services consist of promotion of informed giving; and advocacy on behalf of contributors for compliance with established standards of governance, management and financial reporting by public charities. The promotion of informed giving is accomplished through the development and maintenance of standards in philanthropy, the evaluation of hundreds of national charities in light of these standards and the periodic issuance of reports for each of the charities evaluated. NCIB distributes, usually on a quarterly basis, a *Wise Giving Guide* which contains summary comparisons of each charity's conformity with NCIB's standards in philanthropy. Advocacy activities include NCIB initiatives within the philanthropic community, professional organizations, and regulatory bodies to promote conformity with NCIB's standards, efforts to address specific abuses by individual charitable organizations and still other initiatives designed to promote disclosure of more useful information by public charities to contributors who provide their financial support. Most of NCIB's revenue is derived from contributors such as foundations, corporations and private individuals.

NOTE 2—SUMMARY OF SIGNIFICANT ACCOUNTING POLICIES

A. Adoption of Statements of Financial Accounting Standards—Beginning with 1994, NCIB implemented Statements of Financial Accounting Standards No. 116, *Accounting for Contributions Received and Contributions Made* ("SFAS No 116") and No. 117, *Financial Statements for Not-for-Profit Organizations* ("SFAS No. 117") issued by the Financial Accounting Standards Board. In addition, beginning with 1996, NCIB adopted the provisions of the Audit and Accounting Guide, *Not-For-Profit Organizations* issued by the American Institute of Certified Public Accountants.

Among other things, SFAS No. 117 requires that a not-for-profit organization's statement of financial position report the amounts for each of three classes of net assets—permanently restricted net assets, temporarily restricted net assets, and unrestricted net assets—based on the existence or absence of donor imposed restrictions. In addition, NCIB's statement of activities shall classify revenues, expenses and gains and losses within one of the above three classes of net assets. SFAS No. 116 provides guidelines in accounting for contributions and gifts with donor stipulated conditions and donor-imposed restrictions. NCIB holds no net assets that are considered permanently restricted.

B. Property and Equipment—Expenditures for office furniture and equipment and leasehold improvements have been capitalized at their installed acquisition cost and are amortized over the remaining term of the lease in the case of leasehold improvements or over the respective useful lives of furniture and equipment, using the straight-line method. Service lives for furniture and equipment range from 5 to 15 years. NCIB capitalizes all assets having a useful life of more than one year and a cost greater than or equal to $1,000.

NATIONAL CHARITIES INFORMATION BUREAU, INC.
NOTES TO FINANCIAL STATEMENTS
FOR THE YEAR ENDED DECEMBER 31, 1996

NOTE 2—SUMMARY OF SIGNIFICANT ACCOUNTING POLICIES (Continued)

C. Revenue—All contributions are considered to be available for unrestricted use unless specifically restricted by the donor. Pledges are recorded in the statement of financial position as received, and allowances are provided, where appropriate, for amounts estimated as uncollectible. NCIB reports gifts of cash and other assets as an increase in temporarily restricted net assets if such gifts or contributions are received with donor stipulations that limit the use of such donated assets. When a donor restriction expires by virtue of the passage of time or the purposes of the grant restrictions have been accomplished, temporarily restricted net assets are reclassified to unrestricted net assets in the statement of activities as net assets released from restrictions.

D. Contributed Services—During the year ended December 31, 1995, NCIB received significant pro-bono legal services from external counsel and estimates that the value of such contributed services is approximately $35,000. Such contributed services, which were essential to NCIB's organizational mission, have been recorded as unrestricted contributions and program expense in the statement of activities. Although NCIB benefits from hours of volunteer services in both fund-raising and administrative duties from Board members and other volunteers, no amounts have been reflected in the financial statements for contributed services inasmuch as such services do not require specialized skills nor do they create or enhance nonfinancial assets.

E. Use of Estimates—The preparation of financial statements in conformity with generally accepted accounting principles requires management to make estimates and assumptions that affect certain reported amounts and disclosures.

F. NCIB presents a statement of functional expenses for 1996 using comparative totals only for 1995. Accordingly, certain 1995 comparative information is summarized by functional classification and presented as follows:

| | Total Program Services | Supporting Services | | Total 1995 |
		Management and Administration	Fund Raising	
Salaries	$ 417,166	$ 46,094	$ 41,493	$ 504,753
Payroll Taxes and Benefits	89,597	9,900	8,911	108,408
Consulting Fees	44,420	5,469	34,046	83,935
Occupancy	78,006	15,601	17,830	111,437
Professional Fees	46,926	9,100	-	56,026
Printing and Mail	24,942	10,198	92,187	94,464
Postage	28,626	2,478	29,633	60,737
Depreciation	32,481	6,856	7,836	48,973
All Other	63,548	6,826	6,142	107,579
Total	$ 825,712	$ 112,522	$ 238,078	$ 1,176,312

NOTE 3—PLEDGES RECEIVABLE

As of December 31, 1996 and 1995, contributors to NCIB have made written promises to give, totaling $214,118 and $280,940, respectively. The following is a breakdown of the pledges as of December 31, 1996 and 1995:

NATIONAL CHARITIES INFORMATION BUREAU, INC.
NOTES TO FINANCIAL STATEMENTS
FOR THE YEAR ENDED DECEMBER 31, 1996

NOTE 3—PLEDGES RECEIVABLE (Continued)

| | 1996 | | |
	Unrestricted	Temporarily Restricted	Total
Foundations	$ 50,000	$ 125,000	$ 175,000
Other	39,118	.	39,118
Total	$ 89,118	$ 125,000	$ 214,118

| | 1995 | | |
	Unrestricted	Temporarily Restricted	Total
Corporations	$ 300	$.	$ 300
Foundations	7,900	235,000	242,900
Other	37,740	.	37,740
Total	45,940	235,000	280,940
Less: Current Portion	45,940	135,000	180,940
Non-Current Portion	$.	$ 100,000	$ 100,000

Temporarily restricted pledges which are restricted to purpose, are available for costs to be incurred with the implementation of initiatives presented in NCIB's Business Plan. Unconditional pledges are scheduled to be received as follows:

| | December 31, | |
	1996	1995
Less Than One Year	$ 214,118	$ 180,940
One to Five Years	.	100,000
Total	$ 214,118	$ 280,940

NOTE 4—PENSION PLAN

NCIB sponsors a defined contribution pension plan covering all qualifying employees. Contributions to the plan by NCIB represent 6% of eligible salaries. Employee contributions amounting to $28,207 for 1996 and $25,162 for 1995 are included in payroll taxes and employee benefits in the accompanying financial statements.

NOTE 5—LEASE COMMITMENTS

The minimum annual rental commitment under NCIB's lease for its office at 19 Union Square West in New York City is $75,000 per year through September, 1998. Base rent expense for real property amounted to $75,000 per year for 1996 and 1995.

NATIONAL CHARITIES INFORMATION BUREAU, INC.
NOTES TO FINANCIAL STATEMENTS
FOR THE YEAR ENDED DECEMBER 31, 1996

NOTE 5—LEASE COMMITMENTS (Continued)

The minimum annual rental commitments under operating leases for an office copier and telephone system are $8,550 per year through July, 1999 and $5,171 per year through September, 1998, respectively. Equipment rentals amounted to $18,134 for 1996 and $17,857 for 1995.

NOTE 6—NET ASSETS RELEASED FROM RESTRICTIONS

Net assets which were temporarily restricted at December 31, 1995 and 1994 were either restricted to expenditures in 1996 and 1995, or restricted to specific expenditures by the respective donors. During the years ended December 31, 1996 and 1995, certain time and purpose restrictions were removed because of the passage of time or by incurring expenses thereby satisfying the restricted purposes as follows:

| | December 31, | |
	1996	1995
Time Restrictions Lapsed	$ 57,500	$ 15,000
Capacity Enhancement	-	12,142
Business Plan Initiatives	195,700	242,500
Advocacy Activities	-	10,000
Total	$ 253,200	$ 279,642

NOTE 7—TEMPORARILY RESTRICTED NET ASSETS

NCIB held temporarily restricted net assets at December 31, 1996 and 1995. The amounts and nature of such temporarily restricted net assets are as follows:

| | As of December 31, | |
	1996	1995
Business Plan Initiatives	$ 15,300	$ 86,000
1996 General Operating Purposes	-	107,500
Total	$ 15,300	$ 193,500

NOTE 8—PROGRAM SERVICES

NCIB's program services as presented in the statements of activities and functional expenses for the following major segments of program activity:

| | December 31, | |
	1996	1995
Program Services:		
Promotion of Informed Giving	$ 589,757	$ 636,090
Advocacy	188,932	189,622
Total Program Services	$ 778,689	$ 825,712

NATIONAL CHARITIES INFORMATION BUREAU, INC.
NOTES TO FINANCIAL STATEMENTS
FOR THE YEAR ENDED DECEMBER 31, 1996

NOTE 9—BANK LOAN PAYABLE

On October 31, 1996, NCIB borrowed $95,000 from Chase Manhattan Bank for a period of 100 days at the bank's prime interest rate plus 2.0%. NCIB pledged as collateral for this loan the proceeds of the final grant payment due from the Robert W. Woodruff Foundation on February 10, 1997. This bank loan was repaid on February 10, 1997 upon receipt of funds from the Robert W. Woodruff Foundation.

NOTE 10—CONCENTRATION OF SUPPORT

During 1996 and 1995, NCIB received significant contributions from individuals, corporations and foundations.

For 1996 and 1995, NCIB received single contributions of $100,000 and $250,000 representing 10% and 19% of total support and revenue for 1996 and 1995, respectively.

NATIONAL CHARITIES INFORMATION BUREAU, INC.: FINANCIAL STATEMENTS (1991)

Introduction

**Statement of publicsupport, Revenue and Expenses and changes in Fund Balance
for the Year Ended December 31, 1991 with Comparative Totals for 1990**

	1991				
	Unrestricted Fund	Restricted Fund	Office Furniture & Equipment Fund	1991	1990 Total Funds
PUBLIC SUPPORT AND REVENUE:					
Contributions	$932,340			$932,340	$836,854
Grants(Note 4)		$ 40,000		40,000	40,000
Sales of publications	5,953			5,953	6,767
Interest income	5,613			5,613	9,827
Total	943,906	40,000		983,906	893,448
EXPENSES:					
Program services:					
Standards maintenance and reporting services	571,061		$ 13,954	585,015	568,750
Special projects (Note 4)		41,547		41,547	29,827
Supporting services:					
Management and general	164,184		3,739	167,923	162,273
Fund raising	173,714		3,958	177,672	122,317
Total	908,959	41,547	21,651	972,157	883,167
PUBLIC SUPPORT OVER (UNDER) EXPENSES	34,947	(1,547)	(21,651)	11,749	10,281
Fund balances, beginning of year	115,848	32,229	217,388	365,465	355,184
Fund balances, end of year	$150,795	$ 30,682	$195,737	$377,214	$365,465

See notes to financial statements.

Independent Auditors' Report

National Charities Information Bureau, Inc.:

We have audited the accompanying balance sheets of National Charities information Bureau, Inc. as of December 31, 1991, and 1990 anmd the related statments of public support, revenue and expenses and changes in fund balances and of functional expenses for the year ended December 31, 1991. These financial statments are the responsibility of the Organization's management. Our responsibility is to express an opinion on these financial statments based on our audits.

We conducted our audits in accordance with generally accepted auditing standards. Those standards require that we plan and perform the audit top reasonable assurance about whether the financial statements are free of material misstatement. An audit includes examining on a test basis, evidence supporting the amounts and disclosures in the financial statements. An audit also includes assessing the accounting principles used and significant estimates made by management, as well as evaluating the overall financial statement presentation. We believe that our audits provide a reasonable basis for our opinion.*

Statement of Functional Expenses for the Year Ended December 31, 1991
with Comparative Totals for 1990

	Total Program Services	Supporting Services			Total Expenses	
		Management & General	Fund Raising	Total	1991	1990
Salaries	$290,485	$ 78,632	$ 52,731	$131,363	$421,848	$401,386
Payroll taxes and other employee benefits	54,049	14,631	9,811	24,442	78,491	63,561
Consulting fees	86,392	2,462	0	2,462	88,854	58,197
Professional fees	3,916	23,700	0	23,700	27,616	24,126
Supplies	4,700	1,272	854	2,126	6,826	6,574
Telephone	8,045	2,178	1,460	3,638	11,683	9,153
Postage	17,126	1,903	9,123	11,026	28,152	22,015
Occupancy (Note 3)	81,023	21,933	14,708	36,641	117,664	108,404
Equipment rental (Note 3)	11,495	3,112	2,087	5,199	16,694	11,573
Printing	33,946	3,285	0	3,285	37,231	44,976
Travel	6,355	1,001	4,411	5,412	11,767	7,816
Conferences and meetings	822	5,994	287	6,281	7,103	4,741
Mail service	0	0	77,031	77,031	77,031	48,665
Insurance	5,166	1,398	938	2,336	7,502	7,393
Interest	0	0	0	0	0	0
Miscellaneous	9,088	2,683	273	2,956	12,044	24,590
Total expenses before depreciation and amortization	612,608	164,184	173,714	337,898	950,506	843,170
Depreciation and amortization	13,954	3,739	3,958	7,697	21,651	39,997
Total expenses	$626,562	$167,923	$177,672	$345,595	$972,157	$883,167

See notes to financial statements.

In our opinion, such financial statements present fairly, in all material respects, the financial position of the Organization at December 31, 1991 and 1990 and the results of its operations and changes in fund balances for the year ended December 31, 1991 in conformity with generally accepted accounting principles.

Deloitte & Touche

March 16, 1992

Balance Sheets
As of December 31, 1991 and 1990

Assets	1991	1990	Liabilities and Fund Balances	1991	1990
Unrestricted Funds:			**Unrestricted Funds:**		
Cash	$ 9,681	$ 63,642	Accounts payable	$ 51,093	$ 33,246
Pledges receivable	188,065	98,719	Accrued salary, payroll taxes		
Inventory - publications	2,000	4,000	and vacation	6,736	19,996
Other assets	11,041	4,681	Deferred support (Note 2)	150	305
			Security deposit	1,417	1,417
Total	$210,787	$171,042	Other liabilities	596	230
Restricted Funds:					
			Total	59,992	55,194
Cash	$ 30,682	$ 32,229			
Total	$ 30,682	$ 32,229	Fund balance	150,795	115,848
			Total	$210,787	$171,042
Office Furniture and Equipment Fund:			**Restricted Funds:**		
Security deposit	$ 6,250	$ 6,250	Fund balance	$ 30,682	$ 32,229
Leasehold improvements — less accumulated amortization of $161,753 in 1991 and $141,593 in 1990	140,668	160,828	Total	$ 30,682	$ 32,229
Office furniture and equipment — less accumulated depreciation of $113,922 in 1991 and $112,431 in 1990	48,819	50,310	**Office Furniture and Equipment Fund:** Fund balance	$195,737	$217,388
Total	$195,737	$217,388	Total	$195,737	$217,388

See notes to financial statements.

Notes to Financial Statements

1. ACCOUNTING POLICIES

The accompanying financial statments have been prepared in accordance with the Standards of Accounting and Financial Reporting for Voluntary Health and Welfare Organizations and the Industry Audit Guide of the American Institute of Certified Public Accountants for Voluntary Health and Welfare Organizations.

Expenditures for office furniture and equipment and leasehold improvements have been capitalized. Depreciation on office furniture and equipment is provided on a straight-line basis over the lives of the assets. Amortization of leasehold improvements is provided on a straight-line basis over the life of the lease.

All contributions are considered to be available for unrestricted use unless specifically restricted by the donor. Pledges are recorded in the balance sheet as received, and allowances are provided for amounts estimated as uncollectible.

Revenues from sales of publications are generally recorded net of related inventory costs.

Purchases of suplies and printed materials, generally distributed without charge, are treated as expenses in the year incurred and inventory of such supplies and printed materials is usually not significant.

National Charities Information Bureau, inc. (NCIB) is a New York State not-for-profit corporation, exempt from income tax under Sections 501(c)(3) of the United States Internal Revenue Code. Contributions by donors qualify for the maximum charitable contribution deduction.

Organizations and individuals periodically perform clerical services and donate equipment to NCIB. No amounts have been reported in the accompanying financial statements for these items because no objective basis is available to measure the value of such donations.

2. DEFERRED SUPPORT

Deferred support in the unrestricted fund consists of contributions designated by donors for expenditure in future years.

Changes in deferred support are as follows:

	1991	1990
Balance at beginning of year	$ 305	$ 75
Additions—contributions	150	305
	455	380
Deductions—expenditures during the year	305	75
Balance at end of year	$ 150	$ 305

3. LEASE COMMITMENTS

The minimum annual rental commitment under NCIB's lease for its office at 19 Union Square West is $65,000 through September 1993, and $75,000 through September 1998.

The minimum and annual rental commitment under an operating lease for two copy machines acquired during 1991 is $6,400 through June 1994.

4. PROJECTS

The restricted support received in 1991 and 1990 pertains to the Public Outreach project. This project's goal is-to expand awareness and use of NCIB services.

GLOSSARY

ACCELERATED DEPRECIATION: A depreciation method that, in comparison to the straight-line depreciation method, allocates more cost to the earlier years of service of a depreciable asset and less to the later years. See "DEPRECIATION."

ACCOUNT: A recording device in which is entered, in money amounts, all increases and decreases in an item, whether an asset, liability, or element of ownership equity.

ACCOUNTS PAYABLE: Liabilities of a business to vendors for merchandise purchased on credit.

ACCOUNTS RECEIVABLE: Claims of a business against its customers for goods sold or services rendered on credit.

ACID TEST: One of several ratios designed to measure the liquidity of a business. It measures a firm's ability to convert its current assets quickly into cash to pay its current liabilities. It is computed by dividing the sum of a firm's cash, marketable securities and accounts receivable by its current liabilities.

ACCRUAL: An accounting procedure in which income is recognized when it is earned as opposed to when it is received and expenses are recognized when incurred as opposed to when funds are disbursed.

AMORTIZATION: A method for allocating the cost of an intangible asset over its estimated useful life.

ASSETS: The economic resources owned by an enterprise.

AUTHORIZED SHARES: Shares which the certificate of incorporation authorizes the board of directors to issue.

BOOK VALUE: The value at which an asset or liability appears on a balance sheet. It is also referred to as the "carrying value."

BOOK VALUE PER SHARE: A measurement of the amount of net assets (assets less liabilities) backing each share of common stock. It is a theoretical measurement of the amount an owner of a share of common stock would receive if all corporate assets were liquidated at book value, all liabilities were paid off, and the proceeds were distributed on a *pro rata* basis.

CAPITAL SURPLUS: A category of shareholders' equity equal to the excess of paid-in capital over stated capital.

CAPITALIZE, TO: An expenditure is "capitalized" if its cost is recorded as an asset on the balance sheet. It may then be allocated as an expense over time. This term is to be contrasted with the term "to EXPENSE."

CASH BASIS: A method of recording expenses and revenues that records increases in income only when cash is received and records decreases in income only when cash is disbursed.

CONSERVATISM: One of the conventions which comprise generally accepted accounting principles. This convention directs that when two or more acceptable alternatives are available for recording assets and liabilities or for recognizing expenses and revenues, the alternative that results in the lowest net income and net assets should be selected.

CONSOLIDATED FINANCIAL STATEMENTS: Financial statements which combine the financial statements of a parent corporation and its subsidiary(ies).

CONTRA ACCOUNT: An account which is deducted from another account on a financial statement. The contra account "Accumulated depreciation" is deducted from plant assets on a balance sheet.

CONTRIBUTED CAPITAL: See "PAID-IN CAPITAL."

CREDIT: See "DEBIT."

CURRENT ASSETS: Those assets which either are cash or can be converted into cash in the normal course of business operations within an operating cycle or one year, whichever is longer. See "OPERATING CYCLE."

CURRENT LIABILITIES: Those liabilities which mature within a year or within the length of an operating cycle if longer. Current liabilities will be satisfied by the application of current assets. See "CURRENT ASSETS" and "OPERATING CYCLE."

CURRENT RATIO: A ratio designed to measure the liquidity of a business. It is calculated by dividing current assets by current liabilities. See "CURRENT ASSETS" and "CURRENT LIABILITIES." It provides a rough evaluation of the ability of a business to pay its debts as they fall due.

DEBT-TO-EQUITY RATIO: A ratio that compares a business's debts to its total liabilities plus owners' equity. Other expressions of ratios serving a similar purpose are total debt to equity (owners' equity exclusive of liabilities) or the ratio of owners' equity to the total of liabilities plus equity. In each instance, the ratio derived is informative of the protection provided creditors.

DEBIT: Entries into accounts either increase or decrease the balance of the account. Debit entries increase balances of asset and expense accounts and decrease balances of liability, ownership equity, and revenue accounts. Credit entries decrease balances of asset and expense accounts and increase balances of liability, ownership equity, and revenue accounts. When debits in an account exceed the credits, the resulting balance is a debit balance. When credits in an account exceed the debits, the resulting balance is a credit balance. In conventional "T" accounts, debits are entered on the left side and credits are entered on the right side.

DEFERRALS: Non-recognition of revenue for cash received within the current fiscal period because the revenue has not yet been earned. Non-recognition of expense for cash paid within the current fiscal period because the expense has not yet been incurred.

DEFERRED CHARGE: A long-term prepaid expense which is carried on the balance sheet as a noncurrent asset. The prepayment must be made for a future expense for a time period that exceeds the business' operating cycle. *See* "PREPAID EXPENSE."

DEPLETION: The allocated cost of a natural resource as it is exhausted.

DEPRECIATION: The allocated cost of a plant asset over its estimated useful life.

DIVIDEND: A distribution to shareholders of a corporation of the income earned or the gains made by the corporation.

EARNED SURPLUS (RETAINED EARNINGS): The accumulated undistributed net income of a corporation as measured from the inception of the corporation to the present time. In instances where the corporation has experienced net losses, such losses are referred to as a "deficit." While attorneys will frequently use the term "earned surplus," accountants prefer "retained earnings."

EQUITY: The claims of the owners of a business. Equity is equal to the assets of a business less its liabilities.

EXPENSE, TO: An expenditure is "expensed" if its cost is matched against the revenues generated during the period of time in which the expenditure is incurred. This term is to be contrasted with the term "to CAPITALIZE."

EXPENSES: Outflows of assets (without an offsetting inflow of assets) or incurrence of liabilities, or both, arising from the carrying out of the primary activities of a business.

FIFO (FIRST IN, FIRST OUT): A valuation method for inventory which assigns cost to inventory by arbitrarily assuming that goods purchased first are sold first.

FINISHED GOODS: Manufactured goods that are ready for sale. Finished goods are created by the application of labor to "raw materials." The cost of finished goods includes an allocation for overhead in addition to the cost of raw materials and labor.

(Matthew Bender & Co., Inc.)

FUND: Cash and/or other assets which have been set aside for a specific purpose. For an individual, this might be a retirement fund or an education fund. For a business corporation, there may be a bond sinking fund or a pension fund. As to a non-profit organization,, all of its assets minus its liabilities constitute one or more funds to carry out the purposes of the organization. All non-profits have a general or unrestricted fund. There may also be additional funds, such as endowment, building, or restricted funds.

FUND ACCOUNTING: A system of accounting in which separate records are kept for resources associated with specific activities, objectives or restrictions.

GAIN: An increase in net assets resulting from a transaction that is peripheral or incidental to the primary business of an entity.

GENERALLY ACCEPTED ACCOUNTING PRINCIPLES: A set of conventions and rules which guide accountants in determining how to present information on financial statements.

GOODS IN PROCESS: Raw materials to which some labor has been applied but which have not become "finished goods." See "FINISHED GOODS" and "RAW MATERIALS."

GOODWILL: An intangible asset which is reflected in certain advantages which a business might possess arising from factors such as location, reputation, good labor relations, and superior management among others. Goodwill can only be recognized as an asset when a business or part of a business is purchased.

GROSS MARGIN: The excess of sales revenue over the cost of goods sold. From this amount, a business arrives at its net profit after deducting its selling, administrative, and other expenses.

HISTORICAL COST: A method of valuation that records items on a balance sheet in terms of their original cost to an enterprise.

HORIZONTAL ANALYSIS: A method for analyzing the financial condition and results of operations of a business by comparing current financial statements with those from prior periods.

IMPAIRMENT OF CAPITAL: A financial condition of a corporation which exists when net assets (assets less liabilities) are not at least equal to stated capital. The "cushion" of capital upon which creditors rely is not available. See "STATED CAPITAL."

INCOME, NET: Revenues less expenses. The net income (loss) of a business during an accounting period increases (decreases) the retained earnings of that business by an identical amount.

INSOLVENCY: This term can refer either to equity insolvency or to bankruptcy insolvency. Equity insolvency means that a business is unable to pay its debts as they become due. Bankruptcy insolvency means that the liabilities of a business exceed its assets.

INVENTORY: In a merchandising firm, inventory includes all goods which the firm holds for sale in the ordinary course of business. In a manufacturing firm, inventory includes finished goods, goods in process, raw materials, and supplies that will be consumed in the production of goods for sale.

ISSUED SHARES: When the board of directors of a corporation exercises its authority and sells or otherwise distributes the share which it is authorized to issue, the shares are then considered "issued."

JOURNAL: A formal accounting record in which each transaction is recorded in terms of increasing or decreasing an account balance. The entries in the journal are ultimately transferred to the ledger. See "LEDGER."

LEDGER: A collection of accounts. A general ledger includes all of the asset, liability, ownership equity, revenue, and expense accounts. See "ACCOUNTS."

LEVERAGE: Borrowing by a business in situations in which the rate of return on the assets obtained by use of the borrowed funds exceeds the interest cost of the borrowed funds.

LIABILITIES: Claims by creditors against the assets of a business.

LIFO (LAST IN, FIRST OUT): A valuation method for inventory which assigns cost to inventory by arbitrarily assuming that goods purchased last are sold first.

LIQUIDITY: The capability of an asset to be readily converted into cash. The more liquid an asset, the more readily it may be converted into cash. Marketable securities are more liquid than buildings and land.

LOSS: A decrease in net assets that results from ordinary operations or from transactions which are peripheral or incidental to the ordinary business of an entity. (Note: Losses, unlike gains, may result from ordinary, continuing business operations as well as from non-ordinary business activities).

MATCHING: One of the conventions which comprises generally accepted accounting principles. This convention directs that expenses incurred within a fiscal period be charged against revenues earned during that period.

NET ASSET CLASS: A term arising from an accounting model, replacing fund accounting for external (but not internal) reporting which:

1) the equities in groups of assets and related liabilitites are termed "net assets" and

2) the net assets are classified according to donor-imposed restrictions: permanently restricted, temporarily restricted, or unrestricted.

NET WORTH: The interest of the owners in an enterprise. The claims of the owners against the resources of an enterprise.

NONCURRENT ASSETS: Those assets which are either consumed or used in the operations of a business over a period of time lasting longer than an operating cycle. Examples include land, building, equipment, and intangible assets.

NO-PAR STOCK: Stock authorized without a par value. Statutes generally permit directors to assign a stated value to such stock. See "PAR VALUE."

OPERATING CYCLE: The average period of time in which a business entity produces and sells its product, measured from the time of acquisition of materials and services to the realization of cash from accounts receivable.

OUTSTANDING SHARES: Authorized and issued shares still in the hands of the shareholders (*i.e.*, issued shares which have not been reacquired by the corporation). See "ISSUED SHARES."

PAID-IN CAPITAL (CONTRIBUTED CAPITAL): That portion of shareholders' equity (the capital of the corporation) that is contributed to the corporation when the corporation raises funds through the sale of its shares.

PAR VALUE: An arbitrary figure recorded in the Certificate of Incorporation that designates the minimum amount that must be received by the corporation for each share of stock, upon original issuance of such shares, for the shares to be considered fully paid.

PERIODIC INVENTORY METHOD: A method of keeping track of inventory pursuant to which a running record of inventory is not kept. Instead, periodically, a physical count is taken of inventory.

PERPETUAL INVENTORY METHOD: A method of keeping track of inventory pursuant to which a business maintains a continuous record of its inventory.

PLANT ASSETS (FIXED ASSETS): Noncurrent assets which fall into the category of either "land," "building," or "equipment."

PREPAID EXPENSE: Supplies paid for which have not yet been used or services paid for which have not yet been received. Prepaid expenses are assets since cash will not have to be expended during the period covered by the prepayment to be able to use the goods or receive the services. Prepaid expenses generally are treated as current assets since they are payment of expenses that will arise within the next operating cycle or within a year, whichever is longer.

PRICE-EARNINGS RATIO: The number of times by which the per share earnings must be multiplied to arrive at the current market price of the stock. A high ratio tends to indicate that investors believe future earnings will be greater than present earnings.

RAW MATERIALS: Those items of inventory of manufacturing firms that are transformed in the manufacturing process into finished products.

RECEIVABLES: See "ACCOUNTS RECEIVABLE."

RESTRICTED CAPITAL: A limitation placed on the use of retained earnings as a measurement for funds available for distribution by a corporation. Retained earnings will be restricted to the extent of the amount of treasury shares repurchased by the corporation.

RETAINED EARNINGS: See "EARNED SURPLUS."

REVENUES: Inflows of assets (without offsetting outflows of assets) or settlement (payment) of liabilities, or both, that arise in the course of a business entity's primary operations. Revenues typically arise from sales of merchandise or services.

RETIREMENT OF SHARES: Shares reacquired by a corporation may be entirely eliminated by a charter amendment reducing the number of authorized shares of the corporation. Such eliminated shares are said to have been "retired" and they may not be reissued without an additional charter amendment authorizing their issuance.

SALVAGE VALUE: The estimated value of a depreciable asset at the end of its useful life.

SHAREHOLDERS' EQUITY: Ownership equity in a corporation.

STATED CAPITAL: The par value of a corporation's stock multiplied by the number of shares issued. When no-par stock has been issued, the stated value of such stock multiplied by the number of shares issued is added to stated capital. Stated capital is also called "legal capital" or just "capital." Historically, it has been thought of as a financial "cushion" out of which distributions will not be made and upon which creditors can rely in making loans and extending credit to a corporation.

STATED VALUE: An arbitrarily assigned value given to no-par stock to indicate what portion of the consideration given in exchange for the stock will be allocated to stated capital.

STOCK DIVIDEND: A corporate distribution in which current shareholders receive additional shares in the corporation. Since the dividend is distributed on a basis prorated to current holdings, each shareholder's proportionate interest in the corporation remains constant. No assets leave the corporation and the net effect is that the equity of the corporation becomes divided among a greater number of shares.

STRAIGHT-LINE DEPRECIATION: A depreciation method that allocates depreciation expenses equally each year over the estimated life of an asset. See "DEPRECIATION."

TREASURY SHARES: Shares of a corporation which were once outstanding but have been reacquired by the corporation and are being held for possible reissuance.

TRIAL BALANCE: A listing and totaling of the balances of all of the accounts in a ledger in terms of debit balances and credit balances. See "LEDGER" and "DEBIT."

VERTICAL ANALYSIS: A method of analyzing the financial condition or results of operation of a business that relies upon comparisons of various items within a single financial statement. As an example, the amount for one asset on a balance sheet might be computed as a percentage of the total assets on the same balance sheet, or various expenses in an income statement might be computed as percentages of net sales.

WORKING CAPITAL: The excess of current assets over current liabilities.

PROBLEMS

CHAPTER I

Problem I-1

Liabilities of a corporation total $27,000; its assets total $40,000. What is its shareholders' equity?

Problem I-2

Assets of a corporation exceed its liabilities by $15,000; its retained earnings are $6,000. What is its paid-in capital?

Problem I-3

What is the separate effect on shareholders' equity of each of the following transactions?

A. The purchase of merchandise for cash, $20,000.

B. The sale by the corporation of 100 shares of its capital stock for $10,000.

C. Payment of officers' salaries, $3,000.

D. The purchase of merchandise on credit, $40,000.

E. The sale on credit for $15,000 of merchandise costing $10,000.

F. Payment of accounts payable, $7,000.

G. Collection of accounts receivable, $4,000.

H. Declaration and payment of a dividend, $1,000.

Problem I-4

Sales for the period totalled $60,000; cost of sales was $35,000; rent and other expenses totalled $18,000. What was the gross margin for the period? The net income?

Problem I-5

Net income for the period was $11,000; expenses totalled $27,000; and sales were $90,000. What was the gross margin for the period? The cost of sales?

Problem I-6

Assets increased during the period by $10,000 and liabilities decreased by $5,000. What was the net effect on shareholders' equity?

Can you determine the net income for the period from the foregoing information. If not, why?

You are now informed that there was no change in paid-in capital over the period. Can you now determine the net income for the period? If not, why?

Problem I-7

The Trellace Corporation is notified that one of its customers had gone out of business and will be unable to pay anything on the $500 it owes to Trellace. The bookkeeper of Trellace is instructed to "write off" (eliminate) the account receivable of $500. What is the effect of this write-off on the financial statements?

Problem I-8

Given the following transactions of the Ajax Corporation for the period of March 1, 20____ through April 30, 20____:

A. Stockholders invested $30,000, cash.

B. Merchandise was purchased for cash, $10,000.

C. Merchandise was purchased on credit, $40,000.

D. Merchandise costing $6,000 was sold for $10,000, cash.

E. Merchandise costing $27,000 was sold on credit for $50,000.

F. Collections were made on accounts receivable, $30,000.

G. Payment of $25,000 was made on accounts payable.

H. Rent was paid, $3,000.

I. Salaries and other expenses were paid, $7,000.

J. Dividends of $1,200 were declared and paid.

Required:

A. An analysis of the effects on the fundamental equation following the format in Exhibit 1.1.

B. A balance sheet at the end of the period, April 30, 20_____.

C. An income statement for the period, the two months ended April 30, 20_____.

D. A statement of retained earnings for the two months.

Problem I-9

This problem is a continuation of the financial activities of the Best Selling Corporation which was presented in Chapter I. The transactions for the three months ended November 30, 20_____ are summarized below.

A. Merchandise purchases for the period were $1,200 for cash and $163,000 on credit.

B. Sales totalled $260,000, all on credit. The cost of the merchandise sold was $155,000.

C. Collections on accounts receivable, $240,000.

D. Payments on accounts payable, $142,000.

E. Expenses for the period, all paid in cash, totalled $72,000.

F. A dividend of $2,000 was declared and paid.

Required:

A. An analysis of the effects on the fundamental equation following the format in Exhibit 1.1. However, the balances in the fundamental equation for the Best Selling Corporation as of August 31, 20_____ should be set up as the first line in this analysis.

B. A balance sheet at November 30, 20_____.

C. An income statement for the three months ended November 30, 20_____.

D. A statement of retained earnings for the same three months.

CHAPTER II

Problem II-1

Laminall Plastics Inc., an expanding plastic laminating business, bought a heavy duty plastic sheet press for $25,000 in 20X1. The company intended to maintain the press for ten years at which time it expected to sell the equipment for scrap value and to buy a replacement press. Laminall estimated that the scrap value of the press would be $5,000.

A. What would be the book value of the press in 20X6, five years after it was purchased? Assume a straight-line depreciation method.

(Matthew Bender & Co., Inc.)

B. Assume that, at the end of 20X6, a new type of laminating process is introduced into the market. The process is cheaper and more efficient than the laminating process that was in existence prior to that time. Laminall Plastics recognizes that in order to remain competitive in the laminating business it will have to obtain equipment that will allow it to utilize the new laminating process. Laminall decides that, instead of keeping its now obsolete press for a total of ten years, it will keep it for a total of eight years (*i.e.*, for three more years). Further, Laminall realizes that the scrap value of the old press will now be only $3,000. What will be Laminall's depreciation expense on its 20X1 purchased press for the following three years? Continue to assume a straight-line depreciation method.

Problem II-2

In 20XX, Murray began his own auto repair shop. He leased his shop, bought his tools, and had some workmen construct a work area and a small office. Murray also ran an advertising campaign which cost $10,000 and he bought an automobile ownership list from a local automotive club for $5,000 in order to make direct mail solicitations. Within five years, Murray had a thriving automobile repair business. Instead of charging the advertising and mailing list costs as expenses during his first year of operations, he carried those items as assets under the category of "goodwill." He estimated that the value of the advertising and the mail solicitation to the business would last for about seven years. As a consequence, he chose to allocate the cost of this goodwill expense by amortizing it over a seven-year period.

Was this an appropriate accounting procedure?

Problem II-3

A. In what regards is the LIFO method of accounting for inventory a more realistic method of valuing inventory than the FIFO method?

B. In what regards is the FIFO method of accounting for inventory a more realistic method of valuing inventory than the LIFO method?

Problem II-4

Amalgamated Builders Inc., a building construction firm, buys lumber on a continual basis during the year for its construction needs. During a recent year, Amalgamated made the following purchases of structural lumber at the following prices on the dates specified:

Date	Number of Feet	Cost per Foot	Cost of Purchase
January 10	4,000	$.25	$ 1,000
March 20	8,500	$.30	$ 2,550
June 15	7,000	$.40	$ 2,800
September 5	8,200	$.50	$ 4,100
November 12	6,600	$.55	$ 3,630
TOTALS	34,300		$14,080

Amalgamated began the year with 2,000 feet of lumber in inventory which it carried on its books at $400. During the year, Amalgamated used 33,000 feet of lumber.

A. What would be the differential in net income before taxes for Amalgamated for the year in question if it applied a LIFO method of inventory accounting rather than a FIFO method?

B. What would be the difference in the value of Amalgamated's net assets on its balance sheet at the end of the year if Amalgamated applied a LIFO method of inventory accounting as opposed to a FIFO method? Ignore the effect of income taxes.

Problem II-5

A. The following alphabetical listing contains items appearing on financial statements. Which of these would be classified as:

    A. current assets, and why?

    B. current liabilities, and why?

C. noncurrent assets?

D. noncurrent liabilities?

E. elements of shareholders' equity?

F. Which items would not appear on a balance sheet, and why?

1. Accounts payable

2. Accounts receivable

3. Accrued expenses

4. Accrued income

5. Allowance for depreciation

6. Bank loan

7. Building

8. Capital stock

9. Capital surplus

10. Cost of sales

11. Current installment on mortgage payable

12. Deferred income

13. Dividends declared

14. Dividends payable

15. Equipment

16. Furniture and fixtures

17. Goodwill

18. Interest expense

19. Interest income

20. Investment in stock of subsidiary

21. Land

22. Marketable securities

23. Merchandise inventory

24. Mortgage payable, net of current installment

25. Prepaid expenses

26. Rent expense

27. Retained earnings

28. Salaries and wages

29. Sales revenue

CHAPTER III

Problem III-1

Assets of a corporation are $25,000. Liabilities are $10,000. Par value of the 1,000 shares of outstanding stock is $10. Can we compute retained earnings? Why?

Problem III-2

The balance sheet of the Nouvell Corporation indicates that shareholders' equity is comprised of $10,000 of stated capital, $15,000 of capital surplus, and $15,000 of retained earnings. Does the Nouvell Corporation have adequate current assets to pay its debts as they become due?

Problem III-3

Registered Industries, Inc. issues 1,000 shares of no-par stock which is purchased by several investors for $10,000. No attempt is made by the board of directors to provide a stated value for this stock. In the majority of states, the concepts of stated capital and capital surplus are still viable. What would be the stated capital and capital surplus of Registered Industries, Inc. as a result of the above issuance? For an illustrative statute governing this question, see Del. Gen. Corp. Law § 154.

Problem III-4

The Appreciating Corporation issued 10,000 shares of $2.00 par common stock to Investor A for $30,000. The Appreciating Corporation is thereafter very successful in its business and the market value of its stock rises. Within a year of purchase, Investor A is able to sell the 10,000 shares to Investor B for $50,000, or $5.00 a share. What impact does the sale of stock from A to B have on the capital surplus of the Appreciating Corporation?

Problem III-5

The Certificate of Incorporation of the Ambitious Corporation indicates that the Corporation has authorized 50,000 shares of $2.00 par common stock. At Time 1, the Ambitious Corporation sells 1,000 shares of common stock at $3 per share. At Time 2, the Corporation sells 10,000 shares at $5.00 a share. Immediately after Time 2, what are the stated capital and capital surplus of the Ambitious Corporation?

CHAPTER V

Problem V-1

Prepare a balance sheet from the following data which appeared in the financial statements of Large Corporation for the calendar year 20X2. All of the data is in millions of dollars. However, the six zeros to indicate millions can be omitted. Note that some of the data is not includible in a balance sheet and that the dollar amount of retained earnings will have to be computed.

The item, treasury stock, appears on many balance sheets. Although not discussed in the Guide until Chapter IX, treasury stock has been included in this Problem for the sake of completeness. In order to prepare a proper solution, the cost of the treasury stock should be deducted from the total shareholders' equity.

The titles used in this problem were taken from published financial statements and, since such titles vary, they may not coincide in all cases with the terms used in the Guide. However, the meanings should be sufficiently clear so as to permit proper classification.

Accumulated depreciation on plant and equipment	287
Accrued payrolls, pensions and bonuses	60
Additional paid-in capital	187
Cash	21
Common stock, $5 par value	105
Cost of goods sold	1,751
Current portion of long-term debt	7
Dividends	36
Finished goods	190
Goodwill	50
Income taxes payable	10
Interest expense	37

Long-term debt	165
Marketable securities	19
Net sales	2,600
Other current payables and accruals	65
Other liabilities (noncurrent)	19
Other receivables and investments (noncurrent)	23
Patents and trademarks	3
Prepaid expenses	43
Property, plant and equipment	920
Provision for income taxes [income tax expense]	85
Raw materials	110
Retained earnings, 12/31/X1	?
Retained earnings, 12/31/X2	?
Selling, general and administrative expenses	622
Short-term debt	211
Trade accounts payable	140
Trade receivables, net of allowance for bad debt	340
Treasury stock, at cost	57
Work in process	22

CHAPTER VI

Problem VI-1

A business takes out an insurance policy with an inception date of December 1, Year 1 and, on November 25, pays a one-year premium of $600. It renews the policy at a premium of $660 a year effective December 1, Year 2. Because of interoffice confusion, the premium due December 1, Year 2, was not paid until January 15, Year 3. Despite the delay in payment, the policy continued in force.

With respect to this insurance policy and the financial statements of the business:

A. What should be shown as insurance expense for calendar Year 1?

B. Where on the financial statements for Year 1 would this expense appear?

C. What amount, if any, should appear on a balance sheet at December 31, Year 1, and how should it be titled?

D. What should be shown as insurance expense for Year 2?

E. What amount, if any, should appear on a balance sheet at December 31, Year 2, and what should it be titled?

With respect to this insurance policy and the financial statements of the insurance company:

F. What should be shown as revenue for calendar Year 1?

G. What amount, if any, should appear on its balance sheet at December 31, Year 1, and what should it be titled?

H. What should be shown as revenue for Year 2?

I. What amount, if any, should appear on the balance sheet at December 31, Year 2, and what should it be titled?

Problem VI-2

A business borrowed $30,000 on a mortgage on June 1, Year 1, at an annual interest rate of 12%. Interest was payable semiannually, together with semiannual payments of $1,000 to amortize the principal.

With respect to the business:

A. What payments should be made during Calendar Year 1?

B. What interest expense is incurred by the business during its fiscal year ending March 31, Year 2?

C. What amount, if any, should appear on the balance sheet at March 31, Year 2, and how should it be titled?

D. What payments should be made during Calendar Year 2?

E. What should appear on the balance sheet at March 31, Year 3?

F. What interest expense is incurred by the business during its fiscal year ending March 31, Year 3?

With respect to the bank:

G. What should appear on its balance sheet with respect to this mortgage at December 31, year 1?

H. What is its interest revenue on this mortgage during Calendar Year 1? Calendar Year 2?

Problem VI-3

A business with a five-day work week of Monday through Friday pays salaries every Tuesday for the week ended the previous Friday. New employees, if any, start work on a Monday. Salary increases, if any, are also effective on a Monday. The following salary payments were made:

March 6	500
13	500
20	500
27	550
April 3	550
10	550
17	600
24	600
May 1	600
8	600

A. How much was paid for salaries during March? April?

B. What is the proper salaries expense for March? April?

C. What amount, if any, should appear with respect to salaries on a balance sheet as of March 31? April 30?

Problem VI-4

Refer to the data in Problem V-1 for the Large Corporation.

A. Prepare an income statement for the Calendar Year 20X2.

B. Prepare a statement of retained earnings for the Calendar Year 20X2. Note that the dollar amounts for beginning and ending retained earnings have not been provided. For retained earnings of December 31, 20X2, use the amount you determined in Problem V-1. Derive the proper amount for retained earnings at December 31, 20X1.

CHAPTER VII

Problem VII-1

A Statement of Cash Flows generally is divided into sections dealing with:

operating activities,

investing activities, and

financing activities.

These three sections are summarized to arrive at a net increase or decrease in cash and cash equivalents. The net increase or decrease is followed by the balance of cash and cash equivalents at the beginning of the period. By addition or subtraction, one then reconciles the beginning balance with the balance of cash and cash equivalents at the end of the period. Following the reconciliation of cash, information is presented, usually in schedule form, about investing and financing activities that affect assets or liabilities other than cash or cash equivalents.

State the effect of each of the following transactions on the fundamental equation and also the section of the cash flows statement affected. Consider each transaction separately and apart from the others.

A. Sale of capital stock at par for $10,000 cash.

B. Purchase of equipment for cash, $7,000.

C. Issuance of capital stock with stated value of $8,000 in exchange for equipment with a fair market value of $12,000.

D. Recording of depreciation expense of $5,000.

E. The borrowing of $11,000 on a bank loan repayable in three months.

F. Collection of accounts receivable, $9,000.

G. Payment of accounts payable, $4,000.

H. Payment of salaries of $2,300.

I. Sale of merchandise costing $1,100 on credit for $1,900.

J. Issuing of bonds at face value for $75,000 cash.

K. Declaration of a 50% stock dividend, resulting in an increase in capital stock of $20,000 and a decrease in retained earnings of $20,000.

L. Purchase of a building for $25,000 with $5,000 paid in cash and the balance covered by a mortgage payable for $20,000.

M. Sale for $20,000 of land carried at a cost of $14,000.

Problem VII-2

Prepare a Statement of Cash Flows from the comparative balance sheets, the income statement, and the additional information provided below.

Problematical Corporation
Comparative Balance Sheets

	Ending Balance Sheet	Begining Balance Sheet
Assets		
Cash	18,000	15,000
Accounts receivable, net	43,000	40,000
Inventories	47,000	48,000
Land	27,000	41,000
Buildings	110,000	50,000

	Ending Balance Sheet	Begining Balance Sheet
Equipment	53,000	30,000
Allowance for depreciation	(26,000)	(20,000)
	272,000	204,000
Liabilities		
Accounts payable	20,000	25,000
Income taxes payable	1,500	2,000
Interest payable	500	1,000
Bank loans, current	5,000	4,000
Mortgage payable, noncurrent	70,000	30,000
Equity		
Capital stock	105,000	90,000
Additional paid-in capital	28,000	20,000
Retained earnings	53,000	32,000
Treasury stock, cost	(11,000)	-0-
	272,000	204,000

Income Statement

Net Sales		205,000
Cost of sales		152,000
Gross margin		53,000
Selling expense	15,100	
Administrative expense	11,200	26,300
Income from operations		26,700
Interest expense		3,200
Income before taxes		23,500
Income taxes		3,500
Income before extraordinary items		20,000
Gain on sale of land (net of taxes)		5,000
Net income		25,000

Additional information:

1. Land costing $14,000 was sold at a gain of $5,000, net of applicable tax. The sale was for cash.

2. Cash dividends were $4,000.

3. A building was purchased for $60,000, of which $40,000 was raised by mortgage.

4. Equipment was acquired for $23,000 in exchange for capital stock. The capital stock was issued at a premium of $8,000.

. . .

Note that one can prepare a statement of cash flows without an elaborate worksheet. Sketch the format of the statement as a starting point. Then systematically run through all of the items listed in the comparative balance sheets, the income statement, and in the additional information and insert the proper amounts into the sketches. Working carefully, one should arrive at a Statement of Cash Flows with all its several subdivisions.

It would be useful to key each set of source figures by a reference letter, (A, B, C, etc.) and each solution figure by the same letter as the source figures.

CHAPTER VIII

Problem VIII-I

Refer to the financial statements of the H.J. Heinz Company in Appendix B and compute the ratios listed below.

Utmost precision in computing ratios can be unnecessarily time-consuming and may add little or nothing to the significance of the results. To simplify calculations, one might well round out the data before computing a ratio. For example, in dealing with a figure of 47,086,127, one could well drop the last six digits and work with 47. If the original amount is 47,845,833, one might round to 48. In some instances, even greater roughing out of the calculations can provide useful approximations.

However, in the solutions to this Problem, the authors have for the most part used precise figures, but only because this makes it easier for the reader to locate and identify in the Heinz financial statements the figures being utilized to compute the ratios.

A number of ratios involve the use of some average. For example, accounts receivable turnover is computed by dividing sales by the average balance of accounts receivable. Similarly, the denominator in computing earnings per share is the average number of shares outstanding throughout the period. If all of a company's internal data were available, one could obtain a more accurate average with monthly rather than quarterly or annual data.

    A. Current ratio

    B. Acid test ratio

    C. Debt to equity

    D. Times interest earned

    E. Book value per share

    F. Accounts receivable turnover

    G. Inventory turnover

    H. Asset turnover ratio

    I. Earnings per share

    J. Price earnings ratio

    K. Return on total assets

    L. Rate of return on investment

    M. Ratio of net income to sales

    N. Gross profit ratio

CHAPTER IX

Problem IX-1

The Eager to Please Corporation has a balance sheet that in simplified form appears as follows:

EAGER TO PLEASE CORPORATION

Balance Sheet as of December 31, 20XX
(in thousands)

Assets		Liabilities and shareholders' equities	
Cash	$ 25	Short term loans	$ 40
Inventory	20	Long term loans	10
Plant and equipment	80	Stated capital	10
		Capital surplus	25
		Earned surplus	40
Total assets	$125		
		Total liabilities and shareholders equities	$125

As of the date of this balance sheet, would the Eager to Please Corporation be able to make a cash distribution to its shareholders if it were governed by the laws of a jurisdiction which employed an earned surplus test? What of an earned surplus test in conjunction with a solvency test? What of a jurisdiction which had adopted the RMBCA? What would be the maximum permitted distribution(s)?

Problem IX-2

The Less Than Lucrative Corporation has had a poor earnings record during its three years of existence. In fact, the Corporation has an accumulated deficit. However, the Corporation's managers are eager to court the favor of its shareholders by distributing a cash dividend. The Corporation is incorporated in a jurisdiction which has adopted the distribution restriction provisions of the RMBCA. Assuming that a simplified version of the Corporation's balance sheet appears as below, can the Corporation issue a dividend? Is there anything troubling about your answer in light of traditional corporate principles of distributions?

LESS THAN LUCRATIVE CORPORATION

Balance Sheet as of December 31, 20＿＿
(in thousands)

Assets		Liabilities and shareholders' equities	
Cash	$ 20	Short term loans	$ 40
Inventory	30	Long term loans	20
Plant and equipment	50	Stated capital	50
		Capital surplus	10
		Earned surplus (deficit)	(20)
Total assets	$100		
		Total liabilities and shareholders equities	$100

Problem IX-3

The Good and Bad News Corporation has current assets of $5,000 and total assets of $65,000. The short-term debts of the Corporation are $12,000 and its total liabilities are $50,000. Can the Good and Bad News Corporation make a distribution of dividends in a jurisdiction employing a solvency test?

Problem IX-4

If a corporation is newly organized and has no operating history and no record of earnings as of yet, is it permitted to make a distribution?

Problem IX-5

The Credible Corporation has an accumulated deficit. It would like to raise capital through additional share issuance, but its managers know that, for the share issuance to attract capital, the Corporation needs a recent history of dividend distribution to its shareholders. The jurisdiction in which Credible Corporation is organized permits distributions to be made only out of earnings. Can the managers issue a dividend in the present situation?

Problem IX-6

The Fantastic Corporation has had a remarkable earnings record. It has retained earnings of $1.5 million. Most of its earnings have been used for growth in acquiring new plants and equipment. The company keeps very limited amounts of its assets in cash and inventory. Its current assets total $100,000. The Company's short-term obligations total $125,000. The company seeks to make a distribution of $2.00 per share to holders of its 10,000 outstanding shares. The company has the available cash. Can it make the distribution?

Problem IX-7

The Lucrative Corporation has decided to make a cash distribution to its shareholders. It will pay a dividend of $2.50 per share to all holders of the 10,000 outstanding shares of the Corporation. What impact will this distribution have on the balance sheet of the Corporation?

Problem IX-8

The directors of the Cosmetic Impact Corporation want to make a distribution to the shareholders, but the cash assets of the company are presently very diminished. As a consequence, it is decided to make a distribution of one new share of stock for every 10 shares of common stock outstanding. The common stock has a par of $1.00 and is currently trading at $4.00 per share. There are 50,000 shares outstanding. What effect will the distribution have on the balance sheet of Cosmetic Impact?

CHAPTER X

Problem X-1

An investor buys 1,000 shares of $10 par common stock in Corporation ABC by giving the Corporation his delivery truck worth $10,000 in exchange for the shares. What kinds of questions of liability for the investor might exist in some jurisdictions with regard to the issuance price of the stock? What protections regarding valuation of the truck are frequently afforded the investor? What change in the capital structure of the Corporation would have provided the investor with an additional margin of protection?

Problem X-2

The incorporators of the Tentative Corporation are uncertain of the amount at which to set par for the stock they plan to have authorized in the Certificate of Incorporation of the Company. They know that there will initially be a number of shareholders, some of whom will be active participants in managing the corporation and some who will not be active. They also know that the Corporation might, in the near future, have additional capital needs and so the incorporators plan to authorize more shares than what they will initially issue. What considerations should impact upon the incorporators' decision in determining par.

Problem X-3

The shares of the Proper Corporation were authorized with a par value of $50 per share. When the Corporation was first organized, five years ago, the various investors who purchased shares from the Corporation paid for these shares with cash in an amount equal to the aggregate par value of the shares issued. The Proper Corporation has conducted business for five years since it was organized. It has not issued any additional shares. Does the Corporation necessarily still provide its creditors a "cushion" of stated capital.

CHAPTER XI

Problem XI-1

The capital balances at January 1, 20X1, of the partnership of Adams and Bailey were $40,000 and $35,000. Drawings for the year were $29,000 and $32,000. The partnership net income of $70,000 for the year was shared 60% by Adams and 40% by Bailey.

A. Prepare a statement of capital for the year 20X1.

In order to expand their operations, the partnership borrowed $25,000 on a note payable to a bank, pledging new equipment as collateral; Adams invested an additional $15,000; and Bailey borrowed $20,000 from an aunt and invested it in the partnership. Net income for 20X2 was $90,000 and was shared in the same 60/40 ratio. Drawings for 19X2 were $33,000 and $31,000.

B. Prepare a statement of capital for the year 20X2.

Problem XI-2

Quincy, Redman and Seidler are partners doing business as The Sensible Hardware Company. In regard to sharing of profits (and losses), the articles of partnership provide that:

1. the profit-sharing calculation be made on a quarterly basis,

2. interest be allowed at the rate 8% per annum on capital balances at the beginning of each calendar quarter,

3. monthly salaries be allowed of $1000 for Quincy, $800 for Redman, and $1,200 for Seidler, and

4. the remainder be allocated in the ratio of 40%, 40% and 20%.

Net profits for the second calendar quarter were $41,000 and capital balances at the beginning of the quarter were $35,000, $40,000, and $25,000.

A. How should the profit of $41,000 be shared?

B. Drawings were made in addition to salaries of $2000 by Quincy and $3,000 by Seidler. Prepare a Statement of Capital.

Problems XI-3

The partnership of K, L and M has not been prospering and the partners decide to liquidate. Their assets total $245,000 at book value including cash of 15,000 and there are liabilities of $67,000. Capital balances and profit and loss sharing ratios are as follows:

	Capital	P & L ratio
K	$ 55,000	20%
L	45,000	50
M	78,000	30
	$178,000	100%

Assets with book value of $110,000 are liquidated for $90,000, in cash; the liabilities of $67,000 are fully settled by payment of $64,000 cash. The partners wish to distribute the available cash, retaining $3,000 in the partnership account to cover expenses of liquidation and contingencies.

A. How much cash is available for distributions?

B. What are the capital balances at the end of this first stage of liquidation?

C. How much should be paid out to each partner?

D. Assume that in the continuation of the liquidation the available cash is distributed and that the remaining non-cash assets are sold for $41,000 and of the cash that had been held for contingencies, $2,000 was paid out for expenses incurred in liquidation. To conclude the liquidation, the entire balance of cash is to be paid out.

How much is now available for distribution?

E. How much should now be paid to each partner?

CHAPTER XII

Problem XII-1

The Biloric Disease Foundation annually prepares a set of financial statements for external distribution following the patterns recommended in Statement No. 117 as illustrated in:

Exhibit 12.1 -Statement of Financial Position (Balance Sheet),

Exhibit 12.2 -Statement of Activities (Revenue and Expenses),

Exhibit 12.3 -Statement of Cash Flows (prepared by the indirect method), and

Exhibit 12.4 -Statement of Functional Allocation of Expenses.

The unrestricted funds received by the Foundation are devoted mainly to grants for research focusing on the cause and cure of the biloric disease and also the publication and dissemination of information to alert the public as to the nature of the biloric disease and precautions to be taken to avoid catching the disease.

Two other funds are also maintained: a Fixtures and Equipment Fund , which is entirely unrestricted, and an Endowment Fund. Income earned by the Endowment Fund is available for unrestricted purposes , but the principle of the fund is permanently restricted.

Selected transactions of the current year are listed below. For both the debt and credit elements of each transaction indicate the account (or account group) affected and whether the affected account is increased or decreased. Also indicate which fund and which financial statement are affected, and how.

For convenience, the Statement of Functional Allocation of Expenses is referred to in the solution as Functional Allocation.

1. Payment of Monthly Office Rent.

Illustrative Answer

A. Dr rent expense, an increase in the expense. Cr cash to decrease cash.

B. Balance Sheet: Cash is decreased and the unrestricted net assets are also decreased.

C. Functional Allocation: The rent expense is included in the total column and is allocated over the columns, program services, management and general, and fund raising.

D. Statement of Activities: Rent expense constitutes a portion of each of the categories of expense in the unrestricted fund column and in the total of all funds column.

E. Cash Flows: The reduction of cash reduces cash flows from operating activities.

2. Payment of the bill for an annual audit by a public accounting firm.

3. Receipt of donated computer equipment.

4. Sale of informational publications for cash.

5. Receipt of cash contributions arising out of annual drive for funds.

6. Receipt for general purpose of an additional amount from a regular contributor with a stipulation that it be applied to the following year.

7. Provision for depreciation on equipment.

8. Payment of the bi-weekly payroll.

9. Approval of a research grant to Dr. R.R. Cruster, who conducts a research program on the biloric disease at the Meridian Hospital. One-half of the grant is to be paid within 60 days and the balance in 14 months.

10. Payment of the first installment due on the grant described in transaction 10.

11. Payment to a local hotel of a bill for a meeting room and refreshments for the quarterly meeting of the Board of Directors of the Foundation.

12. A block of securities was received from a contributor to add to the Endowment Fund.

APPENDIX

Problem App-1

Prepare entries in general journal form to record the following transactions. If in doubt about the proper format, refer to Exhibit App. 7. You may also wish to refer to the tabular presentation in the Appendix listing the debit and credit effects on asset, liability, ownership equity, revenue, and expense accounts.

1. An account receivable of $3,700 is collected.

2. A $950 sale is made on credit.

3. Merchandise is purchased on credit, $5,100.

4. A truck is purchased for $18,000. $6,000 is paid in cash and interest-bearing notes given for the balance.

The notes are payable $3,000 annually for the next four years.

5. Salaries are paid, $950.

6. Payment of $2,973 is made to the bank on a mortgage payable, including $973 for interest and $2,000 as an installment on principal.

7. Adjustment is made for salaries owed but not yet paid, $330.

8. Depreciation expense is set up for the year, $2,200.

9. The sales revenue account, carrying a balance of $413,000, is closed.

10. The salaries expense account, with a debit balance of $27,400, is closed.

11 The credit balance of $37,800 in the income and expense summary (profit and loss account) is transferred to retained earnings.

SOLUTIONS TO PROBLEMS

Chapter I

Solution to Problem I-1

The fundamental equation usually is stated as

assets = liabilities + shareholders' equity

It can also be stated as

assets − liabilities = shareholders' equity

The deduction of $27,000, the total liabilities, from $40,000, the total assets, leaves $13,000 as the amount of shareholders' equity.

Solution to Problem I-2

Assets minus liabilities equals shareholders' equity. In this exercise, it is given that assets exceed liabilities by $15,000. Therefore, assets minus liabilities equals $15,000 which is shareholders' equity.

Shareholders' equity can have two components — paid-in capital and retained earnings. Having computed a total shareholders' equity of $15,000 and given that one component, retained earnings, is equal to $6,000, the other component, paid-in capital, must equal $9,000.

Solution to Problem I-3

A. There is no change in shareholders' equity. The asset, merchandise, is increased by $20,000, but the asset, cash, is decreased by the same amount. The fundamental equation remains in balance without any change in liabilities or in shareholders' equity.

B. Paid-in capital, an element of shareholders' equity, is increased by $10,000 with a corresponding increase in the asset, cash.

C. Shareholders' equity in its component, retained earnings, is decreased by $3,000. There is an offsetting decrease in the asset, cash.

Note: One may raise the question of whether the $3,000 salary payment does not really represent payment of a liability owed for services already received. In fact, it probably does. However, in most situations there is not likely to have been a formal entry to set up the liability for officers' (or other employees') services. Most commonly, the expense is recognized only when payment is made. If there had been an entry to recognize a liability, it would have been to show a decrease in retained earnings of $3,000, offset by an increase in the liability for salaries owed (accrued salaries). The actual payment of the salaries would then be entered as a decrease in the liability for salaries owed, offset by a decrease in the asset, cash. The net effect of the *two* entries would be as in the answer, above, a decrease in retained earnings of $3,000, offset by a decrease in the asset, cash.

D. Merchandise, an asset, is increased by $40,000. The fundamental equation remains in balance with an increase in the liability, accounts payable. There is no change in shareholders' equity.

E. The consequence of a sale on credit is an increase of $15,000 in the asset, accounts receivable. The transfer of the merchandise to the buyer reduces the asset, merchandise, by $10,000. There is a net increase in assets of $5,000 and an increase of the same amount in retained earnings, an element of shareholders' equity.

F. There is no change in shareholders' equity but cash, an asset, and accounts payable, a liability, are both reduced by $7,000.

G. No change in shareholders' equity. The asset, cash, is increased by $4,000 and the asset, accounts receivable, is reduced by $4,000.

H. Retained earnings or earned surplus, a component of shareholders' equity, is reduced by $1,000, with a corresponding reduction in the asset, cash.

Prefatory explanation to Problems I-4 and I-5

These problems relate to the income statement. The relationships in the income statement can be expressed as:

I. sales − cost of sales = gross margin, and

II. gross margin − expenses = net income.

Solution to Problem I-4

Utilizing the foregoing equations, we have:

60,000 (sales) − 35,000 (cost of sales) = 25,000 (gross margin)

and

25,000 (gross margin) − 18,000 (expenses) = 7,000 (net income).

These figures can be presented in the form of an income statement as:

Sales	$60,000
Cost of sales	35,000
Gross margin	$25,000
Expenses	18,000
Net income	$ 7,000

Solution to Problem I-5

The equations in the prefatory explanation are stated in forms derived from the income statement. However, Equation II can be restated as follows:

gross margin = expenses + net income.

Substituting in this equation, gross margin is determined as $38,000, the sum of $27,000 and $11,000.

Equation I can be restated as:

sales − gross margin = cost of sales.

Sales are given as $90,000 and gross margin has now been computed as $38,000; therefore, the cost of sales must be $52,000.

If presented in the form of an income statement, these data would appear as follows:

Sales	$90,000
Cost of sales	52,000
Gross margin	$38,000
Expenses	27,000
Net income	$11,000

Solution to Problem I-6

Assets = liabilities + shareholders' equity.

This equation always holds. It is true before any particular transaction and remains true after that particular transaction or after any group of transactions.

It is given in this exercise that, over a period of time, assets increased by $10,000. Therefore as a result of all the transactions over this period of time, the total of liabilities plus shareholders' equity must also have increased by $10,000, equal to the total of the assets.

It is also given that liabilities decreased by $5,000. It follows, then, that, for the fundamental equation to remain in balance, shareholders' equity must have increased by $15,000. Summarizing the transactions in the form of an equation:

assets		liabilities	shareholders' equity
+ 10,000	=	− 5,000	+ 15,000.

It has been determined that shareholders' equity increased by $15,000, but this is not necessarily equal to net income. Some of the increase in shareholders' equity may have been the result of a sale of capital stock.

There is further information that there was no change in paid-in-capital over the period. It is still not possible to determine net income from the facts given, for there might have been a dividend. For example, even with no change in paid-in-capital, an increase in shareholders' equity of $15,000 might have resulted from net income of $17,000 and a dividend of $2,000.

Solution to Problem I-7

The write-off is a recognition of the fact that an account receivable has become worthless. Actually, the reduction of asset value has already occurred. However, it has not yet been entered on the "books." The write-off constitutes a formal entry to reflect this reduction of value.

As a consequence of the formal entry, the asset, accounts receivable, is decreased by $500; there is no change in liabilities. For the equation to balance, it follows that shareholders' equity must be reduced by $500.

As a result of this write-off, the asset, accounts receivable, in the balance sheet is shown at $500 less than it was stated before the write-off; shareholders' equity is also shown at $500 less.

This $500 reduction in shareholders' equity constitutes recognition of an expense, usually termed "bad debt expense." This expense would appear among the expenses in the income statement for the period in which the bad debt was recognized (*i.e.*, taken into account).

Solution to Problem I-8

A.

AJAX CORPORATION
Summary of the Effects of Transactions on the Accounting Equation
For the two months ended April 30, 20—

| | ASSETS | | | = | EQUITIES | | |
	Cash	Accounts Receivable	Merchandise	(Liabilities)	Accounts Payable	Paid in Capital	Retained Earnings (Earned Surplus)
a. Investment	+ 30,000			=		+ 30,000	
b. Merchandise Purchased for cash	− 10,000		+ 10,000	=			
Balances	20,000		10,000	= 30,000		30,000	
c. Merchandise purchased on credit			+ 40,000	=	+ 40,000		
Balances	20,000		50,000	= 70,000	40,000	30,000	
d. Sales for cash	+ 10,000		− 6,000	=			+ 4,000
Balances	30,000		44,000	= 74,000	40,000	30,000	4,000
e. Sales on credit		+ 50,000	− 27,000	=			+ 23,000
Balances	30,000	50,000	17,000	= 97,000	40,000	30,000	27,000
f. Collections on accounts receivable	+ 30,000	− 30,000		=			
Balances	60,000	20,000	17,000	= 97,000	40,000	30,000	27,000
g. Payments on accounts payable	− 25,000			=	− 25,000		
Balances	35,000	20,000	17,000	= 72,000	15,000	30,000	27,000
h. Payment of rent	− 3,000			=			− 3,000
Balances	32,000	20,000	17,000	= 69,000	15,000	30,000	24,000
i. Payments of salaries and other expenses	− 7,000			=			− 7,000
Balances	25,000	20,000	17,000	= 62,000	15,000	30,000	17,000
j. Declaration and payment of a dividend	− 1,200			=			− 1,200
Final Balances	23,800	20,000	17,000	= 60,800	15,000	30,000	15,800

(Matthew Bender & Co., Inc.)

Solution to Problem I-8

B.

Chapter I. Solutions. Problems I-9

AJAX CORPORATION
Balance Sheet
April 30, 20.-000165T

ASSETS		LIABILITIES AND SHAREHOLDERS' EQUITY		
Cash	$23,800	Accounts payable		$15,000
Accounts receivable	20,000	Paid-in capital	$30,000	
Merchandise inventory	17,000	Retained earnings	15,800	
		Total shareholders' equity		45,800
Total assets	$60,800	Total liabilities and shareholders' equity		$60,800

(Pub.642)

Solution to Problem I-8

C.

AJAX CORPORATION

Income Statement
Two months ended April 30, 20_____

Sales		$60,000
Cost of sales		33,000
Gross Margin		$27,000
Expenses:		
Rent	$3,000	
Salaries and other expenses	7,000	
Total expenses		10,000
Net income		$17,000

D.

AJAX CORPORATION

Statement of Retained Earnings
Two months ended April 30, 20_____

Retained Earnings, March 1, 20_____		$ - 0 -
Net Income for the period	$17,000	
Less dividends declared	1,200	
Increase in retained earnings		15,800
Retained Earnings, April 30, 20_____		$15,800

Solution to Problem I-9

A.

BEST SELLING CORPORATION
Summary of the Effects of Transactions on the Accounting Equation
For the three months ended November 30, 20..

	ASSETS					EQUITIES				
						Liabilities		Shareholders' Equity		
	Cash	+	Accounts Receivable	+	Merchandise	=	Accounts Payable	+	Paid in Capital	+	Retained Earnings (Earned Surplus)
Beginning Balances	1,600	+	23,000	+	35,000 = 59,600	=	20,000	+	25,000	+	14,600
a. Merchandise purchases	− 1,200	+		+	164,200		+ 163,000				
Balances	400	+	23,000	+	199,200 = 222,600	=	183,000	+	25,000	+	14,600
b. Sales		+	260,000	−	155,000					+	105,000
Balances	400	+	283,000	+	44,200 = 327,600	=	183,000	+	25,000	+	119,600
c. Collection of accounts receivable	+ 240,000	−	240,000								
Balances	240,400	+	43,000	+	44,200 = 327,600	=	183,000	+	25,000	+	119,600
d. Payments of accounts payable	− 142,000					−	142,000				
Balances	98,400	+	43,000	+	44,200 = 185,600	=	41,000	+	25,000	+	119,600
e. Payment of expenses	− 72,000										72,000
Balances	26,400	+	43,000	+	44,200 = 113,600	=	41,000	+	25,000	+	47,600
f. Declaration and payment of a dividend	− 2,000									−	2,000
Final balances	24,400	+	43,000	+	44,200 = 111,600	=	41,000	+	25,000	+	45,600

Solution to Problem I-9

B.

Chapter I. Solutions. Problems I-9

BEST SELLING CORPORATION

Balance Sheet
November 30, 20__

ASSETS			LIABILITIES AND SHAREHOLDERS' EQUITY		
Cash	$ 24,400		Account payable		$ 41,000
Accounts receivable	43,000		Paid-in capital	$25,000	
Merchandise inventory	44,200		Retained earnings	45,600	
			Total shareholders' equity		70,600
Total assets	$ 111,600		Total liabilities and shareholders' equity		$ 111,600

C.

BEST SELLING CORPORATION

Income Statement
Three months ended November 30, 20____

Sales	$260,000
Cost of sales	155,000
Gross Margin	$105,000
Expenses:	72,000
Net income	$ 33,000

D.

BEST SELLING CORPORATION

Statement of Retained Earnings
Three months ended November 30, 20____

Retained Earnings, September 1, 20____		$14,600
Net Income for the period	$33,000	
Less dividends declared	2,000	
Increase in retained earnings		31,000
Retained earnings, November 30, 20____		$45,600

Chapter II

Solution to Problem II-1

A. The annual depreciation expense under the straight-line

method is equal to $\dfrac{\text{cost-salvage value.}}{\text{estimated life.}}$

Initially the annual depreciation expense would equal $\dfrac{\$25,000 - \$5,000}{10}$ or $2,000.

After five years, the allowance for depreciation would amount to $10,000. The book value would equal the actual cost of the press, less the allowance for depreciation or $15,000.

B. Generally accepted accounting principles direct that when a revision is made in the estimated life of a fixed asset or in its salvage value, the change in depreciation charges be reflected only prospectively, not retrospectively. Thus, Laminall would now have to depreciate in three years an asset with a current book value of $15,000 and an estimated salvage value of $3,000. The annual depreciation charge would rise to $4,000.

Solution to Problem II-2

Goodwill should not be carried as an asset unless it represents the excess over net asset value paid by a purchaser for an ongoing business. Since Murray developed the goodwill in question through his own efforts, he must charge the advertising and mailing costs as expenses during the period of time in which they were incurred. Were they legitimate goodwill costs paid for as a premium for a continuing business, they should be amortized over a period of time equal to the expected usefulness of the goodwill, but, in no event longer than 40 years.

Solution to Problem II-3

Under the LIFO method, the cost of goods sold reflects recent price changes. This is because the cost of goods sold is determined by the cost of the most recently purchased inventory. Under the FIFO method, one has to wait a longer time for the cost of goods sold to reflect price changes. This is because the cost of goods sold is determined by the cost of the earliest purchased remaining inventory.

However, under FIFO, the cost of remaining inventory more accurately reflects current prices for inventory than what is reflected in LIFO. This is because the cost of the residual inventory, under FIFO, is determined by the cost of the most recently purchased inventory.

Solution to Problem II-4

A. Under the LIFO method, we would allocate the cost of lumber on the basis of that lumber which was purchased most recently. Essentially we would add up the number of feet of lumber purchased in November and then September and then June and so on until we accounted for 33,000 feet of lumber. We would have to include a portion of the January purchase to account for the total 33,000 feet. The cost for this lumber would be $13,755.

Under the FIFO method, we would allocate the cost of lumber on the basis of that lumber which was purchased earliest. Since Amalgamated had a beginning inventory of 2,000 feet, we would need to start with this amount of lumber and add on to it the cost of the purchases in January and March and so on until we have accounted for 33,000 feet of lumber. We would have to include a portion of the November purchase to account for the total 33,000 feet. The cost of this lumber would be $12,665.

Since the cost of lumber used, as tabulated under the LIFO method is $1,090 greater than the cost of lumber used under the FIFO method, net income before taxes under the LIFO method would be $1,090 less than net income under the FIFO method.

B. To determine the difference in value of net assets remaining at the end of the year, we would have to determine the difference in value of the residual inventory as computed under the LIFO method as opposed to the FIFO method. To make this computation, we would need to know the amount of inventory remaining at the end of the year. Amalgamated began the year with 2,000 feet of lumber. It purchased an additional 34,300 feet of lumber during the year. Thus, it had available a total of 36,300 feet of lumber for use during the year. It used 33,000 feet of lumber. It thus had 3,300 feet of lumber remaining in its inventory.

When we compute the value of remaining inventory under the LIFO method, we assign to the remaining assets the cost of the earliest purchased inventory. Since Amalgamated began with an inventory of 2,000 feet of lumber with a cost of $400, that cost would be included in our valuation of our residual inventory as would the cost of 1,300 of the 4,000 feet of the lumber bought in January. The total cost of the residual lumber inventory under the LIFO method would be $725 ($400 for the 2,000 feet of initial inventory plus $325 for the 1,300 feet bought in January). (Since we have already computed the cost of lumber sold under the LIFO method, there is an alternative method for computing the cost of the residual inventory. We could compute the total cost of lumber available for sale which would include the cost of the beginning inventory ($400) plus the cost of lumber purchased during the year ($14,080), arriving at a sum of $14,480. From the total cost of lumber available for sale we would subtract the cost of lumber sold as computed under the LIFO method ($13,755), arriving at a cost of the residual inventory of $725.)

Under the FIFO method, we assign to the remaining assets the cost of the latest purchased inventory. We would thus compute the cost of the 3,300 remaining feet of lumber on the basis of the price of the lumber purchased in November. The total cost of the residual lumber inventory under the FIFO method would be $1,815.

As with the LIFO method, we could compute the cost of the residual inventory under the FIFO method by subtracting the cost of lumber sold from the total cost of lumber available for sale. We would subtract $12,665 from $14,480 to arrive at a residual inventory cost of $1,815.

Thus assets under the FIFO method would be valued at $1,090 more than under the LIFO method. The company's net assets would also be greater by the same amount (ignoring the impact of income taxes).

Solution to Problem II-5

A. Current assets are those assets which are either already in the form of cash or which can be readily converted into cash in the normal course of business operations within the operating cycle of the business. (Operating cycle is used in this answer as a period of at least one year. See discussion in Chapter II, Section B.) Thus, current assets are those assets that a business entity has available in the normal course of business to pay off short-term obligations as they become due. The following items are classified as current assets:

(2) Accounts receivable generally are collectible in cash within the operating cycle.

(4) Accrued income includes such items as interest and rents receivable. These amounts would normally be received in cash within the operating cycle.

(22) Marketable securities are understood to constitute temporary investments readily convertible back into cash whenever required. Securities intended to be held beyond the operating cycle might be termed permanent investments and would be classified among noncurrent assets.

(23) Merchandise inventory, in the normal course of business, would be sold and the resulting accounts receivable collected within the operating cycle.

(25) Prepaid expenses include such items as supplies to be consumed as part of the business operations and rent or interest paid in advance. Prepaid expenses are not really convertible into cash. However, prepaid expenses to be consumed within the operating cycle are as a matter of practice included among current assets. The rationale is that if these expenses had not been paid for in advance, the incurring of the expenses would require the use of current assets during the operating cycle. In this respect, they constitute a current asset equivalent.

B. Current liabilities are obligations which fall due within a year or within the length of an operating cycle if longer. The following current liabilities are included in the list of items presented in the problem:

(1) Accounts payable are normally due within 30 or 60 days, although, in some industries, the credit period may extend for six months.

(3) Accrued expenses include such items as unpaid wages and salaries, accrued rent, interest and taxes, and miscellaneous expenses incurred but not yet paid. Interest might not be payable for as long as a year but usually it would be payable within six months, three months, or even sooner. All of the other items would generally be due currently or within a short period of time.

Liabilities for merchandise purchased are termed accounts payable, not accrued expenses. Where a note has been given to cover a liability, the liability would be shown on the balance sheet as a note payable among current liabilities unless the term of the note ran beyond the operating cycle or one year, whichever is longer. In such case, the note payable would be included among noncurrent liabilities.

(6) A bank loan generally is due within a year and is to be included among current liabilities. However, long-term loans which mature beyond the longer of the operating cycle or one year are treated as noncurrent liabilities.

(11) The liability on a mortgage generally does not mature for an extended number of years and normally is treated as a noncurrent liability. However, for many mortgages, the principal is payable in installments. The installment amounts due within the current period (the longer of the operating cycle or one year) are treated as current liabilities.

(12) Deferred income exists when payment has been received for services to be rendered after the balance sheet date, such as subscription payments received by a magazine publisher. Since subscriptions

are paid in advance, a portion of the subscription remains unfulfilled. The income allocable to the unfulfilled subscription is deferred and represents a current liability at the balance sheet date. The liability is that services have to be rendered. (A portion of long-term subscriptions may be treated as a noncurrent liability.)

(14) A liability for a dividend payable exists when a corporation has declared a dividend but has not yet paid it. When the dividend was declared, the effect on the fundamental equation was to reduce shareholders' equity by the amount of the dividend and to increase liabilities by the same amount. When the dividend is paid, the liability will be extinguished and there will be a corresponding reduction of the asset cash, except in the rare instance when the dividend is paid by distribution of some other asset.

The date a dividend is declared is the "declaration date." The dividend will be paid to those shareholders on record as owning the stock at the "record date" (an arbitrarily selected date which falls some time after the date of declaration). Inasmuch as it takes some time to prepare dividend checks, actual payment will not be made until the "payment date," some convenient period after the record date. Once a dividend has been declared, there is a liability of a dividend payable which is not extinguished until paid. The period of time between the declaration date and the payment date is almost invariably within the operating cycle, so that a dividend payable is a current liability.

A balance sheet dated after the declaration date but before the payment date should include a dividend payable among its current liabilities.

C. Noncurrent assets are those assets which do not fall into the category of current assets. Noncurrent assets include:

(7) Building

(15) Equipment

(16) Furniture and fixtures

(17) Goodwill

(20) Investment in stock of subsidiary

(21) Land

Building, equipment, furniture and fixtures and land are often referred to as "plant assets." They would appear on the balance sheet at historical cost reduced by an allowance for depreciation.

(5) The allowance for depreciation is not an asset but is a reduction of the historical cost of the depreciable assets. The allowance for depreciation is the accumulation of the amounts which have been allocated as depreciation from the date the plant assets were acquired until the date of the balance sheet. (An alternative title for "allowance for depreciation" is "accumulated depreciation.") The allowance for depreciation is applied as a reduction of the asset value of buildings, equipment and furniture and fixtures. Since depreciation does not apply to land, there is no allowance for depreciation for land.

(17) Goodwill is an intangible asset which is created only when a business has acquired another business with part of the acquisition price designated as payment for goodwill. Under today's accounting rules, the cost of goodwill acquired after October 1970 is to be amortized over a period of time not to exceed 40 years. Many companies amortize the cost in a much shorter period. The unamortized balance of goodwill would be shown as a noncurrent asset.

(20) Although it may be marketable, the stock of a subsidiary would not be included as a marketable security under current assets since it was not acquired as a temporary investment. The investment in a subsidiary would be treated as a separate item among noncurrent assets.

D. (24) As indicated in the answer to section B, item (11), the liability for a mortgage payable is usually long-term and, accordingly, includible among noncurrent liabilities. Installments on mortgage principal due within the current period, however, would be shown as a separate item includible among current liabilities. The balance of the mortgage, after the current installment has been deducted, is a noncurrent liability.

(Matthew Bender & Co., Inc.)

When a mortgage matures within the current period, it should be included among current liabilities unless the business intends to refinance the mortgage and demonstrates an ability to conclude such refinancing, or unless the mortgage is to be paid from funds accumulated for that purpose and included among noncurrent assets.

E. (8) Capital stock, (9) capital surplus and (27) retained earnings constitute the shareholders' residual equity in the assets of the corporation after provision for liabilities. The liabilities have been listed in sections B and D.

Capital stock represents the contribution of stockholders designated as par value or stated value of no-par stock. For no-par stock without stated value, the entire capital contribution of the shareholders is designated as capital stock.

Amounts contributed by stockholders in excess of par or stated value are treated as capital surplus.

Earnings of the corporation increase shareholders' equity and, if not paid out as dividends, remain as retained earnings. In legal circles, retained earnings are often referred to as earned surplus.

F. Revenues and expenses do not appear on a balance sheet. There are several revenues and expenses included in the items listed in the problem. Revenues increase retained earnings and expenses decrease retained earnings. The revenue items are (19) interest income and (29) sales revenue. The expense items are (10) cost of sales, (18) interest expense, (26) rent expense and (28) salaries and wages (expense). Revenues and expenses appear on an income statement (profit and loss statement). The net income for the period would also be shown on a statement of retained earnings. The final balance of retained earnings appearing in the statement of retained earnings also appears as an element of shareholders' equity on the balance sheet.

There is one item in the listing in the problem which affects retained earnings but appears neither in the balance sheet nor in the income statement. Item (13), dividends declared, would be included in the statement of retained earnings. Dividends declared reduce retained earnings and thus affect the final balance of retained earnings.

Chapter III

Solution to Problem III-1

No. We know that total shareholders' equity is equal to assets less liabilities, or $15,000. Further, we know that stated capital is equal to par times the number of shares outstanding, or $10,000. Thus, we can compute "surplus" ($15,000 − $10,000), but without more information we cannot know how much of that surplus is attributable to capital surplus and how much to retained earnings.

Solution to Problem III-2

The answer to this question cannot be determined from the information provided. The classification of equities on the right-hand side of the balance sheet does not permit a reader to make determinations regarding the composition of the assets on the left side of the balance sheet. It would appear that the Nouvell Corporation has prospered, as witnessed by its accumulated earnings. However, it is conceivable that these retained earnings have been reinvested and that there now are insufficient liquid assets to satisfy the company's debts as they mature.

Solution to Problem III-3

Typically, in those jurisdictions where stated capital remains a viable concept, when no par stock is issued the board of directors may designate a portion of the consideration contributed in exchange for the no-par stock as stated capital. The amount of consideration that exceeds the stated capital is deemed capital surplus. If no designation is made regarding stated capital within a specified period of time (within 60 days under Del. Gen. Corp. Law § 154), then the entire consideration contributed for the shares shall be considered stated capital.

Solution to Problem III-4

Although the sale of stock from A to B was at a price of $3.00 per share more than the par value of the stock, this sale has no impact on the equity accounts of the Appreciating Corporation. The transfer of funds between B and A does not accrue to the benefit of the Appreciating Corporation. The capital surplus of the Appreciating Corporation is unaffected by the transaction. The only effect that the transaction would have on the Corporation would occur when purchaser B requests that the ownership of the 10,000 shares be transferred to his name on the record books of the Corporation.

Solution to Problem III-5

Although, the Ambitious Corporation has 50,000 shares authorized, it is only when the shares are issued that consideration is received by the Corporation in exchange for the shares.

Since par is $2.00 per share, the sale at Time 1 of 1,000 shares of common at $3.00 per share resulted in stated capital of $2,000 (1,000 shares × $2.00 par) and capital surplus of $1,000 (1,000 shares × $1.00 premium per share in excess of par).

At Time 2, the sale of the additional 10,000 shares resulted in an additional $20,000 of stated capital (10,000 shares × $2.00 par) and $30,000 of capital surplus (10,000 shares × $3.00 premium per share in excess of par).

Thus, immediately, after Time 2, the Ambitious Corporation had stated capital of $22,000 and capital surplus of $31,000.

Chapter V

Solution to Problem V-1

LARGE CORPORATION
Balance Sheet
December 31, 20X2

ASSETS

		Millions of Dollars
Current Assets		
Cash		$ 21
Marketable securities		19
Trade receivables, net of allowance for bad debt		340
Inventories:		
Finished goods	190	
Work in process	22	
Raw materials	110	322
Prepaid expense		43
Total current assets		745
Other receivables and investments		23
Property, plant and equipment	920	
Less accumulated depreciation	287	633
Goodwill		50
Patents and trademarks		3
Total Assets		$1,454

LIABILITIES AND SHAREHOLDERS' EQUITY

Current liabilities		
Short-term debt		$ 211
Current portion of long-term debt		7
Trade accounts payable		140
Accrued payrolls, pensions and bonuses		60
Income taxes payable		10
Other current payables and accruals		65
Total current liabilities		493
Long-term debt		165
Other liabilities		19
Total liabilities		$ 677
Shareholders' Equity		
Common stock, $5 par value	105	
Additional paid-in capital	187	
Retained earnings	542	
	834	
Less treasury stock, at cost	57	
Total shareholders' equity		777
Total liabilities and shareholders' equity		$1,454

Since the dollar amount for retained earnings was not provided, it was necessary to calculate what it should be. The calculation follows:

Total assets		$1,454	
Deduct total liabilities		677	
Total shareholders' equity			777
Add the amount to be deducted from shareholders' equity for thecost of treasury stock			57
Total amount for capital stock, additional paid-in capital and retained earnings			834
Deduct:			
Common stock	105		
Additional paid-in capital	187	292	
Balance, which is the amount for retained earnings			$542

Chapter VI

Solution to Problem VI-1

A. Although the premium was paid on November 25, the policy did not take effect until December 1. During Calendar Year 1, the insurance was in force only for the month of December. With an annual premium of $600, the expense for the month of December would be prorated as $50.

B. The insurance expense of $50 would be included among the other expense items on the income statement for Calendar Year 1.

C. The insurance premium paid on November 25, Year 1, covers the period through November 30, Year 2. As of the balance sheet date of December 31, Year 1, insurance coverage remains in force through the eleven months ending November 30, Year 2, and the premium for this coverage has been paid. Accordingly, there is a deferred expense of $550 (eleven months at $50 per month). This amount of $550 should appear among the current assets on the balance sheet with other deferred expense items. An alternative title for deferred expense is "prepaid expense." With respect specifically to the insurance, alternative titles might be prepaid insurance or unexpired insurance expense.

Under one conventional accounting practice, the $600 payment for insurance on November 25, Year 1, would be recorded as insurance expense. However, at year end, an adjustment would be made to set up an asset for $550 for the unexpired portion of the insurance premium. As a counterbalance in the accounting equation, the expense would be reduced by $550.

D. The expense for Calendar Year 2 is $605. Eleven months at $50 plus the month of December, Year 2, at $55. (660 divided by 12 equals 55.)

E. At December 31, Year 2, there was no prepaid insurance. In fact, a premium of $660 was owed. As of December 31, Year 2, the liability for unpaid insurance premiums would be shown at the prorated amount of $55. This liability of $55 would be included among current liabilities on the balance sheet as an accrued expense. (As an alternative, if one were to show a current liability of $660 for the entire premium due, then one would also have to show a deferred expense for the $605 representing the insurance premium from January 1 to November 30 of Year 3).

F. With respect to this insurance policy, the insurance company should show revenue of $50 for Calendar Year 1.

G. Although the insurance company received $600 premium on this policy in Year 1, only $50 was earned. The remaining $550, applicable to the months of January through November of Year 2, will not have been earned until the eleven months have passed. As of December 31, Year 1, the insurance company should show a deferred (or unearned) income of $550 on its balance sheet.

H. For Calendar Year 2, the insurance company should show revenue from insurance premiums of $605. The $550 deferred income at December 31, Year 1, has now been earned in Year 2. In addition, there have been earnings for the month of December, Year 2, of $55, even though this $55 has not yet been received in cash.

I. Reflecting the earning of $55 for the month of December, Year 2, on which payment has not yet been received, the insurance company should show on its balance sheet as of December 31, Year 2, an amount of $55 as accrued income.

Solution to Problem VI-2

A. The first interest payment is due on December 1, Year 1. The interest on $30,000 for six months at 12% is $1,800. Including the $1,000 due on the principal of the mortgage, the total payment to be made on December 1, Year 1, is $2,800. There is no further payment due until June 1, Year 2.

B. The interest expense for the year ending March 31, Year 2, includes six months from June 1, to December 1 of Year 1. As computed in A above, this is $1,800, plus the interest on a principal balance of $29,000 at 12% for the four months from December 1, Year 1, to March 31, Year 2. The interest for this latter period is $1,160. ($29,000 times 12% times 1/3 of a year). The total interest expense for the fiscal year ending March 31, Year 2, is $2,960 (1,800 plus 1,160).

C. On the balance sheet at March 31, Year 2, there should appear three items relating to this mortgage and the mortgage interest.

There is a liability for accrued interest expense of $1,160. This should appear among current liabilities. Although additional interest beyond $1,160 will be due later in time, only $1,160 has been earned by the lender at the balance sheet date. Thus $1,160 is the only interest liability as of that date.

There is also a current liability for the two principal payments due within a year from the balance sheet date. These principal payments of $1,000 each are due on June 1 and December 1 of Year 2. Thus the current liabilities should include $2,000 for current installments due on the mortgage payable. The remaining principal balance on the mortgage of $27,000 should appear as a noncurrent liability under a title such as "mortgage payable net of current installments." Notice, there is a present liability for future principal payments whereas there is not a present liability for future interest expense not yet incurred. This is because from the moment the loan agreement was entered into and the loan was received there was an obligation to repay the principal amount. On the other hand, interest payment obligations only arise after the passage of time.

D. Payments are due during Calendar Year 2 on June 1 and December 1. The interest due on June 1 is for six months at 12% on $29,000. This comes to $1,740. With the principal installment added, the total due on June 1 of Year 2 is $2,740.

On December 1, Year 2, the amount due will be less than that due on June 1, Year 2, by $60 which is the reduction of interest due to the $1,000 reduction of principal. The amount due on December 1, Year 2, is $2,680 (interest of $1,680 plus principal of $1,000.)

E. Again there should be three items for the balance sheet. A current liability of $2,000 for the current installments due on the mortgage, a noncurrent liability for $25,000 as the amount due on the mortgage net of current installments, and a current liability for the accrued mortgage interest expense. This last item should be $1,080 (four months at 12% on $27,000.)

F. The interest expense to appear on the income statement for the fiscal year ending March 31, Year 3, is $3,340. This may be computed as follows:

Interest at 12% for the -

two months of April and May, Year 2, on	29,000	= 580
six months, June through November, Year 2, on	28,000	= 1,680
four months, December, Year 2, through March, Year 3, on	27,000	= 1,080
Total		3,340

The calculation can also be made in terms of the accounting entries which would have been made.

During the fiscal year ending March 31, Year 3, there would have been two payments made for interest expense:

on June 1, Year 2 (computed in part D)	1,740
on December 1, Year 2 (computed in part D)	1,680
Total	3,420

However, since the payment on June covered the interest accrued at March 31, Year 2, this total should be reduced

by the amount of that accrual (computed in part B) —	1,160
Interest payments reduced by accrual at beginning of period	2,260

There is one further adjustment. The interest accrued at March 31, Year 3, should be added.

This amount (computed in part E) is	1,080
Total interest expense	3,340

G. On the balance sheet of the bank at December 31, Year 1, included among its assets together with other mortgage loans would be the principal amount due on this mortgage of $29,000. The principal amount due on December 31, Year 2, would be $27,000. The accrued interest receivable at December 31, Year 1, would be $290 (the one month of December at 12% on $29,000.) At December 31, Year 2, the accrued interest receivable would be $270 (one month at 12% on $27,000.)

H. The interest revenue for the Calendar Year 1 would be $2,090 computed at the annual rate of 12% as follows:

six months, June through November, year 1,	on 30,000 =	1,800
one month, December, year 1,	on 29,000 =	290
Total interest revenue Year 1		2,090

For the calendar Year 2, the interest income would be $3,400.

Calculations follow:

five months, January through May, year 2,	on 29,000 =	1,450
six months, June through November, year 2,	on 28,000 =	1,680
one month, December, year 2,	on 27,000 =	270
Total interest revenue, year 2		3,400

Solution to Problem VI-3

A. There were four salary payments during the month of March, three at $500 and one at $550, for a total of $2,050.

There were also four payments in April, two at $550 and two at $600, for a total of $2,300.

For parts B and C, it would be convenient to be able to refer to a calendar. Based on the information given that all salary payments are made on Tuesdays, the following calendar has been constructed:

March

Su	M	Tu	W	Th	F	Sa
				1	2	3
4	5	6	7	8	9	10
11	12	13	14	15	16	17
18	19	20	21	22	23	24
25	26	27	28	29	30	31

April

Su	M	Tu	W	Th	F	Sa
1	2	3	4	5	6	7
8	9	10	11	12	13	14
15	16	17	18	19	20	21
22	23	24	25	26	27	28
29	30					

B. There were 22 days during March for which salaries were paid. Saturdays and Sundays are excluded. There were 21 days in April for which salaries were paid. The daily salary expense was $100 through March 16. Since the weekly salary payment was $550 on March 27, we know that the daily rate became $110 on March 19 (The payment on March 27 was for the five days of March 19 through March 23.) The daily rate remained at $110 until it became $120 on April 9.

The salary expense for March included:

two weeks and two days at $100 a day	1,200
two weeks at $110 a day (or $550 a week)	1,100
Total salary expense for March	2,300

The salary expense for April included:

one week, April 2 through April 6 at	
$550 a week (or $110 a day)	550
three full weeks plus one day, April 30,	
at $600 a week (or $120 a day)	1,920
Total salary expense for April	2,470

(Matthew Bender & Co., Inc.)

Another approach to the calculation of the monthly salary expense will be presented after the answer has been given to part C.

C. The amounts that should appear on a balance sheet with respect to salaries comprise the liability that exists for salaries earned but not yet paid. The amounts for unpaid or accrued salaries should be included with other accrued expenses as one of the current liabilities.

Accrued salary expense at March 31 was $550, the salary for the week of March 26 through March 30. This salary was not paid until April 3.

Accrued salary expense at April 30 was $720. Salary of $600 for the work week of April 23 through April 27 was not paid until May 1. Salary for April 30 at the daily rate of $120 was not paid until May 8. At April 30, a total of $720 was owing for salaries.

As indicated above, there is a different approach to the calculation of monthly salary expense, based on conventional accounting techniques.

For purpose of demonstration let us assume that this company keeps its books on a calendar year basis, that it had paid salaries at the rate of $500 a week for several months prior to March and that it was not a leap year and there were 28 days in February. From these assumptions, one could determine that:

there were five Tuesdays in January with salary payments totaling $2,500,

there were four Tuesdays in February with salary payments totaling $2,000,

the accrued salaries expense at December 31 of the preceding year was $500,

and the accrued salaries at February 28 was $300.

Monthly and cumulative salary payments are shown below:

January		2,500
February		2,000
	Cumulative total salary payments	4,500
March		2,050
	Cumulative total salary payments	6,550
April	Cumulative total salary payments	2,300
		8,850

Under conventional accounting techniques, the salary expense for monthly income statements might be determined through a routine process which takes into account the following calculations:

	February	March	April
Total salary payments through end of month	4,500	6,550	8,850
Deduct unpaid salaries at Dec. 31	500	500	500
Salary payments which apply to current year	4,000	6,050	8,350
Add unpaid salaries at end of month	300	550	720
Salary expense through end of month	4,300	6,600	9,070
Deduct salary expense through end of preceding month	xxx	4,300	6,600
Salary expense for month	xxx	2,300	2,470

Solution to Problem VI-4

A.

LARGE CORPORATION

Statement of Income
Calendar year 20X2

		Millions of Dollars
Net sales		$2,600
Cost of goods sold		1,751
Gross margin		849
Selling, general and administrative expenses	622	
Interest expense	37	659
Income before income taxes		190
Provision for income taxes		85
Net income		$ 105

B.

LARGE CORPORATION

Statement of Retained Earnings
Calendar year 20X2

		Millions of Dollars
Retained earnings at December 31, 20X1	$473	
Net income for the year		105
Total		578
Dividends		36
Retained earnings at December 31, 20X2	$542	

Note: The retained earnings balance at December 31, 20X1 was computed by working back from the balance at December 31, 20X2.

CHAPTER VII

Solution to Problem VII-1

To reduce wordiness, the statement of cash flows will be referred to here as SCF and the several sections of the SCF may be referred to as operating, investing, financing or schedule.

A. In terms of the fundamental equation, this transaction results in an increase of $10,000 in cash, which is balanced by a $10,000 increase in capital stock.

As for the SCF, the transaction will be reported among financing activities as proceeds from issuance of common stock, a cash inflow.

B. The fundamental equation will show an increase in the asset, equipment, of $7,000 and a decrease in the asset, cash, of the same amount.

The transaction will be reported in the SCF as a cash outflow in the investing section as a purchase of equipment or perhaps a part of a broader category of capital expenditures.

C. The asset, equipment, is increased by $12,000. To balance this, capital stock is increased by $8,000 and capital surplus (additional paid-in capital) is increased by $4,000, representing the excess amount received for the stock over its stated value.

This transaction does not involve cash but should be reported in the SCF in the schedule of noncash investing and financing activities.

D. The recording of depreciation expense of $5,000 reduces net income by that amount. The reduction of net income, in turn, reduces the amount to be transferred to retained earnings. The offset in the fundamental equation to the decrease in retained earnings is a decrease in the book value of the depreciable assets. Actually, there is a $5,000 *increase* in the allowance for depreciation (or accumulated depreciation). Since this is a contra account to be deducted from the depreciable assets, the effect of the increase in the allowance for depreciation is to decrease the book value of the depreciable assets.

The depreciation expense reduced net income but did not represent an outflow of cash. On the SCF, in the operating section, $5,000 is added back to net income as an expense not requiring the use of cash, thus, increasing the cash flowing from operating activities.

E. As a result of the loan, cash is increased by $11,000 and the current liability bank loan is increased by the same amount.

The cash inflow is reported in the SCF among the financing activities.

F. The asset, cash, is increased by $9,000 and in the fundamental equation there is a corresponding decrease in the asset, accounts receivable.

This transaction constitutes an operating activity. Under the indirect method, the initial source of cash inflow is the net income. The amount for net income is then adjusted for the decrease in accounts receivable, signifying an inflow of cash from the collection of accounts receivable. This $9,000 transaction would not stand by itself in the SCF but would be included with many similar transactions and with opposing transactions. The opposing transactions would be sales on credit, giving rise to an increase in accounts receivable.

(Under the direct method, the $9,000 would be included under operating activities as part of the cash received from customers during the period. However, when the direct method of presenting the SCF is employed, a reconciliation is required which essentially is identical to the operating activities section of the SCF prepared by the indirect method.)

G. The liability, accounts payable, is reduced by $4,000 and the asset cash is also reduced by $4,000.

Similar to the preceding transaction, this transaction constitutes one of the many transactions included in operating activities. Under the indirect method, the cash outflow because of the payment of the accounts payable is evidenced by the adjustment to net income for the decrease in accounts payable.

(Under the direct method, the payment of an account payable would be included among operating activities as part of the cash paid to suppliers. Bear in mind, however, that the reconciliation required when the direct method is employed will also account for the cash outflow as an adjustment to net income because of the decrease in accounts payable.)

H. The payment for salaries constitutes a recognition of an expense of $2,300 (assuming no liability had already been set up for accrued expense) and reduces net income and consequently reduces retained earnings by $2,300. The offsetting element in the fundamental equation is a reduction in the asset, cash, of $2,300.

The recognition of an expense reduces by $2,300 the net income which is the starting amount in the operating activities section of the SCF under the indirect method. The net income, of course, nets many operating income and expense activities, ultimately, as a rule, involving cash inflows and outflows.

(Under the direct method of presenting the SCF, payment of salaries might be included in a category under operating activities designated cash paid to employees.)

I. The asset, accounts receivable, is increased by $1,900. Offsetting this in the fundamental equation is a decrease of $1,100 in the asset, merchandise, and an increase in net income of $800 which serves to increase retained earnings.

This transaction, by itself, does not involve any cash flow. However, because of its format, the SCF is affected in two counter-balancing aspects. The income of $800 increases the net income for the period which is the first element in the operating activities section of the SCF. The net income as a rule is treated as a cash inflow. However, it has to be modified by various adjustments. The adjustments resulting from this transaction are an increase in accounts receivable of $1,900 which reduces cash inflow, and a decrease in inventory which increases the cash inflow arising from net income.

To summarize:

increase in cash through net income	800
increase in cash because of decrease in inventory	1,100
decrease in cash because of increase in accounts receivable	(1,900)
Net cash flow	-0-

Note that the effect on cash flow is analyzed here in terms of this single transaction. However, during any normal reporting period, there are many transactions. Not only are there sales on credit but there are collections of accounts receivable and there are purchases of merchandise. Thus among the adjustments applied to net income to arrive at the cash flow from operating activities are: net change in accounts receivable, net change in inventory, and net change in accounts payable.

J. The asset, cash, is increased by $75,000 and the liability, bonds payable, is increased by the same amount.

In the SCF, this cash inflow is to be reported in the financial activities section, perhaps as proceeds from the issuance of long-term debt.

K. Retained earnings are reduced by $20,000 but the fundamental equation remains in balance because capital stock is increased by $20,000.

This transaction does not represent either cash inflow or outflow, nor does it affect net income. There is still one further test, however, to be considered. That is, investing or financing activities affecting assets or liabilities are to be reported even if cash is not involved. Such transactions are to be reported in a supplemental schedule. Since this transaction involves neither an asset nor a liability, it does not meet the last test. Accordingly, this stock dividend transaction is not to be included nor appended to a SCF.

Of course, this is a significant transaction to be included in a set of financial statements. Whether as a separate formal statement or as a schedule among notes to financial statements, there would be a reconciliation of balances of retained earnings and of common stock at the beginning and end of the fiscal period. This transaction would be included in such reconciliation.

L. The asset, building, is increased by $25,000. This is balanced in the fundamental equation by a decrease in the asset, cash, of $5,000, and an increase in mortgage payable of $20,000.

This transaction involves an investment in a building and a net cash outflow for part of the purchase price. However, investing activities are reported in one section of the SCF and financing activities in another. Accordingly, in the investing activities section, a cash outflow would be reported of $25,000 for purchase of building or as part of a larger category of capital expenditures. The increase of $20,000 in mortgage payable would be an element in the financial activities section, perhaps netted with mortgage amortizations during the period.

M. Cash is increased by $20,000. The offset in the fundamental equation is a decrease in the asset, land, of $14,000 and an increase in retained earnings of $6,000, representing the gain or sale.

In the SCF, this transaction would be reported as a cash inflow among investing activities of $20,000. However, the gain of $6,000 would have been included as a element of net income. Thus, under the indirect method, there is a duplication of $6,000 of inflow which requires rectification. This is accomplished by an adjustment in the operating acitivities section to reduce the net cash inflow from net income by $6,000.

Solution to Problem VII-2

In this solution, each set of figures in the comparative balance sheets and the additional information is systematically examined, as are certain figures in the income statement. These figures are labelled with key letters to correspond to items in the Statement of Cash Flows (hereinafter referred to as SCF). The comparative balance sheets, the income statement, the additional information and the SCF are all presented at the end of this solution with key letters inserted.

A. The first item in the balance sheet is cash. It has increased during the year $3,000. This net increase of $3,000 appears in the SCF as a final reconciling item, but before the noncash activities.

B. Accounts receivable, net (of allowance for doubtful accounts), the second item has also increased by $3,000. This is entered in the SCF in the operating activities section as an adjustment to net income in order to arrive at the net cash provided by operating activities. Note that the $3,000 has been enclosed in parentheses. The increase in receivables diminishes the amount of net income that was turned into cash. The enclosure in parentheses indicates a subtraction.

C. The next item on the balance sheet is inventories, which have decreased by $1,000 during the year. This decrease has the effect of increasing the cash derived from operating activities and is a plus adjustment to net income.

D. The amount for land on the balance sheet has decreased by $14,000, from $41,000 to $27,000, and is keyed in the balance sheet with (D). One may infer that there has been a sale of land and item 1 of the additional information confirms that. Further, one is informed that the land was sold for cash at a gain of $5,000 after allowing for income tax applicable to the gain. (Income tax increase or reduction applicable to an extraordinary transaction is customarily netted against the gain or loss arising out of such transaction so that remaining income tax represents tax on ordinary operating activities.) Thus, the proceeds of the sale of land (net of the applicable tax or gain) can be taken as $19,000 ($14,000 plus $5,000). The $19,000 is shown on the SCF as proceeds from the sale of land among investing activities. The gain or sale of $5,000 appears in the SCF as an adjustment in the operating activities section eliminating from net income the extraordinary gain on the sale of land.

E. The amount for buildings has increased by $60,000. However, a question immediately comes to mind. Did Problematical Corporation have the $60,000 available in cash or, as usually is the case in the purchase of real estate, did it raise some of the purchase price through a mortgagae loan. Reference to the additional information confirms that $40,000 was raised by a mortgage to enable Problematical to pay $60,000 for the building.

Under the standards set by the Financial Accounting Standards Board, the purchase is to be shown on the SCF among the investing activities, but the cash raised by the mortgage is to be recorded as one of the financing activities.

The key letter (E) has been marked on the balance sheet on the lines for buildings and for mortgage payable. The same letter has been keyed into the SCF for the purchase of building for $60,000 among the investing activities and against the $40,000 proceeds from mortgage as an item among financing activities.

Note that the $60,000 for the purchase has been enclosed in parentheses to indicate a cash outflow.

F. The next item on the balance sheet is for equipment. The amount has increased by $23,000. Reference to Item 4 of the additional information discloses that the equipment was acquired in exchange for capital stock. It further discloses that the capital stock had been issued at a premium of $8,000. Thus we can see that the increase in equipment of $23,000 is offset by the increase on the balance sheet of $15,000 in capital stock and $8,000 in additional paid-in capital. Actually, there was no cash involved in this acquisition of equipment in exchange for capital stock. However, "information about all investing and financing activities of an enterprise during a period that affect recognized assets or liabilities but that do not result in cash receipts or cash payments in the period shall (*are required*) be reported. . . ." (Statement of Financial Accounting Standards No. 95, paragraph 32.)

All of the related elements in this transaction have been keyed with (F), the equipment line on the balance sheet, the lines on the balance sheet for capital stock and for additional paid-in capital, Item 4 of the additional information, and the noncash investing and financing activities section in the SCF.

G. The allowance for depreciation on the balance sheet has increased by $6,000. Unless we have information to the contrary, this increase can only have come about as a result of including depreciation expense of $6,000 in the income statement for the past fiscal period. Thus, insofar as this item is concerned, cash provided by net income must be increased by $6,000 to counter the $6,000 noncash depreciation expense. Both the line in the balance sheet for allowance for depreciation and the adjustment in the operating activities section of the SCF have been keyed with a (G).

H. The next line on the balance sheet, skipping the totals for assets, is for accounts payable. These have decreased during the year resulting in additional cash outflow of $5,000. As an outflow, the adjustmentg in the operating activities section of the SCF is enclosed in parentheses.

I. The next item on the balance sheet, income taxes payable, reveals a $500 decrease in liability. Similar to the decrease in accounts payable, this decrease in liability represents additional cash outflow. It is included among the adjustments in the operating activities section enclosed in parentheses.

The item of income taxes is also involved in supplementary disclosures covered under key letters (O).

J. Interest payable has a consequences similar to income taxes payable, immediately above. It is keyed as (J) among the adjustments and the decrease is enclosed in parentheses to indicate additional cash outflow.

Supplementary disclosure as to interest payments is covered below under key letter (N).

K. Bank loans have increased during the year by $1,000, resulting in additional cash inflow. This item is required to be shown among financing activities.

L. The next open line on the balance sheet is for retained earnings, which have increased by $21,000. Reference to the income statement and additional information (item 2) regarding dividends enables us to fully account for the increase. In order to make sure we understand what took place, we can reconstruct the following analysis of the change in retained earnings:

Retained earnings at the beginning of the year		32,000
Add:		
Net income from regular operations	20,000	
Gain on sale of land	5,000	
	25,000	
Deduct for dividends declared	4,000	
Net increase in retained earnings		21,000
Retained earnings at the end of the year		53,000

There are three items we can key with an (L): the line on the balance sheet for retained earnings, the net income on the income statement, and item 2 of the additional information.

In the SCF, the net income shows up as the first and major item accounting for cash inflow from operating activities and the dividend of $4,000 is enclosed in parentheses representing a cash outflow among financing activities.

M. The last change on the balance sheet is in the treasury stock at cost. It is clear that stock was reacquired during the year at a cost of $11,000. With no additional information to the contrary, this represents a cash outflow and is classified on the SCF as a financing activity.

N, O. The SCF in this solution has been prepared by the indirect method. When the indirect method is used, the cash outflows for interest and income taxes are to be disclosed as supplementary information. These amounts have been calculated as follows:

Interest expense, keyed with an (N) on
  the income statement   3,200
Add: reduction in interest payable
  (2,000 minus 1,500); keyed with an (I)
  on the balance sheet   <u>500</u>
Total cash outlay for interest, key with
  an (N) on the SCF   <u>3,700</u>

Income tax expense, keyed with an (O)
  on the income statement   3,500
Add: reduction in income taxes payable
  ($1,000 minus $500); keyed with a (J)
  on the balance sheet   <u>500</u>
Total cash outlay for income taxes,
  excluding taxes applicabe to
  extraordinary gain on sale
  of land. Keyed with (O) on the SCF.   <u>4,000</u>

There now follows with keyed letter references inserted:

  the original comparative balance sheets,
  the income statement,
  the additional information, and
  the SCF.

Problematical Corporation
Comparative Balance Sheets

	Ending Balance Sheet	Beginning Balance Sheet	
Assets			
Cash	18,000	15,000	(A)
Accounts receivable, net	43,000	40,000	(B)
Inventories	47,000	48,000	(C)
Land	27,000	41,000	(D)
Buildings	110,000	50,000	(E)
Equipment	53,000	30,000	(F)
Allowance for depreciation	(26,000)	(20,000)	(G)
	272,000	204,000	
Liabilities			
Accounts payable	20,000	25,000	(H)
Income taxes payable	1,500	2,000	(I)
Interest payable	500	1,000	(J)
Bank loans, current	5,000	4,000	(K)
Mortgage payable, noncurrent	70,000	30,000	(E)
Equity			
Capital stock	105,000	90,000	(F)
Additional paid-in capital	28,000	20,000	(F)
Retained earnings	53,000	32,000	(L)
Treasury stock, cost	(11,000)	-0-	(M)
	272,000	204,000	

Income Statement

Net sales		205,000	
Cost of sales		152,000	
Gross margin		53,000	
Selling expense	15,100		
Administrative expense	11,200	26,300	
Income from operations		26,700	
Interest expense		3,200	(N)
Income before taxes		23,500	
Income taxes		3,500	(O)
Income before extraordinary items		20,000	
Gain on sale of land (net of taxes)		5,000	
Net income		25,000	(L)

Additional information

(D) 1. Land costing $14,000 was sold at a gain of $5,000, net of applicable tax. The sale was for cash.

(L) 2. Cash dividends were $4,000.

(E) 3. A building was purchased for $60,000 of which $40,000 was raised by mortgage.

(F) 4. Equipment was acquired for $23,000 in exchange for capital stock. The capital stock was issued at a premium of $8,000.

Problematical Corporation
Statement of Cash Flows

Cash flows from operating activities				
Net income			25,000	(L)
Adjustment for differences between income and cash flows from operating activities				
Increase in accounts receivable	(3,000)	(B)		
Decrease in inventories	1,000	(C)		
Depreciation	6,000	(G)		
Decrease in accounts payable	(5,000)	(H)		
Decrease in income taxes payable	(500)	(I)		
Decrease in interest payable	(500)	(J)		
Gain on sale of land	(5,000)	(D)	(7,000)	
Net cash provided by operating				
			18,000	
Cash flows from investing activities				
Proceeds from sale of land	19,000	(D)		
Purchase of building	(60,000)	(E)		
Net cash used in investing activities			(41,000)	
Cash flows from financing activities				
Net borrowing on bank loan	1,000	(K)		
Proceeds from mortgage	40,000	(E)		
Dividends paid	(4,000)	(L)		
Purchase of treasury stock	(11,000)	(M)		
Net cash flows from financing activities			26,000	
Net increase in cash			3,000	(A)
Cash at beginning of year			15,000	
Cash at end of year			18,000	
Noncash investing and financing activities				(F)

Acquisition of equipment at a value of $23,000 by issuance of capital stock at a premium of $8,000.

Supplemental disclosure of cash flow information

Interest	3,700			(N)
Income taxes	4,000			(O)

Chapter VIII

Solution to Problem VIII-1

Note that most of the amounts in the H.J. Heinz financial statements are in thousands of dollars. The same figures will be utilized in this solution, but one should understand that they represent thousands of dollars.

A. The current ratio is computed by dividing total current assets by total liabilities. Referring to the balance sheet for Heinz, the ratio is:

$$\frac{\text{current assets}}{\text{current liabilities}} = \frac{3,013,106}{2,880,415} = 1.05$$

B. The acid-test or quick ratio includes in the numerator cash, marketable securities, and receivables. The denominator consists of total current liabilities. For the numerator we have:

Cash and cash equivalents	156,986
Short-term investments	31,451
Receivables, net of allowance for Doubtful accounts	1,118,874
Total quick assets	1,307,311

The acid-test ratio is:

$$\frac{\text{quick assets}}{\text{current liabilities}} = \frac{1,307,311}{2,880,415} = .45$$

C. The debt to equity ratio is generally taken to be the ratio of total debt to total equities. Since total equities are equal to total assets, this is equivalent to total debt divided by total assets. Total debt is equivalent to total liabilities, that is, current liabilities plus long-term and other liabilities.

For H.J. Heinz, we have:

$$\frac{\text{total debt}}{\text{total assets}} = \frac{2,880,415 + 3,116,951}{8,437,787} = \frac{5,9997,366}{8,437,787} = .71$$

D. Times interest earned. The numerator of this ratio is net income before taxes plus interest expense to arrive at net income that was available to cover payments required for interest.

The ratio to arrive at the number of times interest has been earned is:

$$\frac{\text{net income before taxes plus interest expense}}{\text{interest expense}}$$

$$\frac{479,064 + 274,746}{274,746} = \frac{753,810}{274,746} = 2.7$$

However, Heinz in note 4 reports restructuring charges of $647.2 million which were included in cost of products sold and selling, general and administrative expenses. In a large enterprise, almost always, there is some "restructuring" going on but clearly a major portion of the $647 million should be treated as non-recurring and adjustment might be made for, let us say, 500 million as exceeding normal restructuring costs. With such adjustment, the numerator of this ratio would be computed as follows:

Income before income taxes	479,064
Interest expense	274,746
Adjustment for restructuring	500,000
Total adjusted income before interest and income taxes	$1,253,810

The ratio, then, is

$$\frac{1,253,810}{274,746} = 4.6$$

E. Book value per common share. The numerator is the total shareholders' equity reduced by the amount allocable to preferred stocks; the denominator is the number of common shares outstanding.

The total shareholders' equity, from the balance sheet, is 2,440,421.

The amount allocable to preferred stocks can be computed from data in note 7 to the financial statements. There are 24,100 shares of the $1.70 series preferred at a redemption price of $28.50 per share. This is equal to $686,850. To make this compatible with the amounts used in the financial statements, we will use 687 thousands of dollars.

Shareholders' equity applicable to the common stock outstanding, thus, is calculated at 2,440,421 − 687 which equals 2,439,734 thousands of dollars.

The number of common shares outstanding can also be readily ascertained from the balance sheet. At the end of the year, April 30, 1997, the shares issued totalled 431,096,485. But 63,912,463 of these shares had been reacquired and were held in the treasury. Shares outstanding are computed as 431,096,485 minus 63,912,463 which equals 367,184,022. Note that this figure is not in thousands but is the actual number of shares outstanding.

To compute the ratio, since H.J. Heinz dropped three zeros from the dollar amounts in the financial statements, we have to restore these digits. Thus, the book value per share is:

$$\frac{\text{shareholders' equity applicable to common shares}}{\text{common shares outstanding}} =$$

$$\frac{\$2,444,421,000}{367,184,022} = 6.65 \text{ per share.}$$

Of course, we could have avoided all of these calculations by referring to the 11-year summary of operations and other related data provided by the company in its annual report immediately following the independent accountants' report (opinion). The book value per common share is one of the data given.

F. Accounts receivable turnover is computed by dividing sales by average accounts receivable.

$$\frac{\text{sales}}{\text{average accounts receivable, net of allowances}} =$$

$$\frac{9,357,007}{(1,118,874 + 1,207,874)/2} = \frac{9,357,007}{1,163,374} = 8.04$$

G. In computing accounts receivable turnover, both the numerator and the denominator are figures determined on the basis of selling prices. The situation is different in regard to inventory turnover. The inventory figures in the balance sheet are at cost. The numerator, then, should also be at cost. For this reason, we use cost of goods sold, not selling price of goods sold (which is sales).

Inventory turnover, then is:

$$\frac{\text{cost of goods sold}}{\text{average inventory}} = \frac{6,385,091}{1,432,511 + 1,493,963)/2} =$$

$$\frac{6,385,091}{1,463,237} = 4.4$$

H. The asset turnover ratio is computed by:

$$\frac{\text{sales}}{\text{average total assets}} = \frac{9,357,007}{(8,437,787 + 8,623,691)/2} =$$

$$\frac{9,357,007}{8,530,739} = 1.1$$

I. Earnings per share. This ratio is given in the H.J. Heinz report at the foot of the statements of income and retained earnings as .81 per share. In order to compute this ratio, it is necessary to determine the average number of common shares outstanding during the year and also the amount of net income allocable to the common stock.

The net income for the year was $301,871. From this amount, however, we must deduct the dividends on the preferred dividend of $43, which leaves $301,828 allocable to the common shares.

The average number of common shares can be derived from the data in the balance sheet and note 7. At the end of the year, there were 431,096,485 share issued, of which 63,912,463 were held in the treasury, leaving 367,184,022 outstanding. At the beginning of the year, there were the same 431,096,485 shares issued but 62,498,417 in the treasury, leaving 368,598,068 outstanding.

Based on this annual data, we have an average of shares outstanding of 367,891,045.

Continuing the calculation, earnings per share is determined by:

$$\frac{301,828,000}{367,891,045} = .82 \text{ per share}$$

Why did we arrive at .82 when the financial report shows .81 (actually .8077 before rounding)? There are two reasons. In computing the average number of shares outstanding, H.J. Heinz took into account the common stock equivalents applicable to the outstanding stock options and, as disclosed in the eleven-year summary of operations and other related data, arrived at a total of 373,703,246 shares to be used in computing earnings per share. The calculation of the common stock equivalents is quite complex and the report does not contain all of the data required for such calculation.

A second and much less significant factor is that the company had available quarterly data and may even have employed monthly data. Such more refined averaging techniques may very well have given results somewhat different than obtained by averaging beginning-of-year and end-of-year data. Accordingly, 301,871 minus 43 for preferred leaves [301,828].

$$\frac{301,828,000}{373,703,246} = .8077 \quad \text{(rounded to .81) as stated at the foot of the income statement.}$$

J. The price earnings ratio, expressed as a multiple, is shown daily by a number of newspapers in their financial pages together with the trading prices of securities. The multiple changes as the price of the security rises or falls. The base for the multiple would be the latest 12-month earnings. The data base changes with each published quarterly financial report.

As stated in the H.J. Heinz eleven-year summary of operations and related data, the price range of the common stock during the year ended April 29, 1997, was within a high of 44⅞ and a low of 29¾ per share. Based on earnings of .81 per share, the price earnings multiple would have ranged from a high of about 55.4 to a low of about 36.7. Bear in mind, however, that the earnings base actually applied by the reporting newspapers would have changed with each quarterly report. The .81 constitutes the base obtained from the annual report, which represents the last of the four quarterly reports.

There have been several stock splits in the past decade or thereabouts. These splits have no effect on price earnings ratios because the splits reduce both earnings per share and market price in proportion to the split. The per share financial data in the eleven-year summary of operations and other related data has been similarly adjusted.

K. Return on total assets takes into account total earnings generated by the assets of the company. These earnings include interest earned by the creditors as well as the earnings of the shareholders. As explained in the solution to part D, the net income before taxes may be adjusted for a portion of the extraordinary restructuring costs included in cost of products sold and in selling, general and administrative expenses.

The return in this case is computed by:

$$\frac{\text{net income before taxes (as adjusted)} + \text{interest expense}}{\text{average total assets}} =$$

(Matthew Bender & Co., Inc.)

$$\frac{479,064 + 500,000 + 274,746}{(8,437,787 + 8,623,691)/2} = \frac{1,253,810}{8,530,739} = 14.7\%$$

L. For the rate of return on investment, we want the net income after taxes which appears in the income statement as 301,871. But, this is after the extraordinary restructuring charges. In earlier calculations (see part D) arbitrary adjustment was made for 500,000 before taxes. Heinz does not indicate the income tax allocable to restructuring costs. However, again arbitrarily, we can estimate income taxes allocable to income before income tax in the ratio of the provision for income taxes divided by income before income taxes, i.e. 177,193/479,064 = 37%. The arbitrary adjustment to net income after taxes would then be 63% of the adjustment before taxes. The computed adjusted net income after taxes for the ratio is:

$$479,064 + (.63 \times 500,000) = 479,064 + 315,000 = 794,064]$$

The rate of return on investment, then, is determined by:

$$\frac{\text{net income after taxes (as adjusted)}}{\text{average shareholders' equity}} = \frac{794,064}{(2,440,421 + 2,706,757)/2} = \frac{794,064}{2,573,589} = 32.1\%$$

M. As explained in the solution to part L, the net income after taxes was adjusted to eliminate part of the net-recurring gains.

The ratio of net income to sales takes this adjustment into account and is:

$$\frac{\text{net income after taxes (as adjusted)}}{\text{sales}} = \frac{794,064}{9,357,007} = 8.49\%$$

N. Because of the extraordinary restructuring cost, an arbitrary adjustment of $500 million was made in several of the ratios computed above: D. times interest earned; K. Return on total assets; L. Rate of return on investment; M. Ratio of net income to sales. Adjustment would be equally appropriate in computing the gross profit ratio and a portion of the $500 million should be added back to gross profit. As stated in note 4 of the Heinz report, of the total of $647.2 million of restructuring costs $477.8 million was charged to cost of products sold.

The amount to be added back would be computed by:

$$\frac{\text{restructuring costs charged to cost of products sold}}{\text{total restructuring}} \times 500,000 =$$

$$\frac{477.8}{647.2} \times 500,000 = 73.8 \times 500,000 = 319,000.$$

Gross profit of 2,971,916 as stated in the Income Statement is to be increased by 369,000:

$$2,971,916 + 369,000 = 3,340,916$$

The adjusted gross profit ratio is computed as:

$$\frac{\text{adjusted gross profit}}{\text{sales}} = \frac{3,340,916}{9,357,007} = .357 = 35.7 \text{ percent}$$

CHAPTER IX

Solution to Problem IX-1

There clearly is adequate earned surplus that, under an exclusively earned surplus test, would permit distributions up to $40,000.

When the earned surplus test is combined with a solvency test, one must ask whether it is an "equity" solvency test or a "bankruptcy" solvency test. Under the latter, one need only examine the extent to which assets exceed liabilities. In this instance, assets exceed liabilities by $75,000 ($125,000 − $50,000). As long as the distribution did not exceed this amount, we know that, after the distribution, there would still be an amount of assets equal to liabilities. Since under the earned surplus test, the corporation could only distribute $40,000, the bankruptcy solvency test presents no additional limitation.

However, under the equity insolvency test, which asks whether a corporation is able to pay its debts as they become due, if the corporation paid out more than $5,000 worth of dividends (current assets − current liabilities or $45,000 − $40,000), its current liabilities would exceed its current assets. Consequently, in a jurisdiction applying an equity insolvency test in conjunction with an earned surplus test, the corporation could distribute no more than $5,000.

In a jurisdiction that has adopted the RMBCA, which employs an equity insolvency test in conjunction with a bankruptcy insolvency test, the corporation could distribute the lesser of the two amounts permitted under those tests, or $5,000. The corporation's surplus would be irrelevant in that instance.

Solution to Problem IX-2

The distribution provisions of the RMBCA require only that a corporation be solvent both in an equity and a bankruptcy sense before and immediately after the distribution of the dividend. The Less-Than-Lucrative Corporation would be able to make distributions of up to $10,000 (current assets less current liabilities or $50,000 − $40,000). Beyond that amount, the Corporation would be unable to pay its short term obligations as they mature. Notice that in terms of bankruptcy insolvency, the Corporation's assets exceed its liabilities by $40,000 ($100,000 − $60,000).

The ability of the Less-Than-Lucrative Corporation to declare a dividend is inconsistent with traditional principles of corporate distributions, since the capital of the Corporation is already impaired even before any distribution (i.e., there is not a cushion of assets, beyond all liabilities, equal in amount to stated capital).

Solution to Problem IX-3

The answer would depend upon what type of solvency test was employed. Here, the Corporation is solvent in the bankruptcy sense, but it is insolvent in the equity sense because it does not have adequate short term assets to pay its immediate obligations as they fall due. If an equity insolvency test were applied, the Corporation would not be permitted to make any distributions.

Solution to Problem IX-4

A number of jurisdictions permit corporate distributions to be made out of any "surplus," whether capital or earned surplus. A newly organized corporation might have capital surplus even though there have not yet been any operations and there is no earned surplus. As an example, were the corporate shares issued for consideration in excess of the par value or stated value, that excess would give rise to capital surplus, permitting distributions to be made.

In other instances in which a jurisdiction permits the reduction of capital, perhaps by reducing the par value of the outstanding shares, there also might be capital surplus available to the corporation even in the absence of any operating history.

Finally, a limited number of jurisdictions permit assets to be revalued to reflect appreciated worth. In a limited number of instances, the resulting revaluation capital can be distributed to shareholders (often with special restrictions on the distribution, such as requiring shareholder approval).

Solution to Problem IX-5

The term "earnings" can include both current earnings and accumulated earnings. The Credible Corporation obviously does not have accumulated earnings. However, if it has earnings for the current financial period and if the distribution statute so permits, "nimble" dividends can be paid out of current earnings within a specified time after the end of the fiscal period in which the earnings are generated.

Solution to Problem IX-6

Even though the Corporation has a very good earnings record, it is technically insolvent in the equity sense. If a jurisdiction were to apply this insolvency test as a measurement of whether distributions could be made, the Fantastic Corporation would not be able to distribute the desired dividend.

Solution to Problem IX-7

The distribution will reduce the asset cash by an amount equal to what is paid out to the shareholders, or $25,000 ($2.50 × 10,000). This reduction in assets also reduces the shareholders' equity by an equal amount. Specifically, retained earnings (earned surplus) will be reduced by $25,000.

Solution to Problem IX-8

Assets will not decrease since no cash or property will be distributed. However, on the right-hand side of the balance sheet, there will be a change in stated capital. Prior to the distribution, there are 50,000 shares outstanding with a par of $1.00, resulting in a stated capital for the Corporation of $50,000. After the 1-for-10 distribution, there will be 55,000 shares outstanding still with a par of $1.00, resulting in a stated capital of $55,000.

Since there will be no increase in assets, but there will be an increase in stated capital, in order to keep the basic equation in balance, there also must be a decrease in another category of equity. In instances where the total distribution is less than 25% of the outstanding shares of the Corporation, retained earnings will be reduced by an amount equal to the fair market value of the shares issued as a dividend, or $20,000 (5,000 × $4.00). Since this reduction in retained earnings exceeds the increase in stated capital, the differential of $15,000 ($20,000 − $5,000) will increase capital surplus.

CHAPTER X

Solution to Problem X-1

Many modern corporation statutes hold shareholders liable for having transferred to the corporation consideration at least equal to the par value of the shares issued to the shareholder by that corporation. Thus, were the delivery truck over valued, the shareholder could be liable for the differential between the "actual" value of the truck and the $10,000 consideration that state law would require to be paid in.

Because of the difficulties involved in assessing actual value of the consideration exchanged for the shares, many statutes and many courts employ a good faith test in determining whether the value set for the acquired assets is an accurate value. If the directors of the corporation acted without fraud in establishing a value for the consideration exchanged by the investor and if that value equaled the aggregate par value of the issued shares, then there should be no potential shareholder liability.

Had the Corporation issued the same 1,000 shares to the investor but assigned the shares a par value of $5 per share instead of $10 per share, there would be less concern with the accuracy of the valuation of the truck. With the lower par stock, the investor need only pay in $5,000 worth of consideration instead of $10,000. With $5 par stock, the truck would have to be overvalued by more than 100% before any possibility of shareholder liability for the consideration for the shares issued.

Solution to Problem X-2

The incorporators might want to set par at a figure lower than the issuance price or they might want to authorize no-par stock. Since there is likely to be a later issuance of the same stock, the par value of the stock has to be less than any future market value of the stock. Were the market value of the stock in the future to fall to an amount less than the par value, there would be problems in issuing the stock since consideration at least equal to par would not be received by the Corporation for any shares sold.

Furthermore, if a low par value is set or if no par stock is used, there is greater flexibility in providing for the issuance of stock to the anticipated investors for an unequal consideration. In recognition of the service that some investors will provide in managing the corporation, the incorporators might want shares that are sold to the managing investors to be sold for less consideration than shares sold to the non-managing investors. In order to insure that both categories of investors pay consideration at least equal to par, par must be set at an amount no greater than the lower of the two prices at which the shares will be sold. No-par stock would serve similar ends.

Solution to Problem X-3

Not necessarily. If the Corporation has experienced an accumulated deficit from its operations, it is possible that the Corporation's assets less its liabilities would be less than its stated capital. If this were the case, we would say that the Corporation's capital is impaired. In other words, if the Corporation were liquidated, its assets sold off, and its liabilities satisfied from the sale proceeds, the remaining funds would not equal the amount of the stated capital cushion.

CHAPTER XI

Solution to Problem XI-1

A.

Adams and Bailey
Statement of Capital
Year ended December 31, 20X1

	Adams	Bailey	Total
Capital January 1, 20X1	$ 40,000	$ 35,000	$ 75,000
Add: Net Income	42,000	28,000	70,000
	82,000	63,000	145,000
Deduct: Drawings	29,000	32,000	61,000
Capital, December 31, 20X1	$ 53,000	$ 31,000	$ 84,000

B. The loan from the bank has no effect on the capital account balances. In terms of the fundamental equation, the receipt of $25,000 from the bank increased the asset, cash, by $25,000 and increased the liabilities by $25,000.

The fact that Bailey obtained funds from his aunt does not affect the partnership accounts, but Bailey's investment of $20,000 increases the partnership cash account by $20,000 and increases Bailey's capital by the same amount.

The statement of capital follows: [Note: the format for year 19X2 has to be modified somewhat to accommodate the new item of capital investment. The manner of designation of dates, and line titles, however, has been changed merely to illustrate different possible descriptions.]

Adams and Bailey
Statement of Capital
Calendar Year 20X2

	Adams	Bailey	Total
Capital, beginning	$ 53,000	$ 31,000	$ 84,000
Additional Investment	15,000	20,000	35,000
Net Income	54,000	36,000	90,000
	$ 122,000	$ 87,000	$ 209,000
Withdrawals	33,000	31,000	64,000
Capital, end of year	$ 89,000	$ 56,000	$ 145,000

Solution to Problem XI-2

Interest is allowed at the rate of 8% per annum. For each quarter, then, interest is to be taken at 2%.

The following Statement of Capital has been designed to answer both part a and part b.

Sensible Hardware Company
Statement of Capital
Quarter ended June 30, 20____

	Quincy	Redman	Seidler	Total
Interest on Capital	$ 700	$ 800	$ 500	$ 2,000
Partners' salaries	3,000	2,400	3,600	9,000
Share of remainder	12,000	12,000	6,000	30,000
Total profit	15,700	15,200	10,100	41,000
Add Capital balances				
4/1/20—	35,000	40,000	25,000	100,000
Total	$50,700	$55,200	$35,100	$141,000
Deduct Drawings including salaries	5,000	2,400	6,600	14,000
Capital balances 6/30/20_____	$45,700	$52,800	$28,500	$127,000

Solution to Problem XI-3

A. Schedule 1

Initial cash balance	$ 15,000
Cash received to date on liquidation	90,000
	$105,000
Payments in settlement of liabilities	$ 64,000
Cash balance	41,000
Cash to be retained	3,000
Available for distribution	$ 38,000

B. Schedule 2

	K	L	M	Total
P&L ratios	(20%)	(50%)	(30%)	(100%)
Initial capital balances	$55,000	$45,000	$78,000	$178,000
Add: gain on settlement of liabilities (67,000 − 64,000)	600	1,500	900	3,000
	55,600	46,500	78,900	181,000
Deduct for realized losses (110,000 − 90,000)	4,000	10,000	6,000	20,000
Capital balances before first distribution	$51,600	$36,500	$72,900	$161,000

C. One might suggest that the $38,000 be distributed in the P&L ratio or perhaps in the capital ratio. However, neither procedure would be correct. We have taken into account the realized gains and losses but must also consider the maximum potential additional gains or losses. Distribution should not be made to a partner whose capital balance could be completely wiped out by future losses. Distribution should be made only on capital balances that would survive all possible future losses.

As for potential additional losses, we must assume that the remaining non-cash assets may be worthless and also that the cash to be retained for contingencies might be entirely expended and result in additional loss of $3,000. Thus:

Schedule 3

Assets at beginning	$245,000
Cash at beginning	15,000
Non-cash assets at beginning	230,000
Assets liquidated, at book value	110,000
Non-cash assets remaining	120,000
Add possible contingent expenses for which cash is to be retained	3,000
Possible further loss	$123,000

Before any distributions, this possible further loss is to be allocated, as follows:

Schedule 4

	K	L	M	Total
Capital balances before first distribution, from Schedule 2	$51,600	$36,500	$72,900	$161,000
Possible further loss	24,600	61,500	36,900	123,000
Potential capital balances	$27,000	$(25,000)	$36,000	$ 38,000

Note, now partner L has a sizeable capital deficiency. If the potential loss were actually realized, L would be liable to K and M for $25,000. But L might be unable to pay, and for the purpose of computing this first distribution we do not count on this $25,000 but allocate this deficiency to the capital accounts of K and M in their relative profit and loss ratios, that is 20 to 30, or, 40% to K and 60% to M.

Schedule 5

	K	L	M	Total
Potential capital balances from Schedule 4	$27,000	$(25,000)	$36,000	$38,000
Allocation of L's deficiency	(10,000)	25,000	(15,000)	—
Cash to be paid out	$17,000	$ - 0 -	$21,000	$38,000

D.

Schedule 6

Cash realized in final sale	$41,000
Cash remaining from contingency fund (3,000 − 2,000)	1,000
Cash available for distribution	$42,000

E. First calculate the losses to be recognized in this second, and final, stage of liquidation.

Schedule 7

Book value of non-cash assets at end of first stage from Schedule 3	$120,000
Cash realized in sale	41,000
Losses to be recognized	79,000
Expenses of liquidation	2,000
Total of losses and expenses to be recognized	$ 81,000

After determining the total of losses and expenses to be recognized, one is then prepared to determine the amount to be distributed to each partner.

Schedule 8

	K	L	M	Total
Captial balances before first distribution, from schedule 2	$51,600	$36,500	$72,900	$161,000
Cash paid out in first distribution,from schedule 5	17,000	—	21,000	38,000
Catital balances after first distribution	34,600	36,500	51,900	123,000
Losses and expenses to be recognized from Schedule 7, in P&L ratios	16,200	40,500	24,300	81,000
Capital balances	$18,400	$ (4,000)	$27,600	$42,000
Allocations of L's deficiency in 40%, 60% ratio as computed after Schedule 4	(1,600)	4,000	(2,400)	
Final cash distribution	$16,800	$ -0-	$25,200	$ 42,000

Note that partner L's final deficiency was allocated to partners K and M. Thus, partners K and M did not receive a full return of their capital balances. Partners K and M now have a claim again Partner L for this deficiency. Partner L may or may not be able to satisfy these claims.

Chapter XII

Solution to Problem XII-1

1. This has been covered in the illustrative answer.

2. A. Dr professional fees, an increase in the expense. Cr cash to decrease cash.

B. Balance Sheet: Cash is decreased and the unrestricted net assets are also decreased.

C. Functional Allocation: The professional fees expense is included in the management and general and in the total columns.

D. Statement of Activities: Professional fees are included only in management and general in the supporting services category and in the total column.

E. Cash Flows: The reduction of cash reduces cash flows from operating activities.

3. A. Dr an asset account to show an increase in assets. The account might be entitled computer equipment or it might carry a broader title encompassing fixtures, furniture and equipment. Cr contributions, to record an increase in contributions. The account might be entitled contributions of equipment or contributions in kind.

B. Balance Sheet: In terms of the titles employed in Exhibit 12.1, there would be an increase in the equipment account and an increase in the unrestricted net assets.

C. Functional Allocation: Contributions are not reflected in this statement.

D. Statement of Activities: It is generally assumed that contributions are received in cash unless otherwise indicated. It would be desirable, then, to add a line in the Activities statement for contributions in kind or contributions of equipment. The contribution would appear in the unrestricted column and the total column.

E. Cash Flows: As a non-cash transaction, it should be shown in supplementary data as a contribution of equipment.

4. A. Dr cash to show an increase. Cr sale of publications, an income account.

B. Balance Sheet: Cash and unrestricted net assets are both increased.

C. Functional Allocation: Neither asset nor income accounts are reflected in this statement.

D. Statement of Activities: Income from sale of publications is included in the unrestricted and the total columns.

E. Cash Flows: The receipt of cash increases cash flows from operating activities.

5. A. Dr cash to increase cash. Cr contributions to increase contributions.

B. Balance Sheet: Both cash and the unrestricted net assets are increased.

C. Functional Allocation: Contributions are not included in this statement.

D. Statement of Activities: Contributions are increased in the unrestricted and the total columns.

E. Cash Flows: The receipt of cash increases cash flows from operating activities.

6. A. Dr. cash to increase cash. Cr a temporarily restricted income account.

B. Balance Sheet: Cash and temporarily restricted net assets are both increased.

C. Functional Allocation: Contributions are not included in this statement.

D. Statement of Activities: Contributions are increased in the temporarily restricted and total columns.

E. Cash Flows: the receipt of cash increases cash flows from operating activities.

7. A. Dr depreciation expense to set up this expense. Cr accumulated depreciation on equipment, an account that is deducted from the equipment account. The effect is to decrease the book value of equipment.

(NOTE: A similar entry would be made to depreciate furniture and fixtures.)

B. Balance Sheet: The net value of equipment in the fixtures and equipment fund is reduced as is the total of unrestricted net assets.

C. Functional Allocation: Depreciation expense is allocated among the three functions, program services, management and general, and fund raising. The total appears in the total column.

D. Statement of Activities: This expense is included in the unrestricted and the total columns among the expenses for programs, management and general, and fund raising.

E. Cash Flows: It affects, negatively, the first item, i.e., the increase or decrease in net assets. This change is offset by an increase in depreciation expense among the reconciling adjustments so that there is no effect on the net effect on the cash used by operating activities.

8. A. Dr salaries expense, an increase in this expense. Cr cash to decrease this asset.

B. Balance Sheet: Cash and unrestricted net assets are both reduced.

C. Functional Allocation: Similar to transactions 1 and 7, this expense is included in the total column and is allocated among the functions for program services, management and general, and fund raising.

D. Statement of Activities: The allocated portions of salaries will be included in each of the four categories of expense and in the total column.

E. Cash Flows: As an expense, this expenditure negatively affects the change in net assets, the first item in the statement, increases the net cash used by operating activities; and decreases the balance of cash at the end of the year.

9. A. Dr Research grants, an expense account, to increase this expense. Cr grants payable, a liability account, to increase this liability.

B. Balance Sheet: Increase the liability and decrease the balance of unrestricted net assets.

C. Functional Allocation: The grant expense applies only to program services. It appears also in the total column.

D. Statement of Activities: In the unrestricted fund column, the grant expense is included in the figure for program services. It is also included in the total column.

E. Cash Flows: As an expense, this grant negatively affects the change in net assets, the first item in the statement. However, there is an offsetting effect among the reconciling adjustments in the change in accounts payable. If the liability remains unpaid at the end of the fiscal year, the net cash used by operating activities and the year-end cash balance are both unaffected.

10. A. Dr grants payable to decrease the liability. Cr cash to decrease asset.

B. Balance Sheet: In the balance sheet, both the asset and liability are reduced. The balance of unrestricted net assets remains unchanged. This balance was reduced when the grant was approved and recorded. The balance of unrestricted net assets is not affected by the payment of the liability.

C. and D. This transaction involves neither revenue nor expense and has no impact on either the Functional Allocation or the Statement of Activities.

E. Cash Flows: This transaction affects the change in accounts payable included among the reconciling adjustments, increases the net cash used by operating activities, and decreases the cash balance at the end of the year.

11. A. Dr Conferences and meetings expense to recognize the expense. Cr cash to decrease asset.

B. Balance Sheet: In the balance sheet, both the asset, cash, and the word deleted balance of unrestricted net assets are reduced.

C. Functional Allocation: Usually the entire expense is charged to management and general. Of course, it is also included in the total column.

D. Statement of Activities: The cost for the meeting room and refreshments would be included among management and general in the unrestricted fund column and in the total column.

E. Cash Flows: This transaction has a negative impact on the change in net assets, the first item in the statement; the cash used by operating activities; and the year-end balance of cash.

12. A. Dr Investments to show an increase. Cr contributions to the endowment fund.

B. Balance Sheet: The asset, investments, and the balance of permanently restricted net assets will both be increased..

C. Functional Allocation: Not affected.

D. Statement of Activities: Contributions are increased in the endowment and the total columns.

E. Cash Flows: This transaction does not involve cash, but it should be reported in the supplementary data.

APPENDIX

Solution to App-I

The following entries in general journal format indicate the debit and credit effects of the several transactions on the accounts in the general ledger. The student is reminded, however, that in practically all real-life business situations: (i) the entries involving cash would be made in either a cash receipts or a cash disbursements journal; (ii) the entries for credit sales would be recorded in a sales journal; and (iii) entries involving purchases on credit would be found in a purchases journal or a voucher register. Relatively few entries are actually made in a general journal. On the other hand, in situations involving debit and credit analysis without actual entries in a set of books, it is usually more convenient to work with general journal entries than with several specialized journals.

Explanatory comment follows each journal entry.

General Journal Entries

	Debit	Credit
1. Cash	3,700	
Accounts receivable		3,700

(The debit to cash records the increase in the asset account for cash. The credit to accounts receivable reflects a decrease in accounts receivable.)

	Debit	Credit
2. Accounts receivable	950	
Sales		950

(The debit to accounts receivable records an increase in that asset. The credit to the sales account records an increase in sales revenue.)

3. The solution in this case depends on whether the company maintains a perpetual inventory on its books or functions on a periodic inventory basis. With a periodic inventory, the entry would be:

	Debit	Credit
Purchases	5,100	
Accounts payable		5,100

(The purchases account always carries a debit balance. The debit to this account increases this balance. Inasmuch as the purchases account is a mixed account, this debit may be viewed as reflecting: an increase in a temporary account representing an increase in the asset merchandise; or an increase in the expenses for cost of sales; or a combination of both. The credit to accounts payable reflects the increase in the liability to trade creditors.)

With a perpetual inventory, the entry would be:

	Debit	Credit
Merchandise inventory	5,100	
Accounts payable		5,100

(In the case of a perpetual inventory, the debit reflects an increase in the asset, merchandise inventory, while the credit to accounts payable has the same effect as in the entry under a periodic inventory system, that is, it reflects the increase in the liability to trade creditors.)

	Debit	Credit
4. Truck	18,000	
Cash		6,000
Notes Payable		12,000

(The debit to the truck account indicates the increase in the asset, truck. The credit to the cash account records the decrease in cash, while the credit to notes payable reflects the increase in the liability on notes.

When a balance sheet is prepared, part of the notes payable would be treated as a current liability and the remainder as a noncurrent liability.)

(Matthew Bender & Co., Inc.)

5. Salaries expense   950

     Cash   950

(The debit to the salaries expense account reflects an increase in the expense. This is offset by the credit representing a decrease in the asset, cash.)

6. Interest expense   973

     Mortgage payable   2,000

     Cash   2,973

(The debit of $973 to the interest expense account records the expense and the debit to mortgage payable reduces the liability. The credit to cash records the decrease in the asset, cash.)

7. Salaries expense   330

     Accrued expenses   330

(The debit recognizes the salaries expense incurred and increases the balance in the expense account. The credit records the liability for salaries earned but not yet paid. The specific account title for the liability account might be accrued expenses, as above. Such account could be utilized for such items as accrued interest payable, accrued rent payable, or accrued salaries. An alternate treatment would be to use a title representing the salaries liability only, such as accrued salaries payable.)

8. Depreciation expense   2,200

     Allowance for depreciation   2,200

(The debit to the depreciation expense account records the expense for the period. The credit to the allowance for depreciation (accumulated depreciation) increases the balance in that account. As a contra asset account (see Chapter II, Section G, paragraph 1), the allowance for depreciation carries a credit balance and is to be presented on the balance sheet as a deduction from the asset being depreciated. The effect of the increased credit balance in the allowance for depreciation account is to decrease the net book value of the asset being depreciated.)

9. Sales   413,000

     Income and expense summary   413,000

(This entry is part of the process of closing the books in which all of the revenues and expenses are transferred to the income and expense summary (profit and loss account) and then to retained earnings. The purpose of this entry is to transfer the accumulated credits in the sales account, representing sales revenue. The debit to sales brings the account balance down to zero and the sales account is closed. The credit reflects the transfer of the sales revenue to the income and expense summary account.)

10. Income and expense summary   27,400

     Salaries expense   27,400

(The debit to the income and expense summary account transfers the salaries expense to the summary account and serves to reduce the net income (or increase the net loss) for the fiscal period. The credit to salaries expense offsets the debit balance in the account and brings its balance down to zero. The salaries expense account is now closed.)

11. Income and expense summary   37,800

     Retained earnings   37,800

(The balance in the income and expense summary account represents the net effect of the transfers to that account from sales revenue (and perhaps also from one or more other revenue accounts) and the transfers from all of the different expense accounts. The debit to the income and expense summary serves to close this account and reduces its balance to zero. The offsetting credit to retained earnings represents the increase in that shareholders' equity account arising from the net income for the fiscal period.)

INDEX

[References are to pages and appendices .]

A

ACCOUNTING PRINCIPLES (GAAP) (See GENERALLY ACCEPTED ACCOUNTING PRINCIPLES (GAAP))

ACCOUNTING PROCESS

Generally . . . 1-2
Attorney's interaction with . . . 1-2
Basic equation (See BASIC ACCOUNTING EQUATION)
Mechanics of accounting (See MECHANICS OF ACCOUNTING)
Terminology . . . 2

ACCOUNTS RECEIVABLE

Generally . . . 24
Average age of . . . 80
Bad debts, methods for treating . . . 24
Turnover of . . . 79-80
Uncollectible accounts, accounting for . . . 24

ACCRUAL BASIS ACCOUNTING

Generally . . . 58-59
Accrual defined . . . 59
Accrued expenses . . . 59-60
Accrued income . . . 60
Deferral defined . . . 59
Deferred expenses . . . 60
Deferred income . . . 60

ACID-TEST RATIO

Liquidity, as measure of . . . 78

AICPA (See AMERICAN INSTITUTE OF CERTIFIED PUBLIC ACCOUNTANTS (AICPA))

AMERICAN INSTITUTE OF CERTIFIED PUBLIC ACCOUNTANTS (AICPA)

Role in codifying GAAP . . . 40

AMORTIZATION

Generally . . . 20
Goodwill . . . 27-28

ASSETS AND LIABILITIES

Generally . . . 2; 11
Acid-test ratio . . . 78
Amortization (See AMORTIZATION)
Balance sheet (See BALANCE SHEET)
Banks, of . . . 14; 15
Basic equation, in (See BASIC ACCOUNTING EQUATION)
Book value (See BOOK VALUE)
Contingent liabilities . . . 14-15
Current assets (See CURRENT ASSETS)
Current liabilities . . . 14
Current ratio . . . 78
Defined . . . 2

C

[References are to pages and appendices .]

[References are to pages and appendices .]

(Matthew Bender & Co., Inc.)

[References are to pages and appendices .]

[References are to pages and appendices .]

H

I

[References are to pages and appendices .]

[References are to pages and appendices .]

[References are to pages and appendices .]

NOT-FOR-PROFIT ORGANIZATIONS

Accounting equation applicable to . . . 114
Balance sheet . . . 116-117
Board-designated funds . . . 115
Endowment funds . . . 115
Equity interest . . . 114
Financial statements
    Generally . . . 116
    Balance sheet . . . 116-117
    Illustrative statement . . . App. C
    Statement of Activities . . . 117-118
    Statement of cash flow . . . 118-119
Fund accounting; generally . . . 113-114
Fund balance . . . 114; 116
Net Asset Class model for external reporting . . . 113
Net assets . . . 116
Plant and building funds . . . 115
Profit-seeking corporations compared . . . 114
Restricted funds . . . 115
Statement of Activities . . . 117-118
Statement of cash flow . . . 118-119
Statement of Functional Allocation of Expenses . . . 119-120
Time restricted funds . . . 115
Types of funds . . . 115
Unrestricted funds . . . 115

P

PAID-IN CAPITAL

Generally . . . 31-32
Additional paid-in capital defined . . . 32
Balance sheet listings . . . 34
Components of . . . 34
No-par stock . . . 33
Par value stock, issuance of . . . 32-33

PARTNERSHIPS

Allocation of Profit schedule . . . 108
Balance sheet . . . 105-106
Income-sharing agreement . . . 107
Income statement . . . 108-109
Interest withdrawals . . . 107; 110
Liquidation
    Generally . . . 110-111
    Assets unequal to book value, realization of . . . 111
    Dissolution defined . . . 110
    Residual assets, effect of . . . 111-112
Net income, distribution of . . . 107-108
Profit allocation among partners . . . 107-108
Salary withdrawals . . . 107-110
Statement of Capital . . . 106
Winding-up (See subhead: Liquidation)

PAR VALUE

Generally . . . 32-33

[References are to pages and appendices .]

[References are to pages and appendices .]

S

[References are to pages and appendices .]